THE PERVERSE
GAZE OF SYMPATHY

SUNY series in
Feminist Criticism and Theory
Michelle A. Massé, editor

THE PERVERSE
GAZE OF SYMPATHY

Sadomasochistic Sentiments from
Clarissa to *Rescue 911*

Laura Hinton

State University of New York Press

Cover photograph:
Film Still, *Wuthering Heights* (Samuel Goldwyn 1933)
Courtesy of Arts Library—Special Collections,
University Research Library, UCLA

Published by
State University of New York Press, Albany

© 1999 State University of New York

For information, address State University of New York Press
State University Plaza, Albany, New York 12246

Production by Dana Foote
Marketing by Fran Keneston

Library of Congress Cataloging-in-Publication Data
Hinton, Laura.
The perverse gaze of sympathy : sadomasochistic sentiments from
Clarissa to Rescue 911 / Laura Hinton.
p.   cm. — (SUNY series in feminist criticism and theory)
Includes bibliographical references (p.   ) and index.
ISBN 0–7914–4339–6 (alk. paper). — ISBN 0–7914–4340–X (pbk. :
alk. paper)
1. English fiction—History and criticism. 2. Sentimentalism in
literature. 3. Flaubert, Gustave, 1821–1880. L'Education
sentimentale. 4. Brontë, Emily, 1818–1848. Wuthering Heights.
5. James, Henry, 1843–1916. Portrait of a lady. 6. Richardson,
Samuel, 1689–1761. Clarissa. 7. Television Criticism—United
States. 8. Sadomasochism in literature. 9. Feminism and
literature. 10. Sympathy in literature. 11. Sadomasochism.
I. Title. II. Series.
PR830.S45H56   1999
823.009′353—dc21   99–28288
                                                                           CIP

10   9   8   7   6   5   4   3   2   1

For Bernard,
Cynthia,
and Paul D.

Contents

ILLUSTRATIONS

ACKNOWLEDGMENTS

A book written over one decade, on two coasts and two continents, necessarily embodies the collective geographies, the wit and the wines, of a large
number of landscapes and the friends they inspire. First, I would like to
acknowledge the northern California contingent, beginning with a most
wonderful Ph.D. advisor, David Halliburton of Stanford University, who
coached an "offbeat" (his word) dissertation into birth, and praised its
rapprochement into something entirely other. I would also like to extend
special thanks to other Stanford faculty who supported this work at various
stages over the years, including Sandra Drake, Ron Rebholz, and Diane
Wood Middlebrook—whose own feminist prose has been inspirational.
Several Bay Area friends gave analysis, praise, and humor when it was
most needed: Herb and Grace Schmidt, Carol and Mark DeZutti, Susan
Kulakowski, Nancy Noe and Eric Nedervold, Becky Adams, Dana LaRue,
and Dana Backman. I am also grateful to Shoshana Weschler, who told me
to give it the tabloid grist, as well as to Lyn Hejinian, who stated an early faith
in this project.

For long years of help and guidance, I thank Cathy Humphers, Laura
Hume, and my parents, Barbara and Richard D. Hinton. The insight and wit
of Susan Hardy Aiken and Chris Carroll, mentors and deep friends both of
the University of Arizona, first fostered the courage in me to reveal my own.

In New York City, the manuscript would not have seen its "rebirth"
without the fine, intellectual camaraderie of the Columbia Film Seminar at
the Museum of Modern Art, and the members who encouraged the work's
earlier inculcation: Charles Musser, Jerry Carlson, Krin Gabbard, E. Ann
Kaplan, Maren Stange, and Charles Hobson. At The City College of New
York, I am indebted to former Dean of Humanities Paul Sherwin for believ-
ing in the idea early on, making possible its development through the first
City College Pforzheimer Fellowship during 1991–93, and for reading the
manuscript with interest and support even as he confronted new duties as
dean at Long Island University. I furthermore am indebted to colleagues
Joshua Wilner, CCNY Deputy Dean of Humanities and a Romanticist, who
first pointed out the relevance of "sympathy" to my claims; to Betty Rizzo, an
eighteenth-century scholar who, early on, supported my work in that field;
and to Jane Marcus, Distinguished Professor of Women's Studies, who pro-

vided enormous feminist intellectual-political wisdom. I also thank the following special colleagues who read and saw what was then in the dark: Barbara Fisher, Leon Guilhamet, Mary V. Jackson, Jennifer Roberts, Gordon Thompson, the late William Matthews, and Liz Mazzola (who helped at a particularly dark time by demanding the movie version). Former philosophy colleague Juliet Floyd, now at Boston University, encouraged my meditations on Hume by discussing his radical edges over Northern Italian cuisine; she and her husband, Professor Burton Dreben (who pointed me toward Hutcheson), have supported my explorations in the boundaries between philosophy and literature over the years, as has Carol Gould and the late Marx Wartofsky. I also thank Sybil Schwarzenback of the Baruch College Department of Philosophy for sharing her feminist perspectives on sympathy.

Feminists scattered far and wide, but whose repartée at conferences from Cancun to Toronto has made all the difference include Karen Brennan, Jacqueline V. Brogan, Maria Damon, Jeanne Heuving, Wendy Martin, and Laura Mumford. Feminist poet and critic Cynthia Hogue supported this manuscript through so many stages it is difficult to enumerate them: she taught me the concept of "inviolable time," she tutored me in proposals, she read the whole thing, she argued, conceded, and made me laugh at myself.

Pat O'Donnell, Lloyd Michaels, and Neal Brickman helped at crucial junctures. Anthony Burry kept me focused on the writing, and provided personal-political analyses in times of strain. Mark and Terry Antman provided "porch" sessions in Woodstock, New York; they saw to it that I had the forest into which was born the first full draft.

Moving to France, I cannot thank enough the hospitable friends and family who housed me during periods of intense writing and research in that country, including Mary and Marcel Floris of St. Germain-en-Laye and Ibiza, Spain; Madame Anna Merle D'Aubigné of Paris; and the late Renée Roy of Vence. The Olivier Roy family provided hospitality and phone lines in the South of France, as did the generous family of Jacqueline Boutillier. I wish to give special acknowledgment to Madame Marie Gouttepifre and the staff at the Grand Hôtel in Bormes-les-Mimosas, to whom I owe more than I can express in French for giving me, after Woolf, a "room" for my burgeoning manuscript.

Several libraries extended special courtesy in my effort to explore popular-culture research. I thank the staff at the Bibliothèque Nationale in Paris for helping me explore the topic of nineteenth-century French spectacle, as well as the Bibliothèque de la Ville de Paris for granting me such pleasurable access to historical documents on nineteenth-century Parisian world fairs. Brigitte Kueppers of the Research Library at the University of

California–Los Angeles was especially helpful in providing access to the William Wyler Collection there. New York University's Bobst Library has been my mainstay; I especially thank the Friends of Bobst staff for their support. Funding for research was provided by a two-year grant from the PSC-CUNY Research Foundation, for which Joyce Mullan was my very helpful contact. Funding for research also was provided by two Eisner awards from the City College Division of Humanities and Rifkind Center. To these institutions all, I am grateful.

Thanks to the publishers of *Women's Studies: An Interdisciplinary Journal* 28.3 (June 1999) and *Eighteenth-Century Studies* 32.3 (Spring 1999) for permission to reprint material incorporated into the introduction, chapter 1, and chapter 3. And I extend thanks for permission to reproduce other material essential to the production of this book: to Laura Mulvey and the editors at *Screen,* for permission to reprint significant passages from "Visual Pleasure and Narrative Cinema," *Screen* 16.3 (1975); to the University of California Press, for permission to reprint passages from Daniel Dayan's "The Tudor Code of Classic Cinema," *Film Quarterly* 28.1 (Fall 1994); to Cambridge University Press, for permission to reprint Samuel Bentham's "Panopticon House of Industry" from Robin Evans's *The Fabrication of Virtue: English Prison Architecture 1750–1840;* and to both Cambridge and *The Illustrated London News* for permission to reprint the "Panopticon rotunda, Isle of Pines, Cuba," also from Evans's book. I would like to thank Mrs. Robin Evans for her help with permissions, and to extend special thanks, again, to the Research Library at the University of California–Los Angeles, which provided photo stills of William Wyler's *Wuthering Heights.*

Ron Davies of Stanford generously pored over the manuscript with his eagle eye and prepared it for publication. Editor James Peltz of SUNY Press encouraged this manuscript through the arduous stages of publication, as did production editor Dana Foote.

Artist Paul D. Lyon lent his talent in preparing photo reproductions, and philosopher Bernard R. Roy inaugurated my deeper intellectual venture into Enlightenment texts. Bernard also served as advisor on the French translations, steered me (literally) through his native city of Paris and its libraries, and read manuscript portions from start to finish. To him, and to my son, Paul, my greatest debt is due. They gazed upon the worker and laughed at the absurdities. They, along with Cynthia, were the audience whose sympathies were always perfectly pitched to the ironic. To these three devoted friends, I dedicate this piece.

The Failed Mirror of Sympathy

I looked through her keyhole at my going by her door, and saw her on her knees, at her bed's feet . . . and in an agony she seemed to be, sobbing. . . . as if her heart would break . . . Divine excellence!

—Lovelace on June 8, *Clarissa*

Felicia Mungo, a guard at the prison where Ms. [Susan] Smith has been held since her confession, said a camera pointed at her cell sometimes caught her weeping. "She'll be kneeling in her cell, reading her Bible, crying," she said.

—*The New York Times,* July 28, 1995

When Lovelace, having raped Clarissa, peeps "through the keyhole" and sympathetically views her distress, he illustrates the modern taste for sadistic visual perversions, those befitting a female sentimental incarceration. Voyeurism and fetishism finally kill the fictitious Clarissa. However, they may have saved confessed child-killer Susan Smith from death row. So would suggest the script-like testimony of Felicia Mungo during Smith's presentencing hearing in a South Carolina courtroom. Reading like a page from *Clarissa*, this testimony substitutes Samuel Richardson's keyhole for a surveillance-monitor apparatus.

While the Smith trial went untelevised during the summer of 1995, when the O. J. Simpson trial dominated the airwaves, Smith's infanticide trial incurred its own reproduction of cybernetic monitors in nightly news replays of a video crime re-enactment, through which a camera positioned inside Smith's car created a simulacrum of the point of view of children drowning. And Smith's own image moved swiftly through the gyrations of media spin: from that of a latter-day Medea strapping babies into car seats and watching them sink into a lake, to a female victim of sexual molestation.

In the end, Smith's only "defense"—she confessed her guilt—employed epistolary testimony by her stepfather alluding to the alleged abuse.[1] Sentenced to thirty years, not the electric chair, Smith seemed destined to become a heroine of *Rescue 911*, the prime-time reality show in which mothers cry and pray next to hospital monitors before television cameras, co-victims of their children's spectacular accidents.

My comments do not seek to minimize the tragedy of sexual abuse, nor the possibility that it may have helped to motivate Smith's crime. Nor do they seek to render lightly the murder of Smith's children. But they do seek to call attention to the sympathetic monitors we focused upon Smith and her crime, and to a culture at large that both demonizes and sentimentalizes women. Novels may imitate life, but life also imitates novels. The Susan Smith murder trial is but a recent case in point in the reproduction of sentiment through its visual monitor of sympathy. This has been an excessive reproduction since the mid-eighteenth century.

The Reproduction of Sentiment

The reproduction of sentiment calls forth images of femininity, sympathy, and virtuous moral feeling. But the reproduction of sentiment also relies upon a visual power structure gendered male, and a sympathetic spectator whose "sentiments" are sadomasochistic. This book is a study of the symbolically masculine features of sympathy, from *Clarissa* to modern media trials to television "reality" shows like *Rescue 911*. It argues that sentiment is reproduced by sympathy's endorsement of sadomasochistic, scopophilic practices: in short, by the perverse gaze. While sympathetic spectatorship creates identification—with women and other feminized underclasses—sympathy, this book argues, is a strange phenomenon, indeed.

I treat sympathy as the primary structure underlying sentiment and its related form of melodrama in literature, television, and film.[2] Considered one of the primary "moral sentiments" by eighteenth-century philosopher David Hume, sympathy is the centerpiece of his concept of the "passions." I turn to Hume's account of sympathy, for Hume, perhaps better than any other ethical philosopher, describes sympathy's ironic effects. At issue for Hume is natural moral law, and the perception that reason regulates moral judgment. Hume's revolutionary *Treatise Concerning Human Understanding* (1739–40) describes moral law not as the product of reason but rather as the product of the unstable passions. Sympathy is one of these unstable passions or "moral sentiments." Hume introduces the concept of a sympathetic spectator. Through the spectator, he suggests, sympathy becomes an expression of visual pleasure. The desire for visual pleasure makes the sympathetic spectator a fetishist and a voyeur. In this book, I reread Hume's proto-psychological critique of sympathy through modern theories of gendered spectatorship and its visual perversions. Studying the tradition of popular sentiment that Hume and other Enlightenment philosophers inspired, I suggest that sadomasochistic desire underlies the experience of sympathy, through the perverse narrative spectator who creates and reflects sentimental image-making.

Traditionally, literary scholars have viewed sentiment as an "excessive" mode of fiction, an emotive style limited to the eighteenth-century British novel and to the less "realistic" novels of the American nineteenth century—both genres associated with women as readers, writers, and fictive subjects. This "excessive" mode has been condemned, or, more recently, celebrated, for presenting and appealing to female subjects, for politically championing the cause of women and other groups marginalized by white Eurocentric culture. One classic critique of sentiment is Ann Douglas's *The Feminization of American Culture* (1977), which argues that nineteenth-century American sentiment was coercive and anti-intellectual, the commodified product of lady writers and their Protestant ministers. Feminist criticism in the 1980s, responding to critics like Douglas, salvaged sentimental novels from the critical trash bin. For example, Jane Tompkins's *Sensational Designs* (1985) suggests that women's sentimental novels of the nineteenth century contain a subversive feminist content.[3] My own study, however, reconsiders the assumption that sentiment is largely the product of and about women. It suggests that the formal structures of sentiment are based upon symbolically masculine ideals. We might consider that the propensity in feminist literary and often film criticism to emphasize sentiment's relation to women reproduces the very fetishistic codes of sexual difference these theories critique. If a culturally masculinist bias is at work in such critiques, that same bias may have blinded us to the depth of sentiment's relation to male symbolic structures, as well as to the number of actual male artists who have reproduced sentiment's themes.[4]

My account of a symbolically male form of sentiment—which follows Adam Smith's notion that the moral sentiment of sympathy is a male-identified practice—couples Hume's classic analysis of "the sentiments" with contemporary theories of masculine spectatorship and the figural apparatus of the gaze. Drawing upon the Lacanian tradition in cinema studies, as well as Michel Foucault's writings on perversion, I explore eighteenth- and nineteenth-century novels in light of this gaze, and their sentimental reliance upon it. I also explore the contemporary visual media, whose technology embodies the gaze and enhances the perverse privilege of the spectator.

In doing so, my study reconsiders the narrow historical periodization that has dominated scholarship on sentiment and sympathy. In an important volume of essays on "the culture of sentiment" in nineteenth-century America, Shirley Samuels describes a "habitus" of sentiment—she imports Pierre Bourdieu's sociological term—that enveloped and consumed its popular-textual images.[5] My own study engages with sentiment as a reproductive phenomenon; it embraces the idea of a "habitus," but expands its social-historical boundaries. Moving along the interdisciplinary lines explored in Samuels's volume—especially noteworthy are the essays on sentimental ideology in Native American photographs and murder-trial texts[6]—my own approach also explores the motivation of the psychoanalytic, narrative subject. On both fictive and enunciatory levels of the sentimental text, the narrative subject reasserts what Jean-François Lyotard has called *les grands récits,* the master narratives of the post-Enlightenment West. The master narratives continue to flower and propagate themselves in multiple narrative media within multiple national cultures of the post-Enlightenment. Generating and regenerating the Enlightenment ideal of the "self," the master narratives adapt and readapt themselves in formally transformative media. Differences of media and historical epoch should not dissuade us from examining the common features of the sentimental subject, in its slippery representational duality.

This study also reconsiders the usual claim that sentiment is unrelated to realism. Fictions of sentiment and realism have long been perceived as structurally, historically, distinct—the eighteenth-century epistolary novel and the nineteenth-century novel of realism viewed at a wide remove. These seemingly unconnected traditions, I argue, are unified by the role of the spectator. "Realism," as I treat it here, is another sentimental illusion related to the antirealism of melodrama and its mass-culture narratives, like those of classic cinema and U.S. commercial television. Conversely, the sentimental epistolarity, as I treat it in chapter 1, strives for a type of verisimilitude, or "realism," of its own. Literary epistles fanned the desire for immediacy, directness, and a camera-like visual agency. Hence, I see the novel of realism as one of the epistolary tradition's literary legacies. A sympathetic spectator inhabits novels of realism and sentiment alike; but this spectator maps a perverse historical trajectory. Sentimental identification disguises the sado-masochistic visual desire that frames Richardson's epistolary tradition. And the identification strategies upon which "realism" relies disguise the sentimental, sadomasochistic moralism behind the Flaubert or James schools. The perverse, deviant route of sympathy allows technologies of sentiment and "reality" to thrive. A very bold sado-erotic "reality" spectator is reproduced by women's "weepies"—for example, in Douglas Sirk's late-50s film

Imitation of Life—or by the classic "reality" dramas of Reagan-era television— for example, in CBS's *Rescue 911.*

Not only do I deconstruct the critical binarism undergirding the distinction between sentiment and realism, demonstrating a relationship overlooked, perhaps, because of social beliefs about gendered male and female authorship. But I also deconstruct another critical binarism, one that has initiated its own deconstructive forces. This is the "dismantling" of the binary opposition that exists in early sexology, including Sigmund Freud's early writings on sadomasochism, and which many contemporary writers on popular culture and perversion have recently reassessed. The intellectual leader of this work, Gilles Deleuze, has argued forcefully that sadism and masochism are *not* functionally unified perversions, but, in fact, operate differently and distinctively, historically as well as structurally. Deleuze's argument has been taken up by many critics writing about cinema's relationship to scopophilia and masochism.[7] While I am grateful for the groundbreaking work of these critics on sadism and masochism, I ultimately treat these perversions as dialectically and functionally unified. In this approach, I follow Foucault's writings on perversion, claiming perversion as a unifying device of power. Foucault emphasizes that it is the nature of perversion, which he perceives as a social-sexual methodology and "discourse" of the post-Enlightenment, to disguise and divert sources of aggression and power in order to enhance both. Foucault follows Freud's later writings. For the later Freud, sadistic and masochistic subjectivity is vicissitudinous, always reconceptualizing the sexual subject's shifting relation to an object of desire. In short, Freud suggests that aggression and the desire for control motivate *both* sadism and masochism. Foucault, too, describes perversion, in general, as a vicissitudinous process.

I draw upon Freud when analyzing the unconscious drives of the sadomasochistic subject. But I turn to Foucault to explain the social nature of these drives, specifically the aims of the scopophilic pervert. This figure is a purveyor of sympathy within and around narrative texts, a sentimental figure who defuses but also reasserts power and control. Through the figure of the sentimental pervert, sadism and masochism are united in duplicitous union. This pervert is a gazer who is both controlling and controlled. He is a symbolic subject who is both seeing and unseen.

The "E(ye)nlightened" Subject

The works of both Freud and Foucault instigate a critique of the post-Enlightenment subject, bringing into the picture that subject's perverse visual strategies for self-definition. My book, thus, turns to some of the actual treatises of the philosophical Enlightenment in order to further this critique. These treatises, at times, can be read as proto-sentimental texts themselves, predating the later developments of literary sentiment. To associate Enlightenment philosophical texts with an emergent post-Enlightenment sentimental literature in England, America, and France, of course, is not to stake out new ground; the topic has been admirably covered by R. F. Brissenden, Ian Watt, Fred Kaplan, and Janet Todd, among many others. Yet these classic approaches to sentiment's relationship to the Enlightenment do not treat philosophical texts as sentimental texts in their own right. And they do not raise issues like subjectivity and scopophilia—in fact, rarely is the divided notion of the psychoanalytic subject brought to bear on Enlightenment philosophy at all.[8]

To understand the relation between visual perversion and sympathy, we need to set both contemporary perversion studies and Hume's eighteenth-century theory of sympathy within the context of the "Enlightenment" self, and its historical development through philosophical optimism. In its tendency to dramatize the individual's psychological autonomy, sentimental fiction has promoted the "self" as a whole, independent, and rational being. This concept of Western "Enlightened" subjectivity is based upon the idealization of the human individual, whose use of reason solidifies moral intention and representational divisions. French linguist Emile Benveniste has shown the concept of the subject as whole and undivided to be an illusion of language, a faulty mirror of an identity that, after all, never exists within and through the language from which it emerges. The phrase "Enlightenment subject" is itself an oxymoron, for the "subject" is a narrational impulse whose "identity" is always shattered by the very instability of pronouns ("I" or "you") used to register shifting narrative positions.[9] Jane Flax sums up the modern critique of the Enlightenment subject when she writes that "the existence of a stable, coherent self" is the product of "the ideal of reason" that maintains "privileged insight into its own processes and into the 'laws of nature'" (41). One who reveals such "privileged insight," as we shall see, is the sentimental heroine Clarissa, in her introspective musings upon her "faults." In contrast, the would-be sentimental heroine Susan Smith was criticized in media accounts for *not* maintaining "privileged insight" into her culpability in her children's murders, although one such "insight"—her history of alleged sexual abuse—was precisely the posture taken by her legal defense.[10]

That the "stable, coherent self" exists through "privileged insight" suggests a consistent view of "human nature" prevalent within Enlightenment ethical as well as empirical writings—and in the works of contemporary critics who have analyzed fictive sentiment's roots in Enlightenment philosophical works.[11] Strangely, the concept of the Enlightenment "self" as autonomously reasoning and internally *self*-controlling would appear to challenge other widely held views about sentimental fictions in general. By its very label, "sentiment" invokes "feeling," and is known to create emotiveness to the point of excessiveness. "Sentimentality," in one conventional literary handbook, is defined as "an overindulgence in the 'tender' emotions of pathos and sympathy."[12] This modernist pejorative view of sentiment survives even its recent feminist re-evaluations. My own theory, that sentiment is a divided subject keyed to many Enlightenment precepts, supports a small group of critics who have focused on "overindulgence" as sentiment's *structural* feature. These critics avoid modernity's dismissiveness toward sentiment while nevertheless allowing for the exploration of the formal implications of sentiment's "excessive" character. Following a suggestion of one of these critics, I define sentiment as "a response out of proportion to its object."[13] The disproportionate "response" resembles another subject in psychoanalytic theory, the subject of sadomasochism.

The Subject of Sadomasochism

Sadomasochism is an excessive subject within the object-relations branch of psychoanalytic theory. Object-relations studies of sadomasochism describe a similar "out of proportion" response for a subject performing master-slave roles. Object-relations theory upholds the importance of a child's early environment in psychological development. Most important to this bed of theory is the relationship of the child to his or her primary caretaker, and the corollary importance placed upon the child's ability to obtain a sense of his or her own autonomy through recognition. Much has been written in object-relations studies about sadomasochistic desire. These accounts suggest that sadomasochism itself is a social subject's response "out of proportion" to an object, the repressed drama of social dependency.

If dependency creates what Lynn Chancer's sociological study *The Sadomasochism of Everyday Life* has called "the sadomasochistic dynamic," encoding the paradox between independence and dependence, then dependency is a displaced expression of self-control, social aggression, and domination. Dependency is that which generates the excessive, exaggerated response, subject to object. This response, according to Chancer, is the result of the subject's inability to experience existential recognition, and a less totalizing dependency based upon mutual reciprocity with the "other." Chancer, of course, borrows from Jessica Benjamin's discussion of sadomasochism, which suggests that its psychical origins lie in the early childhood bonds between a child and caretaker.[14] In patriarchal-familial systems, the mother or mother-substitute acts as the child's primary caretaker. Benjamin hypothesizes that an exaggerated aggression results when the child fails to receive psychical recognition from the mother—since the mother is a figure poorly positioned to respond to the child's demands and attacks, because of her own patriarchally instilled passivity and recognition-lack. A complicated dynamic unfolds by which the child may increase his or her sadism toward the mother, but may also incorporate the mother's masochism into his or her subjectivity.

Benjamin's hypothesis is reread by Chancer as structuring an overarching social fabric, in which a socialized sadomasochistic dynamic lies at the core. Chancer emphasizes that the sadomasochistic dynamic is a means of guaranteeing the continued presence of the other. The sadist and masochist depend upon one another for their ontological status based upon the performance of controlling roles. To guarantee the presence of the other is to guarantee the illusion of the self *through* control. But while the self is at issue in Chancer's theory, the sadomasochistic dynamic she describes is a social text that informs and constructs interpersonal relations, those of the nuclear family and other capitalist-patriarchal structures like the post-industrial workplace. The dependency drama, she suggests—quoting Eric Fromm—is the ironic result of a "'denial of dependency,'" promoted by capitalistic social institutions (69). These institutions breed "profound feelings of isolation" that stir desire for sadomasochism to ever-heightening levels.

Recent media murder trials, like that of Susan Smith's, bear testimony to this sadomasochistic social schema. They also bear a sadomasochistic culture's endorsement of *women's* dependency, especially upon patriarchal family institutions that support social sadomasochism and its call for "rational" violence. In the Susan Smith narrative put forth by the media, violence was sentimentally reproduced in the drama of heterosexual romance. A "family" romance evolved, in the spin-off narrative about Smith's alleged sexual abuse. Violence was the result.

From the media, we learned in the aftermath of Smith's murder confession that Smith's stepfather reportedly made unwanted sexual advances toward Smith, which this "good" patriarchal daughter eventually, supposedly, welcomed. The dutiful daughter acted according to what the media psychologized as "feelings of abandonment" due to her *natural* father's original suicide; a naturalness to the father-daughter romance drama thereby was asserted. While the private domestic-family thread of the Smith narrative became a national media sensation—Smith's stepfather was a prominent businessman in a South Carolina town, and Smith herself was a white middle-class girl and local babysitter who appealed to racist stereotypes when she initially blamed her children's disappearance upon a black male kidnapper—these very public and publicized acts continued to be mediated through sentimental images of "private" media: the stepfather's epistolary confession, Smith's jail-cell swoonings, and a personal "diary" published in *People Magazine* attributed to David Smith, Susan Smith's estranged husband and grieving father.

For all their differences in narrative elements like character and plot, the even more publicized media murder trial of O. J. Simpson drew upon similar sadomasochistic features. The narrative details were rearranged, but they were not so very different in their effects, as a rags-to-riches black football hero marries a white waitress and would-be Hollywood starlet, and violence erupts in the privacy of their Brentwood home. In what became yet another narrative of heterosexual coupling and violence, a paucity of what Chancer calls "existential needs" seemed to emerge on both sides. Through months of televised legal proceedings including witness testimony, and the use of audiotapes and photographs to confirm domestic violence, Nicole Simpson was sermonized by the prosecution as the victim of wife beating— and I do not suggest here that she was not a battered wife. What ultimately concerns me is Nicole Simpson's victimage, as both battered wife and murder victim. But if we uphold Chancer's analysis as a lens through which we might review the trial narrative of a crime that captivated millions of spectators through the medium of television, we peer steadily into the larger master narrative of female victimage. The source of this narrative may lie within patriarchy itself—that is the big picture and the easy answer. We need to ask further: what led Nicole Simpson to remain in, to repeatedly return to, a marriage whose multiple separations had already ensured her financial support, a marriage in which she was beaten by her husband in more than one confirmed incident? The syndrome of the trauma of the beaten wife was the interpretation put forth rather baldly by the L.A. County District Attorney's office, whose own motive, of course, was to build jury sympathy for the victim. We might conclude that, indeed, Nicole Simpson was controlled and dominated by some irrational force, including the star charisma of her ex-husband. But she seemed also controlled by her own desire for control, and in her repeated efforts to control, or "recover," a violent marriage.

"Nicole," in the narrative of the battered wife that emerged from the trial, became the image of the sentimental heroine of fiction. As such, her image reproduced popular, social sadomasochistic longings. For this reason, viewers of the "O. J. Trial," as it came to be known, experienced both sympathy for the victim and sadism toward her, as the details of a bloody murder scene unfolded at the trial. America seemed glued to its collective TV set to discover these sensational details, and also "the truth" of the verdict—whether or not its superhero O. J. would be found guilty of the heinous murder of his former wife and her friend, Ronald Goldman. But "America" also became the image of a unified mass spectator who re-experienced again and again, in serial fashion, like Nicole, the sadomasochistic story of violence and heterosexual romance. A Hollywood romance unfolded for the spectator, like a cinematic remake of *Gone with the Wind*—

the image of the battered, bruised face of Nicole Simpson alternating with glamour-girl poses on covers of tabloids like *The Enquirer* and *Star,* propped up against supermarket check-out shelves.

Fetishistic images of female victimage were again reproduced by the prosecution in its closing argument, ironically when replaying a "911" tape that proved the victim called for law-enforcement help. The replaying of Nicole Simpson's "911" call was accompanied by the projection of crime-scene photographs hidden from (but always indirectly present for) television viewers. The prosecution may have emphasized the master and slave aspects of the heterosexual romance. But it attempted to repress the master and slave story of American racism, an attempt that notoriously failed. A nearly all African-American jury returned a verdict of not-guilty after the shortest of deliberations. Many surprised (and usually white) observers blamed this verdict upon the theme of police racism and violence inserted by the defense through the now-infamous "Fuhrman tapes." These tapes reproduced white L.A.P.D. officer Mark Furhman's racist diatribes, which he supposedly reproduced for a television script. The division between fact and fiction—always suspect from the beginning of this case—was erased as a would-be television script became real-life evidence in this televised court-room drama. The narrative of racial oppression collided with that of sexual subjection. Both were sadomasochistic narratives that, together, heightened viewer fascination and the level of entertainment provided by the trial. The "O. J. Trial" (called only slightly hyperbolically "the trial of the century") was certainly the tabloid-television sensation of the year—and the main subject of *Larry King Live* for many months.

Clarissa, what this book considers sentiment's ur-text, might be one of the longest English novels ever written. But the "O. J. Trial" is on record as one of the longest and most lavishly expensive murder trials in L.A. County history, its daily televised coverage replete with excessive lawyers, verbose and raucous sidebars—a case excessively reported upon by network nightly news, by prime-time news magazines, by hour-long network "specials," by its own nightly CNN "recap" program, and by its full, daily, serial, live documentation on CNN as well as Court TV. Two typical sentimental tropes emerged from this excessive event treated as a text. These tropes not only typify narratives of sentiment but also of sadomasochistic desire.

One trope is that of excessive dependency versus independence invoked by object-relations theories about sadomasochism. The other is the trope of specular excess. The first trope appears in the portrayal of the lifestyle of O. J. and Nicole Simpson. Victim or not, Nicole, like O.J., appears to have revelled in the fetishistic representations of social autonomy, reproduced by the spectacle of displayed wealth in posh Brentwood homes, personal trainers, and Ferraris that became part of the trial. These fetishistic representations also included her own image as "the blonde," as would-be Hollywood movie actress. The second and related trope of specular excess was reproduced in the fetishized commodities made props for the court-room/television drama, like maquettes of O. J.'s mansion and Nicole's condominium-as-murder-scene. It was duplicated in the spinning of the master-slave narratives competing for primary meaning: for both a jury who would decide the verdict and a mass spectator sympathetically exerting a moral gaze. And this trope of specular excess also was duplicated in the spectacular renderings of that narrative through its hyper-media coverage.

Excessiveness, and a dependency parading as social autonomy through conspicuous wealth, contributed to the theme of control that insidiously dominated American airwaves and reshaped '90s tabloid journalism. It entranced and dominated spectators. Perhaps what spectators were buying was a tender Hollywood love story that "somehow" went wrong. Or perhaps spectators were seeking that "fellow feeling" of sympathy, in its tender identification and yet detached ("glad it isn't me") effects. But I would add that spectators of the O. J. trial were drawn to a sadomasochistic scene of mass carnage with a sentimental appeal. The trial as mass-media event reproduced the spectator's own massive, spectacular, excessive longings for sadomasochistic forms of bondage—like spectatorship itself.

Mass spectators were drawn by the trial's "out-of-proportion" effects, made especially perverse and bizarre by the containment and solemnity of the courtroom setting, reproduced on television by a video camera that, by judicial order, could not pivot. A drama "out of control" was, in fact, carefully regulated *and* controlled—through its static courtroom representation, and the rigor of criminal-justice legal proceedings that vied against a rather circus-like atmosphere including famous lawyers, the star-struck Judge Lance Ito, and witnesses who became household names. The sadomasochistic drama *about* control (gone out of control) was monitored both within and without the courtroom by megatropes *of* control. The megatropes of control versus a fear of lack (of control) are inherent to the identities of these strange bedfellows I have been describing, the sadomasochistic and sentimental subjects.

A mimetic bondage exists, I maintain, between the sadomasochist and the sentimentalist. Both subjects assert their desire for control based upon an excessive need for another's objectification in narrative self-creation. Yet sadomasochistic and sentimental narratives are not exactly mirroring representations. The subject of sentiment seeks to control its object within the context of a narrative act; this act, indeed, reflects the underlying sado-masochistic trope of dependence. Dependence, however, for the subject of sentiment takes the form of a *dual* denial. If the sadomasochistic subject is the product of a "stifling individualism" generating overvaluation toward an object, the subject of sentiment openly revalidates "excessive" dependency—the disproportionate response declared a means of the subject's narration. The subject's sentiment and use of sympathy actually *encourage* the overinvestment of the subject toward its object; its narratives thereby appear—at least temporarily—to make up for, to compensate for, the subject's loss of control, but also for lack of recognition and mutual social interdependency. In this manner, the sadomasochistic drama operates in tandem with, but also hidden from, the sentimental one. Sadomasochistic dependency lurks under the surface of every sentimental text. And sympathy enters the picture as a representation of sentiment's mixed motives.

A Perverse Subject

In its sadomasochistic drama of disavowed control and subjugation, the subject of sentiment, employing sympathy, enacts what Louise Kaplan calls the "perverse strategy." This strategy is a circuitous method by which a psychoanalytic subject generates an effect different than its psychical origin would otherwise suggest. The perverse strategy is "a mental strategy," according to Kaplan, "that uses one or another social stereotypes of masculinity and femininity in a way that deceives the onlooker about the unconscious meanings of the behavior she or he is observing" (9). Kaplan further explains the way in which the perverse strategy operates as a circuitous, but exacting, phenomenon—in a language that stresses the clinical-research finding that most bona fide sexual masochists (she doesn't mention sadists) are, in fact, male:

> Very often, the perverse enactment depends for its success on a *double sleight* of hand . . . a secret desire is out in the open distracting the observer from searching for any further meaning. . . . We see the kinky sex, the man being humiliated and demeaned by his dominator, right before our eyes, but we are deceived completely as to his unconscious motives. (13—Kaplan's emphasis)

The subject of sentiment employs this indirect strategy in the deceptive, contradictory reproduction of desire and power through narrative forms. Sentiment conceals, but also reveals, "unconscious motives" that are sadomasochistic within narration. The conventions of sentimental subjectivity—femininity, emotiveness, psychological autonomy and independence—"distracts" the subject from other circuitous effects invoking themes of sado-erotic power: the control of femininity, the artificial manipulation of emotion, and the perpetuation of cyclical interdependencies. These circuitous effects are harbored in images of women, or otherwise culturally feminized subjects like mass-culture entertainment audiences themselves, what Andreas Huyssen calls "mass culture as 'woman.' "[15]

To read the perverse femininized conventions of the sentimental subject and its narrative effects, one must follow this aberrational course. Such a course, again, suggests a Freudian legacy. In "Three Essays on the Theory of Sexuality" (1905), Freud describes perversions that include sadism and masochism, scopophilic voyeurism and fetishism, as "the sexual aberrations."[16] A perversion, according to Freud's reductive literality, is an "aberration" that "hinders or postpones the attainment of the normal sexual aim," defined by Freud as penile-vaginal intercourse.[17] His suggestion that perversion circumvents or prevents "normal" reproductive sex appears a conservative one today. Yet intellectual interest in the "deviant," aberrational nature of the Freudian mechanism continues to inform contemporary discussions about perversion as a sexual but also representational act—like the perverse strategy described by Kaplan.

Kaja Silverman also emphasizes the "diversionary and decentering character" in Freud's perversion theory, in discussions of male masochism and masculine subjectivity. "The notion of a deferred action" may be politically subversive, she suggests, through the polymorphous unbinding of the dominant culture's repressive oedipal sexuality (*Male Subjectivity* 185–86). While Silverman does not endorse the view that some radical writers take, that all polysexualities are cause for celebration,[18] she perceives in some perversions—especially masochism—the capacity to strip "sexuality of all functionality, whether biological or social." She adds that "Perversion also subverts many of the binary oppositions," like male-female or dominant-submissive, "upon which the social order rests" (187). Silverman criticizes the contrasting view of perverse sexualities taken by Foucault, who argues that perversion merely extends "the surface upon which power is exercised," in Silverman's words, creating "no subversive edge" (186).

Silverman's critique of Foucault is informed by Deleuze's important study of masochism, which challenges the automatic complementarity presumed about sadism and masochism ever since Richard von Krafft-Ebing's *Psychopathia Sexualis* (1885) coined the "sadomasochism" term. Deleuze points out that the concepts of sadism and masochism arise from two distinctive historical-philosophical contexts based upon the very different "pornologies" authored by novelists the Marquis de Sade and Leopold von Sacher-Masoch. Similarly, Silverman reiterates that not all perversions are alike, and that sadism and masochism function very differently. Masochism may offer the male subject a position of social transgression, according to this argument, since masochism eroticizes a "lack and subordination" conventionally associated with the female subject. Sadistic desire, contrasts Silverman, does not offer this possibility at all: "It is unfortunate but not surprising that the perversion which has commandeered most of the literary and theoretical attention—sadism—is also the one which is most compatible with conventional heterosexuality" (187). To speak about sadism, therefore, appears tantamount to complying with the dominant order's sexual ideology.

I want to emphasize that Foucault's account of perversion—as Silverman herself notes—is figured in his discussion of the panopticon, and the sadistic gaze that asserts itself behind Enlightenment penal reform. Silverman stops short of recalling what I find to be the most interesting aspect of Foucault's model for sadism: that sadism, as a perversion, operates in circuitous, disparate ways to displace but also to wield power, and that it implicates other perversions, including masochism, in the process. In the manner of Kaplan's perverse strategy, the panopticon is both figure for and a means toward exerting sadistic domination in the guise of post-Enlightenment penal reform, according to Foucault. The spectacular "festival" of "punishment"—the style of torture and execution prior to Enlightenment views of criminal justice—were replaced by "a new legal or administrative practice," writes Foucault, making punishment "the most *hidden part* of the penal process" (*Discipline and Punish* 8–9—emphasis added). The sadistic "process," through penal reform, came to operate more secretly through the self-disavowing methods of the sentimentalist. These methods have allowed tyrannical control to adapt itself to a new era, and to centralize itself around the image of its very perversity—to "reapportion" power:

> As a result, justice no longer takes public responsibility for the violence that is bound up with its practice . . . The apportioning of blame is redistributed: in punishment-as-spectacle a confused horror spread from the scaffold; it enveloped both executioner and condemned. . . . Now the scandal and the light are to be distributed differently . . . the publicity has shifted to the trial, and to the sentence; the execution itself is like an additional shame that justice is ashamed to impose on the condemned man; *so it keeps its distance from the act,* tending always to entrust it to others, under the seal of *secrecy.* (*Discipline and Punish* 9–10—emphasis added)

Not only does the "redistribution" separate sadism from sentiment, masochism from aggressivity and power. The "redistribution" propels a circuitous "secrecy" within the legacy of power, and conveys the necessity for hiddenness in power relations. The "distance from the act" refracts perversion into its disparate parts, like the sentimental figure of the cellular panopticon.[19] Foucault, in other words, suggests that perversion understates the method of power, the totalizing tendency of the gaze.

Sentimental narratives, like medicalized narratives that mirror the multiple perverse sexualities they attempt to diagnose, are structurally perverse because they distract *through refraction* the gaze as centralizing agency. Foucault's comments on perversion in *The History of Sexuality* might be applied to sentimental narratives represented by the growth of the criminal-justice system and penal bureaucracies. His image of the various perversions as divided and distinct reiterates the Freudian "aberrational" effect cited by Silverman. But Foucault concludes that it is "through the isolation, intensification, and consolidation of peripheral sexualities that the relations of sex and pleasure branched out and multiplied." (He speaks, specifically, of the culture of the Victorians.) Therefore, Foucault's argument anticipates criticisms like those of Silverman and Deleuze, that sadism and masochism should be viewed as distinct perversions. Foucault explains: "These attractions, these evasions, these circular incitements have traced around bodies and sexes, not boundaries to be crossed but *perpetual spirals of power and pleasure*" (*History of Sexuality* 45—Foucault's emphasis). The Foucauldian reading of perversion may return "the sexual aberrations" back to a conservative early-Freudian base. For Foucault, however, aberration is never a means of escape—from sexual orthodoxy and other forms of repression. "Escape" only mimics the very power differential that is the basis for a modern style of domination, and, we might add, system of sexual difference.[20]

Deleuze and Silverman are right to question any automatic complementarity between sadism and masochism. The term "sadomasochism," based on sexology's misreading of texts, has led both turn-of-the-century sexual-deviance catalogers and many modern sociologists alike to assume a sociobiological fallacy, one that perceives sadomasochism to be a natural erotica informing biological male-female behavior.[21] I nevertheless employ this unstable portmanteau term when discussing sentiment because it best explains the sentimental subject's reliance upon the sympathetic gaze. I use the term "sadomasochism" in agreement with Chancer's analysis of sadism and masochism as an interrelational social dialectic—and also in agreement with Freud's concept of sadism and masochism as creating intrasubjective vicissitudes. Freud's 1915 essay, "Instincts and Their Vicissitudes," countered his earlier more simplistic, binary concept of sadism and masochism by suggesting that sadomasochism is a tertiary shifting process internalized by a subject's relation to an object. The subject claims an "original" sadism when it seeks to control and inflict pain upon an object; but it can reverse the object of its sadistic attack by directing this control or aggression inward—making the self its object, a masochistic positioning. A fully vicarious or representational sadomasochism is created when the subject enjoys pain *vicariously*, viewing a suffering object. Freud's 1924 essay, "The Economic Problem of Masochism," more fully detailed the way in which masochism is related to sadism, through the underlying drive of aggression, asserting itself inward. Self-aggression, Freud argued in this later essay, manifests itself through erotogenic and more displaced forms of masochism, what he called "feminine" and moral masochism.

The vicissitudinous theory of sado-erotic aggression and domination

scarcely touches upon the subject of social power through the steadfast
cultural gaze. In linking Freud's theory to Foucault's panopticon, I would
emphasize Freud's usefulness in exploring perversion as a method of wielding power. Sympathy is implicated as a particularly perverse, panopticon
strategy. It is particularly perverse because its spectator is supposed to be a
moral authority moved by images; but he is also like the faceless prison
guard who reflects bureaucratic violence in the name of "reform." Sympathy
is supposed to encourage the movement of "feeling," through vicarious
affect and identification with someone else's emotion. Yet the process of
vision prevents any true movement associated with "feeling." Hence, sympathy unleashes its own psychical conflict. Sympathy, even more than the
figure of the panopticon, *conceals* the desire for and use of power through
identification. Through sympathy, the aggressivity of sentiment is safely,
perversely, released.

    While Chancer has shown that sadomasochism should not be per-
ceived as a *socially* aberrant behavior—that sadomasochistic behavior is not
the prerogative of exotic social subgroups but rather structures "everyday
life" under capitalism—Foucault has reinterpreted the consequences of the
"aberration" itself; he suggests that an aberrant "nature" re-enforces the
power of oppressive law. Sadomasochistic sentiments may perform as an
aberration, in the primarily ethical sense of Freud, and in Silverman's concept of "aberration" as deviation from oedipal convention. But sadomasochistic sentiments are not aberrational in any socially regulatory sense, since
the aberrational mode is the perverse strategy of collective and individual
sources of social power. Sadomasochism *does* function as an "aberration,"
however, in yet another secondary sense defined by *Merriam Webster's English
Dictionary:* a "failed mirror," a "refracting surface, or lens" made "to produce
exact point-to-point correspondence between an object and its image." This
failed mirror is the best image, perhaps, for the pervert-spectator of sympathy. This spectator looks outwardly toward discursive-erotic freedom and
sexual-textual invention, but his gaze is refracted back into its own ka-
leidoscopic totality. The "failure" is a moral one, the aberration dividing any
totalizing moral picture of human nature into broken shards or fragments.
But the "failure" is also a representational one: when the "failure" cracks,
but also invites spectators to, the verisimilar lens.

"Human Nature," Sympathy, and the Male Gaze

These moral and representational themes are encoded into discourses
about human nature and reason from the philosophical Enlightenment.
While Chancer has related sadomasochism to a faulty individualism that
critics from Marx to the Frankfurt School have aligned with the capitalist

state, I am relating sadomasochism to the conflicted texts out of which the Enlightenment cult of the autonomous and sentimentalized individual arose. The scholars who have tied the Enlightenment to the development of literary sentiment in the eighteenth and nineteenth centuries emphasize the role of empiricism in the evolution of sentiment; they show the reliance of sentiment upon empiricism, and the role of sensory impression in creating knowledge. Watt, for example, shows that Richardson's epistolary novels evolved out of a need to provide a "continuous" image of the individual, an image that first emerged in empirical thought about sensory impression. What Richardson called in his Preface to *Clarissa* the novel's "instantaneous descriptions and reflections" (35), in Watt's observation, reveals the importance Richardson placed upon the sensory, empiricism's primary epistemological theme. Brissenden also has written that the popular assimilation of empirical themes helped Richardson to establish a phenomenological stage that would exploit "sensation." And Fred Kaplan, shifting his focus to Victorian sentiment, suggests that the Victorians waged "a protest against the increasingly powerful forces of philosophical and scientific realism" that empiricism and skepticism had founded (3). Meanwhile, the Victorians also adopted the Enlightenment optimistic view of "human nature," one that countered seventeenth-century claims about "nature" as a state of "war," best represented in the work of Thomas Hobbes.

While eighteenth- and nineteenth-century optimism was "a reaction against the Hobbesian view of a viciously flawed human nature, which only a repressive state can control and only a god of grace can redeem," as Kaplan summarizes (14), this optimism ironically led to the belief in a "normative" view of "human nature" itself, in the assumption that "such an entity existed," or could be "applied to the generality of mankind, as the innate disposition or character of individuals and of human kind as a whole" (Kaplan 12–13). In other words, the concept of "human nature" emerged from out of its own positive terms. I stress in this book that this belief about "human nature" is related to natural law, and British Moralist School discussions of a "disposition" in human nature to adopt the course of virtue and social harmony. One contemporary writer on this formulation of natural law notes that it emerged from a "tradition of moral enquiry" that inescapably "puts strong emphasis on the role of virtue in moral life."[22] Natural law came to heavily influence British Moralist discussions of human nature, virtue, and the "moral sentiment" of sympathy; and it later influenced fictive sentiment.

Natural law has a long and ancient history. It was Thomas Aquinas who drew upon Aristotlean virtue ethics and the New Testament of the Bible to establish the early modern concept of natural law, that the law exists as a form of innate moral knowledge through the use of reason. Long after Aquinas, the early-seventeenth-century Dutch lawyer and political theorist

Hugo Grotius paved the way for the secular application of natural law that would prove important to the Enlightenment; he declared the "law" to be known through "an intuitive judgement," that which makes known "what things from their own nature are honorable or dishonorable, involving a duty to follow the same imposed by God"—but not *of* God, an important distinction for Grotius.[23] Samuel von Pufendorf, another writer who would become important to the Scottish Enlightenment and the British Moralist tradition, followed this Grotian insight when he distinguished "natural law," knowable through reason, from "divine law," knowable through God's revelation. Yet Pufendorf and later empiricists viewed reason itself as God-given, thereby reverting to Thomisic doctrine while nevertheless suggesting that "man" was free to discern the application of reason for himself. What seemed to be a distinction became a lack of distinction for Pufendorf and the British Moralists. This supposed "distinction" hovered within the image of "nature" itself, which implied a natural, or transcendent, use of reason.

Even the great empiricist John Locke, when writing essays on natural law, had difficulty discerning between the "tradition" of "nature" and the use of "reason or judgement" to determine "nature." Locke discussed a "disposition" or "inner principle" upon which natural law rests. While he did not "deny that some, and nearly all, of the precepts of this law are handed down to us by our parents, teachers, and by all those who busy themselves in forming the character of the young and tender minds with the love and knowledge of virtue" (*Questions* 125), such principles of socialization do not escape the fact that an internal "knowledge of virtue" exists. Internal "knowledge" is the root of the moral sentiments described by the next generation of British Moralists. And it is at the root of the moral sentiments that emerged from Richardson's pen and spawned narratives of fictive sentiment.

Perhaps most closely identified with the moral ideology of Richardson's sentiment is the philosophical work of the Third Earl of Shaftesbury, who perceived virtue as naturally "imprinted" on the human mind. Shaftesbury, too, emphasized that a use of "right reason" would determine knowledge of virtue and the "law." Indeed, Shaftesbury seemed to be describing Richardson's archetypal sentimental heroine Clarissa when he wrote of a "sense" and of a reason through which "Mankind" is possessed of a "just Affection" (*Inquiry Concerning Virtue* 7). Through a "Sound and well-established Reason" (17), Shaftesbury wrote, it is "man's nature" to be kind to his fellows. This link between reason, human nature, and virtuous feeling was a source of intense debate by other members of the British Moralist School as they tried to merge empiricism with cultural beliefs about nature and natural law.

The protestant minister Frances Hutcheson, who would deeply influence Hume, was among the more articulate members of the school who tried to mediate these two points of view.[24] Like Shaftesbury, Hutcheson wrote that human nature contained a native "moral sense" that, if not "innate," was a "determination of our minds to receive" what he called "Ideas of Actions," whether they be of an "amiable or disagreeable" nature (83). Recalling natural law's affiliation with Christianity, Hutcheson's argument cites the Christian image of an all-knowing "maker" or God, and attributes a "uniformity" in human goodness to this "Author of Nature," who "has determined us to receive, by our external Senses, pleasant or disagreeable Ideas of Objects . . . the Pleasures of Beauty and Harmony, to excite us to the Pursuit of Knowledge" (83). Hutcheson, like Aquinas of another age, believed that a Christian God "has given us a Moral Sense, to direct our Action, and to give us still nobler Pleasures." In using this moral sense, "We are only intending the Good of others," Hutcheson added; but "we undesignedly promote our own greatest private Good" (83).

In his own discussion of the "moral sentiments," the more radical empiricist and skeptic Hume would further Hutcheson's perceptual emphases on the human desire to obtain pleasure. But Hume's *Treatise* would underscore a paradox lurking in the use of the term "sense." Developing Hutcheson's language further—especially Hutcheson's rational "sense" based upon "sentiment"—Hume described the way in which the "moral sentiments" were products of "the passions," and not at all the "sense" of reason. Hume insisted in the *Treatise* that "Reason of itself is utterly impotent in this particular. The rules of morality . . . are not conclusions of our reasons"; therefore, "'tis in vain to pretend, that morality is discover'd only by a deduction of reason."[25] In writing thus, Hume radically divorced the role of reason from morality and ethics. And he thereby called into question the regulatory function of natural law.

Arguing that "morality . . . is more properly felt than judg'd of" (470), Hume suggested that moral judgment arises from the subject's felt "impression." Moral approbation of that impression arises from feelings that are "agreeable" or not: "we . . . must pronounce the impression arising from virtue, to be agreeable, and that proceeding from vice to be uneasy" (470). In discussing the passions in Book II of the *Treatise*, Hume did describe a certain "nature" or consistency within human nature. The passions, specifically, of pride and humility, he wrote, are produced by the same objects; "upon the view even of a stranger, we can know pretty nearly, what will either increase or diminish his passions of this kind" (281). "Inconsiderable" variation may occur through "the tempers and complexion of men," according to Hume. But, he asked, "Can we imagine if possible, that while human nature remains the same, men will ever become entirely indifferent to their power, riches, beauty or personal merit, and that their pride and vanity will not be affected by these advantages?" (281). Hume followed this question with a response that distinguishes between the "natural" and the "original":

"But tho' the cause of pride and humility be plainly *natural,* we shall find upon examination, that they are not *original.* . . . that 'tis utterly impossible they shou'd each of them be adapted to these passions by a particular provision, and primary constitution of nature" (281—Hume's emphasis).

Most readings of Hume link his account of human nature closely to that of Shaftesbury and Hutcheson, who both argued for intrinsic moral value—an "unalterability," in the words of one writer.[26] This reading, I would argue, is a sentimental one of Hume, one that divides Hume's work from the Hobbesian view of natural law, in which "nature" is proclaimed a state of war, and human nature motivated by self-interest. Hume did argue that "There is a general course of nature in human actions, as well as in the operation of the sun and the climate" (402–3). We know this "course of nature" by "the observation of an uniformity in the actions, that flow from them," in other words, by the logic of causality that Hume's epistemological work emphasizes. In this statement, Hume echoes the very problem inherent within cause-effect logic, discussed more fully in the epistemological section of the *Treatise.* He thereby laid the groundwork for what would become an early psychoanalytic exploration of the division in the so-called "uniformity" of the human mind—a "uniformity," he argued, that emerges from "necessity" based in human social need. While "Necessity is regular and certain," Hume wrote, human desire may be "capricious." In a rare moment of full candor—for Hume is normally understated and ironic—he declared in this passage that human "conduct" is "irregular and uncertain" (403). This is a very different view of human nature than that posed by Shaftesbury and Hutcheson; the latter had emphasized a universality, a regularity, within human nature, in its "determination" toward virtue as a natural aspect of the soul.

In this book, I explore Hume's writings on the moral sentiments as they first appeared in the *Treatise,* a work that, as Hume himself stated in his short autobiography, "fell *dead-born from the press,* without reaching such distinction, as even to excite a murmur among the zealots ("My Own Life" 234—Hume's emphasis). In tongue-in-cheek fashion, Hume wrote that he had "been guilty" in the *Treatise* "of a very usual indiscretion, in going to the press too early" ("My Own Life" 235). Therefore, he had recast his work "anew" in the two *Enquiries* of 1748 and 1751, as well as his *Dissertation on the Passions* (1757).[27] Notwithstanding Hume's own comments, I turn to the *Treatise* as the more radical and modern work that undermines the conventions of virtue that had dominated discourses on human nature and natural law up until his time and even after. While the *Treatise* suggests that the moral sense is actually an *a*moral "sense," a "passion," the *2nd Enquiry* on the principle of morals made these thoughts more palatable to the tastes of an increasingly sentimental eighteenth-century public. Hume's "public," of course, included Hutcheson, who, in correspondence with Hume, wrote his protégé rather stingingly that the *Treatise* lacked "'a certain warmth in the cause of virtue.' "[28] In retrospect, Hume's *Treatise* appears to have opened the floodgates to the dividedness of the moral sense and perceptions, which Hutcheson had more cautiously sculpted and regulated according to acceptable notions of observable "beauty."[29] Hume's discussion of the moral sense as a production of the passionate "sentiments" exposes moral judgment to an amoral universe full of unstable representations.

Especially dominant in Hume's discussion of the moral sense is the specific "sentiment" of sympathy embodied in the experience of the spectator. Sympathy, Hume wrote in the *Treatise*—he says little about it in the *2nd Enquiry*—is the process of a moral spectator. This spectator makes moral distinctions based upon the psychological experience of "pleasure" or "discomfort," according to Hume, appraising situations *as they are seen.* Through sympathy, Hume's *Treatise* suggested that the moral spectator seeks what is "pleasurable" in order to judge what is "good." This comment underlines what I believe was Hume's most important statement about sympathy: that it is based upon perceptual instability and the desire for visual pleasure.

To read Hume's comments on sympathy thus, I read Hume's *Treatise* ironically, as we might read a literary text. I propose to show that the *Treatise* is a deeply literary as well as ironic work.[30] And I henceforth cast quotations from Hume in the present tense, to suggest that the *Treatise* invites its readers to engage in an ongoing interpretative process of discovery and contradiction, rather than insisting its readers arrive at a determinant set of philosophical concepts. Hume uses irony to undermine our desire, when reading philosophy, to arrive at steady conclusions, almost a symptom of the natural-law discourses that sought to mandate a steady view of virtue-driven human nature. Irony masks some of the more controversial views Hume would put forth about "nature" and sympathy, specifically. He uses irony in the following passage, for example, which describes the spectacle of sympathy that a spectator would appraise:

> There is no spectacle so fair and beautiful as a noble and generous action; nor any which gives us more abhorrence than one that is cruel and treacherous. No enjoyment equals the satisfaction we receive from the company of those we love and esteem; as the greatest of all punishments is to be oblig'd to pass our lives with those we hate or contemn. (470)

Through irony, Hume points out a willingness in "human nature" to perceive that which is "fair and beautiful as a noble and generous action"—but because it serves one's social purpose to do so. Furthermore, in a following passage, Hume alludes to the wholly representational (unsteady or unstable) and potentially theatrical nature of sympathy: "A very play or romance may afford us instances of this pleasure, which virtue conveys to us; and pain, which arises from vice" (470–71). In assessing what is virtuous, Hume concludes that "The very *feeling* [about what we see or witness] constitutes our praise or admiration" (471—Hume's emphasis). For Hume, there can be no original moral claims to good or evil, since it is "absurd to imagine that . . . these sentiments are produc'd by an *original* quality and *primary* constitution" (473—Hume's emphasis). The skeptic's wit and a literary use of irony again emerges when Hume argues against any moral sentiment's innate or natural qualities: it is "impossible," he writes, that "our original instincts should . . . from our very first infancy impress on the human mind all that multitude or precepts, which are contain'd in the compleatest system of ethics" (473). Instead, the moral sentiment of sympathy, specifically, encodes problems attributed to representation. That is, it acts like a vibration-like "disturbance," unsettling any contained image.

In Book III of the *Treatise,* Hume develops his view of the moral sentiment of sympathy further. The word sympathy, of course, conveys from its Greek etymology the idea of being "together with" another's "passion," or *pathos.* The notion that sympathy is a "disturbance" had its origins in Augustine, whose fifth-century work, *The City of God,* condemned most passions, or "pathos," because they functioned as tempest-like "disturbances," signifying "an irrational motion of the soul" associated with anti-Christian demonic forces (323). However, Augustine suggested that the particular passion or "disturbance" of sympathy posed an exception to these demonic forces, since sympathy is based on the Christian principle of "compassion":

> To be indignant with the sinner with a view to his correction, to feel sorrow for the afflicted with a view to his release from suffering, to be afraid for one in danger so as to prevent his death—those are emotions which, as far as I can see, no sane judgement could reprove." (*The City of God* 349)

In his own discussions of sympathy, Hume explores the Augustinian notion that the "fellow-feeling in our hearts for another's misery" is that "which compels us to come to his help by every means in our power" (*The City of God* 349). But for Hume, the disturbing and passionate aspects of sympathy do not necessary lead to moral faith or action. Rather, sympathy becomes a potential "force" through which feelings between independent "human creatures" are simply registered, and through that representation shared. Sympathy, in other words, is a porous medium, a device of human communication. Explaining how sympathy forms communicational links between human beings, Hume uses a musical metaphor: "As in strings equally wound up, the motion of one communicates itself to the rest; so all the affections readily pass from one person to another and beget correspondent movements in every human creature" (576).

But the metaphor he emphasizes throughout the *Treatise* is not musical; it is visual. The sympathetic communication device works not only through "vibration," but mimetically, through visual resemblance and identification. "To receive by communication," the "inclinations and sentiments" of others, "however different from, or even contrary to our own" is sympathy, Hume explains in Book II on "the passions" (316). In Book III, Hume describes in more detail the communication system by which "the *effects* of passion"—arising from "the voice and gesture of any person," combining the auditory and visual metaphors—form "such a lively idea of the passion, as is presently converted into the passion itself" (576—Hume's emphasis). What for Augustinian Christianity is a virtuous quality within human nature—one that might rescue or "save" another from peril or distress—is for Hume a mediatory register of the witnessing of another's affect, *as if it were one's own.*

While Hume used the term "spectator" to refer to the subject of sympathy, it is Adam Smith's *The Theory of Moral Sentiments* (1759)—popularizing this aspect of the *Treatise,* not widely received in its time—that emphasized the spectator's visual role. In *The Surprising Effects of Sympathy: Marivaux, Diderot, Rousseau and Mary Shelley,* modern critic David Marshall examines Smith's explicitly visual paradigm of sympathy in a theatrical context. Marshall notes that while sympathy appears to transcend "the distance and difference between people," it also enacts "a problem" suggested by "the theatrical conditions in which people face each other as spectators and spectacles" (5). My own book picks up on Marshall's theme of the voyeuristic aspect of sympathy, which he derives from his reading of Smith. But while Smith's account of sympathy provides a more digestible account of the spectator's benign use of sympathy, I believe that Smith avoids the problem of sympathy's moral ambiguity. Smith's version is a *sentimental* view of sympathy. I treat Hume's account, in contrast, as the work of an ironist, calling attention to sympathy's moral-representational paradoxes.

It is in Hume's writings that we learn the way in which sympathy acts as a voyeuristic-fetishistic medium. On the one hand, Hume writes, sympathy requires the experience of likeness, of "resemblance," or "vivacity of conception," by which he who experiences sympathy can *identify* with someone else. According to Hume, "Nature has presev'd a *great resemblance* among all human creatures . . . we never remark any passion or principle in others, of which, in some degree or other, we may not find a parallel in ourselves." It is this resemblance that "must very much contribute to make us enter into the sentiments of others. . . ." (318—emphasis added). On the other hand, sympathy requires an experience of detachment, of distance, Hume notes. So that the subject of sympathy can experience those sentiments *belonging* to "others," he gives up those feelings that may be his own, so as to become like the "other." If sympathy is "our own" experience, it is only "our own" as we perceive ourselves to be *like* someone else. Sympathy is that phenomenon "where the mind passes easily from the idea of ourselves to that of any other object related to us" (340). This version of sympathy reveals the spectator's divided self-reflection, and his aberrational, perverse effects.

The application of contemporary visual theories to Hume's theory of sympathy assists us in the analysis of sympathy's duplicity. The conflicted structure of identification and detachment Hume describes in sympathy is precisely that structure Laura Mulvey uses to describe filmic voyeurism in her controversial piece, "Visual Pleasure and Narrative Cinema," the pre-eminent feminist essay of the *Screen* school, first published in that journal in 1975. Linking the cinema spectator to the politically charged, symbolic male gaze, Mulvey's argument has since been criticized for privileging male identity in the acquisition of cinematic meaning.[31] It has also been criticized for limiting sexual desire—in the words of Jane Gaines—to "the imaginary designed exclusively for male satisfaction."[32] Disgruntlement with a certain rigidity in Mulvey's argument in "Visual Pleasure" has propelled a veritable industry of theories about the *female* spectator. These theories include Mary Ann Doane's classic description of female identification and masquerade; Linda Williams's discussion of the multiple positions of identification available to female viewers (in the maternal melodrama as well as in the horror film); and Mulvey's own critique of "Visual Pleasure," in which she suggests that the female spectator experiences oscillation and transvestitism.[33]

These arguments are so well taken that, collectively viewed, they bespeak a truth at the heart of any spectator's viewing experience: that spectatorship is complex and multiply textured, relying upon the social experience of the spectator. Yet these arguments sometimes reassert their own monolithic ideality of the female spectator (the overidentified pre-oedipal daughter, or the "good mother" who, in multiple viewing positions, identifies with "All My Children"). Rather than rejecting Mulvey's bold claim about the presence of a controlling male gaze in the Hollywood text, this criticism actually extends Mulvey's claim—by examining the overarching specter of patriarchal textuality and spectatorship through their effects upon female viewers. Feminist women critics often seek to escape our reflections in the patriarchal mirror. But that surface refracts our reflections, bends them back into its depths and absorbs us. We cannot escape patriarchal icons and their history.

There is a subtle hint of female narcissism in all our attempts to reclaim what Luce Irigaray once called "the speculum" for a specifically female Imaginary. I turn, again, to Mulvey's seminal essay unapologetically, if uneasily, because it is so useful in describing the cultural masculinity and visual perversity of sympathy reproduced in novels and visual media. Not since the publication of Mulvey's essay has the perverse function of the cinema spectator, specifically, been more cogently condensed or more clearly elucidated. And the essay's description of voyeurism and fetishism as a symbolically masculine phenomenon fits uncannily with Hume's description of visual pleasure as experienced by the sympathetic spectator. Applying Mulvey and, thereby, Lacan to Hume's theory of spectatorship, we find in Hume's writing a focus on the paradigm of loss and control through scopophilia, Mulvey's central Lacanian theme.

For Mulvey, perversion involves the pleasure in looking (looking at an object, being looked at), drawing upon Freud first in associating this visual pleasure with the desire to control, "taking other people as objects, subjecting them to a controlling and curious gaze."[34] But in transferring this figure of pleasure and control onto Lacan's mirror of identification,[35] Mulvey associates cinematic processes "with a fascination with likeness and recognition: the human face, the human body . . . the visible presence of the person in the world" (9). Through psychical gyrations of recognition and misrecognition that emerge from the mirror as emblem of the Imaginary's principle identification "stage," Mulvey suggests that "two contradictory aspects of the pleasurable structures of looking" emerge. These include a scopophilic "*separation* of the erotic identity of the subject from the object," and a narcissistic "constitution of the ego," which "comes from *identification* with the image seen."[36] Both separation and identification modes of visual pleasure promote what she calls an "illusion of reality" (11). They "pursue aims *in indifference to perceptual reality,* creating the imagised, erotized concept of the world that forms the perception of the subject and *makes a mockery of empirical objectivity*" (Mulvey 10—emphasis added).

Hume's theory of sympathy alludes to similar processes of identification as part of his larger empirical project. Like cinema-theory's application of Lacan, Hume undermines the "illusion of reality" that would suppose forms of identification and sympathetic spectatorship to create some kind of "empirical objectivity," or narrative "realism." Hume ironically suggests that the sympathetic spectator, like Mulvey's cinema spectator, is a scopophiliac, whose moral subjectivity is only "unified" within competing impulses toward unification and separation, resemblance and difference. The forms of verisimilitude that the sympathetic spectator renders are interpretations based upon the needs of the spectator for *self*-recognition.

Throughout this study, I explore the means by which the two major scopophilic perversions dominate the sympathetic process. Voyeurism and fetishism are cogently, if too briefly, summarized by Mulvey and aptly defined in relation to cultural inscriptions of sexual difference. The "male gaze" is but a cultural effect of these perversions, predicated upon a fear of castration linked, only symbolically, to maleness, and a properly masculine disavowal of that fear. The "first avenue" of castration disavowal for this cultural masculine subject is voyeurism. The second is fetishism.

Male voyeurism "has associations with sadism" (14), Mulvey writes; it reasserts a "pleasure [that] lies in ascertaining guilt (immediately associated with castration), asserting control and subjecting the guilty person through punishment or forgiveness" (14). Mulvey's voyeur operates like the sentimental figure of the panopticon. If her emphasis on sadism is appropriately criticized for putting too much emphasis on patriarchal pleasures of domination and control, I emphasize here the way in which the voyeur also embodies the narrative pleasures of masochism—as perhaps the more perverse means of asserting the same patriarchal pleasures.[37] Freud's vicissitudinous analysis of sadomasochistic desire implies that masochism requires a loss of control, when the subject shifts its object of sadistic attack to that of the self as object. Yet, implied in Freud's analysis is the suggestion that a loss of control, subject to object, becomes a means of enforcing control, or re-enforcing control as a surreptitious, deviant, and disavowed figure.

These figurations of sadism and masochism oscillate within the figure of Hume's sympathetic spectator. That oscillation might be traced as the detached voyeur also undergoes identification with an object, reproducing a "resemblance," in Hume's word, subject to object, and thereby reproducing the moral spectator's own self-ideality. The experience of identification *as* resemblance inaugurates the spectator into what Mulvey describes as the "second avenue" of castration disavowal, fetishism. This Freudian concept of fetishism is a perversion that, at base, performs as a visual experience; in fetishism, the male spectator, fearing his own very graphic loss (that of castration), "builds up the physical beauty of the object, transforming it into something satisfying in itself" (Mulvey 14). If voyeurism is the scopophilic pleasure underlying the viewing of another's scene of affect or trauma, fetishism is the result of that affect or trauma *as viewed*. Narrowly defined in Freudian terms, the fetish is an image that supplements or compensates for the visual absence of the phallus.[38] In emphasizing fetishism as a visual phenomenon, I follow not only its fundamental Freudian definition but also fetishism's recent treatment in discussions of visual-art spectatorship by critics like Hal Foster and Emily Apter.[39]

My discussion of fetishism, as it enhances—perhaps makes possible—the experience of sympathy also emphasizes its sadomasochistic features. Playing upon its implicit spectatorship paradigm, fetishism signifies both control (over representation) and its lack (of representation, the spectator's visual presence). Fetishism achieves this dual agenda through the fetish's excessive, overspatialized figure. The fetish stands in for the (missing) identity of the spectator. The spectator himself comes to embody the irony of the fetish: at once empty and full, absent and (surreptitiously) present.

If voyeuristic "seeing is from the male organ," as film critic Stephen Heath has said, then the fetishistic spectacle *as seen* is a *female*-signifier, indicating sexual difference as the sign of absence of the "organ." To discuss the visual perversions, therefore, is to render an emphasis on sexual difference that is the legacy of all patriarchal texts. The perverse productiveness of sexual difference is reflected in a wide range of writings about classic cinema, realism, and visual culture. What we have not yet considered is the relationship between sexual difference and sympathy. Ultimately, this is the point at which my argument unfolds.

In the eighteenth century, Adam Smith suggested that the act of sympathy is literally a male spectatorial and ethical practice. *The Theory of Moral Sentiments* not only conventionally refers to "man" as sympathy's spectator. But in a number of explicit references to gender Smith employs the metaphor of sexual difference to distinguish acts of sympathetic spectatorship from other acts of what he calls "humanity." Sympathy, unlike simply humanistic acts, he writes, requires nobility and "generosity." "Generosity," according to Smith, "is different from humanity. . . . Humanity is the virtue of a woman, generosity of a man" (274). In the passage that ensues, Smith separates "humanity" from "generosity" by appealing to eighteenth-century social stereotypes about the "female" virtues, whereby women are "tender" but lack the self-reflective quality required for sympathy. Smith implies that a kind of male intellectual difference, a superiority, grants "man" the capacity for reflection, for detachment, and, ultimately, for the more noble "self-denial," which the "public virtue" of sympathy demands:

> The fair sex, who have commonly much more tenderness than ours, have seldom so much generosity. That women rarely make considerable donations is an observation of the civil law. Humanity consists merely in the exquisite fellow-feeling which the spectator entertains with the sentiments of the persons principally concerned, so as to grieve from their sufferings, to resent their injuries, and to rejoice at their good fortune. The most humane actions require no self-denial, no self-command, no great exertion of the sense of propriety. They consist only in doing what this exquisite sympathy would of its own accord prompt us to do. But it is otherwise with generosity. We never are generous except when in some respect we prefer some other person to ourselves, and sacrifice some great and important interest of our own to an equal interest of a friend or of a superior. (Smith 274)

In commenting upon this passage from Smith's treatise, contemporary feminist historian of philosophy Jane Rendell points out that women are depicted as exhibiting a passion close to sympathy as mothers, caring, for example, for a sick child or the newborn. However, Rendell notes, in

Smith's treatise, "There was little suggestion that women might acquire the virtues of public life, lacking courage and the necessary capacity for self-command" required for sympathy (Rendell 59). The production of sympathy, after all, relies upon detachment from self-interest. And "the pangs of the mother," quoting Smith again, "when she hears the moanings of her infant . . . joins, to its real helplessness, her own consciousness of that helplessness, and her own terrors for the unknown consequences of its disorder . . . her own sorrow, the most complete image of misery and distress" (Smith 8). The compassion of the sympathetic spectator, quite differently, requires "the consideration of what he himself [the spectator] would feel if he was reduced to the same unhappy situation"—not instantaneous shared "terrors of the unknown." The self-sacrificial quality required of sympathy makes it a powerful determinant of the ideal masculine self. It is apt, if ironic, that this ideal masculine self was granted powerful fictive representation in a mid-eighteenth century novel about a woman. As I have been suggesting, the perverse convolutions of sympathy know no bounds.

This novel, Richardson's *Clarissa,* depicts the spectacle of a "virtuous" heroine in distress but through the specular powers of male sympathy. I begin my study of the perverse gaze of sympathy in a detailed analysis of *Clarissa,* treating this novel not only as the apex of an epistolary convention historically associated with "feminine" virtues, but as a foundational fiction illustrating the visual pleasure and power accorded "Enlightened" masculine sympathy: as a female heroine-victim is rendered through the male sympathetic gaze. First published in 1747–48—curiously wedged between the decades spanning the publication of Hume's *Treatise* and Smith's *The Theory of Moral Sentiments*—*Clarissa* gives fictive form to sentiment, a budding tradition influencing novels and other "reality" entertainments to come. *Clarissa* gives fictive form to sympathetic spectatorship as a by-product of the moral sentiments, a paradigm of sexual difference.

Basic to the epistolary *Clarissa* is the philosophical groundwork of natural law and its rational virtue ethics. Clarissa herself is an icon of the law. She is, therefore, a representation of natural-law irony. Internal contradictions within the law are mapped onto the contradictions Clarissa specularizes through her rational moral resolutions and proprietary conduct. In *Clarissa,* we move from a vision of the moral sentiments based upon stability and "reason" to the emotional "disturbance" of sympathy, as the libertine Lovelace portrays a voyeuristic spectator. Peeping "through her keyhole" at Clarissa's distress, the Lovelacean gaze directs us to the enunciatory gaze framing narrative epistolary structure. We see the projective, perverse figure of the editorial redactor. And we see ourselves, *Clarissa's* readers, as perverse sympathetic spectators.

If chapter 1 emphasizes the perverse voyeuristic sadism of the narrative spectator, chapter 2 explores the spectator's masochism. The Lovelacean spectator is an overtly sadistic pervert. However, the "eye-witness" spectator of Flaubertian realism more coyly conceals his scopophilic power through masochistic disavowal and its related form of courtly love. The connections between male masochism and a courtly lover of women are well illustrated by that quintessential novelist of masochism, Leopold von Sacher-Masoch, whose novel *Venus in Furs* (1870) offers a gendered critique of the juxtaposition of perversion, sentiment, and power. However, the male masochist in Gustave Flaubert's *L'Education sentimentale (A Sentimental Education*—1869) fetishizes his own masochism, as well as the object of his adoration: "woman," and a worldly visual "reality." *L'Education* becomes a test-case for the sadism underlying voyeuristic masochism, and the supposedly "free, indirect" style for which Flaubert is so well known and that constructs his illusion of realism.

Through this spectator's perverse masochism and sadism, a novel famous for its verisimilar documentation of the 1848 worker riots and their bloody suppression is as subject to sentimental illusions of piety and "realism" as the courtly-love ardors of its male protagonist. Male masochism in *L'Education sentimentale* employs the device of suture, a term usually used in relation to Hollywood film—that figure for the binding of an audience spectator into the fictional level of the text. Chapter 2 suggests that Flaubert's novel models cinematic suture in a precinematic display of sympathy's visual perversions. I argue that Flaubert borrowed from the popular visual-entertainment culture of his time, that a literary writer who supposedly repudiated his popular culture in fact drew upon its entertainment structures. *L'Education sentimentale* is full of sublimated references to Second Empire mass culture and the Parisian love of spectacular entertainments— from shadow theaters to optical-illusion toys to world fairs that promoted these spectacles. All such spectacles required and promulgated acts of sympathy. They were increasingly vast sympathetic spectacles attracting a "universal" mass audience.

While Flaubert's novel helps us to view the way in which the sympathetic spectator's passivity and masochism enhance sadomasochistic visual control, Henry James's Preface to *The Portrait of a Lady* strives to decode the sadomasochistic visual perversions at work in one of his own novels of realism, in the tradition Flaubert helped to establish. The 1908 Preface to the New York Edition of a novel originally published serially in 1880–81 underscores the sadism and masochism, voyeurism and fetishism, that pervade James's own nineteenth-century representational method. James's Preface reveals that the narrative omniscience of the "realist" eye-witness relies upon sympathies colored by the sadism of the spectator. Richardsonian themes of femininity and victimage typify the development of the novel's heroine, the Preface implies. And the Preface intuits future technological uses of sympathy in mass-media entertainment—especially in James's famous extended metaphor, the House of Fiction, too often viewed as a metaphor about novelistic openness and freedom: I will view it as an image of a sadistic movie house.

The House of Fiction is a panopticon visual structure that anticipates the visual perversions structuring sexual difference in classic Hollywood film narratives. In the second half of the book, I turn to the uses of the sympathetic spectator by twentieth-century visual entertainment texts. Chapter 4 analyzes Emily Brontë's novel *Wuthering Heights* (1847) as adapted by director William Wyler into a classic Hollywood film (Goldwyn, 1939). I discuss the means by which a maverick nineteenth-century novel—one that I argue defies the visual codes of masculine spectatorship, sentiment, and sympathy—is totally reworked by Wyler's deft and perverse cinematic eye into a sentimental, sadomasochistic love story set on the Yorkshire moors of popular imagination. I read Brontë's novel as a narrative dismissal of the "realism" of fictional nature, as well as a narrative dismissal of the moral agency of sympathy through natural law; the novel challenges representational certainty and the benign motives of its sympathetic spectators. Through a disjointed textuality and an eerie multiple narration that implicates sympathetic witnesses in sadistic activities, *Wuthering Heights,* the novel, fails to provide either a morally stable picture of humanity or a visually intact universe. The Wyler film, however, restores classic verisimilitude to the *Wuthering Heights* text—just as it restores our repressed sentimental illusions about the benign spectator.

What is fascinating about the Wyler film are the ways in which this "restoration" occurs through the explicitly visual acts of continuity editing and cinematography. My chapter is a study in these visual arts literalized by the Hollywood apparatus and constructing before our very eyes sympathy's identification processes. Through Hollywood, narrative techniques are shown to embody principles of natural law and the moral sentiments. The chapter on *Wuthering Heights* suggests that sympathy becomes a *metaphor* for the deceptive cinematic screen. The metaphor of sympathy, through its deceptive duality, informs the development of the classic Hollywood maternal-melodrama, as well.

Chapter 5 is a study of the use of female fetishism in this classic genre, also known as the "woman's film" or "weepy." I choose Douglas Sirk's *Imitation of Life* (Universal Pictures, 1959) as an exemplary maternal-melodrama text, comparing its sympathetic strategies to the contemporary daytime television talkshow *Sally Jessy Raphaël*—a latter-day maternal melodrama. *Imitation of Life* draws upon the excessive representation of women as excessively conflicted mothers and daughters, as well as excessive visual fetishistic icons of beauty and female "power." This excessiveness illustrates the sadomasochistic sentiments underlying a spectator culture that sentimentally eulogizes women through their physical objectification. "Femininity" in this film is metaphorically fetishized through the excesses of maternal sympathy, as well as the physical excesses of the female body.

The female fetishism at the heart of the maternal-melodrama textual strategy—which I conclude is based in culturally masculine desire—is repeated in the contemporary *Sally* television show. Ostensibly a spontaneous talk format, the *Sally* show actually provides staged tableaux of hugging and fighting mothers and daughters—*real* mothers and daughters, indeed, who, nevertheless, reproduce the body of the socialized female fetish through macabre and excessive depictions of female emotions. This show suggests that women enjoy their fetishistic fascination—for spectators who are supposed to be women but who, too, deploy a male gaze. A different kind of study of the so-called "female" gaze, I show the relationship of that gaze to a culturally masculine sentiment, and to the male sympathy that structures these melodrama images.

In a final chapter, I explore other sympathetic, fetishistic and voyeuristic roles constructed for contemporary television viewers, turning to the issue of the mass spectator at large. In doing so, I examine the genre of the prime-time "reality" drama, focusing on the rescue "reality" show, *Rescue 911*. Emerging out of the 1980s Reagan-era obsession with crime-drama "reality" TV, CBS's multi-seasonal *Rescue 911*—now syndicated and available to viewers in cable reruns—is fascinating as an elemental, serialized, sentimental television text.

This text obsessively and repeatedly re-encodes, through each sequence on each program, sympathetic and sado-erotic themes typical to early sentimental literatures. Special to *Rescue 911* are the sentimental spectacles of *domestic* "crime scenes," disasters with bleach buckets and faulty furnace switches. Like the rescue-"reality" genre, in general, *Rescue 911* depicts miraculous rescues from the danger of these evil agencies in the home—rescues evocative of the rescue of sentimental heroines in Richardson's epistolary novels.

As law enforcement and technology intervene to rescue domestic and feminized victims in distress, the show reinvents eighteenth-century conceits about control, scopophilia, and sentimental victimage. Ultimately, I read *Rescue 911* as an parable for and about the mass spectator, a sympathetic witness constructed as white and middle-class, an "average citizen" depicted through carefully plotted continuity-editing devices and scripts. In viewing the show with sympathy, the mass spectator is a voyeur who identifies himself as a victim. Like the fictional victim in each *911* episode, the viewer-victim is miraculously sutured, salvaged (raised from the death throes of commercial television viewing), and saved from difference: from the ravaged body and social death posed by sexual difference and American multiculturalism. Rescue fantasies about domestic disaster and survival appeal to fantasies of white patriarchal cultural hegemony in an increasingly scopophilic society, which commodifies vision through entertainment technology, and uses monitors on every urban-suburban street corner to enforce "safety" and "justice." The *Rescue 911* fantasy shields the mass viewer from these signs of a greater authoritarian spectator, and from his own sadism and dependency upon that authority. Meanwhile, the viewer acts as an inverted mirror. He is the proverbial plugged-in couch potato, passively, sympathetically, watching domestic television.

Sentiment traditionally has portrayed itself as a politically progressive genre. Certainly, sentimental texts address progressive themes, like social access and populist reform. These themes permeate mass-media reality melodramas and sentimental literature alike. They emphasize the plight of the downtrodden, like women and accident victims.

But sentiment and its methodology of sympathy invariably generate sadistic voyeuristic pleasure in the name of identification. Douglas notes in her critique of nineteenth-century American literary sentiment, which she associates with the rise of mass culture, that sentiment historically bred a political resistance to the very social issues it purported to raise—what Douglas calls "a form of dragging one's heels" (12). I am suggesting here that the political ineffectualness of sentiment descends from those Enlightenment philosophical ironies that continue to reverberate in Western politics and media culture. Immanuel Kant once articulated one of these Enlightenment ironies when he described a "free" but never revolutionary use of reason. When Kant encouraged the Enlightened thinker to "exercise [his] own understanding," thereby asserting his mental-spiritual "freedom," Kant called upon this "release" from tyranny in the realm of public debate only. For reason, he wrote, should never be used to generate acts of disobedience toward the state, to create political insurgency or revolution.[40]

Foucault offers the best critique of what he aptly calls Kant's "contract of rational despotism." Through the contract, which distinguishes between public and private actions, "the public and free use of autonomous reason will be the best guarantee of obedience" to an oppressive state, writes Foucault. This state is figured in the oppressive conformity of "universal reason" itself.[41] Foucault's critique of Kant reveals the deep relationship that exists between the imaginary use of a transcendent "universal reason" and the sentimental ideals of the sympathetic moral spectator. As we move through these selected texts of fictive sentiment, we view the contradictions of this reasoning but "feeling" moral spectator again and again, performing according to the logic of the spectacle. Through the machinery of sympathy, a very *unreasoning* moral spectator is rewarded with the rationalism of ever-perfected technologies of vision, technologies that reproduce the spectacular euphemism of male desire. Rational efficacy gives the spectator's sadomasochistic sentiments their verisimilitude, a "force and vivacity," in the phrase of Hume.

This "force and vivacity" pervades the sympathetic image—at the expense of the spectator's own. Such rational efficacy, however, can never quite liberate the masculine purveyor of vision from the tunnel-like vision directed at the female star, or any spectacle of victimage. And why not? That is the provocative metaphor of this book, as it attempts to "Tell all the Truth"—I borrow from Emily Dickinson—while suggesting, already, "every man be blind."

ONE

Clarissa through the Epistolary Key-hole

*How selfish so ever man may be supposed, there are evidently
some principles in his nature, which interest him in the fortune
of others, and render their happiness necessary to him, though
he derives nothing from it except the pleasure of seeing it.*
—Adam Smith, *The Theory of Moral Sentiments*

*I had a view . . . to give her an high opinion of her own
sagacity. I love, when I dig a pit, to have my prey tumble in with
secure feet and open eyes; then a man can look down upon her,
with an O-ho, charmer, how came you there?*
—Lovelace to John Belford, *Clarissa*

Critical analyses of Samuel Richardson's *Clarissa* ask the oedipal questions
that are also visual-narrative ones. What is the nature of the heroine? And
whose vision does she represent? Fielded through the sympathetic vector of
Richardson's own sentimental vantage point, answers to these questions
tend to reconfirm Clarissa's identity as paragon of virtue or quintessential
victim of male sovereignty. Alternatively, they view Clarissa as a haughty
member of the bourgeoisie, a daddy's girl.[1]

Plunging into the critical fray, I ask again: when we peep through the
keyhole—the heroine is often behind locked doors—what do we see? What
is the *representational* nature of the heroine at the bottom of the entrapment
"pit," a figure Lovelace, and the rest of us, love to watch?

For all that we know about Clarissa comes from watching: watching
(reading) Clarissa being watched by Lovelace and others; seeing her
trapped, tormented, raped (and reading about it second-hand). Looking
once again at Richardson's paradigmatic sentimental heroine, I will examine the epistolary sentimental genre from which she emerges. The epistolary is historically associated with sympathy toward women. But the woman of
this novel, sympathy's object, is also the object of sadistic attack.

In *Clarissa*, it does not take great powers of speculation to see that what is at the bottom of the pit is the subjected female body. Given the heroine's harassment, I do not quibble with the opinion that Clarissa is a victim, either martyr-like saint championing the Christian faith or proto-feminist championing female consciousness and sovereignty. *Clarissa* may be composed of "ciphers," a "body" of fragmented writings, as Terry Castle observes.[2] And Clarissa's own body generously, perversely, accommodates a multiplicity of views. Yet we can never view "Clarissa"—in either her epistolary or physical corpuses—without asking how she got there, down in the pit, or "through the keyhole," in the first place.[3] Possessed by epistolary sentiment, Clarissa herself remains slave, not mistress, to all these views, the porousness of her body as subject relegated to the subjugated position.

Morris Golden has written about the sadism Richardson inflicted upon his female characters, in general. And Watt has suggested that Richardson's "'keyhole view of life' . . . undoubtedly [was] used on occasion for unwholesome ends," a keyhole likened to—here Watt quotes Samuel Coleridge—"'a sort of *camera obscura*'" that "'transmits the moving phantasms of one man's delirium'" (200). My own focus picks up on the images of sadism reproduced through the Coleridgean cinematic effect. "Through the keyhole," quoting Lovelace, is not only the framed and plotted (against) sentimental image of womanhood, but also the sympathetic viewpoint itself.

The novel *Clarissa* is a fictive working out of sympathy's moral-representational paradoxes. As described by Hume, sympathy is a moral but also representational process based in the ideal of natural law. What has been called the "Clarissa ideal" also is grounded in natural law and its hidden authoritarian impulses. The libertine's attack upon the heroine is a critique of the law and its ideal moral rationality. Just as Hume's *Treatise* suggests that the "moral sentiment" of sympathy divorces morality from reason, Richardson suggests in the figure of the libertine that moral feeling is not regulated by reason but rather is stimulated by visual pleasure. However, the libertine is also a hypocrite, a fetishist who builds up the heroine's ideality as image. Through the libertine's perversion, we gaze into sympathy's perverse and distorted practices. As we gaze upon a sympathetic but also sadistically controlling redactor-narrator in this epistolary novel of sentiment, we gaze upon ourselves, sentimental, sadomasochistic readers.

The Heroine's Subject(ion)

In writing about "the autonomous individual" of Richardson's novels and the early stages of the British novel's development in general, Watt comments that, "without allies," Clarissa "is the heroic representative of all that is free and positive in the new individualism" of Puritanism, as well as the post-Enlightenment era. However, the "autonomous" subject of Clarissa is also *subject to* the political demands of another. Her subjection is the result of a natural-law subjectivity and the optimistic view of human nature.

Natural law is a theory of the individual, but it is also a theory of the civil state. In the state, autonomous subjects maintain natural rights, but often at the expense of the rights of others. The heroine's subjection reflects the dualities within natural law as both personal ethic and social contract. By corollary, natural law creates the social conditions for Clarissa that psychoanalytic theories attribute to sadomasochism, through natural law's hidden authoritarian propensities. When Clarissa acts according to natural law's rationality and moral precepts, she illustrates the tug and pull between the dominance and submission characterizing a sadomasochistic dialectic. Her independent moral position, therefore, is radically compromised by the very foundations of that position.

However, typically perceived as "all that exists beyond mere rationalism" (Leslie Fiedler's phrase—36), Clarissa also is embraced as the quintessential representation of rationality's opposite: the sentimental "heart." Many critics writing about Clarissa refer to the "heart," for instance, Linda Kauffman, who suggests that the heroine's "discourse" presents "the supremacy of the heart . . . antithetical to the logic enforced by men."[4] Others have viewed the sentimental "heart" as a more ideological structure; most noteworthy among them is William Warner, who reads the "heart" of Clarissa as a "locus of virtue . . . planted with principles that are the laws of God and man."[5]

While Warner does not comment specifically upon natural law, his deconstructive critique of Clarissa's "heart" alludes provocatively to the "principles" of the law that form a bridge between "God and man." Discussions about natural law have long employed the image of the "heart," a metonomy for human nature as pure and kind. Aquinas, from whom the modern concept of natural law descends, quotes the Pauline scripture Romans 2.14–15 when arguing for a universal and benevolent gauge for the human soul: "'the Gentiles, who have not the law, do by nature those things that are of the law,'" proving the existence of "'the law written in their hearts'" (Romans quoted in Aquinas 15–16). The "law," in Aquinas's thirteenth-century view, is innate to human nature, regardless of one's social heritage. The "heart" in this scriptural passage is used as evidence for the law: that human beings are virtuous if they adhere to the law—universally so.

The Thomistic concept of natural law as both deeply rational and universally acknowledged—known by all "in their hearts"—influenced later writers on natural law, like Richard Hooker, whose late-sixteenth-century treatise *Of the Laws of Ecclesiastical Politie* argued that the "law" is written upon the human "heart" by God, and that, through reason, one discovers it. This concept of natural law also influenced Pufendorf, the seventeenth-century Saxon jurist and historian, who also alludes to Romans when conflating human nature, reason, and the "heart":

> The common saying that law is known by nature, should not be understood . . . as though actual and distinct propositions . . . were inherent in men's minds at the hour of their birth . . . the common and important provisions of natural law are so plain and clear that they at once find assent, and grow up in our minds, so that they can never again be destroyed. . . . For this reason in Scripture too the law is said to be "written in the hearts of men" . . . we are imbued from childhood with a consciousness of those maxims.[6]

In this passage, Pufendorf suggests that a central contradiction exists within natural law. The law is both natural *and* socially scripted—a contradiction that continues to appear in natural-law theory during the moral Enlightenment. One Enlightenment commentator on natural law was Locke. Written early in his career and remaining unpublished during his lifetime, Locke's essays on natural law suggest that the law is based upon an "inner principle" or human "disposition." This point clearly contradicts his better-known views in the *Essay Concerning Human Understanding*, that there are "no innate principles in the Mind," that the mind exists as a kind of *tabula rasa*, or blank slate, awaiting sensory impressions (*Essay* 55). In his discussions on natural law, Locke also echoes Thomistic reference to Scripture and the language of the "heart": "this law . . . inscribed in his [man's] heart" is discoverable through "the right use of reason and the native faculties with which he is provided by nature." Echoing Aquinas and other philosophers, Locke insists that, through reason, one "arrives at a knowledge of this law without a teacher to instruct him."[7]

Locke further recalls the Thomistic tradition when he argues that natural law is a "universal" law, known through the autonomous use of reason. Through "the right use of reason," humans naturally discern "the social virtues," which include for Locke "truthfulness, clemency, liberality, purity of morals" (125). Through "right reason," one also illustrates "obedience towards . . . superiors" (107). In defining these rather general and rigid versions of "the social virtues" mandated by Locke's Christian culture, a philosopher best known for his empirical views seems to be describing a sentimental heroine like Clarissa, just as her own author perceived her. It may be the Puritan elements to which we attribute Clarissa's conduct-book appeal, an early-day "Miss Manners," or an "exemplar to her sex," as Richardson wrote in his 1759 Preface to the novel.[8] And it may be empirical reason to which we attribute Clarissa's "continuous" self-image, what Watt claims are "thought processes within the individual's consciousness" that appear to make the modern novel "an authentic account of the actual experience of individuals" (27). But it is Clarissa's belief in a universal moral law and the use of transcendent reason in knowing the law that makes Richardson's "girl . . . good . . . upon principle," quoting the author in personal correspondence.[9]

Richardson's commentary suggests Clarissa's "principle" is based upon her rational and intuitive understanding of right and wrong, and a capacity for thought that leads to powers of insight and introspection. What makes Clarissa "good," Richardson emphasizes, is her ability to be thoughtful and truthful in admitting to personal error. What seems important to Richardson is that truthfulness is her guide, her natural course of action. Richardson's reading implies that Clarissa embodies a "moral sense." This "sense," or "sentiment," was considered by most British Moralist philosophers to be deeply rational, but also emotionally felt.

The "moral sense" is a "determination of the mind," as the philosopher Hutcheson writes, through which virtue is "naturally imprinted."[10] Joining Shaftesbury in countering Hobbesian cynicism toward human kind, Hutcheson does not stress Shaftesbury's faith in a deist's global universe, of "all Things and a Universal Nature" (Shaftesbury 6). Rather, Hutcheson draws upon the more traditional and authoritarian conventions of Christian doctrine, writing that the "uniformity" of virtue is the product of an all-knowing "Maker" or "Author."[11] I view Clarissa as a fictive example of Hutcheson's Christianized moral sense, itself a product of natural law. Clarissa applies the moral sense both through her use of reason and through her Christian faith. Clarissa's moral sense enacts in the novel a "determination of the mind" that insists upon its own radical autonomy. But in heeding orthodox Christian moral values as if they are universal, Clarissa's radical autonomy grants her not only "purity of morals," but the view of a Father figure, her Maker-Author.

Throughout the course of her captivity and harassment by Lovelace, Clarissa holds onto her belief in the uniform conduct implicit in the law, and in the belief that reason reveals the law to everyone. That all are provided with "the right use of reason" is suggested by Clarissa when questioning Anna about Lovelace. She asks her chief female correspondent how this persecutor could revel in such "evil habits": "How could this man, with such powers of *right thinking,* be so far depraved by evil habits as to disgrace his talents by wrong acting?" (461—emphasis added). If Lovelace has the capacity for reason, he has the capacity to know right from wrong, Clarissa suggests. In this passage, Clarissa illustrates her absorption of the contradictions of natural law. Her moral indignation at the "evil habits" of Lovelace are part of her rousing assertion of personal autonomy. Yet her notion of a universal law, reproduced through "right thinking," is dependent not so much upon "thinking" as upon imitation—of the social codes of propriety and bourgeois manners.

Lawrence E. Klein has shown the historical relationship between landed wealth and the eighteenth-century British notion of propriety and "personality." He writes of "a politics of personal traits, indeed of personality" tied to property ownership, in which the landed asserted an image of autonomy and stability "against more 'fleeting' forms of property" attributed to commercial wealth.[12] It is as a member of the landed bourgeoisie that Clarissa asserts her radical autonomy as a form of propriety— whose "uniformity," using Hutcheson's term, gives Clarissa her moral edge. She asserts: "'Mr. Lovelace, is this a proper occasion to give yourself these high airs to me, a young creature destitute of protection?—It is a surprising question you ask me," to become his lover to retaliate against her brother.[13] Clarissa's autonomy, what is referred to as her "resolve," precludes a whole set of natural-law beliefs that circulate the concepts of bourgeois identity, property, propriety—and treat the virginal female body as common signifier.

For Clarissa's "determination of the mind" is also a determination of the body, determined as she is to remain a virgin. Her virginity is like a symbolic vessel that graphically signals both her moral propriety and her status as male property. Anna suggests a correlation between moral "determination," radical autonomy based on reason, and virginity among women of their bourgeois class. She writes Clarissa on the subject of "persons of discretion," the (bourgeois) women who would "resolve" against marriage:

> would it not surprise you if I were to advance, that the persons of discretion are generally single?—Such persons are apt to consider too much, to resolve— Are not you and I complimented as such?—And would either of us marry, if the fellows and our friends, would let us alone? (*Clarissa* 277)

"To resolve," in Anna's mind, is both to "consider too much"—to rationalize—and to remain "single," "alone." Clarissa will repeat the word "resolve," in both its verb and noun forms, throughout her ordeal with Lovelace. She writes Anna upon one particularly grueling confrontation with Lovelace: "I was *resolved* not to desert *myself*" (489—emphasis added). Anna's earlier statement anticipates Clarissa's mental-physical "resolve" throughout her entrapment by Lovelace, during which she uses her virginity as a moral weapon. Clarissa's use of female virginity reflects traditional, patriarchal use of female sexuality: a commodity in the symbolic male network of property exchange. The references to female virginity, autonomy, propriety, and property are particularly dense when Clarissa asserts her will in reference to *the* will, the bequest of her grandfather's estate.

Clarissa declares to her undesireable suitor Solmes, who courts her early in the novel while she is living at Harlowe Place: "Take my estate . . . with all my heart, since you are such a favorite in this house!—Only leave me *myself*—The mercy you ask for, do *you* show to others . . . What I ask you for is mercy to myself. . . ." (319). Still properly "placed" in her father's house, valued for her virginal propriety as well as her property, Clarissa may not illustrate the virtuous orthodoxy of "obedience towards . . . superiors" Locke suggests is a function of natural-law tradition. Her father, after all, mandates Clarissa to marry Solmes, to become Solmes's legal sexual property in an exchange that would enhance the father's real-estate property. But Clarissa's declaration to Solmes does illustrate her steadfast obedience to the natural-law belief in rational autonomy. She treats her "self" *as if were the property*, "*my* estate" (emphasis added). In that phrase, Clarissa both distinguishes herself from property and likens herself to it.

In her declaration, Clarissa invokes the political concepts of property and selfhood that historically emerged from natural-law virtue ethics. In the view of some commentators on natural law, most notably Grotius, natural law extends beyond an internal "determination of the mind" to create the conditions of "a natural state," which functions according to the ideals of personal liberty and autonomy. Natural law, according to Grotius, provides a set of "natural rights," which include the right to personal sovereignty and property ownership. Paving the way for the secular application of natural law that would later be embraced by Enlightenment writers, Grotius helped to establish the claim—now important to Western democratic theory—that the autonomous individual through the law should possess such rights deemed natural within the state.

In the early-modern history of natural law, Grotius states one of its central contradictions: the autonomous individual may have rights to own himself and his property; but it is the state's right to supersede these rights on behalf of the larger social good. This contradiction appears when Grotius discusses the charge of the natural state as social protectorate. Because the state in which the individual exists acts as such a protectorate, rebellion against the state is discouraged or prohibited—even if the state limits or represses an individual's rights and freedom, as in slavery. Grotius expresses the contradiction thus:

> all Men have naturally a Right to secure themselves from Injuries by Resistance. . . . But civil Society being instituted for the Preservation of Peace, there immediately arises a superior Right in the State over us and ours, so far as is necessary for that End."[14]

Clarissa reveals these contradictions between the "natural" individual and the state. While she uses her moral sense to defy the tyrannical and unreasonable authority of her father, she also invokes the language of patriarchal property laws to justify a moral presumption of personal autonomy and freedom. Property laws during the eighteenth century economically and politically subordinated women, making women dependent upon men through such legal devices as the entail in wills.[15] Laws concerning married women's property ownership during the period, as Susan Staves notes, had as their "principal feature" a deep-seated "patriarchal structure," ensuring that "women functioned to transmit wealth from one generation of men to the next" (4). Embedded in the strange logic of the declaration Clarissa makes Solmes about her "estate"—in which she *separates* herself from the estate while *retaining* its proprietary self-image—is the problem of the autonomous female subject. The female subject of the natural state does not politically exist. Therefore, Clarissa's autonomy is a false autonomy, masking the maelstrom of contradictions that swirl around her as a *female* subject—whose status as property owner is created by a family patriarch's bequest.[16]

Throughout the plot, Clarissa challenges but also surrenders to paternalistic familial designs. This is part of Clarissa's larger pattern of contradictory behavior, alluded to when Richardson interprets her moral thought in his personal correspondence. He refers to Clarissa's chaste and rational reconsideration of a key disobedient act: corresponding with Lovelace, leading to her ill-conceived flight from Harlowe Place. Richardson quotes Clarissa writing Anna: "'Your Clarissa's mind was ever above justifying her own failing by those of others.'" It is true that, in the original text, Clarissa emphasizes her Christian clemency: "God forgive those of my Friends who have acted cruelly by me!" (*Clarissa* 381). But Richardson's quotation of Clarissa is also used out of context, since the heroine, in the novel, also condemns Lovelace: "Oh the vile encroacher! how my indignation . . . rises at him!" (381). Richardson's use of Clarissa's "words" (*his* words, after all) suggests only that she has given considerable thought to her own error, that she has used her natural capacity for reason. Richardson again quotes his heroine: "'but their Faults *are* their own, and not Excuses for mine. And mine began early: for I ought not to have corresponded with him'" (*Selected Letters* 202; *Clarissa* 381—Richardson's emphasis). We should note that Richardson's audience is a young female correspondent. He uses Clarissa's language selectively, to exemplify his heroine's clemency and right use of reason in a prelude to the lecture he delivers his correspondent on the necessity of female subordination and obedience:

Clarissa says, "Condescension is not Meanness. There is a Glory in Yielding that hardly any violent Spirit can judge of. . . ." [These] little Histories [of]

several women who had failed in common Prudence and common Modesty
. . . shew that Women are safest when *dependent*. (*Selected Letters* 203—emphasis
added)

In arguing that women need to be dependent and to "yield" to social
authority, Richardson constructs a Clarissa who is reliant upon his own
"author-ity," as her father figure, her author.

Paternal authority is fictively rendered by Clarissa's father/Heavenly
Father. It is also rendered by other members and associates of the Harlowe
family, male and female alike, who uphold the symbolic male law. The
contradictions Richardson unwittingly depicts, in his correspondence, between Clarissa's internal thought process and her socially compliant behavior reflect problems that reappear repeatedly in discussions of natural
law. One of these contradictions resonates with the specifically Grotian
theme of property and individual autonomy, or "freedom." Pufendorf, who
builds upon many of Grotius's principles in commentaries on "the state of
nature" and the natural state emphasizes that personal liberty is intrinsic to
the law and the state:

> the chief right attending the natural state is that those living in it are subject to
> no one on this earth . . . that state is usually called a state of natural liberty. By
> virtue of this liberty . . . everyone is taken to be rightful master of himself and
> answerable to no other man. ("On the Natural State of Men" 127)

Pufendorf implies that the natural state guarantees freedom, which
includes one's physical liberty. In *Clarissa*, the use of graphic spatial enclosures, which inhibit Clarissa's physical liberty, signals our entrance into a
morally decadent universe, in which the law of nature becomes perverse.
Clarissa presumes her natural right to freedom. She does so in spite of the
fettered freedom that has marked her life as a female subject. As the plot
progresses, spatial enclosures literally confine Clarissa; she is forced to enter
into various rooms and properties and "plotted" cells. These "plots" become
terrifyingly claustrophobic and tragic when posed against the ideological
grain of a state of nature that Clarissa believes in. She continues to presume
an individual's right to freedom. But, as she moves from one property to the
next, her spatial environments become more and more enclosed: from her
room at Harlowe Place, to which she is banished; to her apartment at
Sinclair's, where she imagines she is free but comes to learn she is entrapped; to prison; to Sinclair's again, where she is raped, the final act of
violation and enclosure.

Lovelace, the novel's "most wicked of plotters," in the words of
Clarissa's aunt, Mrs. Hervey (505), is responsible for plotting out Clarissa's
confinements after she leaves Harlowe Place. Incarcerating Clarissa and,

finally, violating her body spatially through rape, Lovelace also asserts symbolic acts of spatial violation prior to this crime, constantly intruding upon Clarissa's autonomy and freedom. After reporting to Anna a discussion with Lovelace, in which he admits to having let all the rooms in the Sinclair house under the pretence of protecting Clarissa from "an enemy," Clarissa writes her friend: "it was easy for me to see that he spoke the slighter of the widow, in order to have a pretense to lodge here himself. . . . he frankly owned that if I chose to stay here, he could not . . . think of leaving me for six hours together" (526). She indignantly reports Lovelace's suggestion that they cohabitate a house together; Clarrisa tells Anna her response: " 'Fix *our*selves in a house, as *we* and *our,* Mr. Lovelace—pray, in what light—' " (526—Richardson's emphasis). Lovelace's spatial intrusions symbolize the internal intrusions upon her "self." She writes angrily, "He interrupted me. . . ." (526).

Clarissa presumes the right not to be "broken in upon": "I desired that this apartment might be considered as my retirement," that she might "be as little broke in upon as possible. . . ." (525). What Clarissa calls her "retirement" is both her occupation of writing and her inviolate "self."[17] When a servant delivers an invitation to tea, Clarissa declines it, telling Lovelace: "I must pursue my writing . . . I desired him to make my excuses below . . . and inform them of my choice to be retired as much as possible" (525). Clarissa's right to inhabit property spaces under her own free terms echoes the right to personal sovereignty under political formulations of natural law. "You must never urge me against a declared choice," Clarissa heatedly tells Lovelace (525). Her right to "declare" a "choice" reverberates against the right she has already lost, to choose her self-location, her spatial property, her "plot."

Lovelace's *un*natural, multiple schemes and plots violate Clarissa's sovereign ability to write her own plot. The rake's plots lead to the heroine's final and most enclosed "plot," the coffin and its burial place. The heroine's plot about autonomy and moral will becomes an earthly grave marked by the Father's plot, the "Father's House," to which Clarissa presumably ascends in death.[18] We witness the heroine's assertion of autonomy even in that last "state" or "house": the self-fashioned coffin. Her body's funereal "viewing" confines it to the smallest of spatial interiors, which, ironically, although appropriately, is designed by Clarissa herself.

Throughout the novel, Clarissa appears to set herself apart from the social plot while establishing herself more deeply within it. Her actions suggest a fundamental contradiction between autonomous reason and the role of the natural-law state, echoed in the late-Enlightenment writings of Kant. In his pamphlet, "An Answer to the Question: What Is Enlightenment?", Kant wrote of the importance of using one's own reason, of thinking autonomously rather than dependently, declaring the "motto," "*Sapere aude*—'have courage to use your own reason.' "[19] Only through reason might the individual extricate himself from a socialized but also "self-incurred tutelage," the sheep-like dependency human beings tend to maintain upon the "direction of another" (Kant 91).

Clarissa strives for this radical-rational autonomy. What disturbs Clarissa most is having conducted an epistolary discourse with Lovelace, an act which "I might have supposed would put me into the power of his resolution and *out of that of my own reason*" (380—emphasis added). Having one's "own reason" is vital to Clarissa. It allows her to assert her moral-mental individuality and will. But while Clarissa believes she should not have been deceived "out of . . . reason" by Lovelace, she seems quite willing to be deceived "out of . . . reason" by her *un*reasonable father. The dual value of rational autonomy and female dependency—reflected in Richardson's reading of his heroine's plight—is subtly worked out in the plot, when Clarissa asserts autonomy but mirrors dependency upon patriarchal-familial relations.

Clarissa's duality is inherent in Kant's Enlightenment image of the autonomous, rational individual. In a critique of the "stable, coherent" rational individual summed up by Kant, Flax examines its contradictory appeals to autonomy and submission to authority. She suggests that the Kantian image actually conceals the subject's socialized dependencies. Flax writes that Kant's image of autonomy "appears to mask the embeddedness and dependence of the self upon social relations."[20] This masked, or repressed, aspect of Kantian "autonomy" is reflected in sadomasochism, a historical formation of social desire exploited in *Clarissa*.

Sociologist Chancer suggests that the "sadomasochistic dynamic" is rooted in the modern subject's social dependency, a faulty "individualism" prevalent within capitalist social organization. As Chancer borrows from Benjamin's discussion of sadomasochism, so, too, does Benjamin draw upon D. W. Winnicott's analysis of aggression, and its psychical evolution in early child development. Benjamin recounts Winnicott's thesis thus: the child asserts aggression upon his or her caretaker, originally in order to differentiate him- or herself in the developmental process of separation. This process of separation might allow the child to receive important recognition from the "other." But if the "other" does not survive the aggression—rather absorbs or fails to react to it—the child's aggression turns to rage.

Mothers or female substitutes, traditional primary caretakers in capitalist patriarchy, often passively promote the child's rage by absorbing rather than rejecting the child's aggressive attacks, observes Benjamin. The child's initial demands for recognition evolve into sadistic behavior, which Benjamin perceives as the origin of rational violence. Rational violence "is a substitute for the pain and rage of being unable to successfully destroy and rediscover the other," she notes.[21] Benjamin's observations are reread by

Chancer, who examines the overarching social dynamic bred by rational violence, a steady feature of capitalist patriarchy.

This is the sadomasochistic dynamic, which occurs among social subjects who deny a necessary dependency upon each other—who believe themselves fully autonomous and transcendent of social desire. The sadomasochistic dynamic is played out in circuitous and perverse ways; for subjects take on both sadistic and masochistic roles alternatively and at once. Through the sadistic role, the subject exerts control over another by converting a position of dependency into one of seeming autonomy, even privilege. The overt dependency function is performed by the subject taking on the masochistic role. But, as Chancer makes clear, both sadists and masochists depend upon one another for their performative existence; *both* express the desire for control. On the deepest level, the sadist and the masochist operate through a mutual fear of abandonment.[22]

Clarissa's own subject is bound up in the sadomasochistic contradictions between autonomy and dependency, aggression and desire. It is her natural-law claim to rational autonomy and moral universality that denies, but also belies, her native dependence, and leads to the sadomasochistic dialectic. True to the speculations of Benjamin and Chancer, with their deepest sources in the writings of Freud, Clarissa's sadomasochistic dialectic is an internal one, in which she performs, alternatively, sadist and masochist parts. The intersubjective shifts of sadomasochism, discussed by Freud in "Instincts and Their Vicissitudes," mirror a set of the subject's positions regarding an object. Clarissa reflects the Freudian dialectic, first making herself the "simple" sadist in an attack upon the other—the suitors Solmes and Lovelace; and, second, turning the attack upon herself, subjecting herself to a masochistic positioning. Freud later modified his model of the sadomasochistic vicissitudes when he attributed both sadism and masochism to a primary instinct for aggression. In "The Economic Problem of Masochism," he argued that masochism emerges as a "residue" of internal sadism. The moral masochist is, in some ways, the most sophisticated and perverse sadist, having absorbed the aggressive function nearly entirely, directing aggression back toward the self as the only means of control available. In order to *control* the lack of control the masochist experiences, the *moral* masochist appears to *enjoy* suffering—for its own sake. Clarissa is this moral masochist. Her suffering reflects the ethos of natural law. She insists upon her suffering, even as it controls and dominates her.

Clarissa's unacknowledged masochistic aggression emerges within very early scenes in the novel. Clarissa appears to make rational, autonomous entreaties and assertions. But she becomes the masochist when such entreaties and assertions prove unsuccessful. At first, she acts like a sadistic dominatrix, exerting her stern and domineering judgment over Solmes and others. The term "dominatrix" is appropriate here; for the dominatrix is a male projection of the female sadist—and I am arguing here that Clarissa, ultimately, is a masculine cultural projection of sadomasochistic fantasy.[23]

In an early encounter with Solmes, Clarissa unleashes aggression directly and externally—toward him. She reports to Anna that she appeared before the "coward" looking "very saucily," seemingly in charge before a man who appears "cringing to the ground, a visible confusion in every feature of his face" (303). Solmes's "confusion," she reportedly tells Solmes, gives her "hope": she declines his offer of marriage once again, saying cruelly, "give me leave to say, you were miserable by yourself, than that you should make two so" (304). This speech exemplifies, among other things, Clarissa's devotion to the *rational* aspects of natural law, and her desire for autonomy by acting as a reasoning being. Aggressively confronting Solmes, she exhibits little of the "fellow feeling" Hume would call the moral sentiment of sympathy. Rather, Clarissa exhibits the use of reason implicit in the moral sense, and in the Kantian ideal of reason as the basis of freedom.

During Clarissa's speech to Solmes, her uncle Anthony interrupts her, sadistically asserting that she *will* marry Solmes, and ordering her to marry "this gentleman. It shall, it shall, cousin Clary!—And the more you oppose it, the worse it shall be for you" (305). His interruption divides Clarissa's approach both to reason and to aggression. Clarissa's sense of moral rationality and autonomy undaunted at this point in the novel, she continues to offer rational arguments against the marriage, including expressions of disdain for Solmes. Again interrupted, this time by her brother, who bolts "upon me so unexpectedly," and who grasps her hand "with violence" (305–6), Clarissa's rational control is diminished by the overt act of violence. The interruption through physical violence leads her to change strategies. Clarissa continues to protest her treatment through rational claims and entreaties: "Let me go, sir!" she demands; "—Why am I thus treated?—You *design*, I doubt not, with your unmanly gripings, to hurt me . . . wherefore is it that I am to be thus treated by You?" (306—Richardson's emphasis). Yet the voice of the victim, who almost enjoys the spectacle of her own humiliation, emerges when she writes Anna: "He tossed my hand from him with a whirl that pained my very shoulder. I wept, and held my other hand to the part" (306). The violence of her brother's actions still do not move Clarissa to let Solmes intercede, and she declares her need for independence of any "obligation to a man whose ungenerous perseverance is the occasion . . . of *that* violence, and of all my disgraceful sufferings" (306—Richardson's emphasis). But Clarissa endures her "sufferings" by remaining alternatively rational and pleading for a spectator of sympathy, like Anna. In creating a sympathetic spectator through Anna, Clarissa upholds the image of self-control and yet begs for a spectator's moral indignation. This indignation relies upon the fact of her suffering. Clarissa *demands* suffering, Freud's prescription for moral masochism.

Like the moral masochist in Freud's analysis, Clarissa's suffering is an extension of her own sadistic-control tendencies. Indeed, in the course of the plot, Clarissa tries to control others through the assertion of natural law—and by becoming a victim of those who fail to uphold the law. Upon first considering Lovelace's character, for instance, she criticizes Lovelace's aristocratic arrogance in an acerbic manner. In the process, she mirrors that aristocratic arrogance herself.[24] Asked by her uncle Anthony how she likes Lovelace, she writes: "I immediately answered, Not at all: he seemed to have too good an opinion both of his person and parts to have any great regard to his wife, let him marry whom he would" (46). Several times disdainfully noting Lovelace's class "haughtiness," Clarissa illustrates a class haughtiness of her own: "I had a little specimen of this temper. . . ." she writes; "I desired him therefore not to write again on the subject [of his "passionate regards" for Clarissa], assuring him that if he did, I would return both, and never write another line to him. You can't imagine how saucily the man looked" (48, 47). In such passages, she repeatedly asserts her self-determination not to be violated by the man's "look." But Clarissa coquettishly is already caught up in the "look," a "most watchful and most penetrating lady . . . whose eyes will pierce to the bottom of your shallow soul," in the words of Lovelace himself.[25]

Clarissa's "look" finally turns inward. Lovelace, of course, is the more apparent instigator of sadistic control and rational violence. But when Lovelace accuses Clarissa of "thy haughty airs" (148), a mimetic-linguistic championship is set in place that engages Clarissa in the scene of control and violence, as well. A sado-erotic dynamic ensues. That this dynamic is sexy, featuring many principles of culturally sacrosanct heterosexual romantic love, is suggested by Anna. She compares Lovelace to her kind suitor Mr. Hickman, who she complains puts her to sleep. Anna almost praises Lovelace when she writes Clarissa:

> Lovelace keeps up the ball with a witness, and all his address and conversation is one continual game at racquet.
> Your frequent quarrels and reconciliations verify this observation. (466)

Anna's "observation" pays a compliment to Lovelace and his erotic method, which she later refers to a little more critically as "your wretch's [Lovelace's] teasing ways" (498). In contrast to the "good man" Hickman (Lovelace's phrase—753), Lovelace's "racquet" game is dynamic and exciting. At this point in the narrative, Clarissa's own responses indicate that she is caught up, too, in Lovelace's "racquet" game. Her responses fuel the desire for the game. She depends upon it. We see her natural-law moral propriety vying against aggressive, sado-erotic behavior. Repeated exchanges with Lovelace express Clarissa's desire for control and dependency at once.

The "racquet" game continues during Clarissa's entrapment at the Sinclair house. While asserting her moral "resolve" and rational thought, Clarissa also engages in heated debate with the man who has already betrayed her, the man she blames herself for previously corresponding with and who she tells Anna is a "dissembler, odious as the sin of hypocrisy" (451). In this way, Clarissa contributes to what Lovelace calls "the *amorous see-saw;* now humble; now proud; now expecting, or demanding; now submitting, or acquiescing," a "see-saw" he plans to play "till I have tired resistance" (424). Clarissa encourages rather than discourages the "see-saw" effect through her continual volley of words. The very rationality of her arguments fuels the sadist's desire for attack, and for repetition of symbolic and physical violence.

It also fuels the spectator's desire to be sado-erotically entertained. John Belford is such a spectator. As Lovelace's epistolary correspondent, Belford writes: "Thou, Lovelace, has been long the *entertainer;* I the *entertained*" (500—Richardson's emphasis). Reporting Clarissa's "exchanges" with Lovelace to Anna only increases their entertainment value to the reader outside the epistolary fiction, as well; his desires are directed by the "editor" of these epistles, Clarissa's author-father, "Richardson." Like this implied spectator and controlling editor-redactor of letters, Clarissa conceals her own aggression through dependency—and yet reveals it in tones of voice and inflections, exemplified by statements like, "'Excuse me, good Mr. Lovelace (waving my hand and bowing), that I am willing to think the best of my father.'" This statement, repeated to Anna, indicates that Clarissa does not apprehend the mimetic sadism of Lovelace in the patriarchal control of her father—or herself. Lovelace, in turn, reportedly remarks, according to Clarissa: "'Lord! Madam (assuming a drolling air), what have *you* suffered! Nothing but what you can easily forgive.'"[26] Lovelace is attuned to the performative aspects of Clarissa's suffering; he knows that her demand for performance is also a demand for suffering. Readers of the epistles, like Belford and ourselves, function as Freud's vicarious sadomasochist: the third subject position in the vicissitudes of sadomasochistic desire. We watch the scene of rational violence. We enjoy the experience of violence indirectly, perversely, symbolically.

The desire for sadomasochism and its dual dynamic goes on. In the exchanges between Clarissa and Lovelace, it is not always possible to perceive who is the sadist and who is the masochist. Lovelace and Clarissa again mimic one another's language in what Clarissa calls—accusing Lovelace—the "impetuous temper." Their mutual attempts to gain control over the other do not imply mutuality, however, in the distribution of power.

Natural law dominates as a textual ideology arranged by an editorial figure, the epistolary redactor. But Clarissa, from the beginning, is her *father's* natural daughter, and, therefore, she is caught in a political no-win situation. She may illustrate the control function of the dominatrix-sadist. But she is socially disempowered by her "resolve" to uphold natural-law rational autonomy at any cost. Her "resolve," what Lovelace calls her "opposition and resistance," is his "challenge to do my worst"; her "pride" serves to "awaken *mine,*" Lovelace writes (413—Richardson's emphasis). A few letters later, Clarissa will admit that her "pride" has been her downfall. But her admission reflects the "pride" of the moral masochist, who cherishes that most perverse role. She writes Anna that she hopes she will be "an example" through the punitive drama. In doing so, she promotes the call to rational violence:

> How am I punished . . . for my vanity in hoping to be an *example* to young persons of my sex! Let me be a warning, and I will now be contented. For, be my destiny what it may, I shall never be able to hold up my head again among my best friends and worthiest companions. (453–Richardson's emphasis)

A speaking subject like the adaptable Moll Flanders might reappraise the situation strategically, to assess her loss of control. But Clarissa's determination to be an "example," good or otherwise, does not make her a transformable, adaptable subject. Rather, she maintains a "permanence of consciousness" that Benveniste suggests is at the root of the modern-subject's illusion of sovereignty. Masochism has been perceived by Gaylyn Studlar, and others writing on perversion and representation, as a means of giving up this "permanence of consciousness," the totalized "self."[27] But I follow the more Freudian reading of masochism, suggesting that it is inextricably tied to symbolic identity and the instinct for aggression. Through masochism, the subject denies aggression and control. But the subject reasserts aggression and control—and this is the phenomenon of the subject in general—through more indirect means.

Subject to the control of another, who asserts sadistic aggression even more indirectly, Clarissa can only increase her morally watchful "vigilance," as Anna puts it. "Vigilance" is the function of the moral masochist. Masochism is now the only control Clarissa can maintain in her claim to autonomy and virtue. This full turn to masochism is actually illustrated early in the plot, when we are told that Clarissa wishes to die: "how much rather, I think, should I choose to be wedded to my shroud than to any man on earth!" (514). This statement may seems self-directive. But it is voiced by Lovelace. In her attempt to control the sadistic control asserted upon her by others, Clarissa morally "blames herself"—again Lovelace's words—"for having corresponded with me, a man of free character." In self-castigation, "Clarissa"—actually Lovelace's representation of the heroine—shifts the object of aggression to herself, "a turning around [of sadism] upon the self," as Freudian commentator Jacques LaPlanche states about the self-directed vicissitude (111).

But, as LaPlanche notes, this vicissitude is "not yet true masochism," since masochism itself is "an entirely passive phenomenon" (111). In true masochism, the assertive activity of sadism entirely—or nearly entirely—dissipates, becoming only the faint erotogenic imprint. Clarissa does come to represent the "passive phenomenon" of true masochism, a passivity that her earlier dialogic take-over by Lovelace foreshadows. Clarissa, perhaps from the beginning, is "in the pit," to use Lovelace's expression. She is in the pit of the heroine's plot, fabricated for and within the tight enclosure of the sentimental heroine's natural-law text.

Clarissa's renown "insight" is limited to the natural field only. It is a feminized field that leaves her blind, dependent and without defenses. Clarissa's moral "watchfulness" is really more a paranoid attempt to avoid further violation. For Clarissa was never "subject of the action," in LaPlanche's phrase, to begin with.

Contrary to Clarissa's own reading of her predicament, I am arguing that Clarissa's quandary is *not* her "fault." "How is it," writes Lynda Zwinger, ". . . that most of us remember a whey-face goody-goody or a two-faced hypocrite when we think of *Clarissa?*" Zwinger blames "the posthumous text," the product of "the man who couldn't have her and the woman who couldn't be her and annotated by the man who couldn't stop writing her. . . ." (27). I blame the figure of authority dominating the natural-law cultural text, and this figure's prurient and sadistic invitation to sympathy. I believe that Clarissa's radical autonomy is always undermined by the political currents over which she has no control—except by dying. Those currents are forever stirred, everytime we read these epistles, by an authority figure who hovers in these pages and manipulates each line, a figure twisted into the epistolary acts of reading and writing, whose "subject" is much harder to trace.

The Libertine's Perversion

Too many critical discussions of Clarissa fail to note her dependence upon this hidden authoritarian spectator. These discussions help to construct the sentimental architecture through which Clarissa, in turn, continues to be perceived. Warner's controversial *Reading Clarissa,* however, does challenge the sentimental architecture of the Clarissa "heart." The "heart" he views as a matrix of deception and control, forbidding "the entrance of any foreign matter" (17), and thereby structuring the repressive Western binarisms of inside versus outside, or purity versus foreign matter. Warner perceives that the act of domination at the center of the heroine's ideological universe, where only the "pure" self can force an "advantage over others" in the novel's symbolic Christian courtroom (17), is an allegory for self-identity. It is also a missionary colonization over difference.

By suggesting that the "heart" of sentiment, of Clarissa, is a repressive and dominating structure, Warner reminds us, too, that the sentimental heroine is a fictional subject of speech, whose figure can be deconstructed to reveal socially driven forces. Yet it is another fictional subject of speech that Warner makes his deconstructive champion. Through "parody, the lie, the stratagem," he writes, Lovelace displaces Clarissa's sentimental and natural-law heart "onto a surface" (50), provoking her representational striptease. According to Warner, Lovelace's rape is a welcome gesture, "the moment when Clarissa will be undressed, seen, penetrated, and known" (50).

Warner's Lovelace is a pervert, in Foucault's definition of the term. Lovelace engages in "peripheral sexualities," whose aim is not sexual reproduction. His playfulness makes him a "perfect Proteus," in the words of Clarissa herself. Warner's version of Lovelace may offer a necessary critique of the heroine's fictive image. But Lovelace, the pervert, retains his own fictive imagery, and ideologies, too, of a sentimental nature.

These perversions include the seemingly distinct sexual perversions of sadism and masochism. On the one hand, Lovelace lives up to his reputation of sadistic domination over Clarissa by becoming, as he tells Belford, her "master." Having engineered the illusion of pursuit by the Harlowes and ordering Clarissa to flee her home, he writes that he cried: "'They are coming!—They are coming! Fly, fly, my beloved creature' . . . drawing my sword with a flourish. . . . And so I became her emperor!" (400). His ultimate goal may be to triumph over Clarissa's "sex" by subduing her. But Lovelace also loves to play the masochist, and to be dominated by Clarissa when he grabs her hand and declares, "'take me, take me to yourself; mould me as you please.'" In an imitation of the masochistic contract, he tells her: "'I am wax in your hand. . . . Include me in your terms . . . put a halter about my neck and lead me by it. . . .'"[28] Lovelace's masochistic "desires" are not always completely comic or mere artful strategies. Upon arrival with Clarissa at St. Albans, he muses in correspondence to Belford: "I find, everytime I attend her, that she is less in *my* power—I more in *hers*" (402—Richardson's emphasis).

Poor Clarissa, who "can but write according to the shape he assumes at the time," she tells Anna. Priding herself on *not* being the "sex" of "charming contradictions"—depicted thus by Lovelace—Clarissa pleads: "Don't think *me* the changeable person . . . if in the letter I contradict what I said in the same letter for he is a perfect chameleon." But in her response to Clarissa, Anna observes that Lovelace, the sadist, and Lovelace, the masochist, are not different but the same. Anna notes: "I have been looking back on the whole of his conduct . . . and find that he is more *consistently,* more *uniformly* mean . . . than either of us once imagined."[29]

Anna's assessment of Lovelace's perversion is reflected in Foucault's comments on the libertine's perversion. In *The History of Sexuality,* Foucault discusses the "Don-Juan" libertine, a figure whose popularity "three centuries have not erased." The "great violator" of social norms, whose sexual perversity undermines the marriage laws and the conservative codes of erotic repression, is a figure of seeming liberality. But his liberality points to the existence of "a stricter regime." The libertine-pervert may have "overturned" both of the "two great systems conceived by the West for governing sex: the law of marriage and the order of desires," writes Foucault (*History of Sexuality* 39–40). In the example of Victorian medical discourses about perversion, Foucault cautions us to "consider . . . not the level of indulgence of the quantity of repression" that underlies the need to revolt in the first place, "but the form of power that was exercised" (41). Cultural repression is that which, by definition, reveals "an asymptotic decrease in the thing it condemned" (41). Perversion, differently, displays "a simultaneous propagation of its own power and of the object on which it was brought to bear" (42). Of the libertine figure, Foucault writes:

> Underneath the . . . stealer of wives, seducers of virgins, the shame of families, and an insult to husbands and fathers—another personage can be glimpsed: the individual driven, in spite of himself, by the somber madness of sex. Underneath the libertine, the pervert. He deliberately breaks the law, but at the same time, something like a nature gone awry transports him far from all nature. (*History of Sexuality* 39)

Like Don Juan, the Lovelacean libertine represents "a nature gone awry." But this "nature" is one that asserts the rather consistent state of *being* "awry," his perversion replicating perversion as "nature's" phenomenon. Lovelace suggests that nature, indeed, is responsible for the libertine's "sportive cruelty," telling Belford: "We begin with birds as boys, and as men go on to ladies . . . both . . . experience our sportive cruelty" (557). In another passage, Lovelace links images of his natural "cruelty" to the sexual nature of libertinage. He declares himself afraid of having "a vaporish wife" in Clarissa:

> when a man has been ranging, like the painful bee from flower to flower, perhaps for a month together, and the thoughts of home and wife begin to have their charms with him, to be received by a Niobe, who, like a wounded vine, weeps its vitals away while it but involuntarily curls about you; how shall I be able to bear that?" (521)

The sadistic libertine may be a force of nature. But nature is all too consistently sadistic when the libertine compares the sentimental heroine to the "wounded vine," which "involuntarily curls" around him. The libertine, unlike the heroine of nature's law, is a rather immobile, unfixed agent. His nature seems cruel because it is perversely *un*natural. Through the libertine's inconstancy and bee-like mobility, he attacks a "human nature" rigidified by nature's law—a nature that is constant, passive, like a waiting flower (or sitting duck). And Lovelace's libertine nature is a "nature *gone* awry." Like the sentimental heroine, however, the libertine depends upon an original nature—to pervert it. That perversion itself is a function of "nature" is repressed in the image of the "painful bee." If Clarissa represents a kind of static illusion about human nature, Lovelace represents the same "nature"—gone out of control.

In Richardson's portrayal of Lovelace, the inconsistent "sentiments" of passion rule over the rational consistency of natural moral sense. This portrayal fits Hume's description of the moral sentiments in the *Treatise*. Hume separates himself from other natural-law theorists, like Hutcheson, by suggesting that the passions, not reason, guide moral understanding. It is "human nature" to rely upon "our passions and actions," writes Hume, which "go beyond the calm and indolent judgements of the [rational] understanding." Hume's term "moral sentiment," therefore, hinges upon a pun. It is not from the sense of reason that we derive the sentiments, but rather from the sentiments that we derive the "sense."

Through the specific moral sentiment of sympathy, we move, in Hume's *Treatise,* from a traditional, Western philosophical universe of moral determination to a world in which a spectator converts images seen, and interprets them according to shifting, momentary experiences of "pleasure" or "discomfort." The invention of Lovelace probes the problems not only of natural law but also of its moral sentiment of sympathy. These are problems implicitly examined by Hume in the *Treatise,* where we learn that no fixed moral identity constitutes Hume's moral spectator. The spectator is perverse, lacking fixed moral subjectivity or ontological shape. He exists representationally as a kind of mirror, through which moral images are reflected and received.

Lovelace, as the Foucauldian "shape-shifting" pervert, is the perfect sympathetic spectator, in Hume's definition of that term. Clarissa may exhibit the vigilant "watchfulness" of natural moral law and its "insight." But Lovelace fulfills that quality of voyeuristic mobility and perverse, conflicted vision Hume describes for the spectator of sympathy. Foucault comments that perverse pleasure involves a "pleasure that comes of exercising a power that questions, monitors, watches, spies, searches out . . . brings to light"; but it also involves "the pleasure that kindles at having to evade this power, flee from it, fool it, or travesty it" (*The History of Sexuality* 45). Clarissa is "watchful"; but she also is blind—her sentimental "vision" both a prophetic Judeo-Christian "insight" and an internal monitor of moral thought. It is

Lovelace who questions "insight" altogether. His acts of seeing are always externalized, without figural importance to himself. Lovelace turns his view upon an external object, to paraphrase from Hume. His "watchfulness" operates in a sociopolitical field that directs his gaze upon another.

Lovelace's gaze works to "monitor," to "spy" upon, to "bring to light"— Clarissa. In doing so, Lovelace embodies the ultimate a-morality of any "moral spectator." According to Hume, the moral spectator passes moral judgment based upon speculations, which themselves are based upon passionate responses to the object viewed. Lovelacean "watchfulness," his jailing of Clarissa but also his voyeuristic peepings at the scenes of Clarissa's suffering, reveals the logical result of sympathy in a patriarchal textual worldview.

The libertine's "watchfulness" suggests the figure of the male gaze described in studies of classic cinema. This gaze is overtly dramatized by male characters on the screen, who literally watch a female character in such "dark" and oedipally enigmatic genres as the *film noir.* The gaze encodes what narrative theorists in general have called oedipal processes of masculine identity through the opposing feminine symbol of mystery, the *femme fatale.* But the masculine gaze is more richly applied as a metaphor for the artistic representational process itself, typical to the verisimilitude of classic cinema. The masculine gaze is a substitute for the eye of the cinematic apparatus that both asserts and denies the spectator's vision.

The limited but all-embracing "watchful" spectator implied by the figure of the male gaze is a version of Hume's *moral* spectator. The eye of the spectator, described both by Hume and cinema theory, is ever-present but figurally disavowed. True to this spectator's perverse visual strategy, the eyes we never see in *Clarissa* are Lovelace's own. Clarissa's eyes, in their static and moral "watchfulness," are readily described throughout the novel: "we have the most watchful and penetrating lady in the world to deal with: a lady worth deceiving! but whose eyes will pierce to the bottom of your shallow souls," Lovelace writes Belford.[30] The spectating eyes that gaze upon Clarissa's eyes may be invisible, but we witness their penetrating effects.

Both forms of perverse pleasure are asserted by Lovelace's gaze, demonstrated during the scene of the fire hoax. The fire, while fake, renders Clarissa visible. Through the evasive strategy of false smoke and flame, Lovelace "smokes out" Clarissa, who is hiding in her bedchamber; the strategy allows Lovelace to more fully "monitor," or "spy" upon, her. Clarissa begs for invisibility; Lovelace reports, "She conjured me . . . to quit her apartment and permit her to hide herself from the light, and from every human eye." He responds to her desire for invisibility by "bringing her to light," visually in light of the supposed flame. The "fire" may not be real. But as a narrative strategy for Lovelace, it makes Clarissa's body apparent before the eyes of the epistolary reader. Through the visually concrete language addressed to Belford and the novel reader alike, Lovelace now conjures up a visually *luminous* "Clarissa," whose body signals the novel's sympathetic efficacy and visual effects:

> But, oh, the sweet discomposure! Her bared shoulder and arms, so inimitably fair and lovely: her spread hands crossed over her charming neck; yet not half concealing its glossy beauties: the scanty coat, as she rose from me, giving the whole of her admirable shape, and fine-turned limbs: her eyes running over, yet seeming to threaten future vengeance: and at last her lips uttering what every indignant look and glowing feature portended. . . .[31]

This visual description of Clarissa's "fine-turned limbs" scarcely veils Lovelace's voyeuristic sadism. The voyeur, Mulvey notes, masks sadism behind the fetishist's pose. Fetishistic scopophilia is that which "builds up the physical beauty of the object" through the gaze seeking visual control over its object. Hume alludes provocatively to fetishistic scopophilia in the psychological contradictions of sympathy when he writes that sympathy is "a very powerful principle in human nature" that has "great influence on our taste of beauty"—the basis for moral sentiment and distinction.

The Lovelacean incarnation of the masculine sympathetic spectator plays upon the divided motives through which the "taste of beauty" is inspired. Hume writes rather cynically of the phenomenon of "beauty" and the pleasure it invokes for the spectator: "Whenever an object has a tendency to produce pleasure in the possessor, or in other words, is the *cause* of pleasure, it is sure to please the spectator, by a delicate sympathy with the possessor" (576–77—Hume's emphasis). I say "cynically," because Hume insists that what promotes this "spontaneous" feeling is not rationally informed. What is "beauty," like morality, is informed by the inconstant "passions": "Our situation, with regard both to persons and things, is a continual fluctuation" (581). Hume indicates an appreciation for the ideal of a morally stable referent; he writes that, to prevent "those continual *contradictions,* and arrive at a more *stable* judgment of things, we fix on some *steady* and *general* points of view" (581–82—Hume's emphasis). But he stresses that sympathy does not reproduce this morally stable picture. Because sympathy involves visual perception and the reproduction of pleasure for the spectator, sympathy generates contradictions and "difference":

> The *seeming tendencies* of objects affect the mind: And the emotions they excite are of a like species with those, which proceed from the *real consequences* of objects, but their feeling is different. Nay, these emotions are so different in their feeling, that they may often be contrary, without destroying one another; as when the fortification of a city belonging to an enemy are esteem'd beautiful upon account of their strength, tho' we could wish that they were entirely destroy'd. (586–87—Hume's emphasis)

Lovelacean sympathy reflects Hume's paradoxical account. For Lovelace, "feeling" is "different," and "emotions" are "contrary." The "wish" to "destroy" is conveyed in the elements of his look upon the frantic maiden entrapped by it. Lovelace's visual sadism remains concealed behind the sympathetic fetishist's stance. In the scene following the fire hoax, Lovelace describes a drama of sentimental femininity and helplessness meant to elicit his (and our own readerly) experience of sadistic voyeurism by glamorizing, fetishizing, the maiden in distress. He describes a crying, pleading Clarissa, indicating both an appreciation for a virginal "fortification . . . esteem'd beautiful," employing Hume's language, and a desire that the sentimental icon be "entirely destroy'd." Lovelace grasps Clarissa to his bosom, while the heroine falls "upon her knees . . . there, in the anguish of her soul, her streaming eyes lifted up to my face with supplicating softness, hands folded, dishevelled hair" (725). The duality in the motives of Lovelacean vision is doubled in repetitive excess through Lovelace's "sympathetic" (resemblance-producing) descriptive powers:

> her night head dress having fallen off in her struggling, her charming tresses fell down in naturally shining ringlets, as if officious to conceal the dazzling beauties of her neck and shoulders; her lovely bosom too heaving with sighs, and broken sobs, as if to aid her quivering lips in pleading for her. . . . (725)

What makes Lovelace's sympathetic descriptions so overtly sadistic and pornographic behind their fetishism is that they maintain the external positioning of the gaze. This creates what Freud describes as "the instinct for mastery, or the will to power" that is "sadism proper" ("The Economic Problem of Masochism" 278). Freud insists that "Primal sadism is identical with masochism" at its deepest level. Masochism, like sadism, involves the desire for aggression that seeks an object: "After the main portion of it [aggression] has been transposed outward on to objects, there remains inside, as a residuum of it, the erotogenic masochism" that takes "the self as its object" ("The Economic Problem of Masochism" 278). Evidence for the existence of an erotogenic masochism in Lovelace's fetishism increases in the repetitious "keyhole" scenes. Lovelace looks through the keyhole and sympathetically views Clarissa's distress. As both her literal and symbolic jailor, Lovelace sadistically organizes and subdues his prisoner's behavior through tacitly sentimental means. A moral masochism that typifies Clarissa's figure is projected through Lovelace's "concerned" watchfulness in an eye-witness account of his keyhole peepings:

> her voice dying away into inarticulate murmurs, I looked through the keyhole, and saw her on her knees, her face, though not towards me, lifted up, as well as hands, and these folded, deprecating I suppose that gloomy tyrant's curse.
> I could not help being moved. (729)

Through moral masochism, Lovelace appears to identify momentarily with Clarissa's suffering. He exhibits what Smith describes in *The Theory of Moral Sentiments* as that quality in sympathy "representing to us what would be our own," granting "our imaginations copy" of someone's experience: "By the imagination we place ourselves in his [the object of sympathy's] situation, we conceive ourselves enduring all the same torments. . . . His agonies . . . we have thus adopted and made them our own" (258). Smith is more ambiguous when discussing how these "agonies" *actually* become "our own": "Upon some occasions sympathy may seem to arise merely from the view of a certain emotion in another person" (260). The "view" is an "idea of what that person suffers." Lovelace's view "through the keyhole" reveals the sadistic voyeurism implied by this sympathetic conversion of someone else's experience into the spectator's own "idea" of "emotion." The spectator watches his object of sympathy at a distance, at a *re*-move from the moving affect—so that he may monitor his object from the controlled parameters of the keyhole frame. In reporting one of his "keyhole" views of Clarissa's affect, Lovelace expresses the moral ambiguity of "being moved," of making the heroine's "agonies" *his* "own," in the pun he makes on "*pity*-ful," both as a spectator "full" of the pity of sympathy and as a "pitiful" spectator who enjoys witnessing (and creating) Clarissa's distress:

> I looked through her keyhole at my going by her door, and saw her on her knees, at her bed's feet, her head and bosom on the bed, her arms extended (sweet creature!), and in an agony she seemed to be, sobbing, as I heard at that distance, as if her heart would break—By my soul, Jack, I am a *pity*-ful fellow . . . And why, after all, should I thus torment. . . .
>
> The dear creature herself once told me that there was a strange mixture in my mind. (733–35—Richardson's emphasis)

"Strange mixture," indeed. But perhaps not so strange if we recall the steady, *un*moving, directive of the gaze. Mulvey reminds us that the gaze asserts "control," subjects "the guilty person . . . through punishment or forgiveness." These punitive qualities characterize Lovelace's peepings accompanied by his *own* pleadings for Clarissa's sympathy, *his* demands to be "forgiven."

Part of his ruse? Of course. Whatever "strange mixture" the libertine's gaze provokes, its effects are as singularly sadistic as the form of power they assert. This is the power of the visual, "controlling and limiting what can be seen." Meanwhile, this very power denies the limits of vision. In cinema, the gaze is mimicked by the mechanical apparatus, "reproduced by the projector aperture," E. Ann Kaplan notes, lighting up the scene of representation "one frame at a time." This process "duplicate[s] the eye at a keyhole, whose gaze is confined by the keyhole 'frame'" (30). Duplication is an

important word here: the acts of seeing function as doublings of *re*productions, which are secondary *projections* of the presence of the viewer generating sympathy. Through mechanical acts of cinematic projection, the gaze
allows its spectator to concretize his own subjectivity, while negating the
masculine body from the field of representation.

There may be no camera, projector, or mechanical lens in *Clarissa*. But
the structure of projective spectatorship is persuasively duplicated through
the peep-show-like scenes. And, like the cinematic apparatus, Lovelace's
gaze is relayed back "through the keyhole," regressively, toward the spec-
tator-as-reader. Writings on *Clarissa* tend to mimic the spectator's readerly
effect. Warner's, for example, duplicate the sympathetic gaze they would
critique, in their own sympathy with the libertine. Enacting sympathy's
"resemblance" feature, in which the spectator finds his own identity
through the object's "parallel in ourselves" (Hume 318), Warner identifies
with and rhetorically imitates the libertine's perversion, emphasizing the
differential acts of perversity that typify the libertine's coy "distribution" of
power (to use Foucault's terminology).

Warner champions Lovelace as a trickster, likened to the deconstructive effects of literary language itself. And Warner denigrates Clarissa, who
he perceives to be a *female* trickster, a trick-turner, of whom Lovelace "should
beware. For even the commonest slut knows how to weave new veils to cover
the body with a seeming freshness. And Clarissa is *not* common" (50).

But nevertheless a "slut." Clarissa's nature, Warner implies, in its "*seeming* freshness," beguiles the reader through sentimental and sympathetic
deceit. Made up to be a virgin, Warner's Clarissa is made a whore. I would
suggest that this image of Clarissa contradicts Warner's deconstructive purposes. No dismantling of semiotic binarisms can take place in a reading that
appeals to the myth of the virgin and the whore, the conventional binarism
making "woman" a Western sign.

In sympathy with the libertine, Warner debases Clarissa in order to
preserve a sentimental ideal he supposedly deconstructs.[32] Similarly, Lovelace debases Clarissa in order to preserve her ideality, telling Belford: "And
should not my beloved . . . descend by *degrees* from *goddess-hood* into *humanity*? If it be *pride* that restrains her, ought not that pride to be punished?"
(706—Richardson's emphasis). Critics sympathizing with the heroine have
admonished Warner for his liaison with Lovelace—like Lovelace, these
critics argue that Warner refuses to take "moral responsibility," a problem
that "arises from failing to take the story [of Clarissa's rape] seriously."[33]
Terry Eagleton specifically rebukes Warner, for obscuring the moral evil in
Lovelace; Eagleton writes that Lovelace "is for the most part simply a wolf,
and is perceived by Clarissa to be so" (69). But Eagleton's own sympathy—
for the heroine—operates as the flip side to Warner's sympathy for Lovelace. Eagleton attacks Warner and other critics for casting a "slur upon

Clarissa" (69). In the process, however, he restores the debased heroine to the fetishistic ideal; he places her back upon the proverbial courtly-love pedestal.

Furthermore, Eagleton insists that readings like that of Warner's are "fashionably uncomfortable" with the "real" heroism Clarissa stands for— because she is "not only kind, chaste and conscientious but also embarrassingly rich and *real*."[34] She who has been slandered by being made to wear the whore's false accoutrements is divested of all this falsity by a swashbuckling defender of virtue and "realism" in literature. Eagleton's Clarissa "achieves that pure transparency of signifier to signified" (75). But Eagleton's image of "transparency" is also a reflection, or projection, of the critic's own longing for moral "transparency," through his self-reflection in the morally absolute natural-law mirror.

In sympathy with Clarissa, Eagleton, too, illustrates the paradoxes of sympathy in its resemblance effect. Hume likens sympathetic resemblance to the experience of "*great uniformity* we may observe in the humours and turn of thinking of those of the same nation" (316). And, indeed, Clarissa is Eagleton's "nation," an icon for the collective compatriot through which his own authorial subject might find stable moral identity. But this kindred-like "uniformity" reflected by Clarissa reflects the critic's own desire to be his *own* sentimental ideal, to be "kind, chaste, and conscientious" (71)— another masculine champion of sentimental femininity, like Richardson.

Female fetishism may be a comforting representational illusion to our seemingly inescapable male gaze. But female fetishism is also a signifier for the substitutional process that underlies natural law, its moral virtuousness, and the whole(some)ness of its subject. The problem of the fetish is that it reduplicates the anxieties it assuages. Reversing and yet strangely mirroring the libertine's perversion, Eagleton temporarily assuages his own subjective anxieties as critic-subject, viewing Clarissa's public spectacle of death as "a profoundly political gesture." This positive reading of meaning and political significance in Clarissa's death nevertheless reveals the spectator's ontological ambiguity. Writing about the spectator's object fetishism in the context of viewing seventeenth-century Dutch painting, Hal Foster notes that the "female" fetish revels in its own ambiguity. This fetish "allows the viewer"— who is not a woman—"to see *the* woman (the mother) as both whole and castrated" (261—emphasis added). The fetish, in Foster's words, serves "not only as a 'protection' against castration but also as a 'memorial' " *to* it—a "compromise formation that . . . allows the subject to have it both ways."[35] It is this "compromise formation" that allows Eagleton and all of Clarissa's spectators to have it "both ways" in her extended scene of death.

We weep. But we continue to read. Clarissa, in dying, is like the luminous, divided, wedges of fruit about which Foster writes, which he suggests compel the art lover's gaze upon the Dutch *nature morte*. Divided from friends, socially alienated, raped, the dying "Clarissa lives"—quoting Lovelace's words following the rape. She "lives" as a dead "memorial" to the absent but present spectator.

Epistolary Key-holes/Sympathy's Apparatus

Clarissa's body is an ambiguous spectacle at best, as "strange" a "mixture" as the flickering luminosity projected on the silver screen. Her spectacular death encodes the "mixture" of absence and presence that haunts the sympathetic spectator's projected self-image. The spectator's sympathy through the luminous presence of Clarissa (her name means luminosity or light) sustains what Mulvey calls that quality of "to-be-looked-at-ness" associated with the female film star. The glamorized use of white womanhood invokes a luminous fetishism on the screen, to *screen out* the visual presence of a narrative spectator.

Like the spectator of the Hollywood screen, Clarissa's image in Lovelace's epistles is "the leit-motif of erotic spectacle: from pin-ups to striptease, from Ziegfeld to Busby Berkeley" (Mulvey 11). Mulvey speaks, of course, of the literal apparition of white femininity, an icon of female-body specularity through cinema's luminous but divisive lights. I borrow from these discussions of female fetishism in cinema to cast my own light upon the *Clarissa* spectator. The absent-present figure peeks out from within the fetishistic codes of the epistolary text, and its fragmented narrative seams.

Female fetishism was a theme in the epistolary long before Richardson wrote *Pamela* and *Clarissa*. An early "female scribbler" (as Clarissa calls herself) was the sixteenth-century Venetian courtesan Veronica Franco, whose *Lettere familiari* sought to rehabilitate her reputation by making herself seem an "honest woman" through the honesty accorded epistles. Fashioning herself as a "true" lover, mother, and friend, Franco exploited the classical epistolary genre of Cicero and early-Church writers, in which a thoughtful individual revealed personal knowledge of civic duty and social convention,[36] meanwhile manipulating the emotional transparency epistles seemed to convey. Another pre-eighteenth century epistolary text drew upon a different classical source, Ovid's *Heroides*. Repeating the Ovidian portrayal of a woman's excessive capacity for suffering through the love of a man, the French *Lettres portugaises*, first published in 1669 but reissued multiple times due to popularity, made female emotion and suffering the center of seemingly unmediated, authentic epistles.

The supposed correspondence of a Portuguese nun is now believed to have been the literary fiction of a male secretary to Louise XIV.[37] Like

Franco's letters, whose "genuine feelings" were always intended for publication, the *Lettres portugaises* perpetuated a fetishized irony at the heart of "women's" epistles. The epistolary conventions of the French Salon women would embody this masculine fetishism, as well. The Salon women exploited these masculine fantasies about women, emotional transparency and authenticity of feeling.

One celebrated Salon writer, Madame de Scudéry, wrote in *Clélie* (1654–60) that women are the enigma of emotion itself, mimicking the view of femininity from the Ovidian tradition of female suffering and the seemingly inverse tradition of Provençal courtly-love (in which, by some strange conversion, a male poet suffered unrequited love for a woman). Madame de Scudéry insisted that women, representing the vicissitudes of emotion, are naturally emotionally revealing. For Madame de Scudéry, women both revealed their emotions naturally or easily, and were naturally the state of emotion itself. Madame de Sévigné, another Salon writer, was renown for her "natural style." In claiming tight editorial control over letters written by Madame de Sévigné to her daughter,[38] a granddaughter argued that some epistles were too emotionally revealing for publication and never intended for a public audience. The granddaughter's appeal made the fetishistic association between authenticity, womanhood, and a newly emerging image of the natural mother through the presupposition of native intimacy between mother and daughter: "Here is a mother writing her daughter everything that she thinks, just as she thought it, without ever having believed that these letters would fall into another's hands," the granddaughter argued.[39] If the epistolary was linked to "natural" expression through the immediacy accorded the confessional letter, it did so by vying cultural images of female duality and artifice against cultural images of female-inspired artlessness and transparency. No matter how complimentary to women, these images as they circulated in seventeenth- and eighteenth-century epistolary practice, were embedded in misogynistic beliefs about women's artistic and intellectual limitations.

As seventeenth-century writer Jean de La Bruyère wrote:

> women find at the tip of their pens expressions and turns of phrases that often, in men, are the result of long searching . . . they have an inimitable way of putting words together that seem to come naturally and that is *only held together* by the meaning."[40]

But this kind of praise for women-authored letters in an age that had come to admire the seemingly authentic sensibilities of women was mixed with prohibitions that sought to reinforce women's public aspirations. "Praise" for women's supposedly spontaneous and "natural" written expression reassured their readers that these female scribblers did not violate the social norms of femininity. They remained "feeling," but passive and unreflective. They were allowed to be expressive, but only decorative in being so.

Indeed, the· Salon writers helped to reinforce what would become a fetishistic image of bourgeois femininity for the modern age. The epistolary was a genre particularly suited to this image. Not coincidentally, fetishism lies at the heart of epistolary narrative structure, as well. An alternation between the two fetishistic terms, presence and absence, is worked and reworked through the writing, editing, and reading acts that control epistolary enunciation.

In Janet Gurkin Altman's work on "epistolarity," a term she uses to connote "the letter's formal properties [as employed] to create meaning" (4), she writes of this fetishistic quality in epistolary structure. Altman suggests that "the *now* of narration," which is epistolarity's "central reference point," conflicts with the fact that the "*now* is unseizable" (129), haunting epistolary discourse. Unifying or smoothing over the gap that emerges between the present "now" and the absence of the present is the apparition of an editorial figure. I perceive this figure to be a spectator as well as an editor, who tells us how to regard the object through sympathetic projection.

Like Lovelace, the editorial spectating figure does not reveal his own presence directly in the narrative. Rather, he disavows presence, relying upon the indirect route of perversion to make his linguistic and visual mark. This figure vanishes and reappears in the spaces or gaps that exist between letters, and also within the figures for writing mapped out by the content of the letters themselves. One of these figures is the pen. In the letters that describe the fateful scene of Clarissa's departure with Lovelace at the garden door of Harlowe Place, a pen becomes the metonymic substitute for the epistle-writer Lovelace, who, again, is a substitute for the missing editorial figure in the novel at large.

In this scene—itself about Clarissa's "missing" state, or how, through mimicry and substitution, she came *to be missed*—the pen is a fetish for the missing phallus, again substituted by the figure of a key. This scene, as described by Clarissa, is full of references to a "key." The key is symbolic of enunciatory agency and power in the plot, a phallic signifier in the way that Lacan describes this signifier's symbolic but circuitous power.[41] Before the letter describing to Anna her sudden departure from home, Clarissa writes about Lovelace's desires for an "interview": Lovelace, she writes, claims to have "a key . . . to the garden door . . . (if I will but unbolt the door)," letting him "come into the garden at night . . . that he may reassure me of the truth of all he writes" (259). In a following letter, Clarissa again writes Anna that, at Lovelace's insistence, she will "unbolt the door that he might come in by his own key" (262). In another letter dated a couple of days later, Clarissa links the image of key to her locked wardrobe: "Betty had for some time been very curious about my wardrobe . . . I once left my keys in the locks . . . on my return, surprised the creature with her hand upon the keys (281).

Multiple references to the presence or absence of a key or keys continue in the actual scene of the garden meeting, as reported by Clarissa. Starting to take leave of Lovelace and "stooping to take up the key to let myself into the garden," Clarissa tells her version of what we later learn (in Lovelace's version) is a substitutional ruse—Joseph Lehman pretends (Lovelace's scheme) that she is pursued by family members:

> I was offering the key to the lock, when, starting from his [Lovelace's] knees, with a voice of affrightment loudly whispering, as if out of breath, *They are at the door, my beloved creature!* And taking the key from me, he . . . fluttered with it as if he would double-lock it. (379—Richardson's emphasis)

At this moment, "a voice from within cried out" (379). Through the *double* substitution of phallic power invested in the key, from Clarissa's father to Joseph Lehman to Lovelace, Clarissa loses the key symbolically at this moment, resulting in her loss of reputation and, later, in her loss of virginity. Her reputation, like her chastity, is a value for the Harlowe family on the patriarchal marriage marketplace; the loss of the key is a loss within the patriarchal, fetishistic economy that imbues Clarissa with her commodity status. As a precious commodity, Clarissa's chastity should be locked up by the key. This view of Clarissa perceives her body as key*hole*. The key is Lovelace's phallic weapon in a masculinist economy, wielding his power over Clarissa's body. The keyhole is his fetishistic substitution, his voyeuristic medium.

Appropriating the key from Clarissa at the garden gate, Lovelace prefigures the robbery he is about to commit, depriving the Harlowes of their sexual-female property. This reading of agency through the image of the key/keyhole suggests Lacan's reading of the absent but present phallus in language itself, an all-powerful signifier that makes its signifying mark through the playful rhythm of a game of peek-a-boo. Behind the missing and reappearing phallus is a system of psycholinguistic structures that some film critics have used to describe the visual logic of the cinematic apparatus: the dissociated use of the camera, the editing equipment, the projector, the screen—all of which mark the circuitous presence of the cameraman or director-auteur making artistic decisions. *Clarissa's* epistolary structure is a proto-visual text whose epistolarity contains elements of these apparati. In the vanishing materiality of the key, the epistles about Clarissa's fateful departure imply the absent presence of a subjectivity overview, a displaced agency holding the master key to Clarissa's narrative, so to speak.

If the seventeenth and eighteenth centuries characterized the epistolary as artless and unmediated, so, too, the twentieth century has continued to interpret the example of *Clarissa*, specifically, as a medium that conveys no "coherent overview," in Eagleton's words. Margaret Doody, for example, has argued that because "freedom is very much at the center of Richardson's novels," this "author does not intrude his control over his characters; he is withdrawn, letting them speak for themselves" (111). More recent poststructural criticism continues this view through a Bakhtinian discovery that "no single voice prevails" in the epistolary; that rather, as Castle notes, the text of *Clarissa* operates as "a continuous gabble of imaginary voices, among which that of the 'Editor' who shares [Richardson's] name is only one more, albeit pompous addition to the cacophony" (149, 148). In this view of the epistolary nature of *Clarissa*, it is

> the reader [who] must construct meaning, impose an order on events. *Clarissa* activates the invention, the "penetration"—the desire of the reader. Any "authority" one may wishfully invest in the historical imago—Richardson—is naught, finally, in the face of this desire. (Castle 149)

I would agree that *Clarissa* offers a metafictional exploration of the hermeneutic challenges and contradictions of any reader of texts. However, I would like to reconsider the notion that *Clarissa's* epistolary narrative method lacks a centralizing "authority," a controlling authorial presence. I suggest, instead, that the seeming *lack* of a controlling authorial presence actually enhances the narrative control of the author-authority, who is the perverse spectator of sympathy. Through the continual but neutral-seeming interventions of an editorial redactor, the epistles are shaped into the framework of novelistic discourse. The redactor is, by definition, a projective figure, who *pre*figures himself onto the sympathetic affect of others. What one recent critic refers to as "the text's openness" in *Clarissa* is precisely that which leads to the text's perverse redistribution of power.[42]

Through the fetishistic excessiveness of doubles doubling doubles (of retellings, increased by our own rereadings), the reader of *Clarissa* glimpses the ontological problem of such an editorial spectator. Sympathy for the heroine's plight is fetishistically reproduced by the absent but present "key," which alludes to the absent-present editorial spectator. The phallic key performs a kind of double substitution, another vanishing act, through the image of the pen. This is an image that pervades Lovelace's letter about the key, that mirrors (duplicates differently) Clarissa's description of the garden-door scene. We recall that Benveniste cautions us to observe more suspiciously the "now" of narration; "the reality to which *I* or *you* refers . . . is solely a 'reality of discourse' . . . a very strange thing," he writes. In Lovelace's letter to Belford that refers to Clarissa's departure from Harlowe Place, the "pen" is a sign of this "strange thing," this "reality" that is twisted, only mimicked, through writing.

The pen is a double of another kind of substitution in the present/ absent dual image of key/keyhole emphasized in Clarissa's rendering of the story. The juxtaposition of Lovelace's letter with Clarissa's—substituting the object of a key for a pen—suggests that there is a manipulator of both key and pen concealed by epistolary fragmentation. Lovelace states that he uses his "pen" to describe Clarissa's visual "illustriousness." If the pen is the phallic mark of the *missing* figure of the narrative agent as spectator, this master-manipulator reveals himself in the sympathetic pen that depicts Clarissa's spiritual, visual light.

In his own version of the garden scene, Lovelace writes Belford: "Indeed, I never had a more illustrious subject [Clarissa] to exercise my pen upon. . . . Nothing, then, but inclination to write can be wanting" (399). The sexual nature of the pen—and its phallic visual description—is implied by the sexual pun, "exercise my pen upon." In this epistle that describes Clarissa's leaving, Lovelace goes on to describe a virginally intact Clarissa in the most *visually* intact descriptive mode possible through the pen. He reproduces Clarissa's attire, visage, and body, beginning, he claims, with "a faint sketch of her admirable person with her dress" as she arrives at the garden door. Lovelace's "sketch," while appreciative of "a native elegance" that allows her "Excellence" in dress, quickly becomes a full dressing of Clarissa, who he can then "undress" through a visual striptease. "Many a one have I taught to dress, and helped to undress," he comments (399). Lovelace's visual representation of Clarissa's "looks" is enacted by a writing that itself looks—under her dress:

> Her wax-like flesh (for, after all, flesh and blood I think she is!) by its delicacy and firmness, answers for the soundness of her health . . . I never in my life beheld a skin so *illustriously* fair. The lily and driven snow it is nonsense to talk of: her lawn and her laces one might, indeed, compare to those; but what a whited wall would a woman appear to be, who had a complexion which would justify such unnatural comparisons? (399—Richardson's emphasis)

Lovelace's "undressing" of Clarissa reflects then-contemporary attitudes about the epistolary writer's self-exposure and aims of realism: Abraham Cowley called his epistles the "undress'd Soul"; Lady Mary Wortley Montagu wrote that she revealed her "mind undressed"; and even Alexander Pope mused upon his epistolary "thoughts just warm from the brain without any polishing or *dress*, the very *déshabillé* of the understanding."[43] This state of "undress," for Lovelace, reflects the virtual reality that Lovelace reproduces with his epistolary pen, exposing not himself (in the flesh), but rather Clarissa's "white" or "fair" body, which, through his pen's twists and turns on the page, almost appears to glow. Like the white femininity literally rendered by cinematic lights, Clarissa "is alive, all glowing," he writes, "all charming flesh and blood, yet so clear, that every meandering vein is to be seen in all the lovely parts of her which custom permits to be visible" (399).

But like Hollywood's projection of white femininity, Lovelace's sympathy toward Clarissa's vision amounts to a psychical projection of masculine fantasy out of "the lovely parts." His testament to sentimental femininity "wholesomeness" is undercut by the divided account of Clarissa's body actually viewed in parts, "A white handkerchief, wrought by the same *inimitable fingers*" that had embroidered "cuffs and robings" (400—emphasis added), fingers "concealed—Oh Belford! what still more *inimitable beauties* did it *not* conceal!—And I saw, all the way we rode, the *bounding heart;* by its throbbing motions I saw *it!* dancing beneath the charming umbrage" (400—emphasis added). The eroticism in this passage relies upon a division of Clarissa that reaches beyond the visible surface, as his eyes—and our eyes—canvas and categorize the female body *in* parts. Clarissa is also a body of mobile parts, a puppet, appropriated by Lovelace as a symbol of his manipulative powers.[44]

She faints into Lovelace's "supporting arms"—and here Lovelace briefly anatomizes himself as puppeteer. In this manipulative role, he generates the action in the text, and directs our gaze onto the spectacle-entertainment of Clarissa's body parts in motion: "What a precious moment that! How near, how sweetly near, the *throbbing partners!*" (400—emphasis added). "Supporting" Clarissa, assisting her and sympathetically sharing in her moment of emotional agitation, Lovelace also manages to peep at the breasts under the bodice. Through animated and sympathetic description, the reader is drawn to the Lovelacean peep show.

Mulvey explains the way in which female erotic spectacle functions "on two levels" in Hollywood narratives: as "erotic object for the characters within the screen story"; and as "erotic object for the spectator within the [cinema] auditorium, with a shifting tension between the looks on either side of the screen" (11–12). This same tension operates within *Clarissa,* I suggest, as Lovelace and Belford, masculine spectators within the narrative diegesis, act as relay points for the epistolary spectator's look inside but also outside the framing of the letters. The "shifting tension" points to both the redactor figure internal to the fictive structure of the novel's collection of letters, but also to the actual letter reader of the novel. The "shifting tension" actually unifies the "two looks," mediated by what Mulvey calls the "device of the show girl." This image of "the performing woman," according to Mulvey, has the effect of unifying "the gaze of the spectator and that of the male characters in the film . . . without breaking narrative verisimilitude" (12).

Verisimilitude, created through these gestures of spectatorial unity, occurs in a classic Hollywood film narrative when a song-and-dance routine performed, say, by Marilyn Monroe—the luminous white female *par excellence*—"takes the film into a no-man's-land outside its own time and space" (Mulvey 12). It does so by momentarily freezing the progression of the narrative, spatializing the narrative "frame" (on celluloid) through the iconic qualities made by the female body. Mulvey also suggests that the "close-up" of a woman's body part, for example, her face or legs, can have the same frozen-frame effect as the total image of the show girl. So, too, a momentary space, or frozen gap, in Lovelace's story about *Clarissa's* departure occurs as he describes her body. Like director Josef von Sternberg's close-ups of Marlene Dietrich's face in the film *Morocco*, or director Billy Wilder's shot of Barbara Stanwyck's ankles as she first glides down the stairway in *Double Indemnity*, Lovelace's close-up of Clarissa's "throbbing partners," as well as other "lovely parts,"

> integrate into the narrative a different mode of eroticism. One part of a fragmented body destroys the Renaissance space, the illusion of depth demanded by the narrative, it gives flatness, the quality of a cut-out or icon rather than verisimilitude to the screen. (Mulvey 12)

Clarissa's body becomes a visual spectacle. Meanwhile, Lovelace's "pen" acts as narrative agency. In classic film,

> the split between spectacle and narrative supports the man's role as the active one of forwarding the story, making things happen. The man controls the film phantasy and also emerges as the representative of power in a further sense: as the bearer of the look of the spectator, transferring it behind the screen to neutralise the extra-diegetic tendencies represented by woman as spectacle. (Mulvey 12)

The epistolary spectator identifies with the "main controlling figure" through the Lovelacean look: "As the spectator identifies with the main male protagonist, he projects his look on to that of his like, his screen surrogate" (Mulvey 12). In this way, the power of the male spectator inside the diegesis "coincides with the active power of the erotic look" outside the diegesis of the Lovelacean epistle (the "look" of the epistolary redactor-spectator). It also coincides with the "erotic look" outside the diegesis of the novel, that of the reader-spectator.

This is convenient for the male spectator, who can conceal his own visual presence and save himself from "the burden of sexual objectification" (Mulvey 12). The visual erasure of the presence of the spectator is made possible by the very value placed upon the eroticized female body, as Lovelace indicates. "*Her* emotions" are the basis for "*my* transports," Lovelace writes (400—Richardson's emphasis). His own visual presence is erased in the name of sympathy, which, we recall, is a "disturbance" and a "passion" for the spectator. Lovelace's memory of these "transports" is graphically transported onto the epistolary text, when he recalls the hoax played upon Clarissa and interrupts his visual rendering by exclaiming:

> "The sex! The sex, all over!—charming contradiction!—Hah, hah, hah, hah!—I must here lay down my pen to hold my sides; for I must have my laugh out, now the fit is upon me!" (400–1)

The "fit" is his *own* "transports," actually rendered within his epistolary text as a wordless gap, a space. The holder of the pen must be holding his sides at this moment. A "holding" act is signified by the gap that occurs before he resumes his version of the story of the key.

Altman suggests that the authorial redactor in epistolary convention, in general, is figured within a narrative "gap," what she calls "the space of structural interplay" left within the gaps between letters (183). Such a space or gap is "the trace of the editor," she argues, "of that very editor who typically claims elsewhere to have played a minor role" (183). The figure of editor-as-gap involves a much more profound experience of spectatorship in the narrative, I would add. We might read such a "gap" or "space" occurring in what Foster calls the symbolic "commodity exchange" that takes place between the spectator and viewed object. Realism like that of Dutch painting, but also of epistolary immediacy, relies upon an "aura"—Foster uses Walter Benjamin's term[45]—to reproduce the object's "luminosity."

The reproduction of the aura is an inverted and disavowed process for the spectator. Foster writes: "People and things trade semblances" in this commodity exchange; "social relations, take on the character of object relations," while "commodities assume the active agency of people" (254). Dutch "techniques of immediacy" may attempt "to 'deanthropomorphize vision,'" in Foster's words, but the appearance of "no fixed viewpoint, an apparent framelessness, a mirror mimesis," are conventions that "serve to negate the artist as maker" while also affirming the subject (262).

What ensues is "a supreme fiction" of the viewer, by which dead objects (in the *nature morte*) are "*endowed with life* to the degree that the viewer is *sapped* of it" (Foster 254—emphasis added). Foster uses the verb "to absorb" in analyzing the exchange-like inversion between subject of the canvas and subject of the disavowed spectator. Richardson also used the verb "to absorb" in disavowing his authorial presence in his fictive portraits: "I am all the while *absorbed* in the character," he wrote in correspondence. "It is not fair to say—I, identifically I, am any-where, while I keep within the character."[46] The writer, notes Richardson, experiences a loss of "self," "absorbed" into the fictive reality of his characters.

The viewer may be "absorbed" by the sympathetic gaze. But, in the process, he is reborn as a "subject." The "gap" signifying the space of the epistolary redactor is a function of a textual system replete with gaps and deletions that allude to a master figure—one who smooths over, fills in, the gaps. The "pen," Richardson comments provocatively, "makes distance, presence" (quoted in Carson 97). The "mosaic" effect (Altman's term) in epistolary correspondence ironically creates an "illusion of realism" like that of classic cinema—an illusion long associated with the presence and immediacy, the "realism" implied by epistles.

Altman has suggested that an implied structure of "discontinuity" versus "continuity" exists in epistolary narrative. This alternating structure is created by both the redactor and the reader. Both agencies, figured as "gaps," create continuity over the broken mosaic as they place letter against letter, or read the letters together, sustaining the forward movement of epistolary plot. Ruptures and disjunctive passages may be smoothed over, but they are registered within the text as signs of the redactive and readerly function.

The classic-cinema textual system operates similarly to create reality's illusion. In a reading of Raymond Bellour's theory of hypnosis and perversion in cinema, Janet Bergstrom describes a similar use of discontinuity and continuity as structuring filmic shots into "segments," or units of meaning. In a reading of what she calls "segmentation" in Alfred Hitchcock's Hollywood production of *The Birds*, Bergstrom illustrates the way in which the segments advance through an "orchestration of these oppositions." They indicate either "difference" (discontinuity or dissymmetry) or "repetition" (continuity or symmetry). Bergstrom recalls the series of shots in *The Birds* that tell us the story of Melanie's boat trip across Bodega Bay. Melanie plays a prank upon her suitor, Mitch, mysteriously depositing a pair of love birds inside his house. Upon her return across the bay, Melanie is violently struck by a seagull, foreshadowing the aviary viciousness to come. The oppositions that shape the implicit message of the segment (a capricious woman who tries to remain unseen, who pursues a man through deception and chicanery, will be punished) include discontinuity (Melanie's movement to the boat, the camera movement as Melanie enters the house) and continuity (a shot of Melanie smiling in the boat; a shot of Melanie watching Mitch; a shot of Mitch watching Melanie through binoculars). An alternation takes place between shots, first indicating movement, then stasis, then movement again. The total effect of this alternation and segmentation reaffirms the image of a "natural continuity" characteristic of Hollywood realism.[47]

Similarly, these binary oppositions alternate in Lovelace's "segment," which describes Clarissa's body in parts. It does so to assert a false "natural continuity." Discontinuity (difference) is created as our eyes rove over Clarissa's "dress," her "skin," her "fingers," her "cuffs," to her "bounding heart" and "throbbing partners" under the bodice. Continuity (sameness) is created by snapshot-like images of the puppet or doll-like Clarissa, her "wax-like flesh," "skin so illustriously fair," like the "lily and driven snow," like the "whited wall." These multiple snapshot comparisons may suggest a "plurality" of images. But, to borrow from Bergstrom, it is a "plurality" that is "not without direction" (170).

Lovelace interrupts the flow of motion he creates across Clarissa's bodice with "—Oh Belford! what still more inimitable beauties did it not conceal!" In doing so, he not only creates a moment of rupture that then becomes a point of erotic contemplation, a moment of stasis. But he also points to the role of the reader in making "direction" out of "plurality," and to Belford as reader, who will generate the novel's sympathetic sentimental conclusion. Lovelace's portrait of Clarissa, after all, is occasioned by the relationship of her image to this spectator. Before his description, Lovelace reminds Belford of a promise the latter had extracted from him to be made "particularly" informed: "Thou claimest my promise that I will be as particular as possible in all that passes between me and my goddess" (399). But for his "supporting arms," Lovelace remains perversely nondescript about himself. Yet it is Belford, Lovelace's own spectator, who remains unseen upon this occasion, and throughout most of the novel.

Belford, the receiver of Lovelace's epistles, represents the most effaced level of spectatorship, a substitute for the unknown reader external to the fiction. By contrast, Lovelace is one model of the readerly spectator, an overt penetrator of other people's letters, an obvious fictional sadist. Lovelace's overt sadism illustrates, for example, in the scene of another "key," a "master key" given by Lovelace to the servant Dorcas, "which will open every lock" in the closet into which Clarissa has put her clothes, "*an ample mahogany repository*," Lovelace comments with glee, "that used to hold the richest suits which some of the nymphs put on . . . dressed out to captivate or to ape quality" (570—Richardson's emphasis) in Sinclair's house of prostitution. The closet holds "*drawers in it for linen*" (570—Richardson's emphasis). Lovelace, through the substitute Dorcas, will penetrate these drawers, symbolically penetrating the body that wears the "linen," as well as the mind that writes the letters concealed in the "drawers." Dorcas's instruction is to transcribe the letters with the help of Sally and Polly. Here the "master key" is a real object in Lovelace's sadistic reading power. It is associated with the duplicity of female masquerade and the prostitutes' disguises—as well as with the duplicity of the letters they transcribe.

The reading status of letters, of course, is always problematic throughout *Clarissa*. Inherited from the epistolary genre in general is the phenomenon of *mis*reading: in the sending of prohibited correspondence; in letters delayed in the sending (enclosed in one envelope together); in letters written as a series of continued interruptions, but read as if a continuously executed act; in fake letters, like that of Lovelace's "Tom Doleman" or others ascribed to his friends and family members; in letters sent to false names (like the letters Lovelace writes Clarissa, addressed to "Mrs. Love-lace" [732]); in letters addressed to pseudonyms, and/or falsely delivered to the wrong person. Both latter acts of misreading/misdirection of and in the letter occur in the passage about "Miss Laetitia Beaumont's" letter, inter-cepted by Lovelace. "Laetitia Beaumont" is a pseudonym used by Clarissa. This letter enacts a perverse journey, by Lovelace's account. Collins tries to deliver the letter to a Clarissa who has disappeared from Sinclair's (he calls twice); he leaves the letter at Wilson's and that receiver delivers the letter into Lovelace's hands—which Lovelace reads with "excited rage" (732). The purloined, misdirected letter is stamped by a myriad of acts of deceit, literally stamped by the double deceit of the woman who is its (false) re-ceiver and yet does not receive it. It is also stamped by the deceit of the man who should not be its deliverer, as well as the man who should not be its reader.

This doubleness reinforces the knowledge of readers outside the fic-tion that we are duplicitous readers of the Beaumont letter, as well. We are complicitous in multiple misdirected and conspiratorial seeing and reading acts. Through the contents of the letter itself, we are made aware that the reading of any novel of letters is an individual act concealing a group act directed by the sadism of a figure like Lovelace. Written by Anna, this letter warns its intended receiver, Clarissa, that she has been watched by fellow parishioners:

> Miss Lardner . . . saw you at St. James's church. . . . She kept you in her eye during the whole time. . . . she doubted not but you were married—and for an odd reason—*because you came to church by yourself*—Every eye . . . was upon you. (745—Richardson's emphasis)

Clarissa's spectacle of autonomy and independence may stimulate the group gaze of the congregation. But the image of the group vies against the image of the individual, the voyeur who reads or gazes at Clarissa in private. In an earlier church scene described by Lovelace, the individual gaze of Lovelace is actually placed in context of that of the group:

> I was exceedingly attentive to the discourse, and very ready in the auditory's part of the service—Eyes did not much wander. How could they? when the loveliest object, infinitely the loveliest, in the whole church, was in my view? (539)

In the letter to "Miss Laetitia Beaumont," the "eyes" of the congregation are transferred onto the "eyes" of the multiple readers, senders, deliverers, and receivers of this particular letter. We, the reader-spectator of all these epistolary events, are the substitutes for the metafictional reader behind, but also beyond, the novelist's visual mise-en-scène.

The one reader who represents the group reader is Belford. He is the shadowy figure who remains unseen throughout most of *Clarissa*, but, at the end, who tells us how to read the story of the harassed maiden. At first a fellow rake who is the sympathetic occasion of Lovelace's letters, Belford slowly transforms before our eyes into a man of sentiment through the sympathetically "disturbing" process. He begins about halfway through the novel to write Lovelace "professedly in her [Clarissa's] behalf" (500). At first he pleads for Clarissa's salvation at Lovelace's hands, on the basis, he then argues, of his concern for Lovelace and his family. Later, however, Belford argues on behalf of Clarissa's virtuous character: "Permit me, dear Lovelace, to be a means of saving this excellent creature from the dangers she hourly runs from the most plotting heart in the world" (555). Belford emerges by the novel's finale at the heroine's bedside, her sympathetic companion as she dies. He comes to resemble the man of sentiment Lovelace cannot be— Anna's boring suitor, Mr. Hickman, for whom Clarissa has argued: "Hickman . . . is a *modest* man . . . he has a treasure in his mind which requires nothing but the key of encouragement to unlock it, to make him shine" (481—Richardson's emphasis).

Belford "shines" as the sentimental spectator at the novel's end. Best positioned to organize the correspondence of Clarissa and Lovelace, he also is best positioned to direct sympathy's ideological meaning at the denouement of the plot. Belford is the figure of the emerging epistolary redactor who gains a face and character in the concluding pages. He also is a substitute for the epistolary reader outside the fictional frame, merging the image of the redactor and the reader together, making the effects of writing and reading the same.

Like the darkened spectator in a movie house, Belford is the strangely "absent" image illuminated by the screen, and, then, again, when the house lights go up. Film critics, following Benveniste's theory of the subject, call the audience spectator a "spoken" subject. Through Belford, the readers of *Clarissa* become this seeing and unseen spoken subject; through Belford, as individuals and as a group, we identify with the protovisual images. In his disassociated, voyeuristic gaze upon Clarissa, Belford illustrates what Leo Bersani and Ulysse Dutoit describe as the remarkable "coolness" of images of hunters in Assyrian sculptural reliefs. Writing about sadism in the reliefs, they describe a "prettification of violence, a view of the hunt *only* from the perspective of its being an esthetically pleasing ritual" (35). The image of the hunters is, of course, itself a visual image, one which has "the important function of telling us *how* to look at the lion . . . The undisturbed human mastery of the doomed lion's energy gives us the image of an ideal, impossible control over the self and the world" (Bersani and Dutoit 35). In "the hunter's impassiveness" (35), we find a clue about how to read Assyrian reliefs. Likewise, in Belford's invisibility and impassiveness, we find a clue about how to read *Clarissa*.

We read like impassive hunters in a group. The epistles of *Clarissa* amount to a "prettification of violence," lending each reader "the image of an ideal, impossible control over the self and the world" (35). We read and watch the scene of the hunt. Passivity is heightened by the fact that reading in the bourgeois era is a lonely pursuit and private act, made possible through technologies of reproduction and mass distribution. Held in figural bondage, we gaze upon our voyeuristic singularity mimicked in each single, reproducible page. We reaffirm what film-critic Heath—referring to Hollywood cinema—calls our "massive investment in the subject."[48] But we do so through the perverse gaze of sympathy, "ourself . . . in reality . . . nothing."

Two

A Masochistic Spectator's
Sentimental Education:
The "Illusion of Reality" in Flaubert's
L'Education sentimentale

*[C]inema has structures of fascination strong enough to allow
temporary loss of ego while simultaneously reinforcing the ego
. . . [It has] evolved a particular illusion of reality in which
. . . contradiction between libido and ego has found a beau-
tifully complementary fantasy world.*
—Laura Mulvey, "Visual Pleasure"

*It is a story completely invented; I put there neither my feelings
nor my life. The illusion (if there is one) flies in the face of the
impersonality of the work . . . The artist must be in his work like
God in the creation, invisible and all powerful. We feel him
everywhere, but we do not see him.*
—Gustave Flaubert, *Correspondence*[1]

When Hume wrote "ourself . . . is in reality nothing," he alluded to the
sympathetic spectator's masochistic tendencies. In this chapter, I probe
further the relationship of masochism to the visual perversions, and to the
illusion of reality reproduced in the process. By masochism, I invoke Freud's
definition of pleasure in pain through which the self becomes its own
object. But I also invoke the more recent suggestion that masochism is
pleasure in the disavowal of self—a pleasure linked to the artistic representation of cultural masculinity. I argue that the very effect of masculine
masochism expands the sympathetic spectator's visionary capacities.

Disavowal of the self sustains the reality illusion particular to classic
cinema but also to the novel of realism, upon whose structures cinema
would draw. Utilizing the spectator's masochism in service of the "free indi-

rect style" ("*style indirect libre*") for which this French novelist is so well known,[2] Flaubert's novels appear to "free" narrative agency from any fixed point of view. Victor Brombert writes that this "free indirect" point of view creates "the ultimate disappearance of the personage."[3] Robert Kellog and Robert E. Scholes explain that such a "personage" becomes "a disembodied spirit who roams freely in time and space, revealing secret thoughts and actions of his characters" (259), thereby constructing a seemingly unbiased portrait of reality. I take Flaubert's *L'Education sentimentale* as an exemplary novel of "the ultimate disappearance of the personage" necessary to the illusion of reality—borrowing that phrase from Mulvey.[4] But I suggest that "disappearance" reflects a kind of *re*appearance, just as masochism reflects a kind of sadism.

Through "disappearance" of narrative persona in Flaubert's novel, the persona actually gains spectacular control. Mirroring the perverse gaze of narrative visual control is the masochism of protagonist Frédéric Moreau, and the self-effacing but also narcissistic sentiments he expresses through courtly love. The connection of courtly love to masochism is well delineated by Flaubert's contemporary novelist Leopold von Sacher-Masoch in the overtly masochistic fantasy *Venus in Furs*. In *L'Education sentimentale*—in contrast to *Venus in Furs*—the masochism of the protagonist is reflected indirectly, perversely, and through a sympathetic male gaze.

A certain visual manipulability characterizes this gaze, which becomes the gaze of another, the "absent one" of the narrative spectator. Through the vicissitudes of the gaze, suture in the novel is born. A technique usually ascribed to Hollywood verisimilitude and its effects upon viewer identification, suture is developed in *L'Education sentimentale* as a proto-Hollywood style. As in the classic film text, suture in *L'Education sentimentale* binds an unwitting spectator into the illusions of the fiction. I treat the cinematic model of suture, as it operates in the novel, not only as a conceptually visual technique but as a sentimental and sadomasochistic narrative ploy. While suture binds the audience into the text's reality illusion, it conversely disavows the presence of the spectator.

In the course of my discussion of suture, I reexamine what film historians call the precinematic spectator. Vanessa R. Schwartz has related fin-de-siècle wax-museum tableaux, the display of crime victims by the Paris Morgue, and the popular Paris press of the 1880s and '90s to the precinema spectator, and, in general, to the evolution of "reality" entertainments. I shift the ground of this study to the mid-century Paris of Louis Philippe, the Second Republic and Second Empire—and onto the fairgrounds of the Paris Champ-de-Mars, the setting of many mid- to late-century world fairs and related spectacles, and at least one important scene in *L'Education sentimentale*. Allusions to Champ-de-Mars entertainments, like dioramas, panoramas, shadow theaters, and other optical-illusion technologies, point to the perverse habits of the novel's spectator. Such allusions reveal that a novel acclaimed for its documentary realism and an accurate "atomistic" vision relies upon the same visual perversions that create identification as commodification in visual mass culture.

This culture is criticized in the novel by the supposedly "absent" but hauntingly present authorial narrator. However, the representational strategies of visual mass culture are exploited in the novel, just the same. In *L'Education sentimentale,* visual perversions associated with mass entertainments conjure up scenes of urban mayhem and violence, depicting the bloody class revolution of 1848. But, like the scenic panoramas of Parisian monuments and the visions of women in fleeting coaches, these graphic scenes are as subject to sentimental duplicity as Frédéric's perverse sentiments in love.

Sacher-Masoch's "Feminine" Fantasy: Frédéric in Love

Through Freud's vicissitudinous model of power and desire, the sadomasochistic subject invites reversals and projective transformations. The vicissitudes will characterize Frédéric's subjectivity as he visually desires and controls women through the gaze, yet also identifies with "woman's" passivity through his own passive masochism. The "vicissitudes," we recall from Freud's "Instincts and Their Vicissitudes," are the stage-by-stage transformations of the sadomasochistic subject with regard to an object of desire. In the first or "original" stage, sadistic aggression overtly targets an object; but in the secondary stage, "the object is given up and replaced by the subject's self" ("Instincts" 127), the subject's masochistic positioning. Frédéric's visual relation to women falls somewhere between the first and second Freudian stages. Frédéric's aggression targets his female object through the idealizing gaze. But through his narcissism, aggression ultimately is aimed backward, toward the male "feminized" self.

Freud provides a richer explanation of the vicissitudinous slippage between "original" sadism and secondary masochism in "The Economic Problem of Masochism." There he emphasizes that masochism is a displacement of sadistic aggression, that sadism is the fundamental instinct. To explain what he means by instinct, Freud goes back to his earlier analysis in *Beyond the Pleasure Principle* (1920), describing a complex interaction between the libido and the death instinct in multicellular organisms. The death instinct, which is dominant, "seeks to disintegrate the cellular organism," creating "a state of inorganic stability" ("Economic" 278). The libido's job is to divert this "destructive instinct" and to make it "innocuous," "diverting that instinct . . . outwards . . . towards objects in the external world."

The "destructive instinct" is "the instinct for mastery," which he also calls "the will to power" ("Economic" 278). "Sadism proper" is the effect of this instinct transformed into the sexual function. Masochism is the "residue" that remains, "libidinally bound" in the organism.

The residue itself Freud names "erotogenic masochism." While erotogenic masochism lies at the instinctual base of sadism's transformation into self-aggression, what he calls "feminine masochism" results in the submissive fantasies played out by the male masochist. Fantasies of feminine masochism render what Freud calls "a characteristically female situation." This "situation" he describes as "being castrated, or copulated with, or giving birth to a baby" ("Economic" 277). It manifests itself through kinds of "performances" that are "a carrying-out of the fantasies in play," whose "manifest content" includes "being gagged, bound, painfully beaten, whipped, in some way maltreated, forced into unconditional obedience, dirtied and debased" ("Economic" 276). While these fantasies are "feminine" in content, they are acted upon by men. Freud speculates that such fantasies "induce [male] potency and . . . lead to the sexual act."[5]

In her contemporary study of gendered perversions, Louise Kaplan echoes the Freudian observation that sexual masochism "is much more prevalent among males" than females (25). Clinical statistics place the male-female masochist ratio at 20 to 1. In typical masochistic scenarios, "a woman is a paid and/or willing participant who has been cast in the role of the sadist, in a sadomasochistic scenario invented and controlled by her male sexual partner" (Kaplan 25). The latter "requests that he be bound, beaten on the buttocks, straddled, and urinated or defecated on. The woman obeys his commands" (25). Contrary to the common belief that masochism is the purview of women, masochism is one of the "male perversions" that deludes the male subject into falsifying his means of control. Like the other male perversions in Kaplan's catalogue, "fetishism, transvestism, exhibitionism, voyeurism, sexual sadism" (12), male masochism "puts the spotlight on unusual or bizarre sexual activities, 'kinky sex,' as a way of triumphing over the traumas of childhood" (12). We recall that, for Kaplan, it is the "perverse strategy" in general that "puts the spotlight" on the perverse *symptom* in order to conceal psychoanalytic *origin*. In the specific case of male masochism,

> It is the special strategy of male perversion to permit a person to express his forbidden and shameful feminine wishes by disguising them in an ideal of masculinity. Macho genital prowess and the impersonation of fantasized, idealized males are hiding places for the man's humiliating feminine strivings.[6]

Freud's vicissitudes are elucidated through Kaplan's analysis; the latter describes male masochism as an elaborate defense mechanism through

which the subject heightens and protects his "maleness." Kaplan emphasizes that "the strange idea that sexual masochism is a male perversion
becomes more understandable when we realize that a crucial aspect of the
perverse strategy is to give expression to a man's feminine wishes and longings while still keeping him in a position of masculine power."[7] The novel
Venus in Furs is the quintessential demonstration of these "feminine wishes
of males" (25), "wishes" that serve to keep the male subject in a position of
relational power.[8] I turn to Sacher-Masoch's novel—published in German
in 1870, just a year after Flaubert's *L'Education sentimentale*—to more fully
probe masochism in its gendered paradoxes.[9]

    To analyze masochism in *Venus in Furs* is to analyze Frédéric's senti-
ments in love. *Venus in Furs* is a self-conscious masochistic fantasy, a "pornol-
ogy," as Deleuze would have it, structuralizing as well as performing the
conventions of a male-masochist script. *Venus in Furs* demonstrates that
aggression and the desire to dominate a female object is fundamental to the
masochist's desire for self-debasement and humiliation. This aggression
and desire to dominate is illustrated in the behavior of Severin, the male
protagonist in *Venus in Furs,* in his relation to Wanda, a most compliant
mistress-dominatrix.

    As Severin tells Wanda, "'I am only truly able to love a woman who
dominates me, who overpowers me with her beauty, her temperament, her
intelligence and her willpower, a woman who rules over me'" (172). He
believes that he is aroused by a *woman's* domination over *him.* But Wanda,
acting as the cold, brutal dominatrix—"her left hand on her hip, the whip
in her right hand" (223)—has been trained by Severin to mirror his "feminine" fantasies. Wanda tells Severin:

> "The game is over. . . . Now we are in deadly earnest, you senseless fellow! . . .
> You are no longer my lover, but my slave; your life and death are subject to my
> whims. (223)

Turning "back her ermine cuffs with a gesture both graceful and savage,"
she lashes Severin "across the back" (223). Severin "shuddered as the whip
cut into my flesh like a knife" (223), emphasizing the violence in Wanda's
act. But the "game" is never "over." Wanda's abuse of Severin, as Kaplan
reminds us, is "grudging" (25).

    In fact, early in their affair, Wanda begs Severin to love her with
"reason," and to treat her as an "equal." Wanda suggests that she wants
Severin to "know" her; she pleads: "'Severin, this is all wrong . . . do you not
know me yet, do you absolutely refuse to know me?'" (170). But Severin
demands that Wanda "'Be a tyrant, be a despot'" (170). Following his
demands, he enjoys his own "feminine" submissiveness: "I prostrated myself
before her and threw my arms around her knees" (170). When Wanda asks,

"'what would be the value of possessing me . . . ?'" (170), Severin responds that he might otherwise lose Wanda to "'another man.'" His fear of loss—of "Wanda," of his possession to be "mastered"—is also perversely what Severin desires most—when Wanda, in fact, *finds* "'another man.'"

The perverse exchange between Severin and Wanda typifies the masochistic contract important to *L'Education sentimentale*. Deleuze discusses this contract in its historical dimensions, commenting on masochism in general; in doing so, he distinguishes nineteenth-century masochism from eighteenth-century sadism. While sadism, he writes, is the expression of upper-class social hegemony, in which an aristocratic libertine possesses and torments an unconsenting victim (as described in the novels of the Marquis de Sade), masochism is "a pact of alliance," through which two parties agree to perform dominant-submissive roles—thereby reflecting nineteenth-century legal reform through the contract.

For the sadist, language *describes;* for the masochist, language *persuades,* suggests Deleuze. But *Venus in Furs* suggests that to *persuade* is also to *manipulate,* and that to create a "pact of alliance" is to perversely redistribute power. Masochistic manipulation is exemplified when Wanda "consents" to behave according to Severin's wishes. Promising to dominate him, Wanda at first declares herself "'relieved of all duties and obligations toward you'" (196). But Severin protests, insisting upon "'a few conditions,'" including that Wanda should never "abandon me" (196). Severin's masochism allows him to assert a surreptitious control over Wanda, a subtle version of Freud's concept of the "destructive instinct," which seeks an object "in the external world" ("The Economic Problem of Masochism" 278). At this moment, Severin reveals the manipulative turns in the so-called "contract," and its relation to a sadomasochistic dynamic that guarantees "by fiat," as Chancer notes, "that the other upon whom one depends will not disappear" (73).

In masochism, the male subject performs both roles: "manipulating or consenting to be controlled," in Chancer's words (73). Wanda is a mirror of the male subject's control—controlling by being controlled herself. Again she tells Severin: "'Do with me what you will . . . I belong to you'" (188). She shouts, "'Slave!'" He echoes, "'Mistress!'" (185). Wanda asks, "'Do I please you?'" He commands, "'Whip me if it gives you pleasure . . . Whip me . . . whip me without mercy!'" (185).

Severin's desires for being whipped derive from youthful encounters with "a distance aunt . . . a beautiful, stately woman with a charming smile" dressed in a "fur-lined jacket," who beat him upon occasion (174). They also derive from his childhood reading, such as *The Lives of the Martyrs,* whose "supersensual beings"—Christian saints—"found positive pleasure in pain and who sought horrible tortures . . . as others seek enjoyment" (172). Moved to "intense pleasure" and the "worst torments," Severin imitates their religious devotion, standing before a pagan statue of Venus and reciting "the prayers I had been taught, the Lord's Prayer, the Hail Mary and the Creed" (173). The cold statue of Venus may be a bizarre and humorous amalgamation of Greco-Roman and Christian deity worship. But out of this image arises a statue-like apparition, Wanda; and also "Venus in Furs," a luminous, visually charged painting on Severin's wall.

The "Venus in Furs" portrait offers a stereotype of Mediterranean and Northern-European cultural paradoxes; it is an emblem of sensuality and frigidity, seduction and unavailability—like the figure who makes her appearance in the dream opening the novel: a "sublime creature [who] had wrapped her marble body in a great fur" (143). Like this figure, "Magnificent in spite of the stony, lifeless eyes," the painting of Venus wrapped in furs represents the sensuous but cold woman of courtly love. As Denis DeRougemont has famously claimed, the myth of courtly love operates "whenever passion is dreamed of as an ideal instead of being feared like a malignant fever; whenever its fatal character is welcoming, invoked or imagined as a magnificent and desirable disaster instead of as simply a disaster" (24). Adultery, of course, is the classic obstacle in courtly love "disasters," like the romance of Tristen and Iseult (DeRougement's favorite). But the obstacle takes other forms and appears in other literary genres, the Petrarchan sonnet, for instance, in which the improbable image of opposition itself forms an obstacle to poetic closure and satiety. The obstacle in the Petrarchan sonnet creates anxiety, which, in turn, creates language—for a *male* poet speaker, exemplified in Sir Thomas Wyatt's Petrarchan lines: "I find no peace and all my war is done./I fear and hope, I burn and freeze like ice." Unmitigated oppositions between "peace" and "war," "burn" and "freeze" are recalled in the female frigidity and warmth of Venus in *Venus in Furs*. Like the Wyatt-Petrarchan speaker, who finds simultaneous oppositions tormentuous, *Venus in Furs*'s Severin declares this "feminine" capriciousness agonizing, saying: "I sometimes find it disturbing to be so totally at the mercy of a woman . . . What senseless apprehension! She is playing a capricious game," stirring within him "agonizing doubt!" (198).

In *L'Education sentimentale*, Madame Arnoux is a Venus figure whose embodiment of oppositions inflames the "capricious game," the masochist's "agonizing doubt." Like Venus and other feminized descendants of courtly love, Madame Arnoux's image torments but also delights Frédéric: "What was he to do? Tell her that he loved her? She would show him out, without a doubt, or, even, indignant, chase him from her house! So he preferred all the pain rather than taking the horrible chance of never seeing her again."[10] Her unavailability only increases Frédéric's courtly-love, masochistic sentiments: "She sometimes smiled, gazing her eyes upon him for a moment" (84). This "moment"—*her* look at *him*—heightens Frédéric's perception that she controls him: "It was a desire to sacrifice himself, a need of immediate devotion, and all the stronger since he could not satisfy it" (84). He preserves the image of her unavailability through the obstacle of the adultery taboo. When Madame Arnoux refuses his weak, passive sexual advances, Frédéric is gratified, seeming to enjoy the image of himself at Madame Arnoux's feet: "He wanted to throw himself on his knees . . . He was prevented from doing so by a sort of religious belief" (199).

In *Venus in Furs,* "woman" actually *is* a vision: a painting, a work of art, which comes to life through Severin's contractual manipulation of Wanda. "Venus" is made up by Severin, a fetishistic fantasy invented out of her nonexistence, emphasized when she appears to the narrator of *Venus in Furs* in a dream. Severin, we recall, is but a friend of the narrator, a figure of transference for the narrator, another masochist. The true narrator remains nameless; we encounter him only at the novel's beginning when he dreams of the heartless female apparition. The Venus creature knows that he is dreaming, that her image is an illusion: "'You are dreaming . . . Wake up!'" she cries; and she grasps his arm "with her marble hand." "'Wake up,'" she says again, "this time in a low gruff voice" (147). The voice turns out to be that of the narrator's "Cossack," his servant, who "stood towering above me" as the narrator sleeps with his "clothes on and a book in [his] hand." Glancing at the book, the Cossack says, "'Aha, Hegel.'" When the narrator later meets Severin for tea, the latter tells him, "'A very curious dream.'" The narrator glimpses Severin's painting, a "large oil painting done in the powerful colors of the Flemish School. . . . A beautiful woman, naked beneath her dark furs." The narrator cries: "'Venus in Furs! . . . That is how I saw her in my dream'" (148). And Severin responds: "'I, too . . . but I was dreaming with my eyes open'" (149).

The tale of *Venus in Furs,* continuing as *Severin's* diary of "supersensualist" pleasures, is a "dream" with its "eyes open." Severin literally spies a woman "clothed in a vaporous white morning-gown . . . a graceful and poetic figure! . . . Her skin is so delicate that her blue veins show through even under the fine muslin that covers her arms and breasts" (158) — evoking later fashionable portraits of society ladies by John Singer Sargent, or the flowing sculpted limbs of Second-Empire decorative marbles by Jean-Baptiste Carpeaux, and returning us to the initial image of the Flemish-School painting. The painting is an image fused with the image of the book through the condensation processes of the dream, turning our attention away from literal vision and toward G.W.F. Hegel's theory of the "master" and "slave" of dialectical consciousness. This theory historically challenged nineteenth-century positivist notions of the sovereign individual while also reinforcing them. Hegel's dialectical model details not only the contract of the slave-like masochist with his "master," but the route of perverse power through vision.

Hegel poses within consciousness a "master," the independent aspect of human consciousness; and a "slave," the dependent aspect of consciousness, reliant upon the master but negating the master, as well. As Hegel explains, "The master is the consciousness that exists *for itself;* but no longer merely the general notion of existence for the self. Rather, it is consciousness which, while existing on its own account . . . is mediated with itself through another consciousness" (404). The subservient figure of the negating "other" *mediates* the dominance of the master. When the "slave" takes up "a negative attitude to things" (405), the slave creates the conditions of the master's self-realization. The negating effect of the "other" is an obstacle to self-realization. And this obstacle, thereby, insures the possibility of the master's pleasure. Explaining this circuitous process, Hegel writes, "To the master . . . by means of this mediating process, belongs the immediate relation, in the sense of the pure negation of it; in other words, he gets the enjoyment. What mere desire did not attain, he now succeeds in attaining" (415).

The social class implications of Hegel's model are suggested in *Venus in Furs* when the Cossack servant "towers over" the narrator, his master. The *gendered* class implications are elaborated upon in the earlier dream scene, through the Venus-like apparition. She critiques master-slave relations in an analysis of gendered social power. "Woman," she declares, is an image, and has no other power than that which she is granted. When the narrator protests "woman's" cruel "principles," the Venus-like apparition answers that such principles are "founded on the experience of a thousand years. . . . The more cruel and faithless [woman] is, the more she ill-treats [man] . . . quickens his desire and secures his love and admiration. It has always been so, from the time of Helen and Delilah all the way to Catherine the Great and Lola Montez" (146). The catalogue of masculine texts about female domination is, however, the ventriloquism of a dreaming narrator— a voice twice displaced when becoming that of the Cossack. Later in *Venus in Furs*, the narrator's own voice dissolves or is displaced by the "Confessions" of Severin, which become the novel, *Venus in Furs*. Relinquishing narrative control, the sleeping-dreaming narrator is an absent figure, lost to an outer narrative frame.

In *L'Education sentimentale,* Frédéric is like Severin and the absent narrator, too: Frédéric spends his waking hours in masochistic fantasies while dreaming with his eyes shut. The narrative structure of *L'Education sentimentale* is focused, or focalized, through Frédéric's point of view. Yet, in many critical scenes, Frédéric's point of view is relinquished, given up. This is illustrated during a dialogue about Venus, a symbol of aristocratic art among Frédéric's artist-intellectual peers. Frédéric's friends engage in a passionate aesthetic-political debate, and the image of Venus reigns at its center. Venus is a sign of the tyranny of upper-class art, according to Sénécal, and the failure of artists to paint "realistically" in late-Regency landscapes, or to depict the reality of the people in post-Revolutionary France. Targeting Pellerin as a painter of archaic Venuses, Sénécal demands:

> "Do we need . . . these Venuses . . . with all their landscapes? I don't see in them instruction for the people! Show us their miseries, rather! Enthuse us with their sacrifices!" (52)

Similarly, the radical Hussonnet views Venus as a signifier of upper-class artistic and political corruption. But Hussonnet is also a male chauvinist, for whom Venus is too chaste: "'Classical things? You servant! For at last, let's see, no kidding! A loose woman [*une lorette*][11] is more amusing than the Venus de Milo! Let's be Gauls, for Christ's sake!'"[12]

Frédéric's voice and point of view is curiously missing from these pronouncements about Venus. Yet Frédéric's own view is organized around Hussonet's misogynist distinctions. Going to the Alhambra, "a public dance hall recently opened at the top of the Champs-Elysées" (70), Frédéric views women in a kind of Moorish theme park: "*Des lorettes,* easy working-class types, and just plain street walkers came there, hoping to find a protector, a lover" (71). His view of society women is not very different. They are fussy Venuses that resemble their dance-hall sisters. Arriving at a party at the Dambreuse house, and standing "at the threshold of the boudoir where Mme. Dambreuse was [located]" (160), Frédéric watches the room filled by women: "one next to the other, on backless seats . . . their breasts on display in blouses revealing a beckoning cleavage. Nearly all of them carried a bouquet of violets in their hand" (160). We learn that "all kinds of beauties one found there: English women with their keepsake profiles; an Italian whose black eyes flashed like a Vesuvius; three Norman sisters dressed in blue, fresh like apple trees in April" (160). However, like the artificial Venuses of Pellerin's paintings, these women are regarded "through his monocle," stilted and objectified. Together they represent a sameness—in Frédéric's monocle-like point of view—a "harem" or a house of prostitution. Their different types of "beauties" are unified through his lens.

Although Frédéric's voyeuristic approach is the same, Madame Arnoux *seems* different. The wife of his art-dealer friend, "She looked like the women in romantic novels" (9). Madame Arnoux is, like Venus in furs, an abstract but also physically visual image: when Frédéric stops "in the Louvre in front of old masterpieces [*de vieux tableaux*]," he "put her in place of the people in paintings [*des peintures*]" (69). "Her" image is a metaphor for the substitutional visual image; and "her" image causes a chain-like series of substitutions and displacements. In Frédéric's fantasy of Madame Arnoux, "Prostitutes that he saw by gaslight, opera singers heaving their trills, equestriennes on their galloping horses, bourgeois women on foot, working-class tarts at their window, all women reminded him of her, in similarity or in violent contrast" (68). His repetition of the possessive pronoun throughout the text, "her," magnifies but also contains Madame Arnoux's substitutional image through Frédéric's vision. The pronoun is a substitute for Madame Arnoux's name, which is itself another substitute, the name of the wife of Monsieur Arnoux. The pronoun builds up the courtly-love ideal; it also reduces the ideal to a hollow narrative signifier.

Madame Arnoux is aggrandized and diminished in fetishistic images: "In the flower girls' baskets in the cobbler's stall, the flowers opened their blossoms for her to choose them in passing . . . the little satin slippers trimmed with swan's down seemed awaiting her foot" (68). Comparing Madame Arnoux to the prostitutes with whom his friend Deslauriers consorts on the Paris quais, Frédéric again substitutes Madame Arnoux with their image, silently making a comparison: "'As if I didn't have one [a love], and a hundred times more rare, more noble, stronger!'" (76). This statement implies that his attraction toward Madame Arnoux reflects Frédéric's narcissism. Madame Arnoux is luminous, larger than life—as a substitute for his own missing image.

If Madame Arnoux is the luminous but unavailable woman of courtly love, Rosanette is the down-to-earth, physically available, bawdy seductress. Frédéric's affair with Rosanette is sexual compensation and substitute for the "finer" romance with Madame Arnoux. But an uncanny resemblance haunts these two women. We perceive this resemblance in their relation to nature, to landscape, and to space.

Upon first spying Madame Arnoux on the steamship making its way from Paris to Nogent-sur-Seine, Frédéric associates her image with the openness of space, the representation of spatial freedom. He thinks that "He wouldn't have wanted to add or to subtract anything from her person. The universe was suddenly enlarged by her. She was the luminous point where everything converged" (9). A figure for nature's plenitude and its visual abundance when viewed from afar, Frédéric associates Madame Arnoux with the winding Seine and rolling countryside.

The relation of the other woman to landscape and to space is suggested in the trip to the countryside Frédéric makes with Rosanette. Leaving behind the revolution brewing in Paris, the lovers stroll the grounds of the Fontainebleau château, bequeathed by Henry II to his own mistress, Diane de Poitiers—a thought which creates in Frédéric "a retrospective and inexpressible sensuality. So to distract his desire, he transferred tender feelings to Rosanette" (322). As Rosanette becomes the substitute of the king's famed courtesan, Frédéric feels nostalgia for what he imagines to be the good old days, when hermits, "with paternal grins . . . kneeling in front of their grotto," received "the good kings of France" (324). Frédéric's benign view of authoritarian monarchs is linked to nature when he transfers onto forest trees "of an unmeasurable altitude" the image of "patriarchs or emperors" (325). Here the relation of landscape's fertile fauna to patriarchal proprietary control is indirectly recalled. The giant trees, like "emperors," allude not only to Henry II; they allude to the more recent "emperor," Napoleon, who made Fontainebleau his home.

The first Napoleon would be followed by Napoleon III, first named president after the bloody suppression of the workers' riots in June 1848, later declared emperor in 1852. In the novel, Frédéric will witness the suppression of the workers by this "future" emperor upon his return to Paris; in doing so, he will witness the beginnings of the Second Empire's authoritarian regime. In the scene of the Franchard Forest, however, Frédéric does not acknowledge dynasties of history and absolute power. He substitutes the subject of history, of power, for personal memory, through a narcissistic image of autonomous personal sovereignty. As he and Rosanette roam the countryside, "They believed themselves far away from everyone else, completely alone" (325). In the setting of the "natural," but artificially groomed landscape, Frédéric's affair with Rosanette takes on the character of his worship of Madame Arnoux. Rosanette is the *natural* substitute for Frédéric's forbidden and *un*natural liaison.

Rosanette may be a flesh-and-blood reversal of the cold and stone-like Venus figure of Madame Arnoux. But Rosanette also shares in Madame Arnoux's fetishistic ironies. Both fertile and fallow, physically sexualized but symbolically out of reach, Rosanette is the substitute of a wife who is herself the product of substitutions. And, like Madame Arnoux, Rosanette belongs to a substitute man, Monsieur Arnoux. Rosanette is *his* courtesan.

The significance of this set of substitutional liaisons is somatically expressed in Frédéric's dream. In this moment of overt sexual masochistic fantasy, it seems to Frédéric "that he was harnessed beside [Monsieur] Arnoux, to the shaft of a hackney-carriage, and that the Marshall [Rosanette], straddling him, was ripping him open with her golden spurs" (128). Rosanette, in her Marshall role, is a flagrant dominatrix in spurs, "topping" Frédéric. But he is "harnessed" to Monsieur Arnoux, a man with whom Frédéric shares a different liaison, through the harness, the instrument of male bondage. In the dream, Madame Arnoux is curiously missing. Her erasure repeats the fetishistic structure Madame Arnoux represents throughout the novel in reversed form. No longer does "she" signify a visual figure of spatial abundance, as when Frédéric first sees her on the steamship. "She" signifies her own status as substitute—that which replaces something missing. In the dream, Jacques Arnoux takes his rightful place, harnessed to Frédéric, "being" the "wife." He displaces his wife, who, in waking life, always is a displaced or transferential image.

There is truth in the dream, loaded with homoerotic connotation and the "feminine" wishes of males. Reading the dream for its repressed content, we reassociate the Venus-like Madame Arnoux, who dominates mistress-like over Frédéric's waking imagination, and Rosanette, the "Marshall," who dominates in the dream. In a later image, we again see Rosanette not as a natural woman who reverses the unnatural, cold image of Madame Arnoux; we see her *like* Madame Arnoux, a made-up image. Like the artificial statue of Venus, Rosanette, too, literally is made a work of art. Dressing and undressing her for a portrait sitting with Pellerin, Frédéric cannot make up his mind about which version of "Rosanette" to represent:

> "Perhaps if I put her in a pink silk dress, if I had her wear an oriental burnous—hell, no! No burnous! or perhaps if I dressed her in blue velvet upon a grey background—too colorful? . . .
> She would have a flame-red velour gown . . . its wide sleeves lined in ermine . . . setting off her bare arms. (150–51)

In this scene, Rosanette literally becomes a Venus in furs, the "ermine" setting off the fetishistic display of skin and fur. The skin and fur reminds us of another site/sight of female skin and fur: that of the female sexual organs. Traditional psychoanalysis perceives this site to be fetishism's origin in male vision. Discussing male masochism, Kaplan presumes this traditional psychoanalytic route, noting that the "feminine wishes of males" are wishes simply because they are "forbidden." But what *is* forbidden? Being "feminine" ("Abused . . . humiliated")? Being "feminine" as a man?

The scene of Rosanette in her ermine-decked gown opens up an ambiguous curtain veiling the "forbidden" scene. Behind one scene is the scene of another. In this secondary scene, the (male) child views his phallic mother. The child so sympathizes with the mother's lack that he imbues her with his own anatomical features. Giving the mother a phallus, he veils his own. But it is in the veiling of the phallus, as Lacan emphasizes, that the phallus emanates its symbolic, transferential power.

The phallic mother evokes the memory of the missing phallus. Never seen again, she is the talisman of "feminine" male domination and agency. The phallic mother is yet another representation of male masochism, upholding male power while disavowing it. The masochist projects the master role onto her; she absorbs it, deflecting her "lack" back onto him. A condensed image of a substitutional exchange system, the phallic mother recycles the Hegelian dialectic meant to preserve male mastery in a complex circuitry of sublimation and projection.

The clinical effects of what I will call the masochistic *dialectic* (as opposed to the contract) are well summarized in a modest book on male masochism based on clinical data. In *Masochism and the Self,* Roy F. Baumeister notes that masochism contradicts fundamental features of the self. He defines the self as a human ideal that "develops a strong orientation toward control" in the "environment." For matters of efficacy, "the self seeks to believe itself in control even when it is not," says Baumeister (6). The "self" seeks "freedom, choice and multiple options," which masochism, again, contradicts. Baumeister summarizes these contradictions: "the self is developed to avoid pain, but masochists seek pain. The self strives for control, but masochists seek to relinquish control. The self aims to maximize its esteem, but masochists deliberately seek out humiliation" (6–7). As the masochist engages in self-defeatism, according to Baumeister, he no longer functions as "an active agent" or "decision maker." What's in it for the masochist? Baumeister concludes that the very "denial of control" that masochism embraces serves to enhance "the complex, long-range" growth of the "symbolic self" (87). Here the Hegelian master-slave consciousness pendulum is reconfigured as social practice, by which the master role is replenished and fed. Indeed, in clinical studies noted by Baumeister, everything about masochism is a misleading illusion:

> A first illusion in masochism concerns the pattern of control. On the surface, the dominant partner is in control. The masochist appears helpless, often being tied up and blindfolded. All initiative, all decisions, are left up to the dominant partner, while the masochist merely obeys and submits. Yet often it is the masochist's wishes and desires that determine the course of the interaction. The script that is enacted is often written by the masochist. Indeed prostitutes complain about the inordinate particularity of some masochistic clients. For example, some men desire to be verbally humiliated with a precise series of insults. If the prostitute deviates at all from her lines, even just forgetting a word or two, the men get upset and insist that she start over. (12)

In *L'Education sentimentale,* Frédéric is always writing the same script. He thinks, however, that he "starts over." In yet another affair of sentiment—with society matron Madame Dambreuse—ties between masochism, mastery, and class economic power become both more veiled and more blatant. Frédéric sleeps with Rosanette by night and courts Madame Dambreuse by day. Agreeing to attend the sick Monsieur Dambreuse on his deathbed, Frédéric think that "A mistress like Madame Dambreuse would set him up well" (364). Later, agreeing to keep vigil over Monsieur Dambreuse's corpse, Frédéric is "ashamed of this pious sentiment," but then admits, "'Maybe it would look better'" (378). His sentiments are not to be distinguished from their social appearance. In this affair, the upper-class etymological roots of *les sentiments* are exposed. *Les sentiments* traditionally are social "feelings," behaviors of artifice attributed to French aristocracy.

Les sentiments are the "feelings" of courtly love. The proper proprietary "sentiments" provide a class-coded imitative script. Frédéric follows the script well. Courting Madame Dambreuse, "He read her pages of poetry, soulfully in order to move her and to make her admire him" (365). We are told that the conversations between Frédéric and Madame Dambreuse "always returned to the eternal question of Love!" (365). Here we are directed to question the nature of Frédéric's sentiments, not only toward Madame Dambreuse but toward Madame Arnoux, as well.

In Frédéric's view, it is only in relation to Madame Dambreuse that it would be "idiotic" to "take everything seriously"; again harkening back to some grander time, Frédéric tells Madame Dambreuse, "'Our grandfathers lived better. Why not obey the impulse we feel?' Love, afterall, was not in itself a thing so important" (367). At the height of Frédéric's feeling for Madame Dambreuse, he imitates the masochistic sentiments inspired by Madame Arnoux. Feigning one of the Dambreuse servants, "In order to amuse her, he offered himself as a domestic, pretending to pass plates around, to dust the furniture, to announce visitors, to be, in fact, a butler or, perhaps, a slave, although the fashion for that had passed" (366). What *does* remain in fashion for Frédéric, however, is his "authentic" devotion for Madame Arnoux. Such devotion relies upon the impossibility that Frédéric's sentiments will ever be requited. At the novel's conclusion, when Frédéric re-encounters Madame Arnoux—and the aging widow with white hair asks him to have sex—he is overcome with "a repulsion . . . a terror of incest." He refuses her, in "a desire not to tarnish his ideal" (423).

Madame Arnoux thinks Frédéric is very noble in his sentiments. She thinks he is "'so delicate,'" so considerate and sympathetic; she says, "'There is no one like you'" (423). By the novel's conclusion, we have come to question the nature of Frédéric's sentiments in love. The conclusion invites us to recall previous moments in the plot, in which we questioned Frédéric's *moral* sentiments, as well.

His moral sentiment of sympathy, in particular, is the theme of the scene in which Madame Arnoux confronts her husband about his sexual philandering. Frédéric, who appears at the Arnoux house unannounced, is caught in the crossfire; and he plays the double agent. Madame Arnoux has learned about her husband's affair with the other woman (Rosanette) because of a "cashmere" delivered to the wrong "Madame Arnoux." Frédéric secretly confirms the wife's suspicions, whispering, "You don't doubt that I share . . . ?"—implying he "shares" her feelings, or that he feels sympathy (183). But the duplicity in his sympathy for Madame Arnoux is suggested when we learn that he defends Monsieur Arnoux "in the vaguest manner that he could find." While he pities Madame Arnoux, a victim of her husband's adultery, Frédéric also "rejoiced, delighting deep in his soul. Out of vengeance or need of affection, she could turn toward him" (165). And, in fact, we know that Madame Arnoux's grief is at least partially inspired by Frédéric's double dealing. Originally persuaded by a revengeful Mademoiselle Vatzez to inform Monsieur Arnoux about *Rosanette's* infidelity, Frédéric admits to himself that "nothing effectively stopped him from going up . . . [Mademoiselle Vatzez's] bullying destroyed any sympathy left in him" (165). Monsieur Arnoux steps out for "a breath of air," following the spat with his wife; and here we see that Frédéric's sympathy toward Madame Arnoux is reminiscent of Lovelace's sympathy toward Clarissa through the keyhole:

> Never had she seemed so captivating, so profoundly beautiful . . . a sigh made her breasts heave; her two staring eyes seemed dilated by an internal vision; and her lips were half opened, as if giving up her soul. Sometimes, she pushed into her handkerchief; he would have wanted to be this small piece of tear-soaked cloth . . . he could scarcely resist taking her in his arms . . . he came nearer to her, and, leaning over her, he greedily looked over her figure. (168)

The duplicities of sympathy continue to unfurl around Frédéric upon Monsieur Arnoux's return to the house. Frédéric describes Rosanette's gratitude for the cashmere to Monsieur Arnoux, hoping, of course, that the affair with Rosanette will continue—ensuring Frédéric's sympathetic position toward Madame Arnoux. Monsieur Arnoux is delighted to hear his gift has met with warm reception; he wants to visit Rosanette right away. Frédéric, however, has been caught in the duality of his sympathy. He dissuades Monsieur Arnoux—knowing Rosanette is in bed with Delmar; he convinces Arnoux to stay home and console his wife. Monsieur Arnoux declares: "What a good man you are." Frédéric's sympathy manipulates Rosanette's bedfellows, and the fictional process itself.

The clue to Frédéric's sympathetic duality is buried in an offhanded remark he makes regarding Rosanette. She has just seen Madame Arnoux and has not been civil. "Wasn't it enough to have outraged Madame Arnoux? As for her, it served her right! Now he hated all women!" (230). Frédéric's sympathy toward one woman is based in his fundamental hatred of "all women." But his hatred of "women" is less about "woman" than Frédéric thinks. At the site of Rosanette's ermine and bare flesh, we come to perceive Frédéric's own *missing* sentiments. What Frédéric "loathes" is his *own* lack: not so much of moral feeling, but of self-representation. Fearing his own reality to be another illusion, he attempts to compensate for it through vision. The ironies of sympathy and the ironies of visual representation are the same. Guiding Frédéric's education in masochistic sentiment are the ironies of representation, of "realism."

Through the Monocle: Sympathy, Suture, and the Realism Effect

Flaubert is considered a great realist through the documentary effects of the "free indirect style." But Flaubert's own correspondence attributes realism to "a certain illusion." Poststructural critics have taken such statements by Flaubert to be proof of his modernity; they suggest he questions the validity of literature's mimetic function and the subject's stability. Many of these critics champion Flaubert as the first great *non*-realist, because of such statements, and because his fiction experiments with language and representation. Roland Barthes perhaps most famously articulates the postmodern view of Flaubert's writing, arguing that Flaubert writes "with an irony impregnated with uncertainty," and achieves "a salutary discomfort of writing: he does not stop the play of codes . . . one never knows if he is responsible for what he writes (if there is a subject *behind* language)."[13] I agree, however, with objections raised to this argument by Brombert; he remarks that, taken as a whole, Flaubert's correspondence reveals "unsteady and constantly shifting attitudes towards the possibilities of art and experience." On the one hand, Flaubert questions the validity of literature's mimetic function; on the other, he suggests a deep concern with representation and the "subject-as-matrix" (Brombert 107).

My own suggestion is that the postmodern "play of codes" is to mimeticism what masochism is to visual power in Flaubert's work. While this work generates linguistic ambiguity and difference, it also creates fetishistic processes of substitution associated with male masochism. Denying his own visual presence, Frédéric gazes upon the women at the Alhambra and the Dambreuse party through the lens of his monocle—and, likewise, he gazes upon nature's landscapes, monuments, bridges, and Parisian avenues. The monocle of Frédéric's gaze is a metaphor for the novel's displaced vision—of a spectator not really present to the fictive arena. A figure for Frédéric's look in the fiction, the monocle is another lens through which visual control is exerted and extended ouside the fictive frame, through the "free indirect" persona. And, therefore, the monocle reproduces Flaubertian irony.

As Naomi Schor points out, "irony allows the ironist both to reject and to reappropriate the discourse of reference" (98). In *L'Education sentimentale,* I would add that what Schor calls the "fetishization of irony" finds its locus in the "free indirect" monocle point of view. The "free," mobile, shifting point of view fetishizes autonomy and detachment: the principles of the realist illusion. Mechanically, it operates through imagistic "shot" displacements—to use the vocabulary of cinema production, shot/reverse-shots, like those later absorbed by the Hollywood machine.

Suture is reproduced through this exchange of shots in *L'Education sentimentale,* an exchange of visual images so concrete as to resemble shots reproduced on celluloid film. Suture is the effect of the shot-by-shot mechanism. An exchange of glances moves the shots from an enunciatory to a fictive level in the text, thereby sustaining the masochistically disavowed, so-called "free" point of view. Meanwhile, the values and assumptions of the enunciatory subject are transferred onto a masochistically "bound" audience.

Suture effectively creates the image of a unified mass spectator, a growing consumer audience for nineteenth-century realist spectacles that *L'Education sentimentale* critiques but also revels in.

In the novel, an absent figure of a narrative spectator literally borrows—piggy-backs onto—Frédéric's point of view. The "exchange" that occurs through the substitution of the gaze occurs at the onset of scene-setting, on page one. We are introduced to the vision of Frédéric viewing the Paris quai from his departing steamship. The illusion of realism and a documentary objectivity is established by the announcement of a time and date:

> On September 15, 1840, around 6 o'clock in the morning, the Ville-de-Montereau, ready to sail, belched big clouds of smoke by the Saint-Bernard quai.

Realism is established in the visual image of the belching clouds of the steamship, which contrasts with the "whitish pall" that "covers everything" (1). This "real" visual concrete image is conjoined with other "real" oral-concrete images, a "hiss of steam" and a "ship's bell" that "clangs away." (3). Following these concrete descriptions, the general view of an unseen, all-knowing figure reveals to us the image of Frédéric: "A young man eighteen years old, with long hair . . . stood beside the helm, motionless (3). The unobtrusive stance of Frédéric is emphasized in the word "motionless [*immobile*]." That he is the perfect "free" viewer is suggested by his own ability to describe but not to name objects: "Through the haze, he observed church towers, buildings whose names he didn't know" (1).

This sentence establishes a relationship between the fictive subject, Frédéric, and the absent narrative spectator-speaker who knows Frédéric "didn't know." This narrator projects Frédéric's internal consciousness onto a point of view adopted as narrative viewpoint in general. More images of Frédéric seeing, perceiving, being a spectator of "reality" (and being a subject defining reality as well as subject to it) continue as "Paris disappeared" (3). The motion of the boat is perceptually owned by Frédéric; the reference suggests that the city, like the landscape, is Frédéric's to manipulate. It is Frédéric's vision that dominates when "he embraced, in a final glance," Parisian vistas and monuments: "*l'île Saint-Louis, la Cité, Notre-Dame*" (1). But their disappearance indicates another disappearance, which characterizes the novel as a whole. Disappearance is embodied, or, rather, disembodied, by the narrative "eye-witness."

Writing, specifically, of *Madame Bovary*, Scholes and Kellog suggest that Flaubert, this "most careful of novelists," starts that novel "with an eye-witness account of Charles Bovary's arrival at school," a figure who "soon fades" in the course of the narrative as he takes on the omniscient perspective, without figuration. The eye-witness, they remark, is that "disembodied spirit" whose seeming neutrality and invisibility lends a quality of verisimilitude. However, they also note that Flaubert "did not hesitate to concoct an eyewitness for the moment and then cause him to dematerialize a few pages later" (259–60). The eye-witness becomes, in these critics' view, "dematerialized," a disappearing view, free-ranging and shifting—likened by Flaubert himself to "God's" view.[14]

Their analysis is similar to that of Alan Spiegel's, in *Fiction and the Camera Eye,* a study of cinematic vision in the novel. Spiegel argues that the Flaubertian eye-witness inaugurated a "new method" in the history of narrative fiction, a "method" that was revolutionary, and contributed to later developments of narrative omniscience in fiction. Spiegel contrasts the "new method," based on visuality and verisimilitude, to an "old method," which is visually nondescript. The latter method is exemplified by authors like Miguel de Cervantes and Henry Fielding, and relies upon an audience holding upper-class values and epistemological precepts derived from a belief in God and social hierarchy—an entire "structural reality . . . synonymous with truth" (Spiegel 15). By contrast, the "new method" is nondiscursive, without overview or narrative commentary, presenting a world experienced through visual perception. Flaubert's "new method," writes Spiegel, is "atomistic," recreating "reality" through multiple points of view. Yet its very "atomistic" quality creates representational continuity. The material world is seen as a continuous field in time and space, through which bodies and objects are seen and in which they are anchored.

Spiegel's description of Flaubert's style is helpful, but I disagree with the claim that the "new method" is "new." I would argue that the "new method" reflects Richardson's eighteenth-century epistolary achievements, through the use of the sympathetic spectator who sees but remains unseen. The so-called "new method" furthers the development of what the epistolary set out to do: to create verisimilitude through visual strategies of sympathetic identification. Yet while the spectator of Richardson's epistles creates identification through the moral sentiments, the spectator in *L'Education sentimentale* creates identification through sympathetic "resemblance"— literally rendered visually. In "resemblance," we recall from Hume, the spectator is seeking his own likeness. The perception of one's resemblance to someone else creates moral sympathy; and sympathy further increases the universalizing ideal of resemblance. We have seen in Richardson's *Clarissa* an attempt to create unity and universality. In Flaubert's *L'Education sentimentale,* unity and universality are even better served—for the very reason that we are supposed to ignore any universalizing point of view.

The implications of sympathy in the novel of realism are overlooked, perhaps because we imagine sympathy to be a moral rather than representational phenomenon. Thus, literary history disassociates Richardson's epistolary sentiment from nineteenth-century "realism" altogether. It is true that the epistolary did not survive as a dominant fictive form into the nineteenth century in England or France. In the textual wars between Richardson and Henry Fielding, the latter's obtrusive narrator is believed to have won out, a narrator evolving into the omniscient narrator—a convention that reigned supreme until twentieth-century experimentation. The epistolary may have died as a major British fictive medium with Fanny Burney's *Evelina* (1778)[15]—submerged, perhaps, into the fictive letters that punctuate Jane Austen's *Pride and Prejudice* (1813), and even Emily Brontë's *Wuthering Heights*.[16] In France, Choderlos de Laclos chose the epistolary as his medium in *Les liaisons dangereuses* (1782), but as a nostalgic method to recreate *les sentiments*—if overtly sadistic ones—of French aristocrats. Nevertheless, the epistolary did grow in importance during the last decades of the eighteenth century for genres of nonfiction. These included "documentary" accounts of serialized travel journals, which ran in English periodicals, for instance, with titles like *A Ramble through Holland, France, and Italy* (1793), and which presented the roving figure of the narrative eyewitness.[17] They included, as well, other forms of early journalism and political histories, because epistles were associated with reality, Richardson's legacy.[18]

Through the roving spectator, eighteenth-century epistles and nineteenth-century "realism" have much more in common than not. The epistolary spectator may not obtrude; in Elizabeth Brophy's words, "the epistolary form intrinsically demanded that the authorial 'I' be eliminated from the novel" (44). Yet the spectator also directs the gaze of representation. Just as epistles were submerged into the narrative framework of many nineteenth-century novels, so, too, was the spectator submerged and incorporated into the structure of nineteenth-century narrative omniscience. Flaubert's novels are an important link between the epistolary spectator and the omniscient narrator. Like epistolary sentiment, omniscient "realism" leads neither to neutrality or realism but rather to the *illusion* of neutrality and a *sentimental* realism through visual identification.

Flaubert wrote in one of his own letters: "We must rise above personal emotions and nervous susceptibilities. It is time to endow it [the novel] with the pitiless method, with the exactness of the physical sciences" (*Correspondence* 164). The "pitiless method" may suggest appreciation for unadorned, "true" reality. But it also suggests a Lovelaceian pride in being "pitifull," watching "sympathetically" at a woman's—at reality's—keyhole. To take such statements of Flaubert's as straightforward declarations of the simplicity, if harshness, of representational art is to adopt the "resemblance" aspect of sympathy wholesale. That is, it is to confuse concrete, physical "exactness" with a non-ideological reproduction of the "real." To interpret Flaubert thus enhances the universalizing program of the spectator. This program is transferred onto the supposedly autonomous desires of the audience spectator, actually created by the text to construct its own image of being a "mass" spectator, a universal spectator. The identification strategies of sympathy that coax into being the image of a universal or mass spectator are rendered in the opening scenes from *L'Education sentimentale*. When Frédéric's view of Paris disappears and becomes that of narrative point of view in general, we see the universalizing strategy of the spectator: to never "disappear," as Scholes and Kellog suggest, but to become submerged by the fictive level of the text—to become accepted by the reader-spectator as part of the make-believe, the fiction.

This substitutional process of fictional and narrative spectators has been carefully analyzed in the context of classic cinema, in discussions about suture. Suture allows the spectator—by the time of Hollywood clearly associated with mass entertainment audiences—to bind the spectator into the fictive level of the text. Therefore, the moment identification takes place, the viewer—who may have had doubts about the veracity of the text's reality—puts hesitation aside and identifies more fully with the fiction, perceiving the fictive world as if it were, in fact, real. Suture is, in Daniel Dayan's words, "the system that negotiates the viewer's access to the film . . . that 'speaks' the fiction" (22).

In examining suture processes more closely, I borrow from Dayan's classic analysis. Dayan suggests that suture is based in the processes of identification and subjectivity summarized by Lacan in the mirror-stage, whose "mirror" is a figure of "a radical desacrialization," suggesting "that the 'I,' the 'ego,' the 'subject,' are nothing but imaginary reflections" (24). And the Imaginary in which the mirror-stage occurs constitutes subjectivity through the "'specular effect' common to the constitution of all images" (24). Dayan refers to Jean-Pierre Oudart's classic work on suture, which, in turn, invokes Foucault's analysis of *Las Meninas,* the Velasquez painting that is a masterpiece about Renaissance space. In *Las Meninas,* the image of the Spanish king and queen are reflective spectators in the mirror of another's image: that of the painting's spectator.

Dayan, after Oudart, suggests that filmic suture is that mechanism hinted at by the Velasquez painting, where the spectator's perverse invisibility is indicated. Again following Oudart, Dayan develops the theory of suture as it works in cinema, reminding us that the fundamental narrative statement of classic cinema is "a unit composed of two terms: the film field and the field of the absent one" (30). Each "field" unfolds in the exchange of two shots. Shot one reveals an image we suppose to be reality: a landscape, a character walking down the street. Shot two reasserts this image of reality "as somebody's point of view" (Dayan 29), thereby reaffirming the presence of a spectator. Through the second shot:

> The viewer discovers that the camera is hiding things, and therefore distrusts it and the frame itself, which he now understand to be arbitrary. He wonders why

the frame is what it is. This radically transforms his mode of participation—the unreal space between characters and/or objects is no longer perceived as pleasurable. It is now the space which separates the camera from the characters. The latter have lost their quality of presence. (29)

For the spectator, this creates a sense of dispossession. The spectator "discovers that he is only authorized to see what happens to be in the axis of the glance of another spectator, who is ghostly or absent" (29). Dayan, again after Oudart, calls this hidden spectator "the absent one" (*l'absent*). In shot one, "the missing field imposes itself upon our [the spectator's] consciousness under the form of the absent-one who is looking at what we see"; and in shot two, "the missing field is abolished by the presence of somebody or something occupying the absent one's field." He concludes: "The reverse shot represents the fictional owner of the glance corresponding to shot one" (29).

This process of the shot/reverse shot creates the illusion of realism because it confirms and accommodates the spectator's suspicions, those that suggest his or her pleasure is "dependent upon his identification with the visual field." It is not the shots themselves that insist upon the spectator's demand for self-knowledge. Rather it is their process of exchange:

> When shot two replaces shot one, the absent-one is transferred from the level of enunciation to the level of fiction. As a result of this, the code effectively disappears and the ideological effect of the film is thereby secured. The code, which *produces* an imaginary, ideological effect, is hidden by the message. Unable to see the workings of the code, the spectator is at its mercy. His imaginary is sealed into the film, the spectator then absorbs an ideological effect without being aware of it. (30)

As the fundamental process of classic-filmic enunciation, suture is viewed by Dayan as special to filmic language: "the system of the suture is to classical cinema what verbal language is to literature" (22). This comparison may be logically faulty; "classical cinema" cannot be compared to "literature"—a huge general category—but rather to the specific genre of nineteenth-century "realism." Adjusting for this problem, I still would argue that Dayan's distinctions between cinema and literature do not hold. In *L'Education sentimentale*, suture occurs on a deep structural level, an effect of realism reproduced in both verbal and visual languages.

In *L'Education sentimentale,* "the film field" is the image of the steamship leaving the Paris quai. After the moment of the ship's departure, we are given a brief history of the long-haired young man who is also in the field—and who gains the name "Frédéric Moreau," who "had recently received his baccalaureate degree, and was returning home to Nogent-sur-Seine" (1).

This history is interrupted by the external vision of passengers "keeping themselves warm around the engine" (2), the river "bordered by sandbags," and a "hill that followed, on the right side, the flow of the Seine"—which then appears "little by little to disappear" while "another [hill] sprang out of it, closer, on the opposite bank" (2). The "field" becomes the point of view of an "absent one," and Frédéric is the spectator guiding both internal and external narrative histories.

The "absent one" of "the missing field" alternates with but also becomes embodied in Frédéric's visual presence, as well as in his ruminations: "'Frédéric was thinking of the room that he would be occupying there,'" in Paris (2). An "exchange" of "shots," or glances, occurs. This "exchange" exposes the figure of the spectator, but it ironically allows the *absence* of the enunciatory spectator to exist—his vision passed off as Frédéric's own. This process of exchange becomes more displaced and fictively complex when we meet another spectator, a man "flirting with a country girl," whom we learn is Monsieur Arnoux. Frédéric immediately identifies with this new fictive spectator, urging our own identification with him as reader-spectators of the fiction. We learn that "Frédéric soon confided much to him [Arnoux] about his future plans" (3). Arnoux is a distracted sympathetic spectator of Frédéric as well as a distracted spectator of technological machinery and natural scenery; he

> approved of them [Frédéric's plans].
> But he interrupted himself to peer up at the chimney stack. Then he mumbled quickly a long calculation to figure out "how many strokes of the piston at so many r.p.m. would become, etc."—And, having found the answer, he started admiring the scenery. (3)

The owner of *L'Art industriel*, Arnoux engages in the aesthetics of what Benjamin has termed "distraction," an aesthetic endemic to mass culture and mechanically reproducible art. Half magazine, half gallery, Arnoux's *L'Art industriel* is located on the Boulevard Montmartre, the district of other theatrical spectacles Arnoux is also so fond of watching: "he knew . . . all the celebrated artists, with whom he was on a first-name basis" (3). A spectator of spectacular women of the theater world as well as of atomistic mechanics, Arnoux is the transference spectator through which Frédéric's own narrative vision slips when he first views Monsieur Arnoux's wife.

If both Monsieur Arnoux and Frédéric are fictive substitutes for the "absent one" of narrative vision, Madame Arnoux is a substitute for the narrative's "missing field," likened to "an apparition" from another world:

> She was sitting in the middle of a bench all alone; or at least [Frédéric] did not distinguish anyone else in the blinding light that her eyes emitted upon

him. At the same time that he passed her, she raised her head. He involuntarily flexed his shoulders. And when he moved further away, along the same side, he looked at her.

She had on a wide-brimmed straw hat. . . . Her dress of light polka-dotted muslin flared around her in numerous folds . . . her straight nose, her chin, her whole body was silhouetted against the background of blue sky.

As she kept the same posture, he took many turns to the right and to the left to disguise his maneuver; then he planted himself near her sun umbrella . . . and he pretended to observe a boat on the river. (4–5)

Frédéric, the substitute spectator, imitates movement and a "free" narrative detachment, concealing his static fixation on Madame Arnoux's image as she works the embroidery:

Never had he seen such splendid brown skin, so seductive a figure, nor such fine transparent fingers. He gazed at her work-basket in amazement, like an extraordinary thing. What was her name, her address? What life did she lead? What was her past? (5)

The unknown woman (who we later learn is Madame Arnoux) is the "missing field," in which the "absent one" finds its own representation. Her gaze is that of a blank: "Madame Arnoux looked far into the distance. . . . When the music stopped, she twitched her eyelids several times, as though coming out of a dream" (6). The image of Madame Arnoux sitting against "the background of blue sky" and evoking Frédéric's "boundless, aching curiosity" suggests a boundlessness in the "missing field," in its free, visual horizon. And yet Madame Arnoux herself is like "the absent one," too, an emptiness that signifies an absent presence.

Madame Arnoux is an image that encodes the problematic of the spectator, and his own *lack* of visual presence—a presence that must be called forth through another, Frédéric. What is notable about Madame Arnoux's presence is the fact that people around her do not "give the impression of noticing her" (7). The silhouette scene depicting Madame Arnoux against the background of the sky shifts in the next paragraph to the scene of another look: "Sometimes, through the portholes, one could see the flank of a boat as it came gliding alongside the ship to pick up or drop off passengers. The people sitting and eating at tables leaned out the windows and identified the riverside towns" (7). In another narrative statement, similar to that of the shot/reverse shot, Frédéric again observes Madame Arnoux under the awning of the boat, "reading a slender volume in a grey binding" (7). The frame of the porthole is transposed or substituted by the frame of the binding of the page, reminding the novel's spectators that *reading* is also *seeing*. But this reminder of the mechanics of enunciation only serves to bind the spectator's vision back, once again, into the fictive level of the text.

The interest Frédéric obtains in watching Madame Arnoux intensifies in the distance Frédéric feels as a spectator: "The more he contemplated her the more he felt between her and him the opening up of an abyss" (7). As "the absent one" in representation, Frédéric's own image is both distant and near. Meanwhile, the gap between distance and closeness enhances Madame Arnoux's image, and her relation to spatial freedom signified by "the missing field." The connection between the voyeuristic perceptions of her image "field" itself is revealed again as we cut, cinema-like, to the seemingly *unlimited* frame "on the right," where "a plain extended itself"; while "to the left, a pasture gently met with a hill, where vineyards can be perceived . . . and narrow trails beyond, forming zigzags on top of the white rock that touches the rim of the sky" (7). Rendering an undetermined expanse of space or field, the gaze of an enunciatory spectator merges successfully with Frédéric's gaze. The merger is so complete that we are not certain if it is Frédéric or the enunciatory spectator who utters the following: "What fortune to climb up there, side by side, his arm around her waist . . . under the radiance of her eyes!" (7). Frédéric's position as fictive viewer is reaffirmed, however, when we are told, "He gave her a look in which he tried to put all of his love." However, Madame Arnoux remains "*immobile*" (8). The fictive level of the text is dominant. The presence of an absence (or absence of a presence) that fills these descriptions continues to mark Frédéric's visual relation to Madame Arnoux.

He first attempts to visit Monsieur Arnoux—as a pretense for seeing Madame Arnoux—at *L'Art industriel*. We are told that Frédéric "waited for Her to appear" (21). However, "the high transparent windows offered a look" not upon Madame Arnoux but upon "statues, drawings, engravings, catalogues, issues of *L'Art industriel*," the magazine (21). This list increases in references to commercial, burlesque forms of art—forms of mechanical reproduction—as Frédéric's eye finally rests upon "the subscription price . . . on the door, adorned in the center with the initials of the editor" (21). The "initials" are the only traces of editorial subjectivity and authorship that exist in this commercial display. They are a reminder that editorial authorship, in general, is motivated by commercial spectacles and financial enterprise. The would-be vision of Madame Arnoux, at this moment, has been transposed onto the "missing field" of reproducible, commercial art. This art is a deceptive art, for a spectator whose own deceptiveness is suggested as he "made it seem that he was examining the drawings" (21). A human substitute (of Madame Arnoux, of the missing field) suddenly appears: "An employee raised the small door, and responded that Monsieur would not be at 'the store' until 5 o'clock" (21). Although Frédéric reflects that he had surely glimpsed "a wash basin in the back" (35), we learn that behind the shop is not the Arnoux home, that Madame Arnoux does not live there.

These evocations of presence and absence are reproduced by the spectator's visual experience reading the novel. They are recreated when, prior to Frédéric's shop visit, he stops to visit Monsieur Dambreuse, carrying a letter of introduction from his provincial neighbor, the old man Rogue. The first image provided of Monsieur Dambreuse is from the perspective of another "missing field." Through another exchange of narrative "shots," suture binds into the fictive reality Frédéric's view of the other elderly man, Monsieur Dambreuse, reading the letter. Frédéric watches Monsieur Dambreuse as "He perused old Rogue's letter" (20). The field of the absent one (here as Frédéric) is rendered as the view of *another,* that of Monsieur Dambreuse as reader. The description of Monsieur Dambreuse continues to ignore but also to exploit the spectator's presence: "From afar, because of his slender build, he could have been young still" except for visual details like "his thin white hair, his frail limbs and . . . the extraordinary pallor of his face" (20). These eyes, too, like Madame Arnoux's, are empty but strangely energetic: "A merciless energy rested in his glaucous eyes, colder than eyes of glass" (20). The contrast between coldness and energy is evocative of the "marble eyes" of the dominatrix in *Venus in Furs.* Monsieur Dambreuse, a transference figure of feminine masculinity in male masochism, is also a transference figure for Frédéric/the absent one. The latter receives specularity only as Frédéric "left by another corridor and found himself in the bottom of the courtyard, next to the coach house" (20).

"The missing field" of the feminized and yet dominating image of Monsieur Dambreuse is substituted by a female "other," Madame Dambreuse—or, rather, *not* Madame Dambreuse, but her coach, which presumably conveys her "passage" through (no) image. We only learn of a trace of her image when Frédéric/the absent one notices "a vague scent of feminine elegances" (21). The literal trace of a "scent" disperses when the coach driver gives a signal, "and everything disappeared" (21). Frédéric, the spectator envisioned by shot two in the narrative statement, is reinserted back into the fictive level of narration in the motion of the coach. We are told, "Frédéric returned home on foot, along the boulevards. He regretted not having been able to see Madame Dambreuse" (21). The connections between "the missing field" designating Madame Arnoux and Madame Dambreuse continue both through the mediation of Monsieur Dambreuse reading the letter (another "missing field"), and through Frédéric's vision of the coach as "missing field," a projection of his own lack of representational image.

Later, walking to the top of the Champs-Elysées and approaching the intersection of the *Rond-Point* (23), Frédéric "felt as if lost in a remote world" (24). His view of other "female faces" recalls the image of Madame Arnoux as he also observes panoramic city views. Frédéric transfers "the missing field" of a woman onto "the missing field" of panoramic, picture-perfect Paris. And he experiences what Dayan calls the "obliqueness" of "the absent one": the illusion of plenitude, of panoramic "freedom."

Frédéric may be "lost" in a self-image of "loss." But this state of loss/ being lost confirms an ideological aspect of his "free" worldview. As Dayan writes, "the subject must be signified empty, defined but left free" (27). Speaking specifically of the Velasquez painting, he says: "Reading the signifiers of the presence of the subject, the spectator occupies this place. His own subjectivity fills the empty shot predefined by the painting" (27). But in Dayan's reading of Lacan, the psychoanalyst "stresses the unifying functions of the imaginary" (27). Such "unity"—borne out through the representational effects of the painting, film, or, in our case, the literary-realist text— comes at a cost: the spectator's imaginary can only coincide with the painting's built-in subjectivity. The receptive freedom of the spectator is reduced to the minimum" (27). "Obliqueness," therefore, is never ideologically "free." The "empty" subject is precisely the subject who, through suture, "systematically encroaches" upon "the spectator's freedom by interpreting, indeed, by remodeling his memory" (Dayan 31). "Freedom," in other words, is a perverse, sentimental means of denying ideological perspective in a text.

"The spectator is torn to pieces, pulled in oppositions," says Dayan (31). The signified faith in perceived "reality" tugs at the spectator in one direction; the signifier of "the absent one" tugs at the spectator in the other. "Brutality" and "tyranny" is the result. The ideological codes in "suturing" processes are violently divisionary.

Yet this violence within suture serves its own ideological purpose, ironically enhancing the illusion of narcissistic wholeness for the spectator. We view this illusion when Frédéric, our substitute spectator, sees himself in the mirror after his first dinner at the Arnoux's: "His face was reflected back at him in the glass. He found himself handsome—and stayed a minute to look at himself" (50). This moment may be ironic. But it also points to the narcissism of the narrative spectator with whom Frédéric identifies. Frédéric's pleasure in self-vision follows the pleasures he has just experienced as the (absent) spectator of Madame Arnoux, who performs a song. The image of "woman"—the "woman" he "needs"—grants him the capacity for a self-portrait, a dual self-image.

Duality takes the form of masochistic self-debasement accompanied by arrogant self-aggrandizement when Frédéric tells Deslauriers early in the novel:

"I would have made something [of myself] with a woman who would have
loved me . . . Love is the fodder and air of genius. The extraordinary emotions
produce sublime works. As for looking for the woman I need, I give up!
Besides, if even I find her, she will reject me. I am of the race of the disinherited." (16)

"Disinherited," Frédéric is also determined to "make something" of himself,
to feel the "extraordinary emotions" that "a woman" should invoke. In one
of his many moments of masochistic "agonizing doubt"—borrowing that
phrase from Sacher-Masoch's Severin—Frédéric wonders if it would be "better to come straight to the point, to declare his love" to Madame Arnoux. He
"composed a twelve-page letter full of lyrical passages and apostrophes,"
then, tearing it up, "did nothing, strove for nothing—immobilized by fear
of failure" (23). Yet Frédéric generates power through his paralysis, his fear.
He generates the power to control representation's future, and to more
fully see.

Technologies of Vision

Frédéric's self-satisfaction upon seeing his image in the mirror suggests that
his simple "monocle" is a very effective lens. It is adaptable to various and
wider—but also singular—methods of vision. These methods of vision are
explored in many contexts throughout the French nineteenth century. Indeed, to understand the ironies of vision emboldening the spectator in
L'Education sentimentale, we must situate vision itself within the larger context of French nineteenth-century technology and invention. The nineteenth century was obsessed with vision; many film and art historians note "a
striking increase in visual awareness" that occurred, especially, in France. As
French film historian Alan Williams notes, the French century "marked a
kind of cultural birth or rebirth of vision," during which there was a "release
and re-evaluation of the sensory . . . observed in all media, beginning some-
time around the Revolution"—notable in the evolution of classical drama to
melodrama, for example, and in the evolution of the realist novel, as well.
    Of particular interest to cinema historians is the emergence of optical-
illusion toys and other technologies of vision from the 1820s on; these are
traditionally considered as precursors to the cinema apparatus developed
before the century's end. The most famous optical-illusion instrument may
be the photographic camera; in 1837, Louis-Jacques-Mandé Daguerre
caused a photographic image to appear on a copperplate within a short
exposure time, marking the advent of serious photography. But the Daguer-
rotype camera represented only one optical-illusion technology that sold by
the mid-century. The Phénakistoscope, invented in 1832, played upon prob-

lems of movement illusion through a revolving wheel containing pictures, which, in motion, appeared to make pictures move simultaneously as a spectator observed them through a mirror. A few years later, the Zoëtrope employed the basic features of the Phénakistoscope but eliminated the mirror lens, permitting group viewing. Other mechanisms invented and marketed during the 1850s and '60s continued to complicate the illusion of motion presented to viewers, and to enhance group spectatorship. Especially important to cinema historians was the popular Praxinoscope, patented by Emile Reynaud in 1888. Through a series of rotating and facing mirrors, the Praxinoscope combined the image of synthesized motion of the Phénakistoscope with the group-viewing position of the Zoëtrope, in its detached cylindrical form.[19]

In his classic account of the development of cinematic realism, André Bazin comments that these devices were "precursors . . . more like prophets" of cinema (19). Bazin's essay on "reality" in cinema suggests that optical-illusion toy developers saw the possibility of

> the reconstruction of a perfect illusion of the outside world in sound, color, and relief . . . The guiding myth inspiring the invention of cinema, is the accomplishment of that which dominated in a more or less vague fashion all the techniques of the mechanical reproduction of reality . . . from photography to the phonograph, namely an integral realism, a recreation of the world in its own image, an image unburdened by the freedom of interpretation of the artist or the irreversibility of time. (21)

Bazin's account of "the myth of total cinema" perceives such "reproduction of reality" to *be* a myth. But while Bazin calls attention to the mythologizing tendency of cinema and its "precursors," he also privileges a different "myth of total cinema," placing cinema at the teleological end of nineteenth-century technologies striving for realism. Recent trends in cinema and visual-art histories have placed less emphasis on the apparatus and more emphasis on the spectator's experience. Jonathan Crary, for example, describes historicized "techniques of the observer," treating optical-illusion technologies as symptoms of shifting conceptual structures for the viewing subject. In *L'Education sentimentale,* I suggest, the occasional allusion to the visual apparatus signifies these more conceptual concerns with the perceptual drama of the spectator—and, by extension, its embodiment in the novel of realism.

Writing of mid-nineteenth century visual experience, Crary emphasizes the importance of the stereoscope. Invented during the 1820s, the stereoscope was widely distributed and popular after the 1850s. Developed independently of photography, the latter representing the reproducible image as static, the stereoscope played upon "the illusion of movement" in

the viewer's binocularity. The stereoscope—like the Phénakistoscope and
the Zoëtrope—considered the problem of binocular parallax, the human
"capacity under most conditions to synthesize retinal disparity into a single
unitary image" (Crary 119), which had fascinated its inventor from a bio-
logical-research point of view.[20] The invention and ensuing popularity of
the stereoscope suggests to Crary a general "reorganization of the observer"
that took place in the mid-nineteenth century. This was part of a larger
collapse of the "linear optical system" and fixed positionality associated with
the camera obscura, which had been both the instrument and the figure
dominating the spectator's experience since the sixteenth century.

In the mid-century setting of *L'Education sentimentale,* the visual-
representational issues surrounding the stereoscope's emergence are explored in the scene of the horse races. This scene describes the Paris Hippodrome, a stadium situated in front of the Ecole Militaire in the area known
as the Champ-de-Mars, the Paris fairgrounds. Horse races and other spectacles, like the flying of an unmanned dirigible from the Hippodrome in
1852,[21] typified mid-century Champ-de-Mars entertainments. By the mid-
century the Champ-de-Mars became the favored site for nineteenth-century
Parisian world fairs, or universal expositions. Through world fairs, Champ-
de-Mars entertainments grew bigger and more spectacular as the century
wore on.

Flaubert would have witnessed the Universal Exposition of 1867 as he
was completing *L'Education sentimentale.* Certainly many of his writer con-
temporaries, including friend Georges Sand, published articles that described and promoted what was then to date the biggest Parisian world fair.
In the novel, as we trace the journey of Frédéric and Rosanette to the
Hippodrome through Parisian streets and quais, pseudo-global themes that
allude to the world fair are remarked upon; we are told Rosanette "thought
Lebanon was in China" (221), so she asks Frédéric to give her "lessons in
geography." In one of many scenes that describe the "geography" of Paris,
we are told that "leaving the Trocadéro on their right, they [Frédéric and
Rosanette] crossed the Pont d'Iéna and finally stopped in the middle of the
Champ-de-Mars, beside the other carriages already parked in the Hippodrome" (203). The trip to the Hippodrome, itself built earlier in the century, serves as its own kind of "lesson in geography."

That is because the description of this trip terminates in an allusive
reference to the central edifice built for the 1867 Universal Exposition, a
large rotunda. The rotunda, as Flaubert would have witnessed, would be
built next to the Hippodrome, between the Iéna Bridge and the Ecole
Militaire. And it provoked a major civic controversy over safety as well as
aesthetic appeal—as did the building of the Eiffel Tower for another world
fair, two decades later. The dominant architectural feature of the 1867
rotunda was the existence of several circular galleries surrounding a central

exotic garden; each gallery rigidly displayed fair products according to type and nationality. The design of the rotunda would have resembled the panopticon prison architecture of Jeremy Bentham in the late eighteenth century (Fig. 2.1), actually rendered in many new prison designs by the mid-nineteenth century. Erected years before the 1867 world fair and its rotunda, the Hippodrome itself suggested a panopticon-like design. In a drawing of the Hippodrome published in the *Paris Guide* for the 1867 fair,[22] a seating diagram is strangely evocative of the panopticon visual ordering principles. Printed for potential Hippodrome spectators to assist in their purchase of seats, the drawing is made from the vantage point of an imaginary spectator, who, at the center of the Hippodrome field, looks at his own Imaginary through individually marked, numbered boxes (Fig. 2.2). The spectator may be missing; but the potential *mass* spectator is commercially enumerated, each number following the horizontal, circular bend of the stadium and vertical floors. Similar to Bentham's prison model, whose watch-figure is the invisible prison guard representing reformist but author-

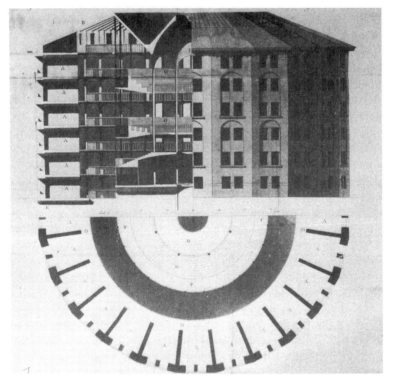

Figure 2.1 Jeremy Bentham's Penitentiary Panopticon

Figure 2.2 Paris Hippodrome Seating Chart, in Victor Hugo's *Paris Guide*, published for the 1867 Universal Exposition

itarian bureaucracy, the imaginary spectator contains both visual capacity and complete invisibility, suggesting control of the absent field.

Like the invisible Hippodrome spectator-prison guard, the narrative spectator in *L'Education sentimentale* lacks imagery but exists as a figural emblem of the watchtower view. The description of the Hippodrome in *L'Education sentimentale,* as Frédéric and Rosanette arrive there in the scene set in 1848, alludes to the watchtower view of both the 1867 rotunda and of the Hippodrome in its 1867 advertisement. The narrator-spectator describes "people swarming over the grassy knoll" and "curious" spectators "on the balcony of the Ecole Militaire," as well as the Hippodrome grandstand (203). These spectators have different but similar panopticon views of the "field." They imitate the panopticon panorama of the narrator, except that they themselves are *seen,* the "well-dressed crowd" (204). The narrator views *them,* from the perspective of the *missing* field. We learn both about the narrator's opinion of the spectators' class through his descriptions of their attire, and his own curious relation to the Hippodrome scene as past event. He remarks that the crowd's fashion reveals a "deference toward this recently introduced sport. The race-going public, more exclusive *in those times,* appeared less vulgar," sporting "velvet collars and white gloves" (204—

emphasis added). The phrase "in those times" reminds us that the narrator exists at some point in the future with respect to the chronology of the novel. Subtle allusions to scopic activity upon the future site of the 1867 world-fair rotunda suggests that this narrator has witnessed the fair. Fast-forwarding to the chronological conclusion of the novel, to the late 1860s, we could surmise that the novel's narrator, having witnessed the 1867 fair, superimposes one panopticon figure, the rotunda, upon another, the Hippodrome, in a commentary upon the duality of vision, a form of binocular parallax.

The scientific exploration of binocular parallax in the 1830s resulted in the invention of the stereoscope. The very interest in binocular parallax, as Crary argues, reconfigured nineteenth-century understanding of what it is to see an object in vision: to see the *appearance* of a singular image, in a multiple-plane reference. The superimposition of dual panopticon models in *L'Education sentimentale,* that of the Hippodrome and the later rotunda, suggests a paradox of vision reminiscent of the stereoscope's binocular-parallax effect. Furthermore, the continuing description of the horse race at the Hippodrome suggests that objects in motion reproduce binocular parallax.

Recalling another popular instrument of binocular-parallax vision, the Hippodrome spectators watch the horse race "through their binoculars" (206). The binoculars are both different to and evocative of Frédéric's "monocle." They remind us that monocle vision relies upon a dual vision embodied by the human spectator. The scene at the Hippodrome reveals the duality of what the spectator perceives, in the *illusion* of singularity through motion as horses and riders fly down the course. But, first, the narrator-spectator is obsessed with other spectators, especially female ones and the visual illusion they create when viewed collectively in the grand-stand: "The women, decked out in brilliant colors, wore high-waisted dresses, and sitting on the tiers of the stands, they looked like large beds of flowers flecked by a black spot here and there, caused by the dark suits of the men" (204). The view of these spectators' own bodily view is emphasized in the next sentence: "But all gazes were turned toward the celebrated Algerian Bou-Maza," a captured chieftan who himself is part of the spectacle and "who remained impassive between two officers of the state, in one of the reserved stands" (204). Here the earlier reference to Lebanon and China—and Rosanette's confusion between them—is recollected in this allusion to another French colony through the reference to the Algerian chieftain. He, too, is a spectator who, like the women, becomes a spectacle for other viewers.[23] In the shift from the missing field of the absent one to the actual eye of the spectators, we have an ironic image of mass spectators themselves as colonizing but also colonized spectacles. Their aloneness in a "reserved" seat is a function of the group view.

The eye-witness or absent one reinhabits this universalized but also particularized view. The spectacle of movement illusion he creates is echoed as the first race starts, from the perspective of the missing field: "At first, they [the horses] stayed condensed in a single mass; soon, the mass elongated and split in two (204). The emphasis in this passage is no longer on the spectator. Rather, it is on the spectator's perceptual illusion of the horses' motion. This illusion continues in the following sentence: "in the middle of the first lap, the jockey who wore the yellow jacket nearly fell off" (204). The jockey is seen as a mechanical moving part, a visual metonymy representing a part, not a human whole, straddling a horse. The description of the second race heightens the motion illusion and binocular vision—especially as a reverse shot shows the spectators, again, and point of view is re-established:

> The grandstand spectators climbed on top of their seats. The others, standing up in their carriages, followed with binoculars the course of the jockeys. They saw them scurry like flecks of red, yellow, white and blue, against all the length of the crowd that bordered the Hippodrome course. From afar, their speed did not seem excessive; at the other end of the Champ-de-Mars, they seemed to slow down and only to proceed by a kind of sliding, where the horses' bellies touched the ground without their extended legs having to bend. But, returning again very fast, they grew larger. (206)

In this passage the problem of binocular parallax and movement illusion is specifically tied to the problem of how to view the horse race. The passage forms a study of the effects *on the viewer* of the horses and jockeys as they form a singular image. It is a scene uncannily evocative of Edvward Muybridge's famous anatomy-of-motion experiment, conducted between 1872 to 1877. Commissioned by railroad magnate Governor Leland Stanford of California, Muybridge's experiment sought to determine whether or not all four legs of a running horse were off the ground simultaneously. Muybridge, a photographer by trade, confirmed Stanford's contestation that the legs were all off the ground, by employing a battery of 12–24 cameras making successive photography stills through a fast camera-lens shutter. To persuade a yet-dubious public, Muybridge gave follow-up lectures about his experiment with the aid of a zoopraxiscope. These lectures created a kind of early motion cinema, as Muybridge projected the still images of the horses in motion in rapid succession through a lantern onto a rotating glass disk.

The use of the zoopraxiscope and Muybridge's experiment is historically important to the development of early cinema. Interestingly, Flaubert's description of the motion illusion of horses predates Muybridge's experiment by more than a decade. This scene is but one of several that comments on motion illusion in a way indicative of precinema technology. For example, in a short scene narratively sliced into the larger scene of the Hippodrome race, Frédéric sees Madame Arnoux, who appears and then disappears in a coach, a motion echoed by the woman's head bobbing in and out of the coach: "a lady appeared in a victoria; she leaned outside the door, then sank back inside quickly. This she did over and over several times" (205).

At first Frédéric cannot determine who the "lady" is. But then, "A suspicion seized him; it seemed to him that this was Madame Arnoux" (205). The motion illusion created by her appearance and disappearance causes great anxiety for Frédéric. But it is not until "the victoria reappeared," later, that he is certain "it was Madame Arnoux" (207). Frédéric panics. His panic is stimulated by his having been seen with Rosanette. It also is stimulated by his fear of not knowing what he has seen, by the illusion of motion of the head bobbing in and out, by not knowing what or whose is this image.

In an allusion to the earlier scene of Madame Dambreuse's coach and that lady's nonappearance, the image of Madame Arnoux's disappearance and reappearance points to the perceptual illusions Frédéric faces as a spectator throughout the novel. The Hippodrome passages, in general, form a complex commentary on the spectacle of moving bodies that attract the spectator. At the end of the horse race, we are told by the narrative eyewitness, "the bored crowd was scattering" (206). Judgment enters the supposed neutrality of his stance when he remarks, "Groups of men chatted beneath the stands. Their discourse was free; the fashionable women left, scandalized by the proximity of the *lorettes*" (206). While this scene differentiates spectators by gender and class, it also combines all spectators into a collective and rather uninspiring mass—summed up by society ladies only concerned with superficial appearances and their own empty fetishism. The lady spectator herself becomes an icon of the missing field, which exists in a moral vacuum. The spectator's attraction to motion illusion is attributed to nothing less than blank curiosity and stupidity, an image the collective *feminized* spectator emphasizes in other instances in the novel.

These include a conversation about female representation among Sénécal, Hussonnet, and friends. At the mention of "the tableaux," performed "at the Gymnase . . . attracting large audiences at the time," Sénécal "griped about them. Such spectacles corrupted the daughters of the proletariat. Afterwards, one saw them flaunting an arrogant finery" (141). The Hippodrome race, like the tableaux spectacles, offers opportunities for group spectatorship that contrast with individual acts of spectatorship that Frédéric enjoys alone, watching Madame Arnoux. But Frédéric's private spectatorship acts allude to a different technology of vision that historically attracted large groups of spectators: shadow theaters.

Frédéric spies the Arnoux family eating in the steamship dining room, and Madame Arnoux becomes a shadow puppet. She "reprimanded her husband for his weakness toward the child. He whispered in her ear a pleasing nicety . . . she smiled. Afterwards he got up to close the curtain of the window behind her neck" (9). At the drawing of the curtain, we are told that "the light reflected from the low white ceiling was extremely glaring . . . from where he was sitting opposite her." The effect of the lights creates an illuminated theater. Then Madame Arnoux herself becomes a silhouette player, a shadow figure: "Frédéric distinguished the shadows cast by her eyelashes. She put her lips to the glass, breaking a little bread crust between her fingers. The medallion of lapis-lazuli, attached to her wrist by a gold chain, from time to time rang against her plate" (9).

The *théâtre d'ombres* suggested by this image of Madame Arnoux's silhouette image were popular spectacles in the French eighteenth and nineteenth centuries.[24] In the mid-eighteenth century, inventor Jean Gaspar Lavater created a machine upon which a human subject sat between a lamp and tracing paper, resulting in black-paper cut-out portraits that would be named "Silhouettes" (for a French controller of finances whose policies were considered cheap). The popular silhouette portraits inspired early live spectacles of projected theater in the mid-eighteenth century: small theater troupes replaced the standard stage curtain with a *toile*, a white sheet, upon which spectators watched the shadowy figures of actors playing between the *toile* and a source of light. These *ombres humaines* were the basis of the famed mechanical silhouette theater of Dominique Séraphin, which started in Versailles in the late 1770s and moved to the Paris Palais Royal in 1784—continuing well after the Revolution and into the nineteenth century, every day, twice a day on Sunday.

Visited by upper and working classes alike, Séraphin's theater was but one of a type of puppetry called the *ombres chinoises*. Shadow puppet theaters originally evolved in ancient Asian cultures; they remain popular in China, Java, and India today. Asian shows are highly allegorical and varied, employing flat hide puppet figures—sometimes colored and jointed—and operated by hand-held rods pressed firmly against a cotton screen, with a light behind the screen to create the shadow effect. However, their French version in the eighteenth and nineteenth centuries employed cut-out figures whose rods and wires were more carefully hidden. As one writer on puppetry notes, this gave "their audiences a quite different illusion."[25] By 1887, many forms of these *théâtre d'ombres* were combined in the shadow-theater cabaret of Montmartre, the Cabaret du Chat Noir. Lasting thirty years, the Chat Noir drew upon the talents of many Paris artists in producing cinema-like shadow theaters.[26]

By the time shadow theaters reached their popular height in nineteenth-century France, puppets generally had obtained an important status in European culture. In literature, as puppet-theater historian Scott Cutler Shershow remarks, puppet theaters had long acted as a metaphor for duplicity in artistic representation, beginning with Plato's allegory of the cave, in which shadowed men, like puppets, present "a particularly clear paradigm of all representation . . . in Plato's famous formulation, mere copies of a copy at 'three removes' from truth."[27] The Greek word for "puppet," Shershow notes, is *thauma*, which means "wonder" or "marvel," probably derived from *theaomai*, meaning, "'I gaze upon or look at'" (Shershow 17). The "wonder" or "marvel" is embodied by and reproduced in what Shershow calls the "inescapable fascination with performing objects" (6). In *L'Education sentimentale*, Frédéric spies Madame Arnoux as one such "performing object"; he gazes upon her behind her screen-like curtain, observing her eyelashes and the glass at her lips and the "crust between her fingers." The "performing object," Shershow adds, is typically feminized as a mammet or doll, a child's plaything "also . . . applied colloquially to a subordinate person, usually a female, as a term either of condescending affection or of abuse and contempt" (28). In the silhouette scene of the dining car, Madame Arnoux is this shadowy, duplicitous figure of the puppet-doll, a figure of both fascination and "contempt."

Her image relies upon the trickery of shadow and light to create a detailed mimeticism: the eyelashes, the crust of bread. But her "alluring dissimulation" is repeated by the spectator, Frédéric. The spectator himself, both like and unlike his "performing object," exists as a shadowed figure watching the play of shadows behind (and in front of) the curtain. As a passive gazer of the theatrical image of Madame Arnoux eating in the dining car, Frédéric is her visual author-manipulator, whose lonely voyeurism constructs the mammet-like vision. Frédéric's embodied, if shadowy, vision leads his own readers-spectators to witness the image of Madame Arnoux in other series of proto-cinematic flows of shadow and light. As in the dining-car scene, they serve to heighten her presentation as a doll-like "performing object"; and they indirectly, perversely, remind us of the absent presence of the spectator.

The French *ombres chinoises* and the other *théâtre d'ombres* were entertainments whose technologies of reproduced shadow and light—and automaton, doll-like mobility in imitation of human mobility—link them to the later emergence of cinema. One such image foreshadows Madame Arnoux's shadow-theatre performance. This is the image of Madame Arnoux on the boat, silhouetted against the blue background, framed by the sky and also by her "big straw hat" (4). Another later scene reproduces another shadow-and-light effect: invited to the Arnoux's house for dinner, Frédéric waits for Madame Arnoux to appear, and "The light globes, covered by an embroidered paper, cast a milky light that softened the color of the surrounding walls, covered with mauve satin. Through the slates of the fireguard, like a big fan, one glimpsed the coal in the fireplace" (46). Following dinner, the narrative pauses while Madame Arnoux, the "performing object," sings. Yet another scene employs images of shadow and light to refer to Madame Arnoux's performative presence and disappearing image. Frédéric visits the Arnoux family at the St. Cloud country house, where he watches as "One side of the horizon began to pale . . . on the other, a wide band of orange color spread itself out against the sky and was glowing red at the crest of the hills, which had become otherwise completely black" (83). This cinematic mise-en-scène of the sunset-lit sky recollects a similar image of the sky earlier in the novel, on the steamship. There, Madame Arnoux's shadow is framed against the colored light of the sky. At St. Cloud, however, Frédéric/the absent one spies Madame Arnoux in clear silhouette form, sitting "on a large rock," a "fiery glow behind her" (83). Then he spies Madame Arnoux "alone by the window casement" (83). Here the specialness of the "performing object," the female star, is most clearly projected through the male viewer's narcissism. Frédéric becomes part of the cinematic image, in language strangely evocative of black-and-white motion-picture photography, when we are told that "They were standing close to one other, in the embrasure of the window recess. The night, in front of them, spread out like some *immense dark veil speckled with silver*" (92—emphasis added).

Yet to be invented at the time of the publication of *L'Education sentimentale* was the cinematic film emulsion of silver halidate grains, which cluster together "to form tiny specks" when struck by light.[28] Yet other filmlike technologies and motion-illusion experimentation emerged with another nineteenth-century spectacle, the diorama. Invented by none other than Daguerre in 1822, the diorama was a kind of precinematic peep show, which borrowed many of its three-dimensional visual and oral "reality" techniques from stage melodrama, like the use of transparent fabrics to create the effect of a proto-cinematic "dissolve"; sound effects; and pyrotechnics, employing small moving models and multiplane coordinated movements. Like shadow theaters, dioramas were popular entertainments at French fairs, which particularly tried to capture the sights and sounds of real events, especially disasters. Diorama titles like "The Earthquake at Lima" or "The Golden Valley Before and After the Catastrophe" (a landslide) reflected the disaster themes of early journalism.

Dioramas created spectacular, very "real" and striking images for a very passive spectator. The force of the image versus the passivity of the spectator recalls a central paradox of sympathy described by Hume. In his *Treatise,* Hume distinguishes "sympathy" from "compassion"; and unlike St. Augustine, who perceived sympathy as leading to compassionate acts, Hume viewed sympathy as a much more inactive phenomenon. That the passivity of the sympathetic spectator is related to the vividness of the tragic image is suggested when Hume makes this distinction. He writes that compassion is evoked when, "safely at land," the potential spectator thinks about "those who are at sea in a storm." He continues: "suppose the idea to become still more lively. Suppose the ships to be driven so near me, that I can perceive distinctly the horror" (594). This "nearness," this perception of "the horror" close to but not encroaching upon the spectator, is sympathy, according to Hume. As he says repeatedly throughout the *Treatise,* sympathy relies upon "the conversion of an idea into an impression." In Hume's earlier epistemological treatment of these terms in Book I of the *Treatise,* he says an "idea" is faint and an "impression" strong, that it is the *perception* of a "near" experience of the disaster or event that reproduces sympathetic feeling. Sympathy relies upon a more "lively" and greater "force and vivacity" of the impression (594) than does compassion. It is sympathy that the diorama spectator experiences. Through technologies of sight and sound, the diorama recreates the "lively" but *reproduced* (real) event; and it is this very "liveliness" that enhances the *lack* of vivacity in the viewer:

> My sympathy with another may give me the sentiment of pain and disapprobation, when any object is presented, that has a tendency to give him uneasiness; tho' I may not be willing to sacrifice anything of my own interest. . . . A house may displease me by being ill contriv'd for the convenience of the owner; and yet I may refuse to give a shilling toward the rebuilding of it. (586)

The contrast between the passivity of the viewer and the vivacity of the sympathetic reality image is sustained, diorama-like, in Flaubert's novel, when Frédéric witnesses the 1848 Paris worker and student riots. Frédéric is a roving observer of these street demonstrations that often turn violent. He is like the passive "dandy" and fellow bystander of one early riot scene in the novel: "a blond young man, a comely figure wearing a mustache and goatee like a fop from the age of Louis XIV" (27). Like Frédéric, this young man does not know "'what the trouble is'"; the gentleman declares that "'neither do they [the workers]! It's the fashionable thing for the present'" (27). This scene escalates into mob violence, anticipating the full-blown civil war in Book III. Frédéric's passivity is again accentuated when we are told that he is asleep (with Rosanette) when he first hears "the noise of gunfire" (286).

Against Rosanette's wishes, he insists on "going to see what was happening" (286). But he is not a participant. Rather, he is like a news reporter or cameraman, watching, passively reporting events, following "some men in smocks" to the Palais Royal, or overhearing a dispute between "a man in a Greek cap" and "a woman wearing a head scarf, about whether or not to fight" (287). The image of Frédéric's neutrality is emphasized when we are left to guess the nature of the relationship between the man and the

woman. It is again reasserted when Frédéric's vision is transferred onto that
of the absent one, a narrator who has seen both past and future events, as we
read: "Last night, the spectacle of carts carrying five dead bodies gathered
among those on the Capucines Boulevard had changed the dispositions of
the people" (286).

Frédéric's own physical image is reinserted back into the missing field
of the narrative when we are told that he is "caught between two deep
masses" of people, and "could not move" (288). He becomes the quintessential spectator of sympathy as the unfolding drama becomes a "lively"
entertainment: "The drums sounded the attack. Shrill cries, shrill screams,
shouts of horns rose up" (288). We are told that "The wounded that fell, the
dead lying around, did not seem to be really wounded, really dead. It
seemed to [Frédéric] that he was attending a show [*un spectacle*]" (288).
Here the image of shadow and light is repeated not in connection with the
performing woman or with the spectator's problems of vision, but with the
authoritarian tyranny of the military suppression of the workers' rebellion:

> here and there torches sputtered; despite the dust that rose, he recognized
> the line of the infantrymen and the national guardsmen . . . They had just
> taken over the square, and had executed many men by firing squad. (334)

Images of authoritarian tyranny, sympathy, and special lighting effects
continue to inflect this scene when, we are told, to save himself, Frédéric
convinces the militia he has come to the city "to the rescue of a wounded
comrade" (334). The soldiers escort Frédéric to the hospital, in yet another
journey through Paris. In this scene, another "lesson in geography" as Frédéric courses the city, he views windows that "flamed like fire" and he
"passed" shadows while under the authoritarian regime of the guard. This
guard is a figure for the soon-to-be elected Republican president, who
would later make himself the authoritarian technocrat, Napoleon III. Repeated scenes of an illuminated but also shadowed Paris before and after
the suppression of the rebellion may be personalized by Frédéric's vision.
But they remark upon the group authoritarian, sadistic power of Frédéric's
culture, and the masochistic disappearance of its group spectator. The illuminated but shadowed Paris also refers to Paris as source of vision. This
Paris is an illusory civic icon of the Second Empire, which served to embellish the sadomasochistic, feminized global spectator.

Paris Like a Performing Woman: World Fairs, World Fetish

Throughout the novel, images of Parisian civic monuments, the Seine River,
and the city's post-Haussmann boulevards are suggestively rendered in the

glow of luminous and silhouette-casting lights. Although most of the novel takes place in 1848, several years before the Second Empire, and the Paris rebuilding project begun under the direction of Baron von Haussmann, Frédéric—in one of many examples—"idly strolled [*flâna*] along the boulevards" (88). As the passive *flâneur,* Frédéric thinks of Madame Arnoux's return from the countryside. Again evoking precinematic lighting images, the novel suggests he views "pink clouds, in the shape of elongated scarves" (88); then he sees cafés, and women with "an indolence to the eye" passing by (88). Frédéric thinks: "Never had Paris seemed so beautiful . . . in the future. . . ." (88).

And we *are* in the future.

Frédéric's vision of Paris reads like an advertisement for one of its many universal expositions, those grand commercial fairs that absorbed the city both before and after the publication of *L'Education sentimentale.*[29] These world fairs, or expositions, touted French products as the world's best, from furs to fabrics to foods, to engines to gas lighting to visual-technology. And these "world" fairs advertised the city of Paris itself as center of a vast specular universe, a global capital of modern industry. They furthermore advertised Paris as an entertainment commodity—to be had in the viewing of it. In the Parisian tourism promoted by world fairs, the city too, became a "performing object."

Like the puppet, the performing woman, Paris was made a visual fantasy of the passive sympathetic spectator. World fairs produced a travel literature that emphasized this Parisian Imaginary, depicted in that literature as both coquettishly feminine and globally unifying. These books and brochures sold as souvenirs for the increasing masses that attended world fairs—5 million during the universal exposition of 1855, and 30 million during the 1867 exposition. The souvenir books and travel literature employ a gaze just like that of Frédéric's. They pander to the same voyeurism and fetishism Frédéric enjoys, looking at Paris and the women of his world. Like Frédéric, who watches as "gaslights turned on, and the Seine . . . tore itself into shimmering silver against the stone piers of the bridges" (24), an Italian tourist, Edmondo de Amicis—who attended the 1878 world fair—described a Paris of glowing lights:

> "windows, signs, advertisements, doors facades . . . silver and gilded and il-
> luminated. . . . [Paris] is not an illumination but a fire, the boulevards are
> blazing . . . the shops cast floods of brilliant light half across the street, and
> encircle the crowd in a golden dust." (quoted in Evenson 6)

And like Frédéric, perceiving the fading grey light behind the silhouetted Tuileries while thinking about *both* Mesdames Dambreuse and Arnoux flying by in their substitutional coaches, yet another writer of a tour guide to the 1889 world fair compared the fascinations of Paris to the fascinations of "a woman": "The city of Paris is like a coquettish woman: confidant in the power of her charms and certain of seducing strangers with all her graces."[30]

Like most Paris travel writers after Haussmann's rebuilding of Paris, for which many poor neighborhoods were razed to make space for upper-class residences and vast commercial boulevards, Amicis described the "'agreeable'" impression Paris made, as one proceeded up "'the wide street,'" which "'grows broader still, the side ones lengthen,'" and in which "'the grandeur of Paris begins to appear . . . the great street . . . extends before us as far as the eye can reach'" (quoted in Evenson 6). Another booklet, entitled, "Souvenirs of Paris," which sold as memorabilia during the 1889 world fair, shows a series of engravings featuring panoramic views of Parisian boulevards and other panopticon sights. The 1889 world fair is perhaps most famous for having produced the Eiffel Tower as its central-visual spectacle, which provided a global view of the city of Paris as symbolic center of a global world. The 1889 world fair also boasted a large exhibit of pavilions on "The History of Habitation," which represented human habitats from the viewpoint of the Western "exotic": the huts of native Samoans, Guatemalans, Moroccans—a global theme park illustrating the virtual village. The fair's scopically charged, supposedly global views of Paris *as the world* are recalled in this "Souvenirs of Paris" booklet, with photo-like engravings of a "Panorama of the Seine" (Fig 2.3). This bird's-eye view of the

Figure 2.3 Engraving titled "Panorama of the Seine," in tourist booklet *Souvenirs de Paris,* published for the Universal Exposition of 1889. Courtesy of the Bibliothèque de la Ville de Paris.

Figure 2.4 Engraving titled "Avenue of the *Champs Elysées*," in *Souvenirs de Paris*. Courtesy of the Bibliothèque de la Ville de Paris.

heart of Paris originates from its central island sector, the *Ile de la Cité*, and extends as the spectator appears to hover above the Seine, from yet another—but wholly imaginary—*Tour Eiffel*.

The Seine River looks like a regulated, cement-carved channel, forceful and authoritarian, like Haussmann's boulevards. Other engravings in the souvenir booklet depict the boulevards themselves, like "The Avenue of the *Champs-Elysées*" (Fig. 2.4). This image repeats the scopic trajectory of the panopticon prison guard from the field of the missing spectator. In the field, the boulevard appears to rise up; the boulevard wends its rigid angularity into apparent infinity because of the diminishing perspective. Scenic representations of other boulevards and historic monuments are juxtaposed in the same souvenir booklet with symbols of industry and commerce, in collages that depict the scenic *Place St. Michel* and the *Place du Châtelet*, along with the edifice of the Palace of Industry (Fig. 2.5). These collages, presented as casually jostled photo-images from a personal album, poignantly render the staid authority of the social panopticon in tandem with "personal," "free," "spontaneous" capital enterprise. They remind us that "the society of the spectacle"—Gilles Debord's famous phrase—is a symbol of the commodity, and that consumer capitalism reproduces masters and slaves alike who bow down before the pictorial commodity fetish. To see down the vanishing point of the *Champs-Elysées*, this souvenir booklet and others like it suggest, is to see into the far reaches of the global economy

Figure 2.5 Engraving-collage titled "The Palace of Industry," in *Souvenirs de Paris.* Courtesy of the Bibliothèque de la Ville de Paris.

as commodity, which, like "woman," like "reality," is reproduced through visual enterprise.

Meta-images of Paris as "the world" are reality's ultimate illusions, as seen through the capitalistic enterprise of the world fair. The fair, the "universal exposition," helped to define the global mass spectator for a changing century of vision, helped to generate the subjectivity of a passive but potent symbolic male masochist, who peers out (bobs his head in and out) between the lines in *L'Education sentimentale.* In his notes for the Introduction to the *Paris Guide* of 1867, Victor Hugo wrote that the city of Paris "does not belong to a people, but to people . . . the human race has a right to Paris." In this statement, Hugo suggests that a global cosmopolitanism exists and is inherent within the Parisian masses who, necessarily, disavow nationhood and narrow chauvinistic identity. Hugo adds that "France, with sublime detachment, understands this." Hugo may have described Paris as the center of a new subject of nonidentity—a masochistic identity for the masses. But his image of "France," in its "sublime detachment," is laced with more than a little French chauvinism.

Charles Baudelaire echoed some of Hugo's duality and a self-deprecating pride, in a series of articles written for *Le Pays* newspaper on how to view displayed products at the 1855 world fair. Baudelaire, on behalf of this early world fair, sums up the concept of a global spectator; he describes a spectator who has given up narrow regionalism in favor of a wider "sympathy." In terms that distinctly echo the words of the eighteenth-century

Hume, Baudelaire describes the perfect "critic" and "spectator" of the fair as a "solitary traveler," who has obtained "the divine grace of Cosmopolitanism," who has become, no less, "a man of the world." It is this "solitary traveler," without a world, who becomes the most worldly spectator, who is best positioned to see, to experience, a sympathy that only the spectacle's "live" and "penetrating" qualities can offer:

> And if I transport him [the worldly spectator] to a faraway country, I am sure that if the astonishments of the arrival are great, if becoming accustomed is long . . . the sympathy will be sooner or later so live, so penetrating, that it will create in him a new world of ideas, a world that will be an integral part of himself and will accompany him in memories until death. (187)

Baudelaire describes a detached *sublime* spectator—using Hugo's term. For this sublime spectator, the spectacle is all, and the vivacity of the performing object is like a woman, "reality" sought after, and, in this search, mesmerizing.

THREE

Giving Isabel an "Ado" (Adieu): Sympathy and Sadomasochism in Henry James's Preface to *The Portrait of a Lady*

Like Flaubert, Henry James seeks to create "the illusion of reality," as one critic notes, through the novel's visual form; he imagines himself a painter who "begins with 'nature,' and then organizes and shapes his perceptions into an aesthetically appropriate form."[1] In James's essay "The Art of Fiction," published in 1884 at the height of his commercial success, he wrote that "the air of reality" is "the supreme virtue of a novel"; therefore, the novelist's job

> competes with his brother the painter in *his* attempt to render the look of things, the look that conveys their meaning, to catch the colour, the relief, the expression, the surface, the substance of the human spectacle. (610—James's emphasis)

In the "look," for James, is "the *sense* of reality" that any "good novel" must "possess."[2] It was the French school of realism, out of which Flaubert's novels emerged, that inspired James's heightened sense of the visual in portraying "reality," in offering a view of life—as James put it in "The Art of Fiction"—"*without* rearrangement" (613—James's emphasis).

The French "realist, descriptive novel," according to James in an essay on Flaubert, "sprang out of Balzac, began in its effort at intensity of illusion where Balzac stopped, and . . . whether or not it has surpassed him, has at least exceeded him" ("Charles de Bernard and Gustave Flaubert" 198). While James consistently heaped praise upon the early nineteenth-century novelist Honoré de Balzac, he was more divided in his appraisal of Flaubert, a "master"—he used the word taciturnly—who followed. His first essay on Flaubert classified the latter author among the "Minor French Novelists," in an essay published by that title in 1876. There James expressed reservations about the school of French realism in general and Flaubert's novels in particular. Even his admiration for what he calls Flaubert's "masterpiece,"

Madame Bovary, is ambiguously stated in this first essay. He describes the novel as the story of "a pretty young woman who lives, socially and morally speaking, in a hole, and who is ignorant, foolish, flimsy, unhappy . . . sinks deeper into duplicity, debt, despair, and arrives on the spot . . . at a pitiful tragic end" ("Minor French Novelists" 80). More critical yet is James's assessment of *L'Education sentimentale,* whose protagonist, Frédéric, "is positively too poor for his part, too scant for his charge," who creates "a kind of embarrassment" for the reader.[3]

These harsh critical views about Flaubert's subjects are more telling about James's own work than that of the French novelist. Read in tandem with the generous appraisal of Flaubert in a revised version of the essay published two years la'er,[4] James's views appear shifting; and they help us to trace James's aesthetic evolution. Re-evaluations of Emma Bovary, in the later essay, begin by adopting the original argument from "Minor French Novelists":

> the reader may protest against a heroine who is "naturally depraved." You are welcome, he may say, to make of a heroine what you please . . . but in mercy do not set us down to a young lady of whom, on the first page, there is nothing better to be said than that" ("Charles de Bernard" 205)

But James then defends Flaubert's "lady," because she is so *real:*

> Madame Bovary is typical, like all powerfully conceived figures in a fiction. There are a great many potential Madame Bovarys, a great many young women, vain, ignorant, leading ugly, vulgar, intolerable lives. ("Charles de Bernard" 205–6)

A novel "prosecuted for immorality," writes James, is actually "the pearl of 'Sunday reading.'" He declares: "Every out-and-out realist who provokes serious meditation may claim that he is a moralist" ("Charles de Bernard" 200–1). Here James's voice is no longer that of a Sunday-school sentimentalist providing proper fictive subjects. It is that of the moral representationalist, for whom even the most scandalous view of reality must be portrayed in the name of a greater moral landscape.

In this chapter, I suggest that James pushed his moral vision even further—to the brink of decay and extinction—in a later essay, the 1908 Preface to *The Portrait of a Lady.* I read the Preface to his New York Edition of the novel as a radical critique of James's own nineteenth-century visual-realism method, whose aesthetic value he once had argued for in "The Art of Fiction." The Preface critiques James's method in a larger statement about masculine sentiment, and its moral but also representational problems of sympathy. The invention of Isabel Archer, an innocent and betrayed heroine, is the legacy of eighteenth-century Richardsonian sentiment, and natural-law permutations into nineteenth-century American Transcendentalism. But the fuller visual method portraying Isabel is the product of nineteenth-century realism, as cultivated by Flaubert. Both sentiment and realism rely upon the sado-erotic perversions of the spectator. The sentimental narrator of Richardson creates identification and "resemblance" by promoting moral sympathy for victims like Clarissa. The omniscient narrator of Flaubert—like the universal eye of the Transcendentalist visionary—creates identification through *visual* resemblance, conjuring up a pictorially identifiable "world." Both narrational methods rely upon sympathy to generate their visually perverse acts. The Preface to *The Portrait of a Lady* calls attention to these perversions, which structure a novel James had written some twenty-seven years earlier and which was a popular success.

The Preface is an astounding, if subliminal, analysis of the sado-masochistic voyeurism and fetishism that pervades sentimental realism as James practiced it in his mid-century novels—and as sentimental realism evolved through fin-de-siècle technological entertainments. I say "subliminal," because what James observes about visuality, sympathy, technology, and power must be read through the poetics of a highly artful and deconstructive rhetoric. While James's prefaces in general to the New York Edition of his novels traditionally are read as remarks upon "the art of the novel" as a form, to paraphrase R. P. Blackmur, critics tend to read them straightforwardly, for their expository content, not their dense poeticism. One exception is Sara Blair, who claims that formal metaphors about "vision" in the Preface to *The Portrait of a Lady* reveal "a convincing self-portrait of the author" as "Master" of vision (90). Blair remarks that Jamesian "Mastery" is tied to surveillance and representational control, an insight echoed by Carol Schloss and Mark Seltzer in connecting themes of photography, visuality, and power in James's novels. I explore these issues as they emerge in the Preface to *The Portrait of a Lady*. But I argue that they do so not only to mask "the foundation of [James's] authorship in more literal forms of surveillance," in visual acts of "insight and recognition," as Blair writes (96), but also to *un*mask "authority" in images about vision-making.[5]

Metaphorical design in this Preface underscores novelistic "design" as a whole: the *designs* upon an ill-used heroine, and a narrative spectator who, like his reader, wants to be spectacularly entertained. In the Preface, James intuits the cinematic theories that would associate the portrayal of the heroine with a male voyeur's fetishism. Through an analysis of visual power, the Preface suggests that sympathetic portraits of female problems are morally-representationally undermined by the much graver problem of sympathy itself.

The Preface's critique of sentiment and sympathy begins as "James" turns the spotlight on himself, the "visionary" author of *The Portrait of a Lady*. In the Preface, "authorship" becomes a problem, too, when authorial point of view is dislocated from its own self-reference. The Preface narrator exists as a subject only in a series of vicissitudinous, shifting subjectivities adopted during the course of the Preface rhetoric. These various subjectivities suggest postures that are sentimental, sadistic, and masochistic, respectively. Reproducing a metaphorical structure that, in turn, reproduces the metaphorical structure in the novel, they loosely trace a beginning, a middle, and an end as we move through the Preface. Their transformability, one into the other, reflects the vicissitudes of sadomasochistic desire described by Freud. And their projective instability recalls the illusionary qualities of the linguistic subject described by Benveniste, in fictive, speaking, and "spoken" subject narrative positions.[6]

Each subject suggests a position, inflected by a controlling visual metaphor. This metaphor serves to recreate and re-envision sadomasochistic visual effects from the novel. These metaphors are actually clusters, or groups of related images. The Preface begins with a metaphor cluster connoting nature: images associated with the sentimental stance of a narrative subject who sympathetically identifies with—who cannot be separated from—the female fictive subject, Isabel. The Preface continues with a metaphor group that suggests visual architecture: images associated with a sadistic voyeur, who gains identity when he symbolically separates from the female subject—and perceives her image as his object. The Preface concludes with a metaphor group connoting money. Through the latter metaphor, the speaking subject re-identifies with the female subject, but as a masochistic "spoken" subject of the mass audience.

The Preface may suggest that the heroine's subjectivity, like her "femininity," relies upon sentimental acts of visual subjugation.[7] But the Preface also suggests that to give Isabel an "ado"—to grant her an entertainment narrative form—does in Isabel *and* her author, the novel's visionary Master. Identified with the "spoken" subject of cultural femininity, a gendered stereotype for mass-entertainment audiences,[8] Isabel's author is both Master of vision and sadomasochistic pervert. The Preface analyzes how sentimental realism works as sadomasochistic form. And it intuits sadomasochism's role in twentieth-century mass entertainment.

Sentimental Nature and Isabel's "Origin"

Following a seemingly *mis*placed meditation on the novel's origin as its author is spellbound by a monumental view of Venice, the Preface's speaker invokes images of origin through nature metaphors like "germ" and "seed." The metaphors emphasize the visual metaphoricity that will flourish throughout the Preface. They also seduce the reader into the Preface's "original" sentimental point of view, one that is identified with the creative emergence of the heroine.

In the sentimental perspective that opens the Preface, the speaking subject is bonded with his heroine's image. Point of view suggests an excessive enthusiasm about the fictive subject, whose bounty is rendered in profuse images of a fertile, innocent Eden, a benign world identified with the "germ" of the female fictive subject. The speaker suggests she is his novelistic origin, his creative source, this "engaging young woman":

> Trying to recover here, for recognition, the germ of my idea, I see that it must have consisted not at all in any conceit of a "plot," nefarious name, in any flash, upon the fancy, of a set of relations, or in any one of those situations that, by a logic of their own, immediately fall, for the fabulist, into movement, into a march or a rush, a patter of quick steps; but altogether in the sense of a single character, the character and aspect of a particular engaging young woman, to which all the usual elements of a "*subject*," certainly of a setting, were to need to be super-added. (4—emphasis added)

This sentence offers not only words about natural growth but its rhetorical image, as the sentence seems to protrude into the crumbling old walls of Venice. Parenthetical clauses and an unrelenting cumulative structure figure a voluptuous vine. Sentences continue to blossom forth, excessively flowery, emerging reproductively from out of the "seed" image itself:

> Quite as interesting as the young woman herself . . . do I find . . . this projection of memory upon the whole matter of *growth*, in one's imagination. . . . These are the fascinations of the fabulist's art, these lurking forces of expansion, these necessities of *upspringing in the seed*, these beautiful determinations, on the part of the idea entertained, to grow as tall as possible, to push into the light and the air and thickly flower there. (4—emphasis added)

While this excessive language of nature establishes the original sentiments of the Preface-speaking subject, the image of excess itself figures sentimental identity as that which is excessively *over*identified. The image of the "upspringing in the seed" may charge the subject of speech with a reproductive excess, suggesting female agency as Mother Nature. However, the speaker's verbose style also charges the speaking subject with an excessive *human* nature, based in natural law and its evolution into sentiment. These enunciatory excesses of speech the speaker attributes to an excess in the "upspringing in the seed." The compacting of images about the speaker's own excess and the natural fictive excess of the female subject of speech renders a resemblance between two levels of narration: the speaker mirrors, and is bonded in sympathetic identification with, *his* Isabel.

The speaker's relationship to Isabel in the first section of the Preface reflects the "resemblance" feature Hume associates with sympathy. Hume writes of "the great uniformity we observe in the humours and turn of thinking of those of the same nation"; such "uniformity" is "resemblance," which arises from sympathy (316–17). Enacting sympathetic resemblance, the Preface speaker emphasizes his bond with Isabel through a theme of mutual "origins." Hume adds in his *2nd Enquiry* that the propensity for "great resemblance" among humans produces the "social virtues," which include "beneficence and humanity . . . natural affection and public spirit" (*Enquiry Concerning the Principles of Morals* 178–79). The Preface speaker who sees Isabel sentimentally constituted by such virtues sees himself constituted this way, as well. His affinity for the feminized "germ" of his fiction builds his own image of "beneficence and humanity" into what Fred Kaplan calls the "man of sentiment," a Victorian archetype of male sensitivity and benign intent. This hero with "the good and moral heart" can be traced back to Henry MacKenzie's protagonist in *The Man of Feeling* (1771); it also can be traced back to figures like Anna Howe's insipid but kind suitor, Mr. Hickman, from *Clarissa*—later reworked by Richardson in *Sir Charles Grandison* (1753–54). James's reconstitution of this literary male figure in the Preface, however, emphasizes the "man of feeling's" inversion of sexual difference. The man of sentiment, or "feeling," is rooted in seventeenth- and eighteenth-century appraisals of "true" feeling—which was associated with women in philosophical discourses linking them to maternal "feeling," tenderness, and emotionality, and thereby disassociating women from reason and public virtue.

But we have been arguing that the man of sentiment—exemplified by Belford in *Clarissa*—can be a voyeuristic sadist, as well. Indeed, the suggestion of sexual inversion in the early section of James's Preface alerts us to the speaker's voyeuristic narrative manipulations of "woman" to come. But at this point in the Preface, the speaker remains more positively identified with Isabel, his gender confusion reflecting a love of his creation—and a desire for self-effacement. She may be *his.* But she is also the author. She seems to "upspring" from "herself," naturally self-generating.

This originating quality of the subject of speech—her propensity for self-authorship—gives the appearance of a wholly independent and original nature, repeating this theme about Isabel from the novel. Other characters in the novel perceive Isabel to be quite original; for example, her sister Lilian is "distinctly conscious" of "two things in life": her lawyer-husband's "force in argument" and Isabel's "*originality*" (37—emphasis added). Isabel herself suggests that it is her originality and social independence that causes her to turn down Lord Warburton's marriage proposal: "the idea failed to support any enlightened prejudice in favour of the free exploration of life that she had hitherto entertained" (101). Marriage to a lord, while enhancing Isabel's financial worth, would subject her to aristocratic tradition and confine her to a landed estate. In the Preface, Isabel's self-image of originality is tied to her freedom, a fact recreated in a prose that invokes the subject of natural "origins"—a prose that itself runs untethered and "free": "the origin of one's wind-blown germs themselves . . . are the breath of life—by which I mean that life, in its own way, breathes them upon us," floating "into our minds by the current of life" (5).

The sympathetic nature that shows Isabel's independent nature to be like "wind-blown" images recalls the historical discourses about "human nature" *within* nature during the English and French Enlightenments. Lord Shaftesbury, for instance, made large claims about a naturally virtuous universe: "one System of a Globe or Earth," whose "strong Principle of Virtue lies at the bottom" (6, 17). Hume, the empiricist, argued cautiously in his *2nd Enquiry* that "the utility, resulting from the social virtues forms . . . a *part* of their merit"; so natural is the utility drive that "when we recommend even an animal or plant as *useful* and *beneficial,* we give it an applause and recommendation suited to its nature" (179—Hume's emphasis). Jean-Jacques Rousseau shifted the emphasis on nature toward man; in *Emile* (1762), his tract on "enlightened" child-rearing and education, the "natural man" was a man literally *out* of nature, born and left to run free within it, uncorrupted by urban civilization.[9] In the nineteenth century, the Transcendental movement borrowed Rousseau's romantic views of nature.

Ralph Waldo Emerson, for instance, presumed human nature to be closely allied with a beneficent natural world. In *Nature,* Emerson suggests that a mutual and mimetic relation exists between man and nature. "Nature," he writes, is "all which Philosophy distinguishes as the not me"— those "essences unchanged by man; space, the air, the river, the leaf" (22). Like Rousseau, Emerson argues here against a human nature that is *un*natural, or separate from nature. Emerson views nature as universally harmonious, presenting a harmony that reflects the natural benevolence in humankind: "In the tranquil landscape, and especially in the distant line of the horizon, man beholds somewhat as beautiful as his own nature" (24).

Yet a paradox exists in Emerson's language about a "man" both in and out of nature, best expressed in Emerson's image of "the Universal Being." This is a figure through which "Standing on the bare ground,—my head bathed by the blithe air and uplifted into infinite space,—all mean egotism vanishes. I become a transparent eyeball; I am nothing; I see all" (24). Emerson's image of the "Universal Being" suggests a human presence within nature that is also an absence, a figure at once objectified within and yet transcended out of nature. It is the Emersonian image of presence and absence within/without nature that best describes Isabel's representational self-image in the novel.[10]

Like the sentimental narrator of the Preface's early section, Isabel views her own sentimental image as if plucked out of a natural landscape, because of her original/originating view. Isabel describes her friend Henrietta Stackpole as "'a kind of emanation of the great democracy—of the continent, the country, the nation . . . she suggests it; she vividly figures it'" (87). This description is a displaced one for Isabel's view of herself—a pastoral vision resonating with Emerson's views of the free and open American range:

> "I like the great country stretching away beyond the rivers and across the prairies, blooming and smiling and spreading till it stops at the green Pacific! A strong, sweet, fresh odour seems to rise from it, and Henrietta—pardon my simile—has something of that odour in her garments." (88)

In this passage, Henrietta is also a figure for the colonialist doctrine of Manifest Destiny. Identified with the "original" virgin American wilderness, Isabel does not acknowledge that this wilderness was subject to systematic appropriation in the late nineteenth century. Instead, Isabel ignores the political-economic implications of her view, taking on the seeming neutrality of Emerson's "transparent eyeball" in her description. This transparent eyeball is that seemingly absent lens through which the perceiver sheds "egotism," and, being "nothing," sees "all." Isabel's description emerges similarly, from behind the enunciating power of the lens, screening the viewer's own persona from view.

Isabel's disregard for the political control of nature is linked to her sentimental view upon and about nature—and herself. James assumes this same disregard in "The Art of Fiction," published just a couple of years after *The Portrait of a Lady* ended its 1880–81 serial debut. James writes in this essay that the "good" novel transmits the "direct impression" of human "experience," reproducing life in an original form.[11] "The Art of Fiction" discursively renders James's sentimental faith in "direct" and "truthful" representation through novelistic realism. In a passage from *The Portrait of a Lady*, Isabel at least hints at possible distortions in her own self-representation, however. She does so in a narrative meditation upon her refusal to marry Lord Warburton:

> She herself was a character—she couldn't help being aware of that; and hitherto her visions of a completed consciousness had concerned themselves largely with moral images—things as to which the question would be whether they pleased her sublime soul. Lord Warburton loomed up before her. . . . a territorial, a political, a social magnate had conceived the design of drawing her into the system in which he rather invidiously lived and moved. (94–95)

Isabel possesses a *visual* awareness of her own original, representational image, not only in "her visions of a completed consciousness," but in her general self-posturing. The figure of Lord Warburton, who "loomed up before her," is also visual, even cinematic; and it exemplifies Isabel's narcissistic relation to others. But the presumption of self-detachment dominates Isabel's image-making. She mimics what Smith, in *The Theory of Moral Sentiments,* calls the "impartial spectator" of sympathy. Smith writes that the spectator is capable of self-judgment because he views himself as others view him: "We can never survey our own sentiments and motives . . . unless we remove ourselves . . . and endeavour to view them at a certain distance from us . . . to view them with the eyes of other people" (297). The "other" is a veritable "looking-glass" for the spectator (299).

Smith writes that sympathy emerges "by conceiving what we ourselves should feel in the like situation . . . by representing to us *what would be our own.* . . . (258—emphasis added). This theme of "other," of "distance," derives from Hume, who writes in the *Treatise* that, while sympathy may be "our own" experience, it nevertheless is founded on feeling for someone else: "relations are requisite to sympathy . . . by their influence in converting our ideas of the sentiments of others into the very sentiments, by means of the association betwixt the idea of their person and that of our own" (322). The "self" who experiences sympathy is relegated to a passive role, sometimes taking the form of masochism, as we have seen in Flaubert's *L'Education sentimentale.* But in *The Portrait of a Lady,* the fictive Isabel is more obvious in her self-aggrandizement and self-posturing than Frédéric. Isabel both *is* a character and views herself *as* a character like Lord Warburton, treating herself as a speaking subject, the controlling narrative figure over "self" and "world." So Isabel resembles—sometimes becomes one with—the novel's omniscient narrator, who hovers passively observant yet controlling over the mimetic landscape, Emerson's "universal being," "nothing" but seeing "all."

In the Preface to *The Portrait of a Lady,* the simultaneous passivity and power of the omniscient figure is suggested by its narrational design. Even as the Preface speaker sympathetically attributes creative agency to the female subject, her creativity is rendered passively: it emerges, plant-like, "into the light and the air" (4). At the same time, the presence of a speaking subject is disavowed; early in the Preface, the narrator-speaker recalls his friend and fellow novelist Ivan Turgenieff speak of "his own experience of the usual origin of the fictive picture" (4). While the theme of *being* a subject is emphasized in this statement, the statement itself seems to belong to Turgenieff: "He [Turgenieff] . . . *saw* them" (5)—those "persons, who hovered before him. . . . soliciting him"—"subject to the chances, the complications of existence. . . ."[12] The narrator's attributions to Turgenieff void any assertions that the Preface speaker might make. His identity has been twice displaced, enabling the narrator to elide responsibility for "the complications of existence" that sub*ject* characters to narrative events (the verb form of "subject," meaning to dominate).

When the Preface speaker cites Turgenieff, a subtle slippage of metaphors takes place. The group of metaphors connoting a free, original nature associated with Isabel and the sentimental point of view is *re*placed by
those metaphors connoting placement, form, and the architectural intervention of nature's "freedom." Significantly, the Preface speaker actually
(supposedly) quotes Turgenieff directly; the speaking subject's *re*placement
suggests a voice of someone who is like but is *not* the author, "James":

> If I watch them ["people" or subjects] long enough I see them come together,
> I see them *placed*. . . . How they look and move and speak and behave, always
> in the setting I have found for them, is my account of them—of which I dare
> say, alas, *que cela manque souvent d'architecture*. But I would rather, I think, have
> too little architecture than too much. . . . (5—James's emphasis)

"To arrive" at a story, in words attributed to Turgenieff, is to visualize a
structure for one's subjects, to "*see* them placed" (emphasis added). "To
place" is like "to see." In visualizing subjects, the speaking subject grants
them narrative form. Otherwise, these subjects of fiction remain vague,
unattached "wind-blown germs."

The slippage of metaphors provides a transition for narrative perspective in the Preface and a "new," more openly sadistic subject of speech. In
images of placement and architecture, which imply walls and separation,
symbolic damage is rendered the fictive Isabel, and her original, mimetic
"nature." The speaking subject now reveals the authorial control he once
exerted over his original "seed." Re-creating biblical patrilineage, in which
female maternity is conspicuously absent from the creation myth, the Preface speaker announces that his authorial task had been to pick up or gather
the "wind-blown germs"—the "seed" transformed into an image of
harvest—and to invest them with "the germinal property and authority" (5).
This shift in metaphorical reference alludes to images of free land versus
landedness from the novel. And it now implicates sentimental, Transcendental views of nature within a patriarchal social hierarchy. The shift in
metaphor, furthermore, introduces an economic image, one that will grow
in significance later in the Preface. At this moment, however, natural images
of "germ" and "seed" are simply exchanged for social images of "ground,"
"property," and "authority." The exchange signals a more general exchange,
from a point of view generated by an original, "natural," female subject and
self-author, to a point of view conferred upon that "subject" by an authoritarian agent of patriarchal narration.

A Sadistic "House": Going to the Movies

Architectural division in the Preface now appears to have separated the
fictive from the speaking subject. This separation actually was implied in the

beginning. But the sentimental voice of the speaker-narrator also denied separation. Now, the fictive female subject—with whom this speaker had seemed so fully identified—is clearly the speaker's external object.

An object, the female fictive figure becomes vulnerable to the speaker's critical, even punitive, stance in the Preface. As a figure of cultural femininity, she was always created passive and vulnerable to begin with, an object upon which the speaker might exert his aggression. But a shift in attitude marks the speaker's ambitions in the mid-section of the Preface. A movement or transaction of position seems to take place, from the speaker's longing for complete narcissistic identification with his female nature to his separation from it, his repudiation. Separation leads to a sense of newfound hostility and sadism toward his object. This hostility may reflect the male speaker's anxiety over his earlier association with femininity, and his anxiety over the loss of an original narcissistic attachment.

Whatever the motive, the shift from internal to external rendering of the object echoes the paradigm of love and hate explicated by Freud in his analyses of sadomasochistic vicissitudes. "Love" and "hate," or "pleasure" and "unpleasure," are structured upon the subject's relation to an object of desire, the (imagined) placement of the object within or without the self, according to Freud. He writes that hate is associated with an object perceived as external to the self, and "derives from the narcissistic ego's primordial repudiation of the external world. . . ." ("Instincts" 139). And he writes that love is associated with that which is internal to or identified with the self, "the relation of the ego to its source of pleasure" as the object is "incorporated into the ego" (135–36). Because hatred is involved in a "preliminary stage of loving," and because "frequent conflicts between the interests of the ego and those of love" exist, hatred can evolve through love itself ("Instincts" 139). These vicissitudes between subject and object create the erotic phenomenon of love and hate, sadism and masochism, in the dialectic. Freud's theory fits well here with Chancer's, suggesting that a sadomasochistic dialectic is created by an odd mixture of dependency and separation.

The vicissitudes of sadomasochism are embedded within the mechanics of voyeurism. Noting voyeurism's source in the desire for phenomenological control, Mulvey has said: "Voyeurism . . . has associations with sadism" (14). But Mulvey has argued that scopophilia, from which voyeurism derives, is a combination of acts of identification and separation. Christian Metz explains that "Voyeuristic desire, along with certain forms of sadism, is the only desire whose principle of distance symbolically and spatially evokes this fundamental rent" (*The Imaginary Signifier* 60). And yet what satisfies the pleasure-seeking voyeur is the concealment of narcissistic identification, of the projection of his own image.

As we have seen in novels by both Richardson and Flaubert, voyeurism is sadistic in its distancing power, which allows it to constrict and objectify a figure confined to "the controlling male gaze," quoting Mulvey's famous formulation (15). This gaze has a narrative function, which James's Preface intuits. Architectural metaphors that seem to loom up in the mid-section of the Preface emphasize narration's voyeuristic and sadistic content. Architectural frames of place, as well as of reference, control and distort "original" and natural forms, the Preface suggests.

We are introduced to the voyeur's socialized sadistic control, inflicted upon Isabel's natural "origins," when we are told that the "seed" has grown in an ungenuine "soil," thereby losing its "value." Such statements recall those of "The Art of Fiction," which insists upon a "true" and "free" representation. In assessing the worth of a given subject," the Preface speaker asks: "is it valid . . . is it genuine, is it sincere, the result of some direct impression . . . of life?" (6), almost mimicking the language of "The Art of Fiction." In the Preface, an allusion to the speaker's identification with the original "seed," concepts of morality, truth, and "value," again are fused with images of natural growth: "the soil out of which his [the author's] subject springs . . . its ability to 'grow' with due . . . freshness and straightness any vision of life, represents . . . the projected morality" (6). That "the quality and capacity of that soil" will *not* bear "due freshness and straightness" of "vision" (6) is suggested in a pun on "mould." The "artist's humanity" can be either "a *rich* and magnificent medium" or "a *comparatively poor and ungenerous* one"; "The *high price* of the novel as a literary *form* . . . tends to burst, with *a latent extravagance,* its *mould*" (6–7—emphasis added). In the dual meanings of "mould"—a frame around an architectural aperture or a fungus that decays organic matter—we remain hinged between two perspectives, two metaphorical systems.

In the House of Fiction extended metaphor, the Preface's "governing metaphor" (Blair 91), the sentimental speaker and the sadistic voyeur meet head on. Images of originality and freedom collide with images of limitation and voyeuristic, panopticon-like, distortion and control:

> The house of fiction has in short not one window, but a million—a number of possible windows not to be reckoned, rather; every one of which has been pierced, or is still pierceable, in its vast front, by the need of the individual vision and by the pressure of the individual will. These apertures, of dissimilar shape and size, hang so, all together, over the human scene. . . . They are but windows at the best, mere holes in a dead wall, disconnected, perched aloft; they are not hinged doors opening straight upon life. (7)

The beginning of this passage might well be read as a statement about the novel's hermeneutic openness and representational form, echoing James's statements in "The Art of Fiction" that a "good" novel invokes "sincerity" and a "direct impression" of life. As the tone of the passage darkens, however, limitation of perspective is tied to novelistic point of view, revising James's earlier statements. The "million" windows "of dissimilar shape and size"—implying an originality and independence of "vision"—become "windows at the best, mere holes in a dead wall, disconnected" (8); a *blockage* of vision is indicated, a *separation* within and from "life." Recalling the pun on "mould," the passage conjures up yet a more ominous implication of the word. In British dialectical usage, "mould," a variation on "mold," is "the earth of the burying ground" (*Merriam Webster's*). The "soil out of which his [the author's] subject springs" is not only a moldy soil full of natural decay but one in which cadavers are "placed." The vision of the "million" windows may be a multiple one. But those windows do not offer "hinged doors opening straight upon life" (8). Rather, they offer the circuitous, perverse "vision" of the dead.

The reference to a *house* of fiction alludes to the many houses that form settings within the novel, each of which become spatial enclosures symbolizing the sadistic entrapment of Isabel in marriage to Gilbert Osmond. Indeed, a chain of houses signifies Isabel's narrative trajectory: from the house in Albany, her literal, figural "origin"; to Gardencourt, in "creepy" but benign antiquity; to the Florentine house, with its "imposing front," where Isabel meets Osmond; to the house shared with Osmond in Rome, "the house of darkness, house of dumbness, the house of suffocation."[13] The Preface's House of Fiction echoes the novel's description of Osmond's Florentine house, whose "heavy lids" have "no eyes. . . . It had a narrow garden. . . . The windows of the ground-floor . . . were massively crossbarred . . . jealous apertures. . . ." (195–96). The "jealous apertures" are architectural, reminding us of Bentham's prison architecture, for example, the design for the Panopticon House of Industry (Fig. 3.1). The multiple "crossbarred" window images, reflected in Samuel Bentham's drawing, are alluded to in the House of Fiction metaphor in the Preface: "in short not one window, but a million . . . every one of which has been pierced, or is still pierceable, in its vast front . . . by the pressure of the individual will" (8). The "jealous apertures" also invoke the structure of photography, especially "moving pictures." The apertures recall the "aperture" of a panopticon viewer. And they recall the voyeuristic apparatus of cinema discussed by Mulvey and Metz.

For the House of Fiction is also a *movie* house, a figure that, by design, is a figure for the novel itself as another panopticon architectural imprint.[14] James had attended at least two films in London by the time he wrote the prefaces, the 75-minute film of the Corbett-Fitzsimmons world championship fight (1897), made on site in Nevada but distributed around the world; and a Biograph short of the Boer War by W.K.L. Dickson (1900), an American who had helped to develop the Edison Kinetoscope, a "peep-show"

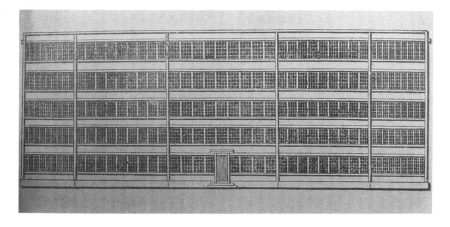

Figure 3.1 Panopticon House of Industry, Samuel Bentham (engineer brother of Jeremy) and Samuel Bunce, 1797.

mechanism that, along with Emile Reynaud's optical-projection theater, generated the first cinematic apparatus, the cinematograph. And James had employed other references to early cinema in his fiction. For example, in a short story published at the time of the New York Edition and their prefaces, James imagistically alludes to the cinematograph. "Crapy Cornelia" introduces its heroine with "a startling and apt visual metaphor" derived from early cinematic photography, as Adele Tinter notes: "the abrupt looming up of figures" as they approach the camera from the rear (*The Museum World of Henry James* 191). When Cornelia appears before the hero White Mason, she seems, according to James, " 'an incongruous object usurping at a given instant the privilege of the frame. . . . The incongruous object was a woman's head . . . that came nearer and nearer, while it met his eyes, after the manner of images in the cinematograph' " (James quoted in Tinter, *Museum World* 188). Furthermore, throughout the production of the New York Edition, James displayed an interest in still photography. Alvin Langdon Coburn was commissioned to photograph a series of architectural monuments for the edition's frontispiece illustrations. And James asserted a "passive watchfulness" over the photography process, Schloss comments, having had a "deep premeditation about the image he wanted."[15]

The "dead wall" in the House of Fiction metaphor suggests the "passive watchfulness" James asserted as *surrogate* photographer over the making of the frontispiece photographs. The "dead wall" also is an image for the photographic image itself, a replacement of an original "natural" view—that, conversely, of a "dead wall," the prison as architectural monument. Given James's fascination with cinema photography, as well as with the photographing of the monuments that "housed" the New York Edition, we might view the "dead wall" of the House of Fiction as a metaphor for a movie screen that also resembles a panopticonic cell. Indeed, a distinctly cinematic voyeuristic scene seems to prevail in the panopticon prison, exemplified by a photograph of one early twentieth-century institution, the Panopticon Rotunda at the Isle of Pines, Cuba, in which each crossbarred cell is illuminated as if a projected image (Fig. 3.2). A distinctly cinematic voyeuristic scene charges the imagery of James's House of Fiction passage, as well. At each individual window stands a peeping Tom,

> a figure with a pair of eyes, or at least with a field-glass, which forms, again and again, for observation, a unique instrument, insuring to the person making use of it an impression distinct from every other. *He and his neighbors are watching the same show,* but one seeing more where the other sees less, one seeing black where the other sees white. . . . And so on. . . . (6—emphasis added)

Figure 3.2 Panopticon Rotunda, Isle of Pines, Cuba, 1932, from *Illustrated London News.* Photo reproduced by permission from Robin Evans, *The Fabrication of Virtue: English Prison Architecture 1750–1840,* Cambridge UP.

The "show" is a *moving* picture spectacle; the shiftiness of the "black" and "white" reproduces for the reader a moving, if also "dead," series of photographic images, evocative of cinema. The figure with a pair of eyes" or "a field-glass" is a complex "figure" representing the multiple technological views required by cinema: that of the camera lens and projector; the window-like frames of celluloid containing the photographed image; the "original" eyes of the cinematographer himself; the eyes of potential audience spectators who view the final product. The infiltration of nonliving technological equipment into the bodily "natural" view of human spectators is yet another sadistic suggestion implied by vision. The distance and yet bodily immediacy of a spectatorial point of view is concretely suggested in the figure of the peeping Tom, whose voyeuristic "passive watchfulness" is reasserted in the image of audience spectators: "He and his neighbors . . . watching the same show . . . one seeing black where the other sees white. . . ."

The image of the "dead wall" suggests the dichotomy of presence and absence that structures the voyeur of the panopticon and also of "sympathy." Theories about voyeurism, specifically as it functions in cinema, are usually ascribed to classic cinema, that genre of films produced by Hollywood studios in the 1930s and 1940s and known for their duplicitous methods of sustaining audience identification. Nevertheless, some of these theories are applicable to preclassic cinema, as well. The early films James saw in London did not employ the so-called verisimilitude style attributed to classic cinema's continuity-editing techniques, which attempt to replicate nature in a smooth-flowing narrative-in-time and to imply a position for the spectator through the close mapping of cinematic shots, thereby easing processes of suture. As we have seen in Flaubert's *L'Education sentimentale,* it is the effacement of the spectator that creates suture, binding the spectator into the apparently seamless filmic world.

Binding the spectator into the "world" creates the appearance of plenitude, the fullness of representational "nature." Metz writes that a "fundamental disavowal" exists in classic films, which strive to obliterate "all traces of the enunciation" ("Story/Discourse" 544, 546). In the preclassic films seen by James, however, narrative enunciation was handled differently. As film historian Charles Musser writes, in films produced before 1907, "the viewer is a voyeur, but not, as in later cinema, apparently effaced" (4). But if the viewer, or spectator, is more obviously present within early films, voyeurism may be more apparent. Many preclassic films rely upon a more obvious spectatorial role, such as the Corbett-Fitzsimmons fight film that James saw in London in 1897 during its sensational, world-wide distribution. In this film, the camera itself was the featured spectator; the fight was actually staged to be filmed, since fights were illegal in most states, and only a widely viewed film could reap significant profits. So the "battery of cameras" filming events "were given the best seats in the house" (Musser 195–96). The film reminds us of the camera's importance because of its straight-on view of the fight scene.

If the obviousness of the camera in the Corbett-Fitzsimmons film somehow detracts from the perverseness associated with voyeurism, another writer on early cinema, Richard DeCordova, speaks of a curiously hidden spectatorial effect in the first film ever produced by the Lumière brothers in Paris, a film showing workers leaving the factory, *La sortie des usines Lumière* (1895). At the end of the fifty-second film, DeCordova writes that "two figures [are] staring out [of the view framed by the camera] as if they, too, were witness to some new sort of spectacle." These figures suggest "the camera, which is absent" (76). As in the enunciatory absence of classic Hollywood films, these two figures of *La sortie des usines Lumière* stand in for a missing camera and, thereby, "naturalize" and humanize—also repress—its technological lens. The repression of the camera, as well as the spectator in the theater, curiously serves to negate but also to heighten the voyeuristic, spectatorial effect.

It is this paradox that psychoanalytic film critics attribute to the illusion of verisimilitude in classic film narratives. Again, by the 1908 publication of the prefaces, James would not have viewed films adopting a "verisimilitude" style—in the formal sense of that term. But well before its stylistic development, "reality" in cinema had become a formal theme. Although perhaps not employing sophisticated continuity-editing techniques, these early films tend to promote a documentary image of themselves. That is, they presume to replicate *events as they were filmed,* a style that generates verisimilitude myths of its own. However awkward these films may seem to viewers today steeped in Hollywood images, the documentary style tends to claim a representation of "reality" face on, as the camera lens records it.

André Gaudreault notes that films need only imply a *sense* of chronology and movement within time to produce a fictive narrative effect. In the example, again, of the fifty-second Lumière film of the workers, Gaudreault writes that it reveals "some structuring" mechanisms—like those of sequencing and transformation cited by narratologists like Tzetvan Todorov—when the factory gates open to let the workers out and then close again. A slightly later narrative-film prototype is Edwin S. Porter's *The Great Train Robbery* (1903), whose action develops "with a clear linearity of time, space and logic," notes David Bordwell and Kristen Thompson (456). And early director D.W. Griffith, in his 1908 directing debut—the year the New York edition prefaces were published—brought "a strong narrative motivation" to film technique, as well. As early as 1910, two years following the publication of the prefaces, several continuity-editing techniques associated with later Hollywood mimeticism were in use. These included the eye-line match, which encodes the key principles of suture and spectatorship, as an initial shot shows a character looking into space and a follow-up shot reveals the image supposedly viewed.

If the concept of "reality" as a style seems to be incipient to cinema as form, James's Preface to *The Portrait of a Lady* reveals the way in which the voyeuristic principles of spectatorship had been operative in the novel as form well before cinema's development. Certainly Mulvey's claim that filmic voyeurism's "sadistic" element "fits in well with narrative" is suggested by the narrative structure of *The Portrait of a Lady*. "Sadism demands a story, depends on making something happen, forcing a change in another person, a battle of will and strength, victory/defeat, all occurring in a linear time with a beginning and an end," Mulvey states (14). The chronological events of James's novel drive home its sadistic aspects: from Isabel's first appearance at Gardencourt framed by "the ample doorway" (25), to the "vision" of various authorial plots that intend to see her married. Isabel is the subject of plots by Mrs. Touchett, who would like her to marry Lord Warburton, and by Henrietta, who would like her to marry Caspar Goodwood.

However, Isabel ultimately is subjected to the more insidious plot of Madame Merle, who claims to have "no natural place," no house, no plot, of her own (171). Throughout the novel, Madame Merle refuses to speak about herself, blaming this fact on her self-effacing modesty. She tells Isabel: "'I'm old and stale and faded. I'm of no more interest than last week's newspaper'" (170). But we also learn that Madame Merle is "never idle" (167), and that she has been "a dweller in many lands," with "social ties in a dozen different countries" (168–69). Her character, like her homes and "plots," is a multiple one, although she disavows her own placement within representation. Madame Merle embodies the perverse, sadistic machinations of sympathy in the novel, a matrimonial agent *par excellence* and the chief novel-plot perpetrator.

Sadism in the novel perversely is enhanced when Madame Merle, along with accomplice Gilbert Osmond, makes her plot invisible. Yet, however invisible her machinations, Madame Merle is the Transcendental witness, a being who "sees all." Another surreptitious, sympathetic plot-perpetrator is Ralph Touchett, Isabel's cousin and friend. Only Ralph warns Isabel against marriage to Osmond, saying, "'you're going to be put into a cage'" (288). Although Ralph seems to escape the role of narrative sadist— the role of plotter against (about) Isabel—Ralph's sympathy toward Isabel actually is a function of his controlling visual image-making. Sharing in Osmond's passion for collecting art, Ralph views Isabel as an *objet d'art*. He is a voyeur who wants to watch her, to literally see what she is "going to do with herself. . . . conscious she was an entertainment of a high order" (64, 63). Ralph fetishizes Isabel's visual nature thus:

"a real little passionate force [Isabel's] to see at play is the finest thing in nature. It's finer than the finest work of art—than a Greek bas relief, than a great Titian, than a Gothic cathedral." (63)

When Ralph tells his father "'I should like to put money in her purse'" (160), he seems not to hear his allusion to *Othello's* Iago. The sentimental passion Ralph bears Isabel is conflicted and also enhanced by his voyeuristic sympathy. Like Madame Merle, he controls Isabel, while appearing "selfless."

Isabel Endowed

Following the House of Fiction metaphor in the Preface, the speaking subject behaves like Ralph, like Osmond, a voyeuristic collector of female art. He suggests that Isabel is "an acquisition" he "had made" (7)—as in making art, making a financial investment, "making" someone (putting something over on someone), or "making" a woman. The speaker is now "in complete possession" of "Isabel," his artistic project. Yet what he calls "the history of the growth of one's imagination" (8) has been "taken over" by strangling images of nature (as weeds), a "take-over" that is also a financial one, when metaphors for money in the Preface "take over" those for nature and architecture. Were one to write a "history of the growth of one's imagination" (which, of course, is what the speaker does):

> One would describe then what, at a given time, had extraordinarily happened to it [the imagination] . . . how . . . it had been able to take over (take over straight from life) such and such a constituted, animated figure or form. The figure has . . . *been* placed—placed in the imagination that detains it, preserves, protects, enjoys it, conscious of its presence in the . . . heterogeneous back-shop of the mind. . . . (7—James's emphasis)

This passage sketches a microcosm of the Preface metaphorical structure: metaphors move from those connoting natural ("straight") representation, to those connoting architectural place—particularly the place of commercial transaction. The speaker's recollection of a "pious desire but to place my treasure right" (8) suggests that his previous sentimental piety toward Isabel is linked to his current sadistic and financially motivated desire to "place" her. Isabel is now an object on a "backshop" shelf, an embarrassing commodity of exchange. Trying to recall his original sentiments in composing Isabel's story, the speaking subject now alludes to his sadistic and commercial motives:

> "Place the centre of the subject in the young woman's consciousness," I said to myself, "and you get as interesting and as beautiful a difficulty as you could

wish. Stick to *that*—for the centre; put the heaviest weight into that scale, which will be so largely the scale of her relation to herself . . . To depend upon her and her little concerns wholly to see you through will necessitate, remember, your really 'doing' her." (10–11—James's emphasis)

In the novel, Ralph's desire "to see" Isabel is related to his question, "what was she going *to do* with herself?" (64—emphasis added). He tries to answer that question by seeing Isabel endowed with an inheritance. In the Preface, the emphasis on the verb "to do" previously had been made a nominal form, when we were told that what the author "was in for" was "for positively organizing an *ado* about Isabel Archer" (9—emphasis added). An "ado" etymologically is related to the verb "to do," a noun in the American vernacular: a "to-do," an event that creates "much trouble or difficulty" over something relatively insignificant (*Merriam Webster's*). The Preface speaker suggests that the plot of *The Portrait of a Lady* was organized around the "question . . . what will she *do*" (James's emphasis). If the novel is that form which makes "an ado about something" (9), the allusion to Shakespeare also suggests that "something" is "nothing": that Isabel's patronage by Ralph is trivial and misplaced. The word "ado" darkens considerably in light of the Shakespeare allusion and through its French homonym "adieu," literally meaning to commend to God (as if in dying), as well as an English archaic literary expression for "farewell." Read through the multiple connotations suggested by etymology, literary reference, and homonymic sound, to "positively [organize] an ado about Isabel Archer" (9)—the authorial task—is to give Isabel a spectacular (specular) demise: "to do" her in.

The sadistic aspect of "doing" the female fictive subject, through representation, is carried out in a further discussion of "doing" other literary female figures. The Preface speaker writes that the "full . . . substance" of what he calls the novel consists of the fact that "the Isabel Archers, and even much smaller female fry, insist on mattering" (9). He seems to grant textual-moral approbation to the "substance" of what he calls "frail vessels" from the nineteenth-century novel tradition, specifically George Eliot's heroines "Hetty Sorrel and Maggie Tulliver and Rosamond Vincy and Gwendolen Harleth" (9). Approbation becomes condemnation, however, in the misogynistic connotation of "frail vessels." Borrowed from Eliot's *Daniel Deronda,* the phrase might imply those female persons infused with a certain grace. But a "vessel" is also a conveyor of fluids: bodily fluids, as in a female body "vessel," the vaginal canal. The Preface speaker implies a graphic reference to female sexuality by using Eliot's phrase as a weapon against her own "frail vessel," "George Eliot's 'treasure' " (10). While "treasure" alludes to his earlier statement, the "pious desire" to place his "treasure right" (8), the second reference to "treasure" operates without sentimental illusions of piety: it associates the work of a great woman novelist with the commodified version of her own female sexual anatomy.

In appearing to overvalue Eliot's achievement, the Preface speaker *de*values it through the sexualized image. He exposes her, in essence, to a kind of literary sexual harassment. Any "value" placed upon Eliot or her female protagonists, therefore, is not a morally laudatory one. Rather, the "value" is a patriarchal one for the unbroken hymen, transformed by capitalist entertainment culture into monetary value through narratives of the harassed maiden (and author).

Early in the novel, Isabel insists that she is immune to problems of money. She tells Mrs. Touchett, " 'I'm not stupid; but I don't know anything about money' " (35). In the novel, Isabel's lack of knowledge about money, of course, leaves her subject to the very monetary issues she believes herself to ignore. In the Preface, Isabel's lack is now a sexually graphic one. The Preface speaker, whose hostility toward Isabel seems on the rise, reports that she is "an intelligent but presumptuous girl," who finds "*itself endowed* with the high attributes of a Subject. . . ." (8—emphasis added). "Like other "frail vessels" who "insist on mattering," Isabel is both objectified here and "endowed." Her financial endowment may have been plundered in the novel by savvy fortune-hunters. But her sexual endowment—her "treasure's" substance—is more "fully" plundered by the Preface speaker.

Her figure is representationally "undone." The sadistic Preface speaker implies that the figure of Isabel, standing in the "ample doorway" of Garden-court (an ironic Eden), is not as "ample" as it may seem. "The ample doorway" is a passageway revealing an "ample" emptiness, within which the natural female figure stands, paradoxical figure of fullness and emptiness. The Preface suggests that Isabel is the "lynch pin" Mulvey writes is "woman" in classic cinema, the image holding mimesis together. In suggesting that the body of woman binds together the fullness and emptiness, absence and presence, at the heart of "realism," Mulvey, of course, draws upon the Lacanian concept of the Imaginary and its integral event, the mirror stage. The appeal of narrative cinema relies upon "structures of fascination" that restage Imaginary events prior to Symbolic division, encoding the contradictions of self-division that the subject anticipates.[16] "Woman" is that figure of figures encoding subjectivity processes, since the female body invokes the castration anxiety of the male subject. The (male) subject's overvaluation and sexual endowment of the female body conceals and reveals (in a game of peek-a-boo) the anxiety the female image contains.

Voyeurism and exhibitionism are interrelated perversions, according to Freud.[17] The fetishistic female is the male voyeuristic subject's "exhibitionist like," notes Mulvey, a psychoanalytic projection through which the male avoids "the burden of sexual objectification" (12). As the male voyeur looks, he creates a "split between spectacle and narrative" (12). "Woman's" intense visuality through fetishism, her overabundant presence as image, "tends to work against the development of a story line, to freeze the flow of action. . . ." (Mulvey 11). Meanwhile, the male voyeur and his look generate the active progression of the story; the male exists as "a figure in a landscape" (13), with whom we identify as subjects, as audience. "Woman," however, remains an emblem, a placeholder, of visual space—as mimetic representation itself.

A Masochistic Economy and the Entertainment Audience

James's Preface treats Isabel like a Hollywood star. Her glamour connotes lost "whole-someness" signified by the pre-oedipal mother, whose larger-than-life mirror projections imitate narcissistic attachment in a divisive interplay of phantom-like lights. Like the female film star lit before the cinematic spectator, Isabel is an exhibitionist for the Preface speaker. Her exhibitionism, however, originates from the desire of the speaker, who views himself perversely, through these projections upon an otherwise blank screen. When the Preface speaker suggests that Isabel's presence in the novel is one of "full . . . substance" (9), he alludes to the irony of her fetishistic exhibitionism. He also alludes to his own substantial anxieties about exhibitionism, as well.

The multiple ironies in his statement foreshadow those of the Preface's conclusion, where the speaker is exposed and then "undone," like Isabel herself—morally, representationally, economically. A somewhat over-exposed Preface speaker emphasizes the economic problems he faced giving Isabel her "ado" in the novel. The "ado," or "to-do," was *too much*, he says, in the economy of the narrative. Creating a cast of characters around Isabel, for example, was like casting "the group of attendants and entertainers who come down by train when people in the country give a party." Representing "the contract for carrying the party on," this group mirrors a "superabundance," "an excess of my [the author's] zeal"—in the manner of the invention of the cartoonish Henrietta (Preface 15). The speaker also confesses that he broke with economic aesthetic restraint to bolster another economic concern: his "special obligation to be amusing" (15). The speaker admits to having been more extravagant than economic, because he must "work but for a 'living wage'" (12). Here the Preface speaker collapses the original image of "living" natural growth into a monetary image of financial solvency. Nature, once the sympathetic umbilical chord tying him to Isabel's innocent image, is fused to the economic commodity.

At this point in the Preface, the speaker brings in another image: that of the audience. "The living wage," he writes, "is the reader's grant of the least possible quality of attention required for consciousness of a "'spell'" (12–13). Suggesting that representation in the novel is but an entertainment commodity whose chief ambition is to create a brief readerly "spell," the Preface speaker dismisses any high-art missions he might have had, adopting a pejorative stance toward his "reality" audience. His attitude toward popular "reality" audiences would be one later reflected in writings by Frankfurt School critics Theodor Adorno and Max Horkheimer. In their 1944 essay, "The Culture Industry," Adorno and Horkheimer would argue that so-called "democratic" entertainments inspired by reproductive "reality" technologies, like radio and film, breed a "ruthless unity" through the media form itself. Like the speaker in the Preface, Adorno and Horkheimer would suggest that a sadistic authority creating this "unity" marks the reproducible "reality" form, which poses as a form embodying democratic inclusion and difference.

The critique of popular, reproducible, "reality" art is a critique of the audience economically generative of such art. Adorno and Horkheimer claim that popular entertainment media seduces and sedates the political masses; the masses, in turn, adopt a passive masochism in their desires to be entertained, they conclude. The Jamesian speaker implies that a similar sadism and masochism exist in the novel's speaking as well as "spoken" forms. In adopting a proto–Frankfurt School stance, the speaker writes despairingly of his novel audience: "The artist may . . . dream of some Paradise (for art) where the direct appeal to the intelligence might be legalized. . . . The most he can do is to remember they *are* extravagances" (13—James's emphasis)

Just such a "Paradise" is alluded to at the very beginning of the Preface, in tandem with the themes of money, masochism, and spectatorship that typify the Preface's end. In the first two paragraphs—paragraphs whose subjects originally had seemed misplaced—the speaker introduces the Preface reader to a view of Venice, seen from his window "in the fruitless fidget of composition" (3). The speaker recalls being an author seeking inspiration, as he looks out from his "rooms on Riva Schiavoni, at the top of a house near the passage leading off to San Zaccaria" (3). The frustrated nature image—"fruitless fidget"—is made in the context of a traveler's vista of urban monuments. The magnificence of old Venice is not blamed for stifling natural productivity. Rather, its grandeur—the "romantic and historic sites, such as the land of Italy abound in"—nourishes it, as does "the waterside life, the wondrous lagoon before me. . . ." (3). In the first paragraph, we are invited to consider Venice as the center of Cosmopolitanism, a movement James subscribed to during the waning nineteenth century. In contrast to a city like Paris, which catered to "vulgar" public tastes from novels to cabarets to cinema, Venice represented the high-art tastes of wealthy American and European expatriates comprising this movement. James saw Venice as the center of Cosmopolitan values; in Tinter's words, Venice was a "free atmosphere" to James, nurturing all the arts.[18]

In his introduction to a volume of James's essays about Italy, *Italian Hours,* John Auchard describes both James's love for Venice, and its progressive image as a metaphor for decay and decline. In an early essay on Venice, in 1872, James had perceived Venice as a source of inspirational moral vision, for which the "mere use of one's eyes in Venice is happiness enough." James uses the image of an American innocent, "a young American painter" as a spectator like himself, who is "unperplexed by the mocking, elusive soul of things and satisfied with their wholesome light-bathed surface and shape" (James quoted in Auchard xx). What Auchard calls James's "intense visual celebration" undergoes a radical shift in tone.in later essays about Venice, however, when James writes of Venice as site of decadence, loss, and ruin: "the essential present character of the most melancholy of cities resides simply in its being the most beautiful of tombs."[19]

But I would argue that the image of Venice as metaphor for alienation is reflected in the earliest of James's writings, in the *irony* of the American painter, for example, who is "'keen of eye; fond of color,'" who perceives "'old lace and old brocade and . . . old furniture . . . happy contours in cheap old engravings . . . shadows of the Basilica . . . as happy as is consistent with the preservation of reason'" (quoted in Auchard xx). The "'shadows of the Basilica'" infiltrate the lightness of the prose.[20] I read the opening paragraphs of the Preface to *The Portrait of a Lady* as similarly laced with shadows and lights.

In these introductory paragraphs, Venice is first created an artist's "Paradise" of the visual, of the aesthetic claims of moral realism. The speaker recalls that he had worked in full view of external city vistas, but had refused to let the external return his gaze, since the monuments might infiltrate and destroy his composition. He writes that monuments and "historic sites" are "*too charged* with their own meanings merely to help" the artist "with a lame phrase" (3—emphasis added). The metaphor of money, economy, and commerce dominating the late paragraphs curiously rises up here as if premature in this first paragraph. The Preface speaker still seems innocent, like Isabel, about money. To "use" the world thus would be as if "an army of glorious veterans" had helped him "to arrest a peddler who has given him the wrong change" (3).

But just as James's early travel writings on Venice celebrate bright visual surfaces also permeated by metaphoric darkness, the first two paragraphs in the Preface put forth the visual itself as potentially denigrating, cheapening: "Strangely fertilizing"—invoking the nature metaphor for the first time—". . . does a wasted effort of attention often prove. It all depends on *how* the attention has been cheated, has been squandered. There are high-handed insolent frauds and there are insidious sneaking ones" (4—

James's emphasis). Increasingly sordid images of minor economic transactions complete the first paragraph: "Venice is too proud for such charities," like the "lending" of the novelist's vision. The speaker adds: "Venice doesn't borrow, she but all magnificently gives. We profit by that enormously"—but only if the novelist ignores his writing task (one type of masochism) and gives himself entirely to "*her* [Venice's] service alone" (4—emphasis added).

The Venetian, feminized view of monuments begins as a soothing source of meditation for the artist's eye—the sympathetic eye of the sentimental realist. In his own all-too-sympathetic portrayal of realism, the novel genre the Preface speaker is about to expose as illusionary, he speculates optimistically: "there is . . . always witless enough good faith, always anxious enough desire, to fail to guard him [the novelist] against their deceits" (4). But, in the view of Venice, in the "fruitlessness" of its composition, the Preface speaker is forced to allude to his own self-deceit, and then to give up his natural view. Here the speaker, as author, aligns himself and also separates himself from the sentimental Isabel (or the American painter); in the novel, we learn that Isabel read in the private chamber of her grandmother's Albany house with the window shades down. The speaker of the Preface, by contrast—another American innocent—reads in full view of the magnificent, nostalgic scene of old Venice below. But, as he does, Venice, for that moment, becomes a city of lost monumentalism, a city of capital-driven spectacles nourishing tourism and commercial travel literature.

Hence, Venice is another city like Paris, vibrant in spectatorship's trade—celebratory of voyeurism and a faulty "reality" entertainment. The capital of high art comes tumbling—or shall we say, crumbling—down. Venetian monumental architecture is now like museum tableaux or photo snapshots. The Venetian scene may be viewed by the speaker of the first paragraphs from the always-protective aperture of the window frame. But, reversing the view, we, the spectator's spectator, see the speaker *in* the frame, too.

At the conclusion to the Preface, the speaker becomes his own spectacle, again resembling, sympathizing with, the female image, with "'woman' as avid consumer of pulp."[21] Like Flaubert, who wrote "*Madame Bovary, c'est moi*"—and in doing so "fetishized his own imaginary femininity while simultaneously sharing his period's hostility toward real women" (Huyssen 45)—the Jamesian speaker suggests that Isabel Archer *is him*. Identified with "woman," his used and abused "exhibitionist like," the Preface speaking subject enters a new vicissitudinous sado-erotic phase. Like Isabel, he becomes the "performing woman," the exhibitionist. Imitating a Freudian denigrated femininity, he adopts the masochistic position.

"Female" nature has had on him a decomposing influence. At this juncture, the Preface speaker appears to have taken on what Mary Ann Doane calls "the female appetite for the image" in melodrama. Doane writes in the context of her larger discussion of the "woman's film," those popular melodramas attracting female viewers through appeals to female identification and commodity fetishism. She suggests that the "woman's film" constitutes a "mirror image" of the dominant cinema described by Mulvey's "Visual Pleasure" (*The Desire to Desire* 197). In the "woman's film," according to Doane, a certain "despecularization" takes place, since women bear a different, objectified relationship to the gaze. Aggressivity is released through "a deflection of scopophilic energy" in these films, she writes (198). One such "release" is "a narrativized paranoia" that is "disintegrative."

"Paranoia decomposes," Doane notes (198). In James's Preface, to *de*compose (himself as speaker, to be decomposed by the natural metaphors of the Preface) is the Preface speaker's final, masochistic act. Having been subject to "extravagances," in an economically motivated desire to entertain, the Preface speaker, as speaking subject, *subjects himself* to a quiet denouement. In the last paragraph of the Preface, the masochistic perspective itself begins to fade. And, as point of view fades, so, too, does the visual-verbal metaphoricity arresting our gaze in the Preface. Metaphoricity crumbles, like so many Venetian monuments—what Jacques Derrida calls "the efficacy of the sensory figure" has been extravagantly overspent through a "rubbing, exhaustion, crumbling away."[22] The Jamesian "Master of vision" winds down a once spectacular rhetoric into an unspectacular conclusion. He says: "There is really too much to say" (15). And he has nothing else to say.

FOUR

Sentimental Nature in *Wuthering Heights;* or, William Wyler Meets Emily Brontë on the Yorkshire Moors

An infant is cast into [the natural state] if through his parents' wickedness he is abandoned in a vast place neither inhabited nor frequented by humans . . . But one whom shipwreck or the violence of others throw naked, destitute, and deprived of every tool onto a deserted, wholly uncultivated island sinks only to a certain degree of the natural state. . . . As Virgil says of Achaemenides . . . "Ghastly in his squalor, with unshorn beard, and garb fastened with thorns, he dragged out his life in the woods among . . . wild beasts . . . plants fed him with their uptorn roots."

—Samuel Pufendorf[1]

It is rustic all through. It is moorish, and wild, and knotty as a root of heath. Nor was it natural that it should be otherwise; the author being herself a native and nursling of the moors.

—Charlotte Brontë[2]

At the end of director William Wyler's 1939 Hollywood film adaptation of *Wuthering Heights,* Catherine Earnshaw-Linton (Merle Oberon) dies an angelic icon of sentimental distress. Seen at a window embraced by Heathcliff (Lawrence Olivier) and gazing upon their beloved Yorkshire moors, Catherine swoons in his arms, her white chemise drooping like heavenly wings. Carefully plotted shots that suggest Catherine's ascent into a Victorian archetype of sentimental womanhood, the angel of the house, are exchanged for shots of an angel's Paradise, the tranquil, panoramic moors. Absorbed by the still passivity of the natural landscape, Catherine's sadistic demons are located elsewhere, in the sadistic finality of her sympathetic spectator's last glance.

But in the novel from which this movie version was inspired, Catherine's death is only half the story, a story punctuated by partialities of natural vistas, of human duplicities sighted only in broken narrative fragments. In previous chapters, I have discussed the way in which novels from the tradition of masculine sentiment, in the name of realism, use a hidden spectator to transmit ideologies about sympathetic identification and sexual difference. In this chapter, I suggest that *Wuthering Heights*—a novel that unnerved its readers when first published in 1847, causing Brontë's sister Charlotte to write a Preface *apologia* to the novel's second edition[3]—radically undermines these sentimental views about sympathy. It does so through a critique of the state of nature and *human* nature under natural law, along the lines we have been discussing in Hume. And it does so—this point counters Charlotte Brontë's reading—by failing to represent nature at all. The novel does not provide a natural landscape upon which the sympathetic spectator exists.

The novel, therefore, refuses visual pleasure, and the sadomasochistic perversions of voyeurism and fetishism. Visual pleasure gives form to narratives of masculine sentiment; it reproduces the illusion of a state of nature not "wild" or "desolate" but which generates bonds through identification. However, while the novel *Wuthering Heights* explores the social ambivalences of sympathetic identification through a "wild" landscape full of mimetic holes, the Wyler film adaptation restores these holes and sentimental views about identification. In this film version of *Wuthering Heights,* which I will contrast to Brontë's novel, sentimental views about sympathy are reinvoked. In the film adaptation, we witness the very machinery of the sentimental narrative process.

Discussing sympathy in Charles Dickens's *A Christmas Carol,* which was published during the same decade as *Wuthering Heights,* Audrey Jaffe suggests that Scrooge regains a culturally sanctioned sympathy by becoming a spectator of his "scenes of Christmases past," a "relation to representation" that is "articulated in terms of absorption and self-loss." Sympathy, for Jaffe, suggests a *process*, requiring a spectator "to supplement his lack" through the "presence projected by the image."[4] We have seen the way in which the supplementary process works in relation to the masculine tradition of literary sentiment—in novels as diverse as *Clarissa, L'Education sentimentale,* and *The Portrait of a Lady.* In these novels the spectator supplements "his lack" through the perverse pleasures of identification. But the sympathetic process in the novel *Wuthering Heights* actually is shown to be a supplementary one, and "dangerous," to use Derrida's word in reference to the supplement.

"Absorption and self-loss" create power for the spectator. The bonds of sympathy are at issue here, when *symbiosis*—a psychoanalytic term for fusion through identification—creates "bonds of love," sadomasochism in the

course of desire. Bondage is reproduced throughout the fictive relationships in *Wuthering Heights*, the novel. And bondage is tellingly reproduced in
the fictive recounting of the sympathetic storytelling process.[5]

But these sadoerotic implications of the spectator's sympathetic bonds
and processes are resublimated within the text of the Wyler film. The classic
film adaptation of the novel represses the sympathetic spectator's conflicts,
sentimentally within the natural plenitude on the silver screen. Bondage
becomes a natural consequence of heterosexual romance between Cathy
and Heathcliff, as they themselves are spectators of the Yorkshire countryside. Although several screen adaptations of *Wuthering Heights* have been
produced, I look to the Wyler version as a case in point in the classic-film
tradition of making novels into films—a tradition that was recently reinvigo-
rated by filmmaking in the 1990s.[6] What Brontë reveals to be a "wuthering"
feature in human nature and mimetic identification is perversely rerouted
in the "process and leap" of novel-to-film adaptation itself.[7]

Whether Wuthering Heights

Charlotte Brontë's sentimental—perhaps slyly undercutting and sadistic—
Preface to Emily's "rustic" novel claims that her sister's work was "hewn in a
wild workshop" out of the "savage" and "sinister" Yorkshire moors. Using the
analogy of a sculptor carving a figure out of natural rock, she writes of her
sister's creative venture in the language of visual representation: "The statuary found a granite block on a solitary moor: gazing thereon, he saw how
from the crag might be elicited a head, savage, swart, sinister. . . . He
wrought with a rude chisel, and from no model but the vision of his meditations" (xxix). Like the "statuary" himself, Charlotte Brontë attempts to
"elicit" her own solid, concrete ("granite block") moors image. This is
Charlotte's picture, supplementing a visual image for that which her sister's
prose lacks. For if one reads the novel *Wuthering Heights* carefully, one
discovers only tenuous descriptions of the moors, or the natural world, in
general. Any description of the moors and its "savage" landscape is quickly
derailed into a reference about the enigmatic, blustery weather and its
"atmospheric" charge. "Description" functions as a transition into another
sort of description, revealing the *interior* status of the Wuthering Heights
house created by its "inmates," as Lockwood calls them.

A brief passage at the beginning of the novel is one of the very few
direct descriptions of the natural landscape upon which the house exists.
This description exemplifies the movement away from a vision of external
nature into a vision of the *human* nature that dominates the house: "Wuthering Heights is the name of Mr Heathcliff's dwelling. 'Wuthering' being a
significant provincial adjective, descriptive of the atmospheric tumult to

which its station is exposed, in stormy weather" (2). This truncated description serves as that which forbids description. It does not reveal any solid picture of a natural state—a state "hewn" out of Charlotte Brontë's "granite"—but rather an unstable supplement for the scene, implied by the ironically "true" description of nature, an "atmospheric tumult." What is important about the "atmospheric tumult" is the way in which it "exposes" the "station" of the house. This first image of the moors is enhanced by the instability of the linguistic "setting" through the word "wuthering." The "provincial adjective" modifies "heights," where the "atmospheric tumult" is located, but never rests or can be placed.

The word "wuthering"—a unique adjectival expression in English literature—is a linguistic frame conceptualizing what the sympathetic spectator sees, or does not. "Wuther" comes from "whither," itself an archaic term replaced, or substituted, in modern English by "where," meaning, "to what place," or "to what result, condition, action, subject, cause." In its general sense, "whither" implies "any place," or "whatever place"; it therefore conveys the sense of the stability of place, and yet, at the same time, a lack of stability, a movement away from fixity of place: the "place or state to which a person or thing moves or tends," as in "whence." The obsolete "whither" is related to "whether" (a homonym of "weather" but apparently not etymologically related, in spite of Brontë's statement about the provincial application of the term). "Whether" is a pronoun that implies another kind of movement, not that of a linear movement through space but rather of a movement that divides in two. As a conjunction, "whether" introduces "a disjunctive direct question . . . a doubt between alternatives." In a related usage, "whether" replaces "either," indicating "undecideability, uncertainty, lack of resolution."[8]

These connotations of "whether," bearing etymological resonance to "wither" and "wuther," subtly frame the reference to the house on the moors, as well as the narrative frames of Brontë's plot. To plunge into this "plot" is to become *un*-moored, to experience a narrative universe charged by "undecideability, uncertainty, lack of resolution." Nature is traditionally a stable icon in the nineteenth-century British romantic sensibility.[9] However, in *Wuthering Heights,* nature does not offer a stable iconographic locus. Our primary narrator-spectator, Lockwood, tries to gain his visual bearings in a description of the moors when leaving the Wuthering Heights house for Thrushcross Grange. But natural referents and imagistic icons are never sighted or have been erased by a snow storm. Like Lockwood, the reader-spectator fails to gain visual bearings.

The visual signs of nature are at the heart of *Wuthering Heights's* hermeneutic processes. We are warned not to trust natural signs from the very onset of the narrative. As Lockwood reports upon emerging from Wuthering Heights, the whole hill-back was one billowy, white ocean; the swells and falls not indicating corresponding rises and depressions in the ground—many pits, at least, were filled to a level; and entire ranges of mounds, the refuse of the quarries, blotted from the chart which my yesterday's walk left pictured in my mind. (25)

And if the geographical image of the moors—having once served as signs of direction for Lockwood—are "pictures" now "blotted from the chart" of his mind, so, too, are the guideposts lost to the narrative chart in the snow:

on one side of the road, at intervals of six or seven yards, a line of upright stones, continued through the whole length of the barren: these were erected and daubed with lime, on purpose to serve as guides in the dark . . . excepting a dirty dot pointing up, here and there, all traces of their existence had vanished. (25–26)

A theme of pictures lost and guideposts visually obliterated is tied to the theme of place and space, as well as to the theme of human identity. The theme of losing one's way recurs during Lockwood's dream the night before the snow. Having been warned that he would become lost if he attempted to journey home during the storm, Lockwood spends the night in the oaken closet, where "I began to dream," he reports, "almost before I ceased to be sensible of my locality. I thought it was morning; and I had set out on my way home, with Joseph as a guide" (18). In the dream, he finds the passage difficult, with snow that "lay yards deep in our road" and without the "pilgrim's stall," which Joseph tells him is necessary to enter the house. Next, in the dream, Lockwood realizes that he is not going home to Thrushcross Grange after all, but rather "to hear the famous Jabes Branderham preach," a sermon "Divided into *four hundred and ninety* parts." When Lockwood protests his innocence, Branderham points accusingly and shouts, "*Thou art the Man!*" (18–19—Brontë's emphasis). To hear this strange sermon, Lockwood and Joseph have arrived at a hidden chapel, located down "in a hollow, between two hills . . . near a swamp, whose peaty moisture is said to answer all the purposes of embalming on the few corpses deposited there" (18). In a following dream, one of the "corpses" seems to rise up from the grave.

The dream reveals a lack of resolute human nature, as that "nature" becomes purer nature, dust. Meanwhile, outside the window of the oaken closet, a female ghost who identifies herself as Catherine Linton cries, "'I'm come home, I'd lost my way on the moor!'" (20). Following the ghost's tentative appearance is its sudden disappearance. When Heathcliff later implores the ghost to return, Lockwood says: "The spectre showed a spectre's ordinary caprice; it gave no sign of being" (23). "It" gave "no sign of being" because "it" is *not* a "being"; "it" cannot be located or visually placed. Again, an image of the moors—or rather *not* an image but rather an image of the effects of the moors's "atmospheric tumult"—stands in the unsteady "place" of the specter's partialized, fleeting image. Lockwood, always a literal eyewitness, recalls that "the snow and wind whirled wildly through, even reaching my station, and blowing out the light" (23). But snow and wind" do not *re*-place the missing image of the specter.

Just as nature has shown itself to be a set of allegorical signs too soon supplemented and lost, the image of the ghostly "Catherine" vanishes, an image whose "material," using the Freudian word, are the bits and fragments of Lockwood's bedtime reading, the young Catherine's books, marginalia, and inscriptions. Lockwood is a spectator who prefers visual certainty. He prefers to grant his "wuthering" visions an imaginary unity and intactness. In the terse opening description of the Wuthering Heights house, possibly the only description of the house in its natural moors setting, solid references are made to the actual structure of the house. Incorporated into Lockwood's description are clues that suggest that acts of spectating can never fully conjure up the natural environment in which this structure apparently exists, or gives cause to:

> Pure, bracing ventilation *they must have up there*, at all times . . . *one may guess* the power of the north wind, blowing over the edge by the excessive slant of a few, stunted firs at the end of the house; and by a range of gaunt thorns all stretching their limbs one way, as if craving alms of the sun. (2—emphasis added)

This description might tease a reader-spectator like Charlotte Brontë into thinking she has *seen* the moors. But the conditional tense used to qualify the observation, made of "ventilation," suggests that any such description is speculative, *specular*—with all the implied paradoxes of the word. Description is like the "spectre" Lockwood says "showed a spectre's ordinary caprice [in giving] . . . no sign of being." As readers, like Lockwood, we are forced to speculate about the nature of the moors enveloping and defining the representation of the Wuthering Heights house. We are forced to read into the vision granted of "a few, stunted firs at the end of the house." But, like the firs, we, spectators, stand at "an excessive slant," observing the world perversely, from a stunted and indirect viewing position.

"Nature" in this description is remarkably *un*natural; token named elements, the "limbs" of "gaunt thorns" and the few fir trees, have been modified by adjectives marking their deformities. And this description never grants us a vision of the open horizon we might associate with the moorish heights. Instead, our spectator continues to guess, to speculate, about the view of nature *in terms of the structure of the house:* "Happily, the architect had foresight to build it [the house] strong: the narrow windows are deeply set in the wall; and the corners defended with large jutting stones" (2). In this passage, the description of nature quickly dissembles into a few "large jutting stones" that defend the house, a fortress-like, constructed shell. Even the most speculative and uncertain of natural description capitulates back into the human facade of description, the artificial form. *There is no natural nature in Wuthering Heights,* this important passage tells us. Upon our very entrance into *Wuthering Heights,* nature exists only in relation to social structures and edifices.

Nature as sign of the impenetrable may be a function of the novel's seemingly impenetrable hermeneutic codes.[10] But *human* nature *is* penetrable, I would argue, as we are invited to analyze the *internal* "atmospheric tumult." What is explored in the novel *Wuthering Heights* is not the wilderness of the landscape but the wilderness of the human "heart," to employ that sentimental term. Here the "wild, remote region" of the "heart" is less mysterious than it seems, part of a tightly woven fabric of social forces that take psychological shape in an individual, but through social relationships. From the moment we step into the interiority of the house, we are forced—like Lockwood—out of nature and into the problem of "the dwelling."

It is there, inside the domestic confines of the house, inside the sentimental tradition of domestic narrative, that the analysis of "human nature" takes place. Discussions about "human nature," in the centuries leading up to the Enlightenment, were interlaced with discussions about a "state of nature," most famously perhaps in Hobbes's *Leviathan,* which claimed that "the natural state" is a violent and self-serving place. But a more optimistic vision of a "state of nature" was put forth by writers like Pufendorf, who challenged the Hobbesian view of nature in his essay, "On the Natural State of Men." He wrote that "natural similarity fosters greatly the association and mutual endearment of individuals in every class of living things" (126). Pufendorf insisted that a concept of "natural similarity," and what he called "mutual need," created a harmonious rather than hostile environment, stressing the natural "bonds" intrinsic to "men": "Because . . . the bond among men results from the similarity of their nature, their mutual need, and the natural law's dictate urging peace, the natural state cannot properly be considered a state of war" (130).

Pufendorf's idea about the natural state as a locus of "similarity" and human bonds informed Hume's own utilitarian arguments about identification through sympathy, and the general role of "the social virtues." In the *Enquiry Concerning the Principals of Morals,* Hume wrote that these virtues—"beneficence and humanity, friendship and gratitude, natural affection and public spirit"—extend from our "tender sympathy with others . . . a generous concern for our kind and species" informed by mutual need (178). Yet, by the writing of the *Enquiry,* the skeptic Hume already had made the underlying principal of similarity, of connectedness, an epistemological problem. It is this problem that Brontë's *Wuthering Heights* explores and exploits in her own theme of human nature and social bonds.

Briefly, Hume's epistemological writings in both the *Enquiry Concerning Human Understanding* and the earlier *Treatise* undermine the use of reason that traditionally had been accorded "similarity" as a mode of "resemblance"—concepts vital to his theory of sympathy. Hume complicates the resemblance feature that undergirds identification processes in sympathy by viewing resemblance as relying upon the logic of causality, which he writes is based upon psychological "custom" or "habit," akin to a "belief." A "belief" is distinct from a "fiction," in Hume's discussion, because belief has the power of sentiment behind it, felt by the mind, and distinguished by the power of judgment from the imagination's fictions. But, essentially, such a distinction is a matter of degree and not of essence: for what Hume suggests about the relations of connection, in general, is that they are determined by a *perception* of or "belief" in connection; we do not perceive in order to connect. What we see, by "habit," we have the habit of calling fact. Applied to his theory of sympathy, the connecting power of resemblance may grant sympathy its emotive power. But if we remember that resemblance involves only the belief or faith in connectedness—like those "resemblances" we feel among blood relations—the emotive power of sympathy becomes tethered to a wholly psychological and, therefore, shifting social experience. The ironies and disturbances that the resemblance feature of sympathy invites can even provoke contrary, or hostile, feeling.

This duality in sympathetic resemblance is at issue in the novel *Wuthering Heights*. The state of human nature may involve "mutual need." But it does not appear to "dictate . . . peace," to rephrase Pufendorf. In fact, the "bonds among men" result both in overt forms of violence as well as in the subtle violence of emotional bondage, suggesting that *too much* "bond" creates sadomasochistic desire. There is a *pleasure* in violence in this novel, V. S. Pritchett notes, a pleasure that is part of the dynamic of human relationships: "Emily Brontë sees two elements in the soul from which, in Nature, we avert our eyes: the pleasure of inflicting cruelty and torture" (xi). I would reconfigure Pritchett's statement to suggest that "Nature" is a philosophical term that Brontë exploits in its multiple and contradictory meanings, as a brilliant social analysis about processes of human identification.[11] If we follow the idea that "the pleasure of inflicting cruelty and torture" operates in a highly socialized arena of family bonds within the novel—and that this is the "unreclaimed region" through which the social drama takes place—we see that identification between Catherine and Heathcliff, or Heathcliff and Hindley, is a compensatory act, leading to frustration rather than satisfaction, to violence rather than "harmony."

The drama of emotional symbiosis, which critics have noted is important to *Wuthering Heights,* is actually a *failure* of symbiosis, a failure manifested through sadomasochism. The identification experience at the heart of the fictive drama is repeated, or supplemented again, by the enunciatory drama of storytelling and witnessing. "The pleasure of inflicting cruelty and torture" most exquisitely exists in the bonds of sympathy between Lockwood and Nelly Dean. Their "mutual need" for each other, revealed through the dual process of narration, sketches out a liminal plane between the internal fictive plot *about* identification and the novel's formalizing of the issues of identification. Through fictional but also enunciatory speakers-spectators, "mutual need" and the bond of sympathy are shown to be the most perverse, most sentimentally-sadoerotically complete.

All fictive subjects of *Wuthering Heights* are unreliable, unstable, subject to sentiment's contraries. Catherine Earnshaw Linton is unstable and restless, if passionately devoted to Heathcliff. In her bond with Heathcliff, she exhibits both the control features of the sadist and the self-destructive masochist. Her version of sadistic cruelty is to reject Heathcliff, as when she returns to Wuthering Heights from Thrushcross Grange. Having just bathed in the Lintons' class finery, Catherine mocks her beloved friend for wearing tattered clothes and a dirty face. But while Catherine has a sadistic streak, her masochistic tendencies are more pronounced, resulting in "brain fevers," when Heathcliff abandons her, and, later, upon his return, when she must choose between Edgar and Heathcliff. This "brain-fever" takes on the character of "feminine" masochism when Catherine dies after childbirth.

"The pleasure of inflicting cruelty and torture" is even more startling in Heathcliff. The adopted and "supplementary" member of the Earnshaw kin embodies the "danger" in the supplement, exerting sadistic hatred toward members both of Wuthering Heights and Grange households— including Hareton, the son of Heathcliff's enemy Hindley, who ironically looks up to Heathcliff as a father figure; and Catherine's daughter, Cathy II, who is punished for being the daughter of his rival, Edgar. Heathcliff also punishes Isabella Linton, whose chief crime is to have been Edgar's sister, and to have mistaken Heathcliff as "'a hero of romance,'" as Heathcliff later mocks. But Heathcliff, too, like Catherine, is contrary, unstable. His sadism slips into masochism when he cuts his hand on window glass, or when he slams his head against a tree.

"To injure themselves too, was natural to them [Catherine and Heathcliff] and an important part of Emily Brontë's strange imagination," Pritchett notes (xi). But I would argue that the "imagination" is not so "strange" if we follow the sadomasochistic logic. On the existential level of Chancer's description of the sadomasochistic dynamic, the sadist and masochist have more in common than not. They both experience a failure to acquire "mutuality in recognition," therefore, seeking to control and dominate one other. What Chancer, after Benjamin, describes as the sadomasochist's existential dilemma is mapped out in infancy and the object relations of children, a mapping or *plotting* out that is represented in very precise terms in the novel and which returns us to the structure of the supplement, in the attempt at human unity through identification. Chancer cites Margaret Mahler's research into infantile psychosis, which details a series of stages that occur before creating, in the subject, what Chancer calls "a sense *both* of separateness and of connectedness" (78—Chancer's emphasis). These stages begin with a "primary autism" through which the child does not separate himself from the mother's body; and they evolve into symbiosis, through which the child experiences his caretaker narcissistically, as a function of the child's "omnipotent system."[12] The successful completion of these two stages results in a third stage, that of separation-individuation. However, in Mahler's schema, this third and all-important stage cannot occur without the completion of several subphases, including a period of "rapprochement," through which the child "seeks reassurance," and demands the caretaker's approval. As Chancer notes, "On the one hand, the child wishes to separate; on the other, the child needs to feel that separation is not achieved at the risk of losing security . . . reassurance is sought that this price will not have to be paid" (77). Only with such reassurance on the part of the caretaker can "consolidation of individuality" take hold, and the child experiences "the beginnings of emotional object constancy" (77).

In writing about the novel, Philip K. Wion has shown the way in which the relationship between Catherine and Heathcliff in *Wuthering Heights* enacts "a version of symbiotic relationship between mother and child."[13] But evidence suggests that this "symbiotic relationship" is an illusory one, relying upon the compensatory structure of the supplement rather than any real "consolidation of individuality," to borrow from Chancer. Symbiosis in *Wuthering Heights* is an attempt to compensate for *lack* of mother-child symbiosis alluded to in the plot—by even more intensely reproducing human bonds as bondage. Wion convincingly illustrates that Catherine and Heathcliff experience symbiosis. He quotes the famous scene in which Catherine tells Nelly, "I *am* Heathcliff," and other representations in the novel of fused boundaries, and of lost or absent mothers who die prematurely (including both Mrs. Earnshaws and Mrs. Linton, and Catherine herself after giving birth). He argues, furthermore, that food and absorption images evoke the infantile orality associated with the symbiosis stage, as do mirror images. Catherine, indeed, is haunted by the mirror in her final illness: "It was *yourself*, Mrs. Linton," says Nelly, responding to Catherine's fear of her mirror reflection; Catherine, on her deathbed, replies, "'Myself! . . . that's dreadful!' "[14] Wion concludes that all these representations generate symbiosis imagery in the novel. But would I emphasize that, like Catherine's mirror image, these self-reflections *are* "dreadful." They are "dreadful" because they represent dishevelled and displaced states of being that are part of the semiotic level of the text. They are "dreadful" because these images of resemblance, of union, of fused identities, are all too "wuthering," disturbed and disturbing, like the novel itself.

At the heart of symbiosis in the *Wuthering Heights* plot is the "dangerous supplement" fostering a sadomasochistic dynamic. This dynamic controls both fictive and narrative interactions. Indeed, Catherine in the mirror—like Heathcliff—seems a victim of what Nancy Chodorow, another psychoanalytic theorist cited by Chancer, suggests is a premature "hatching," leading to an exaggerated dependency through unresolved narcissism. On one level, the story of *Wuthering Heights* is about children too soon abandoned by deceased mothers and fathers. Catherine has no gentle mirror in which to view her self-image as a child. Both Catherine and Heathcliff are, in Chancer's words, "pushed out" of their bond with parental caretakers too early through the death and, hence, abandonment of their caretakers.

This abandonment leads to what Chodorow calls a "socialized masculinity," the controlling and sadistic orientation of the subject. Chodorow, whose contribution to object-relations theory is most provocative and original in its analysis of socialized processes of gender difference, suggests that the male child has a tendency "to adopt the sadistic role" because he is, by social arrangement, "pushed out" of the mother's domestic sphere before psychological maturity has taken place. This causes the male child, Chodorow speculates, to repress emotional bonds and a continuing need for dependency.[15] Borrowing from Chodorow's analysis of the sadomasochistic dynamic, Chancer suggests that to be "pushed out"—we extend this hypothetical potential for "masculine" sadism to both male and female children—lays the groundwork for the dependency drama of sadists and masochists.

While Catherine loses her mother as a young child and her father as an adolescent, Heathcliff's own parentage is more murky. We never learn about his biological parents or family of origin; he is brought into the family by Mr. Earnshaw, who we are led to believe presumes Healthcliff to be a poor orphan but who we also might speculate is Healthcliff's natural father. Heathcliff, the street urchin of Liverpool, never gains Mrs. Earnshaw's maternal approval; she resents this "supplement" to the Wuthering Heights family, dying shortly after Heathcliff's arrival. Mr. Earnshaw grants Heathcliff a fatherly affection but at the expense of affection toward his son Hindley. And from the moment Heathcliff arrives at Wuthering Heights, Hindley retaliates against Heathcliff. We learn from Nelly Dean that Heathcliff's

endurance made old Earnshaw furious when he discovered his son persecut-
ing the poor, fatherless child, as he called him . . . from the very beginning, he
[Heathcliff] bred bad feeling in the house . . . the young master [Hindley]
had learnt to regard his father as an oppressor rather than a friend, and
Heathcliff as a usurper of his parent's affections. . . . (31)

Mr. Earnshaw's early death in the novel leaves Heathcliff more vulnerable to Hindley's sadism and revenge. Citing research by a student of Mahler, Alma Bond, who made a clinical study of a child whose rejection by
parents led to the child's attempt to control both parents and Bond,
Chancer describes "the sadistic child," the child "too vulnerable to acknowledge how desperately the caretaker's love and attention are needed." Such
vulnerability arises from "the traumatic experience of expressing vulnerability and a desire for love and of being met with rejection," notes
Chancer (79). Hindley, rejected by his father, abandoned by both parents
through their premature deaths, is "the sadistic child." Becoming Heathcliff's "master," he makes Heathcliff a servant, sending him away from the
house to the barn with other field hands. Hindley's sadism toward Heathcliff sets up a mimetic chain of sadomasochistic replication.

The social circumstance Heathcliff also faces sets him up to be "the
sadistic child," like Hindley. Brontë complicates this potential interpretation of Heathcliff's behavior by demonstrating how Heathcliff *learns* his
sadism in mimetic imitation of and resemblance toward Hindley. In the
scene of Catherine's return from the Grange, we see Heathcliff as an imitative mirror, viewed in this instance through Nelly Dean's motherly sympathy
toward him. Nelly's sympathy suggests that the supposedly evil urchin rising
from out of unnatural urban squalor might be made an example of virtue,
" 'a gift of God,' " as Mr. Earnshaw first told his wife upon returning from
Liverpool with Heathcliff, " 'though it's as dark almost as if it came from the
devil' " (30). "God's gift" is *made* a "devil," when he is abused as a child, as the
scene of Catherine's return suggests.

Just before the coach's arrival at Wuthering Heights, carrying Edgar
Linton and Catherine in her newly cultivated finery, Nelly soothes a worried
Heathcliff, who is very concerned about his Linton rival and wishes he had
"light hair and a fair skin." Nelly's sympathetic assessment echoes Mr. Earnshaw's earlier racist assertion. Eliciting the symbiotic mother-child theme
Wion says is important to the novel's structure, Nelly tells Heathcliff that it is
Edgar who " 'cried for mamma at every turn' "; here she implies—trying to
coerce Heathcliff into good humor—that Heathcliff is more autonomous
and, therefore, more manly, than Edgar. Yet Nelly also undermines Heathcliff while she soothes him. She criticizes his "black fiends"—his eyes; she
reminds him that he comes from a lower (and racially inferior, in her view)

class status. Invoking the wuthering aspects of the gaze, Nelly alludes to prurience and prejudice when looking at Heathcliff, saying:

> "O, Heathcliff, you are showing a poor spirit! Come to the glass, and I'll let you see what you should wish. Do you mark those two lines between your eyes . . . that couple of black fiends, so deeply buried, who never open their windows boldly, but lurk glinting under them, like devil's spies?" (47)

Nelly here reveals the way in which the gaze is one of white hegemony and a patriarchal masculinity—assimilated and reproduced by a white female.

If Heathcliff's eyes are "devil's spies," what must be Nelly's eyes, which are never illuminated in the fiction, which we never see? In such a passage, we are forced to reflect upon the missing presence of Nelly's always seeing but "wuthering" eyes, which "spy" upon Heathcliff in the course of plotting and plot-making. Perceived by Lockwood as the "bustling," talkative housekeeper, and eulogized by many critics—from Charlotte Brontë on—as "a specimen of true benevolence and homely fidelity,"[16] "good natured, warm-hearted, wholesome," "detached and normal,"[17] Nelly is generally thought of as an impartial narrator who "has no favorites . . . she makes no consistent attempt to white-wash any of the characters or events."[18] However, the novel makes Nelly control sentimental representations of herself, as she controls the representation of events. Her domestic-drama control is revealed from the moment we are introduced to her by Lockwood, in a parenthetical aside: "(N.B. I dine between twelve and one o'clock; the housekeeper, a matronly lady taken as a fixture along with the house, could not, or would not comprehend my request that I might be served at five)" (6). The "benevolent" housekeeper is so zealous about controlling the dining hour that she competes with even Lockwood's conventional understandings. This early novel passage anticipates Nelly's representation as sympathetic master of the storytelling process. Nelly may be a convenient conduit for telling the *Wuthering Heights* story, having observed events in both houses. But we know Nelly to be more than a mere channel of information. Her gossip is loaded with intrigue and prejudice.

Nelly controls the story to suit her sentimental fantasy. These efforts at control are hard to trace, since she so brilliantly controls the "wuthering" narrative process itself, in collusion with Lockwood. We do get momentary glimpses into her manipulative strategies, however, when, upon a number of occasions, she "slips," to use the Freudian term as a verb. In her "slips," Nelly reveals the way in which she is a catalyst as well as a reporter of events. To "slip" is to admit to a certain *narrative* control, leaving us the imprint of her method of operation—of how she shapes events, often with disastrous outcomes.

In one slip, Nelly recalls—in a brief aside—the deep dislike she has always held for Catherine Earnshaw Linton: "I own I did not like her

[Catherine], after her infancy was past" (55). This slip foreshadows a more major "slip" in the plot: when Catherine tells Nelly it would degrade her to marry Heathcliff, and Nelly watches silently as Heathcliff literally slips away—to disappear for many years. In this important scene, Catherine goes on to confess her deep identification with Heathcliff. Through Nelly's *lack* of interference, Nelly shows a steady sadism toward Catherine, albeit in a passive-aggressive form. Again, Nelly reveals her sadism upon Heathcliff's return and Catherine's illness, when she fails to report the illness promptly to Edgar.

And there are many other instances in the novel in which Nelly has the opportunity to redirect disastrous outcomes for the better but refuses to do so. These include the elopement of Isabella Linton with Heathcliff—Nelly knows of Isabella's absence but does not inform Edgar of it until it is too late; and the developing affair between the young Catherine Linton and her cousin, Linton Heathcliff—which occurs against the explicit wishes of Edgar and which Nelly encourages by arranging secret meetings, even as she protests those meetings to young Catherine. In one instance late in the plot, Nelly, by her own words, recalls discovering Heathcliff's dead body and closing his eyes. Are we to speculate that Nelly causes Heathcliff's death? Is *Wuthering Heights,* after all, a murder mystery, Nelly both its sympathetic witness and executioner?

While we speculate about the reasons Heathcliff dies, we need not speculate about Nelly's role as a sympathetic witness in assisting Catherine Earnshaw Linton's demise. Nelly is the indirect cause of Heathcliff's abandonment of Catherine, leaving Catherine emotionally fragile and irresolute, a candidate for complete neurotic disintegration. In spite of Catherine's fragile health, Nelly arranges what becomes the final meeting between Catherine and Heathcliff. Earlier, when the ill Catherine complains that Nelly has closed the window and demands that she open it, Catherine says, "'Open the window again wide, fasten it open! Quick, why don't you move?'" Nelly responds, "'Because I won't give you your death of cold.'" But Catherine is not far from the truth when she says: "'You won't give me a chance of life, you mean'" (107). Nelly reports that Catherine utters this statement "sullenly," more indicative of Nelly's sadism toward Catherine than of Catherine's actual demeanor or behavior. Catherine catches the potential slander in Nelly's sympathetic stance, declaring later: "'Ah! Nelly has played traitor . . . Nelly is my hidden enemy'" (110).

Indeed, the way in which Nelly "plays traitor" is to remain "hidden." For Nelly's sadism requires a perverse tactic; sadism is asserted through sympathy and her sentimental "affection" for the Earnshaw-Linton families. I would reject James Hafley's harsh, if insightful, assessment of Nelly, which suggests that Nelly is the real "villain" of *Wuthering Heights*.[19] His evaluation misses the point about the perversity of Nelly's position, and that it is Nelly

who embodies the contradictions of *all* the novel's spectators, most impor-
tantly, its readers.

Returning to the scene of Nelly's sympathetic consolation of the
young Heathcliff, we see her perversity emerging in her mothering discourse. Nelly tries to sublimate the dualities that potentially lead to "atmospheric tumult" and that threaten to engulf her, just as the wuthering
relations engulf Catherine and Heathcliff. But Nelly projects her own "atmospheric tumult" onto the story as she tries to control the dark racialized
features of Heathcliff's face, telling him he should "Wish and learn to *smooth
away* the surly winkles . . . change the fiends to confident, innocent angels. . . . Don't get the expression of the vicious cur. . . ." (47—emphasis
added). To "smooth away" is Nelly's strategy, through her perverse sympathetic view and discourse. It is only *according to* Nelly that "Heathcliff gradu-
ally lost his frown, and began to look quite pleasant" (48). Through symbiotic intervention, she believes herself to have transformed a "devil's" visage
into the face of an "innocent angel."

The duality of this scene's sympathy and sadism unfolds when the
Linton coach arrives, and Nelly reports that she "urged my companion to
hasten now, and show his amiable humor" (48). Heathcliff's "amiable
humor" quickly dissolves, as Nelly recalls:

> ill luck would have it . . . as he [Heathcliff] opened the door leading from the
> kitchen on one side, Hindley opened it on the other; they met, and the master
> irritated at seeing him clean and cheerful . . . angrily bade Joseph "keep the
> fellow out of the room—send him into the garret till dinner is over." (48)

As Nelly protests, Hindley threatens a "'share of my hand, if I catch him
down stairs again till dark . . . Begone, you vagabond!'" he dismisses Heathcliff (49). A remark by Edgar about the length of Heathcliff's hair is enough
to cause the latter to dump "a tureen of hot apple-sauce" on Linton's fair
head. Enraged, Hindley "snatched up the culprit directly and conveyed him
to his chamber, where, doubtless, he administered a rough remedy to cool
the fit of passion, for he reappeared red and breathless" (49). Catherine is
accurate when she chides Edgar: "'he'll be flogged'" (49). Indeed, Hindley
returns to the group bragging, "'That brute of a lad has warmed me nicely'"
(49).

This complex scene reveals, among other points, that sadism in familial relations is the same as master-slave class relations. Heathcliff is both
brother and servant to Hindley and Catherine. This scene also reveals that
sadism is socially replicated, and that it originates in the stigma assigned
new generations of slaves by their master figures. Masters are socially replicated, as well, which Hindley's comment to Edgar following Heathcliff's
beating implies: "'Next time, Master Edgar, take the law into your own

fists—it will give you an appetite' " (49). At this point, the whole company is complicitous with Hindley's sadism, especially Nelly. The other members of the household treat the sadistic brutality as a natural event, which points to another feature of social sadism: that master-slave relations are made *to seem* natural through the family metaphor.

Nelly reports, "The little party recovered its equanimity at the sight of the fragrant feast. They were hungry, after their ride, and easily consoled, since no real harm had befallen them" (49). But we recall that it is Nelly's descriptive statement, and her "smoothing-over" style, that amplifies—or even creates—the complicit sadistic "atmospheric tumult." It should seem strange to her auditor that Nelly would conclude a narrative about a sadistic beating in the manner of a placid domestic tale—especially given the supposed fact that she had protested Heathcliff's beating. The dual function of Nelly's sympathy begins to rise to the surface in her reportage of this scene. Nelly's role in the plot is to form sentimental but also sadomasochistic bonds with family members, to supplement the loss of their natural mothers—most apparent in her role as nanny with Catherine and Hindley's children. Nelly's *narrative* role is similar: to supplement unfulfilled mother-child bonds, to fill in the gap of the psychical history of events. As mother-figure and sympathizer, Nelly "smooths over" fictive and enunciatory planes of the narrative—just as she "smooths over" the dark symbolic wrinkles on Heathcliff's face.

She "smooths over" the trauma associated with a Hindley-like brutality, and the difference of racial features and class that create the master-slave social hierarchy within the family. Like Chodorow's ideal caretaker, Nelly helps "the child" through symbolic separation processes, assisting "the child" in tolerating trauma, the classic trauma, for example, of the mother/caretaker's departure. Chodorow perceives the maternal caretaker's role as one that should protect the child from "having continually to react to and ward off environmental intrusions and from being [therefore] continually in need" ("Psychoanalytic Perspectives" 9); with the help of a caretaker, she adds, the child learns "a sense of continuity of experience and the opportunity to integrate a complex of (at least somewhat) complementary and consistent images enabling the 'I' to emerge as a continuous being with an identity" (9). There is a sentimental moral edge to Chodorow's work, however, which too readily supports the notion of a mother-caretaker, transformed into the child's "self" in "good relation," the product of "successful" symbiosis. Hume, in writing about sympathy, comments upon the failure of symbiosis, when he writes that sympathy may be provoked by the desire to unify with another, but also by the desire to voyeuristically separate. In *Wuthering Heights*, the demonstration of Nelly's maternal bonding and sympathy steadily unravels the benign image of the good-mother figure. To "smooth over," for Nelly, is also to stir up; to experience symbiosis and sympathy is also to create a breach.

To "smooth over" conceals her own pleasure in power: the pleasure of a mastery over others and events, the visual pleasure of witnessing narrative scenes. Trying to "smooth over" the scene of trauma for her auditor, Lockwood, the "scene" of Heathcliff's flogging is concealed, displaced onto the symptom of Hindley's "red and breathless" face. The reader-spectator, therefore, is spared the direct viewing of violence, and, hence, might sublimate the fact of Hindley's sadistic treatment of Heathcliff—the traditional response to family violence. And the reader-spectator, likewise, might ignore Nelly's failure at intervention—her failure to protect, or even to console, Heathcliff before and after the beating. Nelly's sympathetic duality disrupts, as well as smooths over, the storytelling process. She does ultimately fail, afterall, in rendering sympathetic trauma-control for the reader of *Wuthering Heights*. Otherwise, why would its original publication have provoked such a storm of controversy? Why would Charlotte Brontë—more politically conservative and traditionally minded than her sister Emily[20]— have written her own trauma-controlling Preface apologia to the second edition of the book?

But Nelly *does* succeed in controlling trauma in the overarching drama she maintains with her sympathetic spectator-narrator, "Mr. Lockwood." This gentleman who partakes of sadism in the *Wuthering Heights* story for his own viewing pleasure, much like the little party partakes greedily of the feast, is helped in his assimilation of the story's sadism through Nelly's symbiotic, "smoothing-over," sympathetic method. Whatever we know, or come to assume, of course, about "human nature" in the two houses is fielded through the vision of Lockwood. Even the image of the house on the heights itself tells us more about this spectator than about the house. This spectator is *like* the house, in "bent" or "stunted" natural representations. The attempt to be an eyewitness, to report all events with sympathetic faith and accuracy, becomes an ironic incrimination of the Wuthering Heights "wall." Built to defend the house from the "atmospheric tumult," it proves forever impenetrable. It is impenetrable, that is, if we read "Wuthering Heights" like Lockwood, like a sympathetic spectator.

And yet through Lockwood's diary text, all interpretations of Wuthering Heights/ *Wuthering Heights* must pass. The gentleman diarist from the city tries to give his reader-spectators comforting versions of the visions he hears and sees. His storytelling technique, too, is a sympathetic one, whose sadistic tendencies are only scarcely concealed by his own efforts at "smoothing over" sado-erotic bonds and events. But the supposed verisimilitude of Lockwood's vision is compromised by the instability of the Wuthering

Heights house, images we witness of its "tumult." What characterizes the representational setting of the house, like the psychoanalytic components of the novel, is its *interior* frame, and the divisionary frame of Wuthering Heights and Thrushcross Grange. Any representation of the landscape of the moors is divided by these partitional frames, a "wall" that literally divides the habitations by vision.

After we are delivered the vision of the house on the moors, and "before passing the threshold," Lockwood says he "paused to admire a quantity of grotesque carving lavished over the front and . . . principal door," the date "'1500'" and the name "'Hareton Earnshaw'" (2). Under these inscriptions Lockwood moves as he passes under the frame of the door, as the reader passes, too, into the interior sitting room. Once inside Wuthering Heights, Lockwood's attempt to convince the reader of the realism in his depiction will seem compromised by his own faulty sympathetic gaze. Lockwood sees, and then colors and perverts. Giving a spectator's tour, Lockwood can only describe what is *not* in the Wuthering Heights house, starting with a room that appears to be a kitchen but is not, which contains "no signs of roasting, boiling, or baking, about the huge fireplace" (3).

Following a description of an oak chest and the room's floor, Lockwood's gaze turns, instead, upon his human subject, Heathcliff, "a dark skinned gipsy, in aspect" (3), foreshadowing Nelly's racial representations. The mode of his description moves immediately from the concrete to the abstract, at this moment when Lockwood continues to embellish his description of Heathcliff and says that he is "rather slovenly, perhaps, yet not looking amiss . . . because he has an erect and handsome figure," also "morose" (3). Heathcliff's image reflects not any truth about Heathcliff, but rather Lockwood's racial ambivalences and white patriarchal cultural speculations. Heathcliff is the uncertain mirror of the slave-like other, the swarthy "dark skinned gipsy," whose color and origins threaten Lockwood's certainty about white mastery and hegemony. The spectator's duality toward this particular human figure in the domestic space—traditionally perceived as a stable and contained arena—is projected onto the threatening racial features of Heathcliff, again projected onto the dissembling space of the rooms themselves. But while we are looking at Heathcliff's "misanthropic" identity, we also are looking at Lockwood, our narrative spectator, before the supplementary narration of Nelly is superadded. We are looking at the masculine ideology of the mastering gaze as it tries to fix culturally wayward representations—and yet fails to do so though its own dissembling ironies.

We penetrate further into the Wuthering Heights rooms vis-à-vis Lockwood's tour—moving through the locked gate and the outer door, into the larger sitting room, and eventually into the inner chambers and the oak closet where Lockwood spends his night hallucinating. We become aware that our gaze, too, is loaded with "wuthering" penetration fantasies, when, from the beginning of the novel's fact-obsessed impetus in a journal entry dated "1801," we are given more uncertain information than fact. While many critics perceive Lockwood as "an ordinary observant man," if also a "prig and a dullard,"[21] I suggest that it is his "ordinary" quality (including his obsession with dates and facts) that should make us, as *Lockwood's* spectators, uneasy. If Lockwood brings conventional wisdom and interpretation skills to this "unreclaimed region," to use Charlotte Brontë's expression, he also misinterprets images and events, much as Lockwood misinterprets himself. Suggested in the name that puns upon the notion of repressive fantasies, he "locks up" any sentiments that do not fit his conventionality. When he literally locks himself into the closet to escape the tumult produced by the storm, Lockwood is overpowered by his own "atmospheric tumult."

His repressive fantasies expressed through conventionality are illustrated upon his visits to the house, when he recasts relationships at Wuthering Heights into sentimental clichés. He imagines a pile of dead rabbits to be sleeping kittens. And he imagines the glaring Catherine Linton Heathcliff to be a "sweet maid." Making small talk, he calls the vicious dog Juno "'A beautiful animal'"; when his "amiable hostess" declines an interest in "'the little ones,'" Lockwood spies what he calls her "'favourites,'" the "obscure cushion full of something like cats" (the "heap of dead rabbits"—7). Furthermore, he falsely assumes that "Mr. Heathcliff" and "Mrs. Heathcliff" are a domestic couple, placing their "wuthering" genealogical relationships into a sentimental archetype.

But there is a truth to Lockwood's misperceptions and perverse sentimental visions, a truth that emerges indirectly, through Lockwood's denials, obfuscation, and "white" lies. Like Nelly's "slips," Lockwood reveals the sadism in his sympathetic strategy. He does so, for instance, when briefly imagining his resemblance to Heathcliff, having first perceived Heathcliff as does Isabella Linton: a hero of romance. Lockwood's imagined resemblance to Heathcliff as "hero" serves as a foil for the resemblance Lockwood actually does bear Heathcliff as "the sadistic child."

Having just arrived at the Grange as a tenant, and viewing Heathcliff as a misanthropic, dashing figure of cultural masculinity and social autonomy celebrated by Romantic poets, Lockwood exclaims how very like Heathcliff is to himself, in the beginning of his diary, the novel's opening paragraph:

> In all England, I do not believe that I could have fixed on a situation so completely removed from the stir of society. A perfect misanthropist's Heaven—and Mr Heathcliff and I are such a suitable pair to divide the desolation between us. A capital fellow! (1)

Lockwood identifies this "heaven" in terms of sympathetic bond with Heathcliff. His bond is described in a following paragraph through the image of the "sympathetic chord" evocative of Hume:

some people might suspect him [Heathcliff] of a degree of under-bred pride—I have a *sympathetic chord* within that tells me it is nothing of the sort; I know, by instinct, his reserve springs from an aversion to showy displays of feeling . . . to manifestations of mutual kindliness. He'll love and hate, equally under cover. (3—emphasis added)

Here Lockwood acknowledges a "wuthering" quality in the image of Heathcliff, who possesses a unifying self-autonomy and yet contrary states of feeling. This "wuthering" effect is mirrored in Lockwood, whose own feeling of identification through sympathy is couched in his bond with a man who indicates "an aversion to showy displays of feeling." Lockwood suggests he can compensate for his own wuthering apprehensions toward the difference infusing Heathcliff's image through the supplement of sympathy— that he, too, *is* Heathcliff, as Catherine Earnshaw Linton declares in the diegesis proper.

Lockwood's language alludes to Hume's *Treatise* when he suggests that sympathy is a medium of communication. Hume suggests that the sympathetic figure is not only a visual spectator; he implies that the figure is also a kind of musician, especially when describing sympathy as communication: "As in strings equally wound up, one motion of one communicates itself to the rest; so all the affections readily pass from one person to another" (576). Through the musical metaphor, Hume emphasizes the way in which sympathy acts as a communicational "motion," that which creates "a lively idea of the passion . . . presently converted into the passion itself" (576). Hume here hints as the impossibility of a unifying function in sympathetic resemblance. But he also states that the "lively idea of the passion" seems to be, momentarily, "converted into the passion itself." We might read the word "passion" as another word for "sentiment." In writing, specifically, about the resemblance phenomenon in sympathy, Hume also suggests that a problem exists within it several passages later in the *Treatise:* "No passion of another discovers itself immediately to the mind" (576). For Hume, the "sympathetic chord" is an acoustic mirror, a faulty or bent reflection of "passion."

Turning to Hume's epistemological account of "resemblance" in Book I of the *Treatise*, we note the way in which resemblance functions in paradigms of causality. Through causality, "Every object predicts, produces always some object like the effect," he states. In his famous analogy of moving billiard balls, Hume writes that the relation of objects "plac'd in like relations of succession and contiguity . . . can never operate upon the mind, but by means of custom, which determines the imagination to make a transition from the idea of one object to that of its usual attendant" (170). Going back to Lockwood's sympathetic resemblance with "Heathcliff," we note that it is based upon "custom," the Romantic image of masculinity. To borrow from

Hume, Lockwood's resemblance to Heathcliff "arises from the relations" (320) of the object, Heathcliff, to himself.

Again, quoting Hume: "When any object is presented to us, it immediately conveys to the mind a lively idea of that object . . . this determination of the mind forms the necessary connexion of these objects" (169). Hume warns that "connexion" devices like resemblance, relying upon "custom," are subject to perceptual change: "when we change the point of view . . . in that case the impression is to be considered as the cause, and the lively idea as the effect; and their necessary connexion is that new determination. . . . the uniting principle . . . is as unintelligible as that among our external objects. . . ." (169). The only "uniting principle" undergirding resemblance and, by association, sympathy are social frames guiding perception. Once Lockwood, who values sentiment's civility and propriety, is *dis*unified, or disheveled, by Heathcliff's uncivil dogs—and Heathcliff's incivility in the process—Lockwood changes the point of view, paraphrasing Hume; he makes a "new determination" in regard to his resemblance toward Heathcliff.

Upon his second visit to Wuthering Heights, and chatting with Catherine while awaiting Heathcliff, Lockwood spies a "canine mother . . . sneaking wolfishly to the back of my legs, her lip curled up, and her white teeth watering for a snatch." Attempting to pet her, Lockwood's "caress provoked a long, gutteral gnarl" (4). He views the dogs as paranoid, ill-tempered watchers of the household: "the ruffianly bitch, and a pair of grim, shaggy sheep-dogs" share "a jealous guardianship over all my movements," Lockwood observes (4). Nevertheless, Lockwood provokes the dogs by returning their watchdog gaze, "making faces at the trio." In response, Lockwood reports that the "half-a-dozen four-footed fiends, of various sizes and ages, issued from hidden dens to the common centre." He says he "felt my heels, and coat-laps peculiar subjects of assault." Using a poker to parry "off the larger combatants," he is assisted by Catherine Heathcliff, who shoos the dogs away with a frying pan. This activity provokes Heathcliff's ire as he ascends from the cellar in the house: "Mr Heathcliff and his man [Joseph] climbed the cellar steps with vexatious phlegm" (4). Heathcliff demands, "'What the devil is the matter?'" Lockwood replies, "'What the devil, indeed! . . . The herd of possessed swine could have had no worse spirits in them than those animals of yours, sir. You might as well leave a stranger with a brood of tigers!'" (5).

Lockwood's invective against the attacking dogs, "those "animals" or "tigers," the "pack of curs," is reminiscent of Hindley's description of Heathcliff in the beating scene: "that brute of a lad." The description of "brutes" or "animals" was reflected in Pufendorf's language on human nature, well before Hume's language on sympathy. In Pufendorf's reading of the state of nature, he differentiates human nature from the natural state itself. While agreeing with other more cynical philosophers like Hobbes, that mankind has an inborn sense of self-love and wickedness, Pufendorf writes that "men are nonetheless linked by bonds of natural similarity, mutual needs, and the desire for social relations," and that such bonds have a civilizing force. In his book-length work on natural law, Pufendorf writes that man exists in nature as "an animal superior" to "the brutes":

> the natural state of man is that condition in which he was placed by the Creator, when he willed that man should be an animal superior to all the rest . . . man should . . . recognize and worship his Author . . . and also pass his life in a very different manner from the brutes.[22]

To be in "the natural state of man" is, therefore, both to be an "animal" and to be "superior to all the rest," distinct from animal. A commentator on Pufendorf asserts that, in such a statement, "The failure to be natural in this sense is a failure to be fully human, or fully appropriate to human life."[23]

The scene of the "brutes"—the "pack of curs" or "brood of tigers"—at Wuthering Heights alludes to the view of human nature for which Pufendorf and other "Enlightened" thinkers argued. But this scene also challenges the optimistic expectations their view sets up. Lockwood attempts to personify the superiority of human nature when situated within and contrasted to the "natural" environment by befriending savage dogs. In Lockwood's mind, even these churlish dogs—which he later accuses of having behaved like a "herd of possessed swine," like "animals"—should have received his social courtesies extended through the sympathetic gaze. In the scene of the dogs, not only do the dogs, in fact, behave as "animals," as Pufendorf's "brutes"; but so, too, does the human "animal," in refusing to offer protection and civil courtesies and denying his "natural similarity" with Lockwood. Heathcliff becomes, like the dogs, a "tiger," a "devil." To maintain Lockwood's narrational superiority over "all the rest" (quoting Pufendorf), Lockwood now separates himself from the Wuthering Heights "society" (the "inmates"). But, in this scene, there is evidence that Lockwood, too, belongs to the "pack of curs," is a "brute," through the wuthering effects of his gaze.

In the earlier scene of Lockwood's perceived "resemblance" to Heathcliff, we might laugh at Lockwood's narcissistic attempt to bolster his autonomous self-image. Following the scene of the dogs, Lockwood corrects this "false" image; and he does so in the very context of admitting how he *does,* in fact, resemble Heathcliff, another "sadistic child." This suggestion about his truer resemblance to Heathcliff is encoded in the story he tells about his atrophied romance during a recent visit to the seashore. In a brief aside, Lockwood recalls a young woman giving him "the sweetest of all imaginable looks," which caused him to shrink "icily into myself, like a snail, at every glance retired colder and farther" (4). Lockwood tells of his "deliberate heartlessness" in the affair—resonating with his first image of Heathcliff and projecting Lockwood's belief in his masculine virility through self-autonomy. At the same moment, in this aside, Lockwood conveys his *lack* of masculine virility, through the image of the recoiling "snail." The description of Lockwood's "heartlessness," his supposed emotional self-sufficiency, is couched in his fearful reaction to the female "look."[24] We learn that Lockwood *is* "heartless," like Heathcliff, and that, like Heathcliff, his sadistic tendencies are based upon a fear of losing control—with a female spectator. Lockwood, after all, resembles Heathcliff, another sadistic child. But this resemblance to Heathcliff Lockwood would rather deny, since it implies his hidden dependency and fear.

Thus, Lockwood alludes to his sadism through the displacement and substitutional processes of dreams. It is during the dream in the closet that Lockwood shows us that he is "the sadistic child." He crushes the wrist of the ghost child who wants in, against the sharp edges of the shattered window glass. If that is not enough to warn us of Lockwood's sadistic nature, preacher Branderham—having listed a long catalogue of humankind's sins—accuses Lockwood: " '*Thou art the Man!*' " (19). Lockwood protests his innocence, but Branderham fingers him as "the Man"—of sentiment and of sadism. Lockwood is the "deliberate" hidden sadist in the visual drama of sympathetic fictions. He is the "brute," the "tiger," wrapped in sentiment's sheep skin.

Such moments in the novel are indicative of Lockwood's socialized unconscious. It is in his bond with Nelly, and their "mutual need" for sympathetic spectating and storytelling, that Lockwood's *voyeuristic* sadistic capacities clearly rise to the surface, albeit in repressed form. In a very brief scene that follows the tale of Heathcliff's beating, Nelly asks to be permitted to retire for the night. Lockwood, who is thoroughly enjoying himself, insists that Nelly stay and that her story continue. Lockwood is literally Nelly's master. A repressed, perverse, sentimentalized eroticism in their master-slave bedtime *tête-à-tête* is suggested in the words Lockwood uses to urge Nelly on—in the image of a mother "puss" and her young ones. He says he is in " 'the mood of mind . . . in which, if you were seated alone, and the cat licking its kittens on the rug before you . . . that puss's neglect of one ear would put you seriously out of temper. . . . ' " (52). Nelly chides him, and Lockwood admits to a " 'terribly lazy mood.' " He announces that, on the morrow, he will have " 'an obstinate cold' " and, therefore, has no intention of rising early, but rather intends " 'lengthening the night till afternoon' " (52). Lockwood is like the narcissistic child who imagines his caretaker to be a function of his "omnipotent system," using Mahler's concept: Nelly waits on him, feeds him—with stories, as well as food. And this illusion of intimacy and symbiosis, in the master-slave (servant) bond, creates in Lockwood his self-delusions of sympathetic identification toward other figures in the story, those figures peopling Nelly's bedtime fictions.

Lockwood admits that his sympathetic practice is a dualistic one, invoking a visual-erotic fusion with his maternal Imaginary. The Lacanian Imaginary is that nostalgic infantile wholeness, whose socialized legacy has become the sentimentalized, "feminine" emotional ideal. Lockwood experiences, in his words about nostalgic Imaginary processes, a "deepened attraction not entirely owning to the situation of the looker-on" (52). He idealizes the subjects of Nelly's tale as more real, more "earnest," in their sensations and feelings, saying: "they *do* live more in earnest, more in themselves, and less in surface change, and frivolous external things" (52—Brontë's emphasis). So gratified is Lockwood by this image of "reality" and the "truer" emotions prevailing at Wuthering Heights that he says, "I could fancy a love for life here almost possible; and I was a fixed unbeliever in any love of a year's standing" (52). Of course, his fantasy is the fantasy enacted by *being* the "looker-on," of controlling the direction of the gaze, a habit he learns from Nelly herself. When Nelly protests, "Oh! here we are the same as anywhere else, when you get to know us" (52), for once she speaks the unembellished truth. The characters of Wuthering Heights are *not* special in their symbiotic emotional bonds. They simply reveal the socialization processes of the sadomasochistic dialectic, through which those bonds are constituted.

They depict, openly, unforgivingly, a sadomasochism underlying "natural" familial bonds. And they represent the sadomasochism underlying the spectating practice of sympathy. Rendering the inevitably wuthering aspects of sympathetic identification within nature, Brontë's novel suggests that belief in such "nature," like "natural" human bonds, is based upon a social myth. The novel teaches us to be wary of the sympathetic mother figure and the man of sentiment alike. These "lookers-on" are, of course, displacements of the fitful looker outside the fiction, the darkened figure of the readerly spectator.[25]

"We're All Angels Here": Wyler's Wuthering Heights

Wyler's film version does exactly what the novel cannot: it presents an undying faith in sentimental human bonds, and it sanitizes the motives of its spectator in the process. Nelly, or "Ellen" Dean, and Lockwood have relatively insignificant roles in the film adaptation. Instead, the film's diegetic emphasis is on the heterosexual romance between Cathy and Heathcliff, told in the form of a nostalgic flashback. And the film represents the full mimetic plenitude of the natural moors that the novel refuses us. The film, thus, re-stores—and re-stor(i)es—the efficacy of sympathy as a visual-identification form. It does so through the power of the film image to bind the spectator into the "world," to make the spectator a "figure in the landscape."

In Wyler's film *Wuthering Heights*—which opened simultaneously in New York and Hollywood in the spring of 1939 to great acclaim[26]—sympathy binds and sustains audience identification. The view of sympathy as a unifying methodology is suggested in the words of "Ellen's" voice-over and through the dialogue of other characters. This view is also conveyed through the moving picture itself, in the stunningly photographed shot/reverse shots, which locate the film spectator within Hollywood's false natural setting.[27] The "Yorkshire moors" were filmed in the hills above the San Fernando Valley, a landscape made up of fifteen thousand pieces of tumbleweed topped with purple sawdust, and one thousand imported heather plants for close-ups.[28] This false, if fabulous, mise-en-scène convinces the spectator not only of the authenticity of the romantic and wild Yorkshire landscape but that he, too, is a *figure,* a "figure in the landscape," quoting Mulvey. He is a figure at once benign and perverse, his sadomasochistic prurience arising from the voyeurism and fetishism in his spectatorial role, aggressive tendencies sublimated by the "social symbiosis" (Chancer's phrase) of the heterosexual romance.

In the Wyler film version of *Wuthering Heights,* men are masters and women are angelic slaves. The film spectator's sadoerotic desires are repressed, however, within the slave-like figure that the "spoken" audience of cinema plays out in the dark. A spectator caught up in sympathetic identification with fictive subjects of the film will also be caught within the enslavement of sadoerotic images of love, desire, and the cultural male-female romance—images supposedly only affecting the fictive level of the drama. Ultimately, the spectator is caught up and within what Bazin calls "the diffuse space without shape or frontiers that surrounds the screen."[29] It is through the process of classic-cinema adaptation that Wyler renders a novel of *anti-*sentiment into a wholly sentimentalized Hollywood love story. This process is achieved as Wyler arrests the wuthering tendencies of nature and replaces them with a full mimetic stage, and a spectator who seems but an "angel," too.

The credits sequence immediately reveals the importance of landscape to the film, a depiction of "real" nature that Bazin suggests is one of cinema's "natural guarantees." Bazin writes that "there can be no cinema without the setting up on an open space in place of the universe rather than as part of it. The screen cannot give us the illusion of this feeling of space without calling on certain natural guarantees" (109, 111). In the film's credits sequence, this "natural guarantee" is offered outright, the potentially wuthering or differential aspects of nature closed off, ignored. We are presented, in the sequence, with several still shots offering different views of the house on the moors. A paragraph overlays a final shot in the sequence, and helps to place the film spectator—briefly here a reader—within the Hollywood mimetic conventions of time and space, making reading language a natural-appearing act: on "the barren Yorkshire moors in England, a hundred years ago. . . ." On those moors, we continue to read, once existed "a house as bleak and desolate as the wastes around it. Only a stranger lost in a storm would have dared to knock at the door." The cautionary tale invoked by the images of words on the screen fades to a shot of just such "a stranger lost in a storm." Violent whirls of snow dash around his weather-beaten image, once again confirming the vitality of the "natural" cinematic image.

The "stranger" we learn is Mr. Lockwood, no insipid sentimental Victorian gentleman here, but rather a haggard-looking fellow trudging bleakly through the piling drifts of snow. Lockwood here represents the "reality," the honesty, of the "natural" image. He is the male "figure in a landscape," who authentically sustains natural realism. But it is he who depends upon the "landscape," as well, to give his *own* nature vitality and solidity. And just as the "natural guarantee" guarantees *him* the natural-man image, his fictive gaze gives the film spectator a point of view, a "natural guarantee," as well. The camera pans as if mimicking Lockwood's point of view, and spies the Wuthering Heights house; the film spectator's point of view is transferred onto Lockwood's. Lost to this suturing process is the fact that the spectator lacks the "natural guarantee," as well.

Suture establishes the spectator's look upon Lockwood's look. And so, too, does this look establish identification, in general. The spectator's desire is the desire to become one with the image. Through the "absent field" that the spectator is made to be, his awareness that "nature" is more artifice than fact is, for the two-hour length of the film, fantastically erased. Meanwhile, the "natural guarantee" of the moors landscape—described in the original Charles MacArthur and Ben Hecht screenplay "as devilish and forlorn," a place upon which the "old manor house" stands "like a derelict in the wild night"[30]—may appear to engulf the figure of Lockwood "lost in the snow." But that figure, too, is *distinguished* from nature. A tired, bedraggled but nevertheless heroic Lockwood pushes his way through the stubborn gate and *out* of nature, to enter the relative calm and civility of the Wuthering Heights manor.

Lockwood is greeted by yelping dogs and cold, immobile human stares. But there are no "wild beasts," in Pufendorf's words, in this domesticated space. The dogs, wild and untameable in the novel, are quickly silenced in the film version by their master, who stands a sentry before a blazing hearth fire. The "master" is initially glowering and cruel, telling Lockwood that "I hope my hospitality is a lesson to you to make no more rash journeys on these moors." But then this "master," who turns out to be Heathcliff, apologizes to Lockwood, offering a bed for the night, saying, "Guests are so rare in this house that I hardly know how to receive them."

While nature may be wild and woolly outside, human nature is benign and tame inside. Keeping with the domestic family picture, the feisty Catherine II from the novel is missing in the film, substituted by a worn and passive "Mrs. Heathcliff," who really *is* Heathcliff's wife (the former Isabella Linton, played by Geraldine Fitzgerald). *This* "Mrs. Heathcliff" fulfills her proper domestic role as a slave-like wife who never questions her devotion to Heathcliff, who turns, servant-like, to her husband to ask whether or not she should serve tea.

Meanwhile, "Nelly"—now called "Ellen" (played by Flora Robeson)—replaces the more wily Nelly from the novel. Ellen bears little of Nelly's sadistic intrigue; Ellen, instead, is witless and passive, a perfect "domestic" who knows her place—literally visible but briefly so in this initial episode, sitting next to the other servant in the film, Joseph. Ellen claims few powers of the storyteller to embellish or manipulate. Ellen has a place but a relatively insignificant one in this film version. She may tell the story of Wuthering Heights to a sleepless Lockwood. But her intrusion into the storytelling process fades with that of her voice-over narration.

Ellen's narrative does have a function, however: to confirm rather than to raise suspicions about the transcendent role of the spectator, and that spectator's suture or identification with culturally sanctioned heterosexual and sadomasochistic love. Ellen's role is to fill in the gaps left by any spectator through suturing processes. This role is demonstrated during the episode in which she begins her story. It is informed, however, by the episode immediately proceeding it.

In this prior episode, Lockwood is shown by Joseph to the upstairs bedroom. Falling fast asleep, he is soon awakened by a banging shutter and a voice crying out from the moors. He closes the shutter, and a point-of-view shot reveals Lockwood's startled gaze upon a vision he obviously fears. The lack of an accompanying reverse shot suggests that what he sees is unrepresentable, but neither is it a product of his bedtime reading, a dream-like fantasy, as in the novel. It is interesting to note that, in the original draft of the screenplay, Lockwood first falls asleep as he does in Brontë's novel, reading Catherine's old books and diaries. This part of the screenplay was edited out of the final film cut. The effect was to "edit out" the possibility that Lockwood's vision is fictively informed—instead, identification is made "real" with the image. Only *super*natural explanations can explain the "nothing" of Lockwood's startled vision. And Ellen's role is to confirm these supernatural explanations as, well, natural. When Lockwood seeks her comfort before the kitchen hearth, she explains to him that "there is life after death," that, as she repeats, "there *is* a force that brings them [the Hollywood lovers] back, if their hearts were wild enough in life."

Heathcliff runs to the moors to pursue the vision, and a close-up of Ellen's face reveals her eyes looking wistfully down. Visibly subdued, Ellen says, "*She* calls him. He follows her out on the moor. . . . It was Cathy . . . a girl who died." Lockwood tells Ellen that he does not believe in life after death, nor ghosts. But this faded old housekeeper, a "ghost" of her former Nelly-self, gazes at Lockwood steadily (in a shot from Lockwood's point of view), and sympathetically proposes to tell him a "story," one that will make him change his "mind about the dead coming back." Caught up in the exchange of point-of-view glances, Lockwood pleads, "Tell me her story." Ellen begins nostalgically, "It began forty years ago, when I was young, in the service of Mr. Earnshaw, Cathy's father." The shot fades out and a new shot fades in depicting the Wuthering Heights house on the moor as seen in the credits. Ellen's presence becomes that of a ghostly voice-over, waxing nostalgic: "Wuthering Heights was a lovely place in those days, full of summertime and beautiful, happy voices. . . ."

The voice-over disappears with the shot of happy children playing in the house with a youthful Ellen. This shot cuts to another shot, showing Mr. Earnshaw drawing up to the house on horseback, accompanied by a beggar-boy, the young Heathcliff. He announces to the servant that he has brought home "A gift of god, although it's as dark as if it came from the devil," the dialogue from the novel. But the prior shot of happy children and nanny establishes a more optimistic interpretation of these lines. Heathcliff *is* "a gift of god," an angel, these lines suggest, an interpretation assisted by old Earnshaw's jolly delivery, laughing and pulling affectionately at Heathcliff.

Earnshaw himself is an angel of mercy, having rescued the child from "the streets of Liverpool," where he was found "starving," and "kicked and bruised and almost dead." The benign depiction of the family patriarch will prevail through Heathcliff during the rest of the film. Heathcliff's inherent assumption of a virtuous nature helps to arouse sympathy in the spectator. Sympathy for Heathcliff builds interest in and focus upon the "male figure." The sentimental interpretation of Heathcliff, as well as "Cathy," as she is called in the film version, will make the sadomasochistic nature of their relationship palatable.

In Wyler's *Wuthering Heights,* Cathy is clearly a subordinate "slave" to Heathcliff's male mastery. Their master-slave coupling will be depicted throughout the story of their heterosexual romance. The romance begins, naturally, in childhood. Its depiction takes for granted a cultural view of heterosexuality that encodes master and slave relations, which Chancer describes thus: "Heterosexuality, in fantasy and reality, is often . . . experienced as inseparable from the eroticization of dominant/subordinate relations along male/female lines" (126). Chancer alludes to Freud, who had argued in his earlier writings on sadomasochism in "Three Essays on the Theory of Sexuality" that "the simultaneous presence of the opposites" of sadism and masochism seem connected to "the opposing masculinity and femininity which are combined in bisexuality" (*On Sexuality* 73). In these essays, Freud followed the earlier sexology account of sadomasochism by Krafft-Ebing, who aligned sadism with masculinity and masochism with femininity, viewing these traits as natural to the heterosexual couple and placing this couple in a traditional domestic setting: "Where the husband forces the wife by menacing and other violent means to the conjugal act, we can no longer describe such as a normal physiological manifestation, but must ascribe it to sadistic impulses."[31] Although Freud spoke of sadomasochism as a perversion of "normal" human sexuality, like Krafft-Ebing, he also considered sadomasochism a logical product of sexual-reproductive needs, citing the male's need to aggressively dominate a "reluctant" female to reproduce the species. The engendering of the species, for Freud and the sexologists, relied upon the "engendering" of sadomasochism, to use Chancer's phrase. Freud writes:

> The sexuality of most men shows an admixture of aggression, of a desire to subdue, the biological significance of which lies in the necessity for overcoming the resistance of the sexual object by actions other than mere *courting*. Sadism would then correspond to an aggressive component of the sexual instinct.[32]

Sadism exists in the Freudian account, Chancer notes, "as a primordial vestige of male aggressivity" (127). Like other psychoanalytic feminists,[33] Chancer reads Freudian determininism as "descriptive rather than prescriptive," the result of "sexually repressive patriarchal milieus" (127). These "milieus" breed "social symbiosis," a phrase Chancer coins to imply "the structure of social institutions themselves, and the customary experiences they engender" (92). Through social symbiosis, human beings can become "excessively dependent" upon such institutions. These include the institution of heterosexuality, whose man-woman dyad makes male sadism and female masochism seem a natural fact.

This natural fact is elaborated upon by Wyler's *Wuthering Heights* as a sadomasochistic, heterosexual romance unfolds, in sequences representing lovers on the Yorkshire moors. The sequences begin early in the film, when Heathcliff and Cathy are children. In the first sequence, Cathy calls to Heathcliff, "I'll race you to the barn! The one who loses has to be the other's slave." The children gallop on horseback in a series of long shots revealing them bounding freely over the open range. Arriving first, Heathcliff shouts, "I won! You're my slave. You'll have to do as I say." Then the theme of masters and slaves in the male-female relationship is temporarily displaced onto the male-male relationship in the relationship of masters to slaves, and, implicitly, fathers to sons.

The master figure (and "father" figure) is represented by Hindley, who plays out the father's sadism when he takes possession of Heathcliff's horse—because his own is "lame." The castration image is shown be a violent one, when Hindley hits Heathcliff on the head with a rock. Hindley and Heathcliff enact the father-son sadomasochistic dyad cited by Chancer. Borrowing from Chodorow's theory of gender development in the traditional nuclear family, Chancer writes that "we know that not only gendered roles are reproduced within the family but gendered sadomasochism as well" (150). Sadomasochism may tend to conclude *vis-à-vis* the son's relation toward the mother, and toward women, in general. But the "dominant sadism" reproduced in the son toward the mother becomes the son's *own* "subordinate masochism" in relation to the father, "compared to whom he knows he is relatively powerless within the family structure" (Chancer 151). While the son "mimics the orientation of his father as well as of the patriarchal order in which the family partakes . . . in [sadistic] relation to a woman," the son reveals "his masochistic side in relation to a man" (151). As Hindley takes on the father-sadist role in his violent treatment of Heathcliff, Heathcliff takes on the role of the son and its masochism. The roles of fathers and sons are also superimposed onto the class roles of masters and slaves that Hindley and Heathcliff represent. Meanwhile, Cathy, who had received a horse whip from her father as a gift in an earlier scene, beats her brother with it, complicating her own image as female "slave" (in heterosexual union with Heathcliff): she is a female dominatrix in dealing with Hindley, a "father" figure. She *becomes* the sadistic father—or, rather, the phallic substitute mother—through the use of the father's whip-gift. She performs her more mothering role when she rescues Heathcliff—using her whip.

The importance of the phallus at the text's subliminal level is suggested in both the whip and the symbolic iconography of Pennistone Crag, a phallic-like protuberance that rises above the moors. The Crag is where Heathcliff and Catherine continue their master-slave rhetoric in lovemaking. The first episode at Pennistone Crag takes place when they are "naturally" innocent children, suggesting both the innocence of sadomasochism and its determinism, its naturalness in relationships not only between men and women but also between boys and girls. Riding toward the symbolic referent of the crag, only a veiled referent in the novel—never an actual image—Cathy tells Heathcliff, "You're so handsome when you smile. . . . Don't you know that you're handsome? . . . you're a prince in disguise . . . your father was Emperor of China and your mother an Indian Queen." In this dialogue, the young Cathy emphasizes Heathcliff's natural nobility as well as native sense of mastery and sovereignty, adding, "It's true, Heathcliff." Pennistone Crag is their "castle," upon which, playing Heathcliff's "queen," Cathy symbolically hands Heathcliff her whip (it becomes a phallus as his "lance"), and plays again the phallic mother, ordering Heathcliff to "challenge him," meaning "the black knight" who would deny him possession to his "castle." From atop the Crag "castle," Cathy and Heathcliff continue their sadomasochistic domestic fantasy. Annointed "Catherine of York" by Heathcliff, Cathy is queen of a courtly lover; she bows down before her "lord," saying, "But I'm still your slave" (fig. 4.1). Heathcliff says, "You're my queen. Whatever happens out there—here you'll always be my queen!" It is Heathcliff's saying so that gives the "queen" power, the ironic power of female mastery, holding the phallus because the male figure says she does.

The relationship of the phallic natural landscape to sovereignty, as well as to unchanging master-slaves identities, is emphasized in two following episodes taking place above the moors at Pennistone Crag, after Heathcliff and Cathy are adults. The first sequence takes place following the father's death and other interior scenes at Wuthering Heights that emphasize Hindley's sadistic mastery and Heathcliff's virtual enslavement as stable boy and servant. When Heathcliff meets and embraces Cathy atop the Crag, he tells her that nothing is "real down there, our life is here"; and she answers, "Yes, my lord," suggesting that, through heterosexual romance, Heathcliff can reverse the master-slave paradigm that makes him

Figure 4.1 The young Heathcliff and Catherine at Pennistone Crag, from *Wuthering Heights* (Samuel Goldwyn 1939). Courtesy of Arts Library—Special Collections, University Research Library, UCLA.

slave at the manor. When Cathy suggests that Heathcliff run away to become a "prince," Heathcliff asks incredulously, "Run away? From you? . . . I've been beaten like a dog, abused and cursed and driven mad, but I've stayed just to be near you." His speech openly reveals the dependency he feels for Cathy, and the symbiosis that generates the sadomasochistic dynamic between them. Later, Heathcliff will appear to emotionally renounce his dependency upon Cathy, keep his feelings more hidden, in order to retain "a position of control and superiority," in Chancer's words, when Cathy abandons him in marriage to Edgar Linton. This renunciation is only part of the male heterosexual mastery dilemma.

But in this romantic episode atop Pennistone Crag, Cathy asserts her own upper-class "nature" when she declares she will not run away with him, "live in haystacks . . . go barefoot in the snow," hearing music from the Linton manor. She identifies with the Linton display of bourgeois wealth and artificial sentiment, saying, "That's what I want. Dancing and singing in a pretty world." Her masochistic dependency upon the master, Heathcliff, is temporarily displaced onto her masochistic dependency to be like the good bourgeoise, and, as a woman, to take on the status of the object-fetish. When Cathy and Heathcliff spy on the Linton party, they gaze through a window that reveals fancy clothes and a mansion decked out in the fetishistic finery of the country gentility. The point-of-view shot suggests the artificiality of this world compared to the natural moors, a distinction between nature and culture that will continue throughout the film and privilege the term of the former—as more "real." Cathy absorbs sentiment's fetishism and artifice as she convalesces at the Linton home. When she returns to Wuthering Heights looking like a fashion plate (in Isabella Linton's dress), we see her adopting the role of the female fetish, a role that is supposed to contrast with her more natural role as Heathcliff's "wild" lover.

Point-of-view shots are exchanged between Cathy and Heathcliff in the scene of her return, the tattered and torn garb of Heathcliff standing in stark contrast to Cathy's finery. Identification is momentarily ruptured, and Heathcliff demands to know why she stayed so long at the Grange, while Cathy demands that Heathcliff change his attire. When Heathcliff leaves, Cathy turns against Edgar, and projects hatred of Heathcliff onto her mannered suitor, telling him she "hates the look of [his] milk-white face" and "soft, foolish hands." "Cathy, what possesses you?" demands the gentle snob Edgar (played by David Niven); "That gipsy's evil soul has gotten into you, I think." Cathy replies adamantly, "Yes, it's true." As she throws Edgar out of the house, Cathy, the masochist, becomes the phallic mother once again, and the changeable female, a prototype for the Hollywood *femme fatale* of the *film noir* tradition. Cathy reveals that she, indeed, is possessed by her own sadistic devils and a changeable, demonic waywardness. She rejects Ellen's offer of tea and sympathy, running to her room, where a shot of her image as she stands before a mirror is followed by a shot of her stripping off her fetishistic adornments, putting on the simple dress she wears on the moors. The "real" Cathy sheds her artificial skins, to appear before Heathcliff in another sequence at Pennistone Crag, where the lovers embrace and reconfirm the natural master-slave contract.

Cathy begs Heathcliff to keep her from changing, in relation to her static view of nature from atop the Crag. Cathy tells Heathcliff to "make the world stop right here. Make everything stop and stand still and never move again. Make the moors never change, and you and I never change." Heathcliff responds: "The moors and I never change. Don't you, Cathy." That Heathcliff has such power over the moors and natural eternity is suggested as he asserts his panoptic gaze over the moors (fig. 4.2). Cathy reiterates the unchangeability of the moors when she replies, "Standing on this hill with you . . . This is me forever." She furthers what is essentially a masochistic declaration when she says, "I think I'd die if you hadn't," meaning having aborted his trip to America by jumping ship. Heathcliff proclaims the master role when he says, "Cathy, you're still my queen." A follow-up sequence displaces Cathy's role as the female fetish decked out in glamour-girl finery onto her role as the fetish-fertility symbol. Cathy turns to Heathcliff and says, "Smell the heather. Fill my arms with heather, all they can hold." At the base of the Crag, with the tall heather waving plentifully in the foreground and the plenitude of the open moor in the background, Heathcliff bundles heather into Catherine's arms (fig. 4.3). That the phallic mother is also mother nature is suggested when Cathy and Heathcliff kiss.

This shot fades out and a new shot fades in, depicting the same spot on the moors but without the lovers Cathy and Heathcliff. A voice-over by Ellen warns us of impending division and loss, signalled by female fetishism: "Cathy was torn by the wild passion she had for Heathcliff, and the new life she had found on the Grange." The next shot reveals Cathy bathing, this time stripping off the grime of the moors, to dress, again, in a glamorous gown—a silk one, even more elegant. Cathy now obtains the iconic power of the Hollywood fetish; Ellen comments on the power of this image as she fusses over the lady seated at the mirror, and remarks upon "this change in you, Miss Cathy . . . look at you, you're lovely, Miss Cathy." This *tête-à-tête* between domestic servant and mistress in the boudoir is interrupted when Heathcliff barges in and stands in the door, gazing at Cathy's new image and demanding to be alone with her. Ellen asserts Cathy's class superiority when she remarks that she takes "orders from Mistress Catherine, not stable boys." The sadomasochism between Cathy and Heathcliff leads to a violent confrontation, as Cathy pushes Heathcliff and Heathcliff strikes her. His own masochism resurfaces when he runs out into the pouring rain and returns to the stable, thrusting his hands back and forth through a window. A follow-up shot emphasizes the representational issues of fetishism—the castration

Figure 4.2 The adult Heathcliff (Laurence Olivier) and Catherine (Merle Oberon) at Pennistone Crag. *Wuthering Heights* (Samuel Goldwyn 1939). Courtesy of Arts Library—Special Collections, University Research Library, UCLA.

image of cutting, severed images and bonds—when the bleeding Heathcliff appears before Ellen in the kitchen, who binds his wounds.

But Ellen cannot bind all wounds. Like the parallel scene in the novel, Heathcliff conceals himself when Cathy enters to announce to Ellen that

Figure 4.3 Catherine and Heathcliff romp in the natural heather of William Wyler's "Yorkshire" Moors (filmed fifty miles from Hollywood). *Wuthering Heights* (Samuel Goldwyn 1939). Courtesy of Arts Library—Special Collections, University Research Library, UCLA.

Edgar has asked her to marry him. When Cathy says it would "degrade" her to marry Heathcliff, a close-up shot of Heathcliff's sorrowful face, coupled with a shot of Ellen's sympathetic gaze toward the door, binds the spectator in sympathy with Heathcliff. Ellen's gaze is missed by Cathy not because Ellen is secretive about it, but because Cathy has her back to Ellen, as well as to the camera. Ellen's role in the film is distinctly different than Nelly's role in the equivalent scene from the novel. Ellen, in the film, makes us identify with Heathcliff, through an *uncertain* gaze—the gaze that seeks to know whether or not he is hiding behind the door. A shot of Ellen through the door frame, lit by a bolt of lightning, reveals to the film spectator that Heathcliff is now missing—but Ellen doesn't know. Her sympathy works on Catherine to help the latter to see that Heathcliff is her true mate. Cathy now parallels Ellen and the spectator's identification with and sympathy for Heathcliff when she declares, "Ellen, I *am* Heathcliff!" A second bolt of lightning melodramatically lights her face, but the sound of horse hooves and shouts from afar signal to Ellen that Heathcliff is gone. She tells Cathy, "He [Heathcliff] must have been listening." Ellen plays an angel of mercy in this scene rather than a covert spy and sadistic manipulator. The theme of angels, as well as identification, inflects the scene in the kitchen through dialogue.

In her sympathetic attempt on behalf of Heathcliff to persuade Cathy not to marry Edgar, Ellen remarks to Cathy, "What's to keep you from taking a place among the Linton angels?" Cathy replies, "I don't think I belong in heaven, Ellen." And she then recounts a dream she had in which she visited heaven and cried, making "the angels . . . so angry they flung me out into the middle of the heath on top of Wuthering Heights." This theme of angels, nature, and sympathetic identification with the "heath" and "cliff" of (masculine) nature is alluded to in a later sequence, as well. This is an episode in which Cathy is "happily" married to Edgar, and we glimpse what turns out to be a temporary domestic bliss. Cathy, presiding as matron and Victorian angel of the house is seated and engaged before a *petit point* pictorial embroidery. Edgar remarks, "For me, heaven is bounded by the four walls of this room." Cathy says, "Yes, we're all angels. Even my little *petit point* hero"—and we see a shot of the picture of a half-completed angel— "I'm just putting wings on him." Punning on the term "wings," Edgar says, "Speaking of wings, I'll show you those plans," referring to architectural plans for the house. This pun suggests that the angel's propriety is related to the proprietor's property, the house of domestic felicity containing these mastering terms.

In this episode, Isabella Linton is also an angel of the house, the angel of mercy—like Ellen—who nurses Cathy in her recovery after Heathcliff's fateful flight, a kind and pretty but simple-minded maid who cannot remember whether or not Dr. Kenneth had prescribed "twenty lumps of sugar in claret and one drop of medicine," or "twenty lumps of sugar and one drop of claret." Cathy calls her a "darling," saying to Edgar, "You've all been darlings. Everyone is so nice to me here," in a mise-en-scène depicting a tranquil garden. The angelic "darling" Isabella is also a passionate masochist, we soon learn, a woman who fits the stereotype of female masochism from Freud's "Three Essays"—and the connection of women to masochism still preponderant in psychology theory today. In Isabella's heterosexual relationship with Heathcliff, she reveals the image of *Sweet Suffering* from Natalie Shainess's book by that title; or the image of the female masochist from pop-psychology paperbacks cited by Chancer, with titles like *Women Who Love Too Much* or *The Pleasers: Women Who Can't Say No and the Men Who Control Them*—books that depict women as undying masochists, painting "portraits of destructive dynamics masquerading as love."[34]

Isabella is a classic candidate for the sadomasochistic dynamic, her desire for love stimulated by the sight of her brother's domestic felicity, and her "loneliness," as Heathcliff himself notes, producing a needy dependency. That this relationship has parallels to the relationship of Cathy and Heathcliff is suggested when Isabella promises to be Heathcliff's "slave."

Isabella's role as sentimental masochist, of course, is taken from her novel's depiction. Heathcliff in the novel tells Nelly upon their marriage that Isabella left her family at Thrushcross Grange "under a delusion, picturing in me a hero of romance, and expecting unlimited indulgences from my chivalrous devotion" (128). But Isabella's masochism in the film version is much more clear-cut than in the Brontë text. In the latter, Isabella quickly becomes wise to her delusion. Even Heathcliff admits, in the novel, that he "had actually succeeded in making her hate me!", although he notes sarcastically that Isabella had herself announced this to him "as a piece of appalling intelligence," as if perhaps it had changed his attitude toward her and moved him to sympathy (128–29). In fact, Isabella's romance with Heathcliff in the novel is a cautionary tale for any sentimental reader, who might construe Heathcliff's sadism as romantic charisma. But a wiser sentimental reader, Isabella, in the novel, nevertheless upholds a sentimental understanding of human virtue and sympathy, writing in a letter to Nelly upon arriving at Wuthering Heights, "How did you contrive to preserve *the common sympathies of human nature* when you resided here?" (116—emphasis added). The notion of "common sympathies" rings with Pufendorf's optimistic view of human nature and the natural state. Isabella then suggests a belief in her own intrinsic benevolent nature when she concludes, "I cannot recognize any sentiment which those around, share with me" (116). Still, her "sentiment" is related to her class background in the novel; as Nelly warns Heathcliff, Isabella "has been brought up like an only daughter whom every one was ready to serve" (128). Heathcliff mocks Isabella's philosophical optimism in the following lines from the novel, suggesting that a woman of her class avoids sadistic visions when they are in front of her eyes—to maintain sentimental illusions of piety and the sadomasochistic fantasy of romance. In the novel, Heathcliff tells Nelly:

> "The first thing she saw me do, on coming out of the Grange, was to hang up her little dog, and when she pleaded for it, the first words I uttered were a wish that I had the hanging of every being belonging to her, except one; possibly, she took that exception for herself—But no brutality disgusted her—I suppose, she has an innate admiration of it, if only her precious person were secure from injury!" (129)

The film version builds upon Isabella's conflation of pain and romance from the novel, by developing further her sentimentality as a form of sadomasochistic desire for Heathcliff. In the film, Isabella resembles the stereotyped caricature of the masochistic woman in love, a desire whose "delusion" is inflamed by the bitter treatment she receives from Heathcliff: the more he mistreats Isabella the more she appears to love him. When Hindley tries to convince Isabella to kill Heathcliff, she defends Heathcliff to Hindley, differing significantly from a parallel scene in the novel—where a more cynical Isabella, who has learned to protect herself, uses the fact that Hindley has a gun to keep Heathcliff locked outside and away from herself. In the film, Heathcliff returns home to a devoted and servile wife who takes his hat and coat at the door. Isabella is fodder for Heathcliff's sadistic revenge upon Edgar and Cathy. But his cruelty and indifference seem only to inflame her passion as she pleads, "Oh, Heathcliff, why won't you let me come near you? . . . I can make you happy." In a declaration that echoes Cathy's own atop Pennistone Crag, Isabella declares, "I'll be your slave." She suggests that to be a "slave" is the same as to be a "woman" when she adds, "I'm a woman, and I love you." Isabella in the film suggests that, as a woman, a slave, she has no identity outside that of Heathcliff's, who is "all of life to me."[35]

A sequence of shots taken at the door reinforces this stereotype of female masochism and victimage. Heathcliff flees Isabella, in a point-of-view shot then revealing a grief-struck Isabella propped up against the door frame. A reverse shot then shows the point of view to be Ellen's own sympathetic gaze; the reverse shot builds sympathy for Isabella's feeling in the look of concern on Ellen's face. Through this shot/reverse shot, sympathetic identification is arrested and the bond of suture takes place. As the spectator bonds with Isabella, the spectator also ideologically is bound into the naturalness of the shot, and the "natural" story of female masochism. A follow-up shot reveals Ellen approaching Isabella, in her role as angel of mercy, nurse and consoler in the film. But Isabella flees Ellen and emerges outdoors. An exterior shot reveals Isabella's back to the camera, standing in the foreground, while Heathcliff rides away across the moors in the background.

One reading of this shot's interesting iconography is that Isabella's gaze upon Heathcliff temporarily reverses the traditional subject-object relations ascribed to classic film by Mulvey—who argues that all classic cinema implies the dominance of male agency through the gaze that engenders the active/passive dualism as male/female. In the shot from *Wuthering Heights*, Isabella's female gaze is *in*active. As Heathcliff tells Isabella in the interior sequence prior to this shot, her "eyes are always empty." It is, indeed, the *empty* gaze of Isabella that looks out over the plenitude of nature and the figure in the landscape that is Heathcliff—who rides away like the Western movie cowboy towards the horizon, zig-zagging across the range astride his mount. The woman may own the gaze in this shot. But she stands a stone statue, a kind of Lot's wife looking back, her own back to the camera's gaze. While Isabella's gaze is "empty," Heathcliff, its object, remains the active figure in the field.

It is Heathcliff's motion, his action and passion, that survives this film, especially in the concluding sequence depicting Cathy's death. In this sequence, Cathy's own female masochism is featured, along with Heathcliff's masculine agency. Demonstrating what Dr. Kenneth earlier called "the will to die," Cathy lies in bed rambling on to Edgar about flowers at Pennistone Crag, looks blankly away and recalls nostalgically that there she was "queen once." Her angelic quality is stressed when she clings to Edgar and tells him sweetly and helplessly, "You've been very dear to me, darling, very dear." When Edgar leaves for the doctor, Heathcliff scales the stairwell and enters Cathy's chamber. In an interior shot of the room, he gazes at a sleeping/ dying Cathy, who awakens to his gaze like Sleeping Beauty. The eroticism of this scene—Heathcliff pushes Cathy down on the bed with his kiss—is conflated with Cathy's masochism, her "will to die." When Ellen breaks in to warn them of Edgar's approach, Heathcliff swears, "I won't go, Cathy. I'll never leave you again." Their heterosexual union seems eternal, when Cathy says, "I told you he was my life, my being."

Death cannot rupture this eternal union. Cathy's death is portrayed through a series of suturing point-of-view shots that symbiotically unite the Cathy-Heathcliff couple with their beloved moors. Cathy asks Heathcliff to "look at the moors, once more." He conveys her limp body to the window, and one shot establishes the perspective of the couple framed by the window, the image of the moors in the background (fig. 4.4). Several following shots build on their unity in an excessive representation of point of view that matches the excessiveness of the sentimental melodrama in this scene. One shot reveals a frontal image of Cathy and Heathcliff, expressed from the point of view of the moors. We note Cathy's wild eyes and frantic face; emotion is conveyed through the movement in both lovers' eyes (fig. 4.5). But sympathy is created through the point-of-view shot itself, when our own visual identification—created by the shot/reverse shot—is implied. Nature is imbued with unity and harmony, as well as sympathetic sentiment, and provides the sympathetic glance from which spectators of the film view the lovers. Yet another shot shows the view of the moors from the lovers' point of view. Their symbiosis and sympathy in the shared point of view is connected with Pennistone Crag, the excessive protuberance seen at a distance (fig. 4.6). Cathy emphasizes the role of the Crag when she says in her dying last line, "Do you see the Crag? . . . I'll wait for you."

A new shot again establishes the scene of the lovers at the window as Cathy's arms droop to her side, and a point-of-view shot then reverses this position by 180 degrees. This shot shows a close-up of only Heathcliff's face. The male figure in the landscape is now alone, sympathy's survivor. Cathy, meanwhile, has become a real angel: as Heathcliff carries her to the bed, her body becomes a seraphic white-robed winged figure (fig. 4.7). Edgar, who arrives on the scene, notes, "She's at peace now, in heaven beyond us." Heathcliff insists that Cathy is not at peace but will haunt him. But the

Figures 4.4 and 4.5 Catherine's death scene presents an establishing shot (left) that reveals a view of the lovers from behind. It is followed by another shot (below) in which the lovers face the moors (and camera frontally), framed by the window and looking out onto Pennistone Crag. *Wuthering Heights* (Samuel Goldwyn 1939). Courtesy of Arts Library—Special Collections, University Research Library, UCLA

intention of both Heathcliff and Edgar is the same: to make of Cathy an angelic eternal lover who helps "poor Heathcliff," in Ellen's voice-over, to "tear away the veil between death and life."

The shot of the grieving face of Ellen at Cathy's deathbed fades out into a shot that reveals the present-day Ellen, who then declares to Lockwood, "Cathy's love, stronger than time itself, is still sobbing for its unlived days." Dr. Kenneth bursts into the room, telling Lockwood and Ellen that he "saw Heathcliff on the moors with a woman," but, after losing sight of them, found "Him, only him, alone, with only *his* footprints in the snow." The solitary male figure may lie dead on the landscape. But Ellen sentimentally surmises that life triumphs over death, unity over time—that Heathcliff is

Figures 4.6 and 4.7 Catherine's death scene continues toward its climax, as a reverse shot (from the frontal perspective of the lovers) shows the moors in their natural but unearthly tranquility (left), followed by another shot that suggests Catherine's angelic iconography (below). She swoons into Heathcliff's arms, while Dr. Kenneth looks on. *Wuthering Heights* (Samuel Goldwyn 1939). Courtesy of Arts Library—Special Collections, University Research Library, UCLA

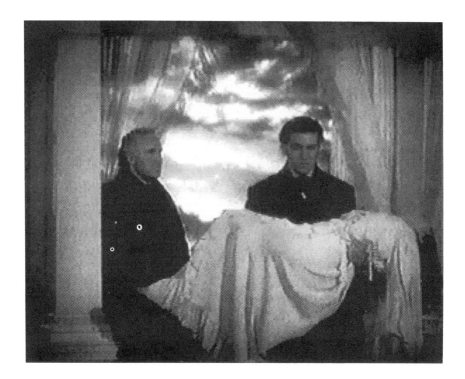

"not dead, Dr. Kenneth, but with *her*." There is a supplement to the portrait of the lone surviving male protagonist, that of the ghostly Cathy wandering the moors. Heterosexual unity is restored in the film as Ellen's image fades out and a still shot of Pennistone Crag fills the screen. Superimposed on this image is the figure of a couple struggling up the Crag—an image superadded to the final cut of Wyler's film.[36] The supplementary image is recalled in the excessive language of the final Ellen voice-over: "Goodbye, goodbye, my wild sweet Cathy." The supplementary process of sympathy, through that excess, is now complete.

FIVE

Excessive Women's Sadomasochistic Sentiments: Maternal-Melodrama Fetishism in *Imitation of Life* and the TV Talkshow *Sally Jessy Raphaël*

"Now is the time to fill what is empty.
Fill my life brim full of charms.
Help me refill these empty,
empty, empty, arms."
　　　　　—Sarah Jane's song,
　　　　　　　Sirk's *Imitation of Life*

"Excess" is that heightened effect within melodrama, giving mythological import to otherwise flat quotidian scenarios in domestic fictions.[1] Speaking of film melodrama, specifically, Thomas Elsaesser describes an "excess" in the "melos" or music of melodrama—a "melos" supplemented by extraordinary and often startling visual effects.[2] In film, melodrama's "expressive code" of sound and light is sustained through the "exaggerated rise-and-fall pattern in human actions and emotional responses" (Elsaesser 521). "Excess" is the dynamic visual intensity of the film form, the luminous mise-en-scène of a Vincente Minnelli or Douglas Sirk picture screen.

In the maternal melodrama, the female image drives the excess of vision, which is also an excess, I will argue, of sympathy. The excesses of female physicality compete only with the excesses of "natural" female sentiment, especially in the roles of mother and daughter. These roles symbiotically bind women, as characters as well as spectators, in mutual identification and dependency. The reproductive intensity between the mothers and daughters of melodrama has a reactionary component, which leads to their conflict and separation. We have seen the way in which the excessive bonds between maternal caretaker and child generate sadomasochistic dependency and conflict in the novel *Wuthering Heights* and its Wyler film version. The maternal melodrama on screen, as I explore it here, takes this effect to its excessive extreme, and, in the process, illustrates "what is empty," as the song lyrics go.

In classic maternal melodramas like *Imitation of Life*—both the original John Stahl version (1934) and the bold Douglas Sirk remake (1959)—and in contemporary daytime talkshows like *Sally Jessy Raphaël*, mothers and daughters fight and embrace, reject one another and tearfully reunite, reproducing the alternating terms between present and absent, full and empty, that define fetishism. This alternating tension underlies the emotional drama of Fannie Hurst's original novel version of *Imitation of Life*, published in 1933 and from which the Stahl version was closely adapted the following year. This novel, like the Stahl film version, tells the story of pancake-mix magnate Bea Pullman, whose career aspirations divide her from daughter, Jessie. Like the Stahl film, the novel also couples the Bea-Jessie mother-daughter narrative with a narrative about Bea's live-in servant, Delilah, and her own daughter, Peola. The African-American Delilah—originator of the pancake mix that makes Bea rich—fights with her own daughter when the light-skinned black girl "passes." An alternation between terms of love and hate, closeness and rejection, typifies the novel and Stahl film version of *Imitation of Life*, as it later does Sirk's rather different scenes and plot. This alternation of terms, responsible for the fetishistic dramatic tension in maternal melodramas in general, is perhaps best recalled in the penultimate scene of the Sirk film: the "passing" daughter, Sarah Jane (played by Susan Kohner), returns to join her mother's excessive funeral procession; and, having formerly rejected the black body of the mother, she sobs and weeps over her coffin while sympathetic spectators look on.

I will suggest that TV talkshow programs like *Sally* play upon the same alternation of terms that *Imitation of Life*, in all its forms, as well as other maternal-melodrama films, helped to make famous. With origins in the nineteenth-century melodrama theater, and director D. W. Griffith's adaptation to the silent screen of the heroine-victim's heavenward glance, the genre of the maternal melodrama—also known as the "woman's film" or "weepy"—became a particularly attractive film medium during World War II to largely female audiences. Social-domestic melodramas of the cold-war '50s, in probing social anxieties about the American family, continued to exaggerate mother-daughter closeness and conflict as a structural conceit—still dominating modern "weepies" like *Terms of Endearment* (1983), *Postcards from the Edge* (1991), and the more recent "chick flick" (a '90s term) *Hope Floats* (1998). The maternal melodrama, however, is perhaps most pervasively part of mass entertainment today through commercial television programming: daytime "soaps," and nighttime domestic dramas—beginning with the 1960s serial *Peyton Place* (based upon the 1957 Mark Robeson film) and more recently including '80s "evening soaps" like *Dallas* and *Dynasty*.

I treat the woman's daytime talkshow as another highly scripted maternal melodrama. The *Sally* show, in particular—which began in the early '80s and is still in production today—revels in the maternal melodrama's fetishistic alternation of terms. On the *Sally* show, mothers and daughters fight and embrace in daily rituals of televised conflict. While it has been observed that the maternal melodrama sheds light on the desires of the female spectator, I argue that it does so only by exploiting this alternation of terms that controls the imitation, the fetishistic image, of women.

I look first at the Sirk version of *Imitation of Life*, and, second, at maternal-melodrama reinvention on *Sally*. In doing so, I focus on the experience of the female spectator, following Doane's analysis, suggesting that the "woman's film" evokes a particular crisis for the female viewer. Doane notes an "opposition between proximity and distance in relation to the image" in male subjectivity, as it inflects "the agency of the look." She contrasts that "opposition" to that which inflects the female look. Because the female body is "so close, so excessive" to the image or icon itself, Doane argues, it is difficult for the female subject to assume "a position similar to the man's in relation to signifying systems."[3] Doane reads the female masquerade often associated with the maternal melodrama—and with classic-cinema, in general—as a female viewer's corrective to the *lack* of distance women experience; "in flaunting femininity, [female masquerade] holds it [femininity] at a distance" ("Film and Masquerade" 23). Through female masquerade, the female subject can *become* a spectator, restoring the *distance* necessary to language. The drama of closeness and separation central to the mother-daughter dyad in the maternal melodrama operates like female masquerade, according to Doane: to open up distance for the female spectator.

The problem is that the female spectator experiences proximity and distance as another alternation of terms, another form of fetishism loaded with connotations about the female image. Fetishism resolves its binary tensions through a rather sadistic glance at this image. I will detail the way in which the maternal melodrama tries to handle this problem for female viewers by displacing, or sentimentally disavowing, its sado-erotic implications—through moral identification and sentimental piety. We recall that a piety about human nature in pre-Hume theories of the moral sentiments emphasize the inherent identification, the connectedness, one human subject feels for his like. Hume called into question sentimental piety, specifically in the field of sympathy, arguing that distance and objectification is also sympathy's function. The maternal melodrama is a fascinating genre because it vies pious and repressive notions about sympathy as pure identification against its more voyeuristic, dissembling effects. We will see how

Sirk's *Imitation of Life* calls upon both repressive ideas of moral sympathy and its sadistic, fetishistic female images. I suggest that a disingenuous form of moral sympathy sustains this supposedly "politically progressive text." Similarly, I will suggest that a disingenuous form of moral sympathy structures the *Sally* talkshow. I will analyze *Sally's* use of female excess—the bodily excess of female obesity, masquerade costumery, and profuse fighting and crying—that both supports and undermines the regulatory sympathies of the talkshow hostess, the "good-mother" figure of Sally herself. Ultimately, I suggest that we are *all* masculine spectators in the dual drama of sympathy, in a maternal melodrama supposedly for and about women.

Sympathy, Fetishism, and the Imitation of Image

Sirk's *Imitation of Life* begins with the novel's bifurcated plot: the dual story of two single mothers raising daughters. This bifurcated plot in all *Imitation of Life* versions pits the concept of closeness against that of distance or alienation, which I am arguing establishes the basic movement of fetishistic structure. In the Sirk film, one plot follows the career of an ambitious white starlet, Lora Meredith (Lana Turner), who experiences a white-feminist struggle to obtain stellar professional success in a theater and film career, overcoming sexual harassment and exploitation. Her daughter, Susie (played by Sandra Dee as an adult), lacks the close and "natural" house-bound mother, becoming alienated from her and bonding, instead, with her black "nanny," Annie Johnson (Juanita Moore)—as well as her mother's suitor, Steve Archer (John Gavin). Susie's alienation from her (unnatural) natural mother, whom I call Lana/Lora to suggest the importance of the "Lana Turner" Hollywood icon "imitating" the Lora Meredith role,[4] presents a theme of closeness and alienation that has sadomasochistic consequences for the mother-daughter duo. Closeness and alienation is expressed in Susie's dual desire *for* the mother (through maternal surrogates), and her sadomasochistic self-alienation from the mother, in competition *against* the mother, expressed through the romantic feelings for Steve.

The other plot follows the drama of Annie and her daughter, Sarah Jane, as the latter tries to pass as white—recalling the origin of this story in the Hurst novel. The mother-daughter conflict between Annie and Sarah Jane is both similar to and different from the conflict between the white mother and daughter. It is similar because a sadomasochistic tension is aroused by an alternation between closeness and alienation, "proximity and distance," to use Doane's phrase, in their relationship. It is different because Annie and Sarah Jane are victims of white racism. Sarah Jane, who looks white, hates her mother's blackness, because it is a visual signifier of Sarah Jane's racial difference. Emotionally close to Susie and Lana/Lora (who uses Annie as a confident and tireless supporter, as well as domestic servant), Annie ironically becomes alienated from her own natural daughter, who is "unnatural" toward her, rejecting her. As Sarah Jane begins adopting the white female image, the bifurcated terms natural/unnatural undergo a reversal. Sarah Jane gives up the close, "natural," real (black) mother to become, like Lana/Lora, a white fetish, the "imitation of life."

In the Sirk film, the reversals and oppositions between unnatural/ natural, closeness/alienation, mother/daughter, white/black, imitation/ real alternate with, but are also bound by, the signifier of female masquerade, the spectacle of burlesque white femininity that Lana/Lora and Sarah Jane enact. It is the Sarah Jane story that is central to what is referred to in feminist film criticism as "the progressive text," and what writers on Sirk have called the "race critique": that which gives this film its political spark. Speaking in an interview a few years after the film's production, Sirk himself insisted that it was the Sarah Jane plot that lent fascination to an otherwise bland American melodrama: "The only interesting thing [in the film plot] is the Negro girl trying to escape her condition, sacrificing to her status in society her bonds of friendship, family, etc., and rather trying to vanish into the imitation world of vaudeville."[5] Most feminist observers of the film have followed Sirk's view in suggesting that Sarah Jane gives the film its social, artistic significance. Marina Heung, for example, in an article entitled, "'What's the Matter with Sarah Jane?': Daughters and Mothers in Douglas Sirk's *Imitation of Life*," argues that Sarah Jane resists bigotry and racist taboos, a resistance that functions as "a catalytic force in the film" to destroy them (318). Lauren Berlant articulates a similar point when writing about the role of black women in both the Stahl and Sirk film versions. But it is Sirk's film, in particular, that "exposes the form of the white woman to the commodification she has for so long displaced onto the black woman's body" (Berlant 129). Likewise, Sandy Flitterman-Lewis suggests that Sarah Jane in the Sirk drama functions like many other "dark sisters" in Hollywood: to show that "the myth of legitimized white womanhood" relies upon a dark racialized other, a figure serving as a "repository for the projection of feminine sexual energy as it is patriarchally defined . . . [through] a fantasy of the non-white woman's hypersexuality."[6]

These superb analyses locate the importance Sirk placed upon Sarah Jane's role in the film, and its effective criticism of American racism. In this sense, Sirk's film achieves what many of the best postwar melodramas strive to do: to subvert traditional American family ideology, to arrest it, to make its spectator call into question the very conventions these films depict.[7] But at the same time, these analyses fall short of interrogating the fetishistic structure that draws the spectator into this specific version of the film, and that made Sirk's *Imitation of Life* one of the biggest box-office hits of all time. Sirk achieves his social points through an alternation of *visual* terms that suggests a moral relation between closeness and reality, alienation and falsity, assigning "legitimate white womanhood" to the second set of terms and blackness to the first. And the film's visual system also revels in the imitative images of "white womanhood" it supposedly critiques, signified by the continuing movement of fetishistic structure. This structure creates a desire for white femininity that goes unquestioned. It makes the ideal "white" mass spectator consider problems of American racism sympathetically while allowing the spectator to deny those problems, as well.

Let me explore further the terms of "legitimate white womanhood" to which Sarah Jane becomes both imitative icon and sign of resistance. The Sirk film plays upon a feminine icon only scarcely alluded to in the Hurst novel—and never seen in the Stahl film: the blonde.[8] In the same interview, Sirk suggests that "Lana Turner's "imitation'" is fraudulent, "not the real life":

> The imitation of life is not the real life. Lana Turner's life is a very cheap imitation. The girl (Susan Kohner [who plays Sarah Jane]) is choosing the imitation of life instead of being a Negro . . . *Imitation of Life* is a picture about the situation of the blacks before the time of the slogan "Black is Beautiful."[9]

Sirk's words articulate the sympathy he intends the film's *white* spectator to feel for Sarah Jane in her struggle with black identity, and the disdain with which he views Lora/Lana as the quintessential Hollywood blonde. The "blonde" is a figure that contains a long semiotic history, which serves to articulate the white slave master's sadism. Following Sirk's point, we need to ask: what does it mean to be "black" and "beautiful" in a maternal melodrama that plays upon the fetishistic alternation between white and black as a *judgment* about falseness versus truth, imitation versus "reality"—and that yet *enjoys* the imitative language of the Hollywood form through the role of the blonde? Michael Selig has pointed out that *Imitation of Life* projects the problem of white American racism onto female representations, thereby blaming women for racism, and failing to expose "the *connectedness* of sexual relations and social determination between the black woman and the white."[10] Selig's point can be taken further if we examine the way in which *white* womanhood (*as* "blonde") is projected onto the desires of the spectator. The spectator experiences the moral-representation in sympathy while simultaneously angry at and arrested by images of white cultural beauty constructed by the Hollywood studio machine of the 1930s and '40s. The spectator's tension is further exacerbated by the sadomasochistic dialectic that fuels competition between mothers and daughters, mothers and mothers, for fetishistic resonance. One example of this occurs between the "white mistress" Lana/Lora and her "black mammy-other," Annie—whose only claim to fetishism is in the excessive funeral she plans before her death. Another example occurs between Lana/Lora and her "black" daughter Sarah Jane, as the latter takes over the former's showgirl, "performing woman" image.

Judith Butler has demonstrated ways in which the white female icon is debunked in the film, perceived as a mask of gender in the illusory hyperbole of the Sirk cinematic style.[11] At the same time, the film attracts the viewer through the mastery of the white icon, a fact Sarah Jane quickly surmises and, in fact, represents, with her straight hair, thin nose, and light skin. (Kohner is a white-Hispanic woman *playing* a black woman.) While the spectator is directed to feel moral sympathy toward the "black girl" and her plight, "white womanhood" is what Sarah Jane seeks to obtain in the film. Sarah Jane's brilliance as a character is that she momentarily escapes the illusion of sentimental piety in the "reality" or "proximity" drama to make herself a copy of white womanhood—in a film narrative that offers her few other options. Using the device of the showgirl to focus and freeze visual attention, her image *becomes* the guiding Sirkian imagery this film employs: a dramatic and symbolic use of mise-en-scène, colors tightly regulated through a "pure" tonal palette.[12] Sarah Jane is the figure that speaks the truth about the ironic *white* "tonal palette," emblematized by the white-blonde figure of Lana/Lora. To obtain cultural power, Sarah Jane *collaborates* with Sirk's system. She learns to successfully exploit her own (imitation of) whiteness.

In this version of *Imitation of Life*, whiteness is associated with the male gaze by the marginal but pervasive presence of white male agents, cameramen, and theater-film producers, as well as the seemingly benign photographer, the Lana/Lora lover, Steve.[13] Their presence signifies that the Sarah Jane plot, and the moral sympathy it invites the spectator to feel, is embedded in the multifaceted episodic style for which film melodrama is known, and which this *Imitation of Life* so well restages. The episodic style signals that seemingly marginal points of view will be rather important. Episodic bifurcation, rather than dismantling a central or controlling point of view, actually enhances that point of view and its sadistic mastery in and of the image. Episodic bifurcation operates like Richardsonian novelistic technique in the epistolary medium: to fragment or empty out point of view, in order to reassert its domineering voyeurism. It *centralizes* point of view, by perversely refracting its very appearance of centralization, the panopticon strategy. Like *Clarissa*, Sirk's *Imitation of Life* offers the spectator a perverse position of centrality, as well, the gaze of sympathetic white paternalism.

The ambiguous nature of this point of view thrives upon the oscillation between identification and distance marked by strategic "breaks" in episodic narration. This pattern of breakage is demonstrated in one early episode in the film, actually composed of two mini-episodes formed out of four sequences, which involve both the "back room" and the little girls' dolls. The first sequence belonging to the first mini-episode reveals Lana/Lora introducing Annie to the "cold-water flat," after she meets Annie at Coney Island and discovers that she and her daughter are homeless. "Nobly" offering them domestic space, Lana/Lora shows Annie the back room conventionally assigned to domestic "colored" help. This mini-episode about the ironies in Lana/Lora's sympathetic offer cuts to another mini-episode, which attacks the theme of generosity and identification in the white family. In what I am calling a second sequence (beginning the second mini-episode), Susie gives Sarah Jane the gift of a black doll. Sarah Jane rejects the black doll, and demands Susie's white doll instead. Susie clings to the white doll, protesting, "I've had her all my life." The girls fight over the white doll as yet another sequence reveals the mothers dealing with the conflict. Lana/Lora enters the room, in what I read as a third sequence, and looks passively on with a benign but uncomprehending, alienated, doll-like smile. Then Annie enters the room from another side and pulls Sarah Jane away, exhibiting a different kind of maternal alienation as she chastises her, asking, "Where are your manners?", and then smooths over the conflict for "Miss Lora," saying, "Everything's going to be all right." The original mini-episode showing Lana/Lora's offer of the back room is connected to the second mini-episode of the dolls when Annie drags *her* "doll," Sarah Jane, to that imaginary (but never represented) "back" space. Sarah Jane complains, "I don't want to live in the back. Why do we always have to live in the back?" At that moment, the camera offers a shot of the black doll, dropped from a fragmented view of the little girl's arm, then sprawled on the floor, abandoned, disheveled. This image, a symbol of female identification and alienation, foreshadows the dual crises of Annie and Sarah Jane in the film, when the daughter abandons her mother because she is the daughter's own visual black signifier, abandons "herself" to become the white doll, the fetish.

The scene of the dolls illustrates the way in which the male gaze, signified by the directive presence of the director-auteur and revealed through mise-en-scène and sequence editing, uses sympathy as a dual gesture of closeness and alienation. Through the gesture of sympathy *as identification,* and directed toward Sarah Jane symbolically through the shot of the black doll, the spectator of the film gazes at the doll, is made to feel identification for the "black doll," and the proprietary rights that black girls should have both to dolls and equally situated rooms. The proprietary theme, suggesting identification and closeness, arises when the white girl, Susie, declares her right to property and propriety in owning the white doll, a doll she has always been as well as owned. The spectator experiences indignation through pity for the rejected and displaced black doll. And the spectator also feels that Sarah Jane deserves spectral as well as proprietary equality with Susie.

The doll itself, however, is a condensation of unequal, subordinating images of females—a sentimental object that contains the suggestion of female masochism and sexual slavery. The doll is an alienated object of an imitation of the young girl, a substitute for the substitute, a baby-imitation that imitates the male phallus in women (Freud's analysis of why girls want dolls/babies). The doll is also an "imitation" that reflects imitative excess like female-masquerade accoutrements—jewelry, high heels, frothy dresses—that cover up "missing" anatomical parts for the male spectator.[14] As a metonomy for the female body as alienated object-fetish, the doll is a reminder to women that they are alienated objects, not subjects. Identification with the doll becomes a training ground for fetishistic femininity, defined as infant-like passivity and objectification. Historically, the doll became a desirable gift for girls in nineteenth-century middle classes. Within bourgeois formulations of the nuclear family, the doll reinscribes a seeming naturalness of social engendering processes, encompassing maternal sentiment and intimate feeling as projected onto the female infant. The doll, in this manner, becomes the young girl's double, miming her supposed longing for imitative identification, for adult femininity and imitative "things." It is presumed inherent, with the gift of the doll, that girls are miniature mothers (a socialization process that Chodorow calls "the reproduction of motherhood"). Young girls, it is presumed by the gift of the doll, want and need the doll, a symbol of their baby selves and reproductive futures.

The social critique implicit in the back-room sequences are neutralized by the "naturalness" of Sarah Jane's desire for the doll, *any* doll, black or white, reinforcing patriarchal conventions of female identification and fetishism. To feel sympathy for the young Sarah Jane *as a black doll*, we must assume that all little girls should have and should want to be "the doll," that they identify with their own alienated and perpetually child-like image. Meanwhile, Lana/Lora is presented as the *real* doll, the "living doll," the white doll come to life—sort of (in imitative form). Lana/Lora *is* the fetishistic duplication the doll image imitates. The duality expressed toward female duplication and duplicity is illustrated in an episode that also appears early in the film, when Lana/Lora poses with a dog in an advertising photography session.

This episode reveals the dual aspects of the spectator's sympathy as sadistic female fetishism is criticized but also reinscribed into the text. Female fetishism itself becomes a kind of humiliating act that evokes the spectator's sympathy for the white woman who must pose as a model in an advertisement for dog-flea powder. What might be seen as a feminist "progressive" critique in the film upon the use of woman as sign, associated with moral sympathy, is a scene that invokes the spectator's indignation: Lana/Lora must stoop to the level of a dog, as well as a minor commodity. The evils of the advertising industry as exploitative of females are well illustrated by the photographer and his humiliating image—we get a brief shot of what he sees through the lens when Lana/Lora sneezes from the dog-flea powder being marketed. While the photographer rubs the head of and compliments the dog, he treats his woman model as something less than a dog, chastising her for sneezing, cutting her off before she has a chance to speak, and telling her curtly that, for her labor, she'll have a check "in the mail."

In this sequence, Lana/Lora may be identified with the dog. But while the spectator feels identification and moral sympathy for her, the spectator feels sentiments of hostility, as well—through the figure the Hollywood blonde represents. The coldly narcissistic, controlling icon of the "blonde" is a cinematic construction with a long Hollywood history; it is a representation of female victimage coupled with the sadism of the white master, for whom this figure is both property and symbol. The blonde is a symbol of white racial purity, to which "Lana Turner"—the platinum-headed signifier of femininity and masquerade—alludes. In early 1930s jungle films, for example, films with names like *Blonde Captive* (1932, Capital Films), a white heroine pursued and captured by a simian monster—half-man, half-ape— stands as both masochistic victim and sadistic oppressor of the "interstitial other." Rhona J. Berenstein suggests that the role of the "radiant blonde heroine" in these films is "ambiguous": "she is under threat and in need of white male care," but is also *like* the interstitial monster, "a liminal character aligned with and likened to monsters." Ann Darrow (Fay Wray) in *King Kong* (1933, RKO) is one such example of the jungle-film blonde; she is a victim of the interstitial ape-man monster but also a personification of the white colonial master who penetrates Kong's jungle and captures *him*. As the white-man's property and bait, the blonde is subjugated, like Kong, by the white male master. As a figure of liminality (both white and symbolically "black," both persecutor and persecuted), she "invokes the risqué and monstrous lures of miscegenation, which places a white woman *between* the black and white worlds."[15]

"Blondeness" in this film, and many others of the genre, is inflected with images of white racial privilege, construed as victimage if the "dark" other (personified by the jungle man-monster from "Africa") is not controlled. The image of the blonde both aligned with and distinctive from the simian African ape-man is famously articulated and parodied in Josef von Sternberg's scene in *Blonde Venus* (1932), during which Marlene Dietrich, playing a cabaret performer billed as "Blonde Venus," emerges from out of an ape suit and puts on a large blonde, "Afro" wig—surrounded by black musicians, white showgirls in black face, and beating drums that emphasize the stereotypes of African-jungle themes and racial "otherness."[16] In other films from the 1930s, however, the identification and alienation division figured by the blonde heroine is repressed, constructed as sentimental virtue, as in James Whale's *Frankenstein* (1934), when a highlighted mise-en-scène emphasizes the blonde fiancée's virtue, in stark contrast to the dark, shadowy mise-en-scène of the Frankenstein lab that gives birth to the monster. The monstrosity and horror connoted by dark and shadowy mis-en-scènes, so well bifurcated in the horror genre, came to depict the blonde woman's alienation and criminality in the Hollywood *film noir* of the 1940s. The darkness of *noir* mise-en-scène enhances the illusion of the *femme fatale,* often played by icy blondes. That archetype of female duplicity and cool narcissism reveals, once again, the dual masochism and sadism of the blonde, whose robotic control through her very dependency and yet hatred of men leads the latter astray, often with dire results. The blonde *femme fatale* continues to convey the white master's sadistic qualities, displaced onto her predatory qualities, which snare and captivate a doomed male lover.

The duality of the *femme fatale* was a duality already conveyed in Hollywood iconography about the "blonde": seducing a man through helplessness and self-destructive masochism, controlling him through her alluring enigmatic narcissism and sadism. The duality in the blonde is rendered in the dual roles played by so many blonde actresses, including Barbara Stanwyck, famous for both her role as the sacrificial mother in King Vidor's *Stella Dallas* (1939) and murderous wife in Billy Wilder's *Double Indemnity* (1946), and Turner herself, who long before her mother role as Lora Meredith played the passive and yet conniving wife-girlfriend in *The Postman Always Rings Twice* (1946).[17] Her famous *femme fatale* role subtly inflects our perceptions of Lana/Lora's sadistic as well as masochistic aspects as *Imitation of Life's* blonde bombshell. In *Imitation,* Lana/Lora is *not* sacrificial, like poor Stella Dallas. She is driven by her career to exploit her good blonde looks; she is too icy and "white" to be a good mother—too interested in fetishistic glamour and lipstick to spend domestic time raising Susie, let alone to sympathize with the lives of the black women living in and oppressed by her household. Sirk plays upon the racism that the figure of Turner represents as she plays out the sentimental but sadistic duplicity of the blonde.

A blonde "helplessness" presented in the Turner character of Cora from *The Postman Always Rings Twice* is coupled with the treachery of this archetypal double-crosser in the figure Lana/Lora offers in the sequence of the photo-shoot in *Imitation.* Lana/Lora plays both captive of the camera and of the advertising industry, and captivator of the spectator's attention as the mastering white image. She is the masochistic victim of capitalist fantasy through visual commodification and the sadistic controlling mistress, who uses her white blonde privilege to "bark back"—at the dog. But any identificational sympathy for Lana/Lora, treated as a sex object, is conflicted by the exploitation she makes of her own blonde looks, and an unlikable self-control and autonomy that makes a victim of her male suitor, Steve, of Annie and Sarah Jane, and of her own daughter.

In a number of sequences, we see Lana/Lora as a victim of sexual harassment—as in agent Alan Loomis's office (Loomis is played by Robert Alta)—or crying on the shoulders of Annie or Steve. Our sympathy goes out to this image of Lana/Lora. Following the harassment, we identify with Annie as the latter gives comfort to the weeping Lana/Lora, then with Steve, to whom Lana/Lora says, "He made me feel so cheap," and he consoles her, "You could never be cheap." Lana/Lora's dual dependency and narcissistic autonomy in relation to a man and the sympathetic spectator is furthered in the marriage-proposal scene. Steve asserts his sentimental but also controlling expectation that she will give up her career, give up the imitation of life to become the "real" image of a mother and wife. But their passionate kiss is followed by a phone call from Loomis, who, having seen the photo with the dog, offers Lana/Lora her first big part in a play, returning her to the alienated "star" role. Lana/Lora's oscillation between dependent "real" womanhood and the star's narcissistic masquerade and autonomy is represented when her bright red lipstick, having been rubbed off in the passionate kiss, "magically" reappears in the Loomis phone-call sequence. This detail alludes to a kissing scene in *The Postman Always Rings Twice,* in which Cora brushes away her own male suitor and puts on fresh lipstick; at the end of this film, Cora actually dies in a car wreck because of a distracting kiss, and a final shot shows her dead arm holding lipstick. The phallic imagery implied in the lipstick *vis-à-vis* the *Postman* allusion is joined to the dominating image of the phallic mother that Lana/Lora's image plays out. As a result of the phone call, which appeals to Lana/Lora's narcissism and "phallic" superiority, she forgets the image of passive wife and mother she has just embraced and informs Loomis she will take the part. The spectator might be startled by the seemingly abrupt shift between the image of female masochistic dependency upon a man, and the narcissistic self-autonomy of becoming again the imitation, the image. The spectator has already been prepared for this shift, however, in the duality that Lana/Lora's blonde image connotes. And Lana/Lora's "divorce" from dependency with Steve only introduces a larger web of male dependency, made up of the male specular institutions that include her male agent and David Edwards, the playwright-producer who catapults her to fame.

The themes of identification and alienation, dependency and autonomous narcissism, masochism and sadism, are expressed through Lana/Lora's various *female* relations in the film's melodrama structure, as well. Her duality is expressed through moments of intense female bonding and identification, followed by moments of alienation in one early episode, when the girls cut their wrists. Lora returns home late to find her sleeping daughter with a bandage on her wrist. Annie, who always attempts to ameliorate Lora's concerns and to sublimate the potential violence in these scenes, tells Lora that Susie's wrist was cut in "just a little experiment," blaming the "experiment" on her own daughter, Sarah Jane, whose schoolmate had told her "Negro blood was different," leading Sarah Jane to compare "her blood with Susie's." Annie assures Lora, "I spanked her [Sarah Jane] good." Sympathetic identification is momentarily with the white mother and her "cut" replication, her daughter. The intense identification Lora experiences for Susie, a budding imitation of her own white femininity, is made at the cost of cutting out Sarah Jane and depriving her of similar maternal sympathy. Similarly, the spectator of the film follows Lana/Lora's identification experience. In this episode, Lora's sympathy is conveyed visually, as she *looks* at her daughter's cut-up wrist with grave concern and then consults Annie. In doing so, and in Annie's own repudiation of her daughter's "experiment," the film successfully *cuts out* the image of the black daughter, Sarah Jane.

In this episode, Sarah Jane is figurally "cut out" of the specter of sympathetic representation. The episode shows the way in which episodic structure will be employed to cut up or out Sarah Jane through much of the film. The episodic bifurcation of the film literally serves to alienate, to "cut out," both Annie and Sarah Jane in several sequences, while fetishistically disavowing that it has not done so. In one sequence later, Annie consoles the now-famous but tired, beleaguered Lana/Lora. In a moment of seeming closeness and intimacy, Lana/Lora declares, "Annie, what would I do without you?" In the following sequence, Edwards, the play-producer and Lana/Lora's lover, enters the room. Annie suddenly blends into the background of the unfocused mise-en-scène, becoming (again) the domestic servant, Lana/Lora's maid.

This cutting-out and alienation of the black woman's image from the foreground of the mise-en-scène is achieved again through episodic editing techniques during the episode of Lana/Lora's celebration party. To help celebrate her serious-theater debut, Steve, long-absent from the household, arrives at the door and teases Susie and Sarah Jane like an old friend. His own male fetishism (and a sentimental repression of that fetishism) is implied when he remarks upon the growth of Sarah Jane's legs. Suddenly, Lana/Lora approaches him and takes one of his arms; he takes one of Susie's arms, in turn, and the three of them walk away from Sarah Jane. Lana/Lora's action literally alienates Sarah Jane from the intimacy previously shown by this group. While Sarah Jane is left to the unfocused background, the three white members of the group form a tableau of the white nuclear family. Their intimacy—they are shown entering the party scene laughing gaily together—is created through the alienation of Sarah Jane from the picture.

Sarah Jane's own image is literally cut out, and she is relegated to the background role of servant in a white household. Unlike her mother, however, whose anger is relayed through a self-denying masochism, Sarah Jane rebels by competing for the powerful white icon that dominates the Sirkian system, which employs "pure" color to sustain irony. Her rebellion occurs in a series of sequences throughout the concluding half of the film, in which she *shows* the alienation posed by the white image. Rather than emphasizing the fullness and excessiveness of the image, Sarah Jane reveals its emptiness within the "fullness" of the verisimilar system. In one famous sequence, Sarah Jane shows the image's emptiness by parodying her black image as plantation slave, having been asked by Lana/Lora to "help her mother" and serving a tray of hors d'oeuvres to the actress's guests. By revealing the truth about the imitative image—that she is *like* the plantation slave—she creates what Heung has called a "shock value" in the film. Sarah Jane also recalls and imitates her mother's "Mammy" image, in the excessive drawl of a Southern black domestic, saying, "Here's a mess of crawfish fo' yo', Miz Lora." When Lana/Lora demands sharply, "Where did you learn that little trick?", the white actress is threatened not only by the allusions to her own racism but by the excessiveness of the parody that calls into question the verisimilitude of the white actress's image. She is threatened, in general, by Sarah Jane's "black" imitation—of herself, as imitative actress. While Sarah Jane "ruptures" the ideological purity of the white master's text, in Heung's word, Sarah Jane also steals the show from her white "mistress," her "trick" a studied performance of the blonde-actress's imitation.

When Sarah Jane responds to Lana/Lora, saying of the "trick": "I l'arned it from my Mammy, who l'arned it from her Massah, 'fore she belonged to you!", she alludes to a series of sadomasochistic mimetic imitations. Flitterman-Lewis writes that the sequence of "the tray of canapés" creates a "grotesque parody of blackness, servitude, and femininity [that] falls into the articulating framework of the film [and] which has established an equivalence between woman and spectacle" (333). In doing so, Sarah Jane generates a "subversive" reading: "a subversive reading of the film . . . sees Sarah Jane in a posture of justified rebellion against her mother's powerlessness and servility," according to Heung (315). I also read the sequence as a moment of "parody" and subversion, but in that it jostles and confuses the conflicted fetishistic terms of identification with alienation. These are the two contradictory aspects of sympathy with which the spectator of the maternal melodrama would relate. Sarah Jane's sequence with the tray of canapés mixes the experience of identification with alienation, because she arrests our attention as spectators, and subsumes the alienated figure of her *own* identification.

She continues to mix modes of excessive identification with clearly voyeuristic, sadistic alienation in two later performances, this time taking to the literal theatrical stage as the "performing woman." Sarah Jane reinterprets the "shock" value of the previous sequence of the canapés in *becoming* the showgirl figure. In these performances Sarah Jane *chooses* to act, unlike the passive Lana/Lora, who is always acting, but seemingly without choice. (Susie once tells her mother to "Stop acting"; she implies that Lana/

Lora is always imitating "in life," and doesn't know the difference between acting and living.) We first see Sarah Jane performing in the song-and-dance-routine of the sleazy nightclub, "Harry's Bar." As glowering male patrons look on, "She becomes the ultimate mimic, manipulating the codes of sexual behavior" in order to dictate her own social position," which Flitterman-Lewis suggests is "an impossible task."[18] I would argue, however, that Sarah Jane's performance, which takes over several minutes of the film frame, wields a great deal of *visual* power as Sarah Jane takes over the frame and figurally stops the show. This scene represents Sarah Jane's growing knowledge of how to take power in the context of the fetishistic structure of the maternal melodrama. She thrusts images of identification *with* the white icon *against* her own alienated image as fetish, as a black woman imitating a (working-class) white woman, calling herself "Judy Brand."

Mulvey's description of the "device of the show-girl" suggests that it momentarily stops narrative flow and casts the film structure "into a no-man's-land outside its own time and space" (12). This can have both negative and positive outcomes for the female image; it nevertheless serves to arrest the film viewer. We have seen the way in which close-up "shots" of Clarissa—or her white limbs and heaving white breasts—create a powerful pause in the epistolary narrative and form the gap that encodes the presence of the sadistic spectator. The gaze exhibited by Clarissa's sadistic voyeur, Lovelace, informs the external spectator how to look, how to view "empty" epistolary narration through the female object of the gaze. In the case of Sarah Jane, the exhibitionist role is taken up by herself. Her unabashed appeal to the fictive male audience and the male gaze of the camera does something similar to but also very different from Clarissa's exposure through the Lovelacean peep show. Sarah Jane reveals a knowledge of how fetishism works. Dressed in a sequined black costume with a mini-skirt and feathered bodice, her plumage alludes to Sacher-Masoch's Venus in Furs, as well as to Dietrich's Blonde Venus performance. Sarah Jane not only takes on the (fake) blonde's sadomasochistic duality. She also alludes to her own castration, her alienation, through the lyrics of her song and in her physical gestures. We are reminded of Venus's missing "two arms" in her song lyrics:

> "Now Venus, you know, was loaded with charms
> And look at what happened to her.
> Waitin' around, she's minus two arms
> Could happen to me, no, sir!"

It could *not* happen to Sarah Jane, losing "two arms," because she is already an imitation, a mime of the castrated woman; she is a body already "minus" its parts. Other lyrics play out the present-absence in fetishistic tension, in the image of cut-off arms, "empty arms," and the "empty-purse" sexual image:

> "The loneliest word I've heard of is 'empty.'
> Anything empty is sad.
> An empty purse can make a good girl bad—
> You hear me, dad?"

Sarah Jane's lyrics suggest that she, too, will have her arms "filled." Holding up her arms in an image of being filled, her body also represents the empty vessel:

> "Now is the time to fill what is empty.
> Fill my life brim full of charms.
> Help me refill these empty,
> empty, empty, arms."

Mulvey points out that "the device of the show-girl allows . . . two looks to be unified technically without any apparent break in the diegesis."[19] These are the "looks" of the spectator within and on the other side of the screen. Through her performance, Sarah Jane forces two other looks to become unified: the look of the moral sentimentalist, expecting identification with the image on the screen, and expecting to be mimetically, representationally fulfilled by that act of identification; and the look of the sadistic voyeur, who expects emptiness and lack. While the moral sentimentalist may question the efficacy of Sarah Jane's imitation of life—it is tawdry and degrading, critics note—he, too, is a voyeur, enjoying Sarah Jane's act.

The voyeur and sentimental moralist are combined in the figure of the watchful mother, Annie, who *we* watch watching her daughter behind a darkened louvered screen in the club. Annie's gaze to which the camera cuts as Sarah Jane performs is full of dual "looks," collected under an ideological notion of maternal sympathy. Its darkened opacity through the screen, and its association with the other gazes in the room, identifies it with the fetishistic fantasy of the male spectator implicit to the film. Annie both identifies with her daughter, but treats her punitively, as a distancing voyeur. After the performance, she chastises her daughter, treating Sarah Jane like a child or doll, saying: "Sarah Jane Johnson! You put your clothes on and get out of this place!" Annie alienates her daughter in this scene; her daughter walks out. Annie's surveillance of her daughter's "imitative" performance continues when she locates Sarah Jane in another showgirl performance, the extravaganza spectacle of L.A.'s Moulin Rouge.

In allusion to both Parisian-style precinema entertainments and Hollywood-based cinema itself, Sarah Jane does not sing in the Moulin

Rouge performance, but becomes a wholly visual image. Her body takes on the cut-out status previously assigned to her by the director figure within the film; she functions as a passive cog in a large-stage routine of moving female doll-like automatons, who hold large chalices and move them side to side. As they lie upon a moving conveyor that circles the stage, they mechanistically move their legs up and down. The total effect is one of a perverse sex machine, in which the women's bodies signify the fullness of the fake chalice, an alienated image of moving female bodies *as parts*, in synchronization. The theme of empty and full from Sarah Jane's previous nightclub act is suggested in the use of the chalice. As Sarah Jane's body arrives on the conveyer machine toward the wings of the backstage, the angle of the camera shifts from the perspective of the theater audience to the point of view of a director-creator, from the "back." This point of view is that of the lonely male voyeur, rarely so poignantly and precisely located in this film. From this viewing position, the film spectator watches Sarah Jane's leg move up and down in a strangely unflattering pose. This image ruptures the prior image of the mass spectator who sees the show as a whole; it emphasizes the alienated motion of the fragmented body parts. Sarah Jane is just another moving anatomical image before an equally alienated mass spectator of the moving-body-part theater, an allusion to cinema. The very artificiality of the moving legs on the stage emphasizes the artificiality of the cinematic image.

Mulvey notes that the sight of the "fragmented body" in the showgirl performance provides a moment of narrative "flatness" that challenges "the illusion of depth demanded by the narrative," lending it "the quality of a cut-out or icon rather than verisimilitude to the screen" (12). In this sequence of the Moulin Rouge act, Sarah Jane again ruptures the authenticity presumed of her "cut-out" image and makes her own moving-picture show, in cut-out relief. In doing so, she may achieve "rupture," a term taken from early feminist-film critics Pam Cook and Claire Johnston, who developed what Janet Bergstrom calls "the rupture thesis."[20] Rupture is that which can occur in moments of subversion, of "denaturalization," to use the term of Cook and Johnston, in mainstream Hollywood texts. Quoting a *Cahier du Cinéma* editorial from the late 1960s, Cook and Johnson define this textual moment as "an internal criticism . . . [taking] place which cracks the film apart at the seams . . . splitting under an internal tension."[21] In her later reassessment of the rupture thesis, however, Bergstrom wisely warns us to examine not just isolated moments in a film text but "to take the narrative movement as a whole . . . rather than arguing, as Johnson consistently does, for the importance of one element, or even of elements chosen . . . as points of rupture" ("Rereading the Works of Claire Johnson" 86). Applying Bergstrom's critique of "rupture" to Sarah Jane's use of it through the device of the showgirl, I would note that, after the early rupture of the sequence with the tray of canapes, Sarah Jane recants her rupture, after she is reprimanded by her mother and by Lana/Lora in a kitchen sequence. Sarah Jane explains her "trick" to Annie and Lora: "You and my mother are so anxious for me to be colored, I decided to be colored." Lora responds, "You weren't being colored! You were being childish!" Sarah Jane responds, "You don't know what it means to be . . . different." When Lana/Lora asks, "Have I ever treated you as if you were different? Has Susie? Has anyone here?", Sarah Jane looks down at the floor and tells her, "No. You've been wonderful." Her response denies that racism exists in the Lora Meredith household. It allows her previous rebellion episodically to be reabsorbed back into the sentimental verisimilitude of the sentimental-racist text. And following Sarah Jane's renunciation of her rebellion, she is physically punished, beaten by a white boyfriend for attempting "to pass." "Rupture" becomes the image of Sarah Jane's black and blue, battered body, abandoned in a "back" alleyway.

At the end of the film, Sarah Jane "ruptures" the film frame for the last time. And this rupture, too, will have conservative sentimental-racist implications. Returning home for her mother's funeral, Sarah Jane flings her arms over the coffin dramatically and cries like a child: "It's my mother! . . . I didn't mean it! . . . Mama! . . . I'm sorry! . . . I did love you." Here she recants, again, having abandoned her natural mother. She literally ruptures the police line that controls the scene of the sympathetic funeral spectators, and demands spectatorial attention in an affective demonstration of profuse language and tears. If this sequence indicates her renewal of her bonds with her mother, the sincerity of that removal must be questioned, since the "mother" is an unseen black body contained by the coffin. Sarah Jane enacts a final "rupture," as she enters the parked limousine containing the white nuclear family: Susie, Steve, and Lana/Lora—who sympathetically looks at and embraces Sarah Jane. As Sarah Jane symbolically "ruptures," or enters, the white nuclear family, she is formally reabsorbed into the visual whiteness of the text. She finally succeeds in the imitation of life, the white life of the image.

A shot of the three women seated together in the "back" recall the back room, the back alley, and the "back" role—the subordinate placement—*all* the women play in the white patriarchal family and its melodrama film. The patriarch himself is Steve, sitting alone in the *front* seat, and glancing approvingly at the back-seated women. His approving glance is "ambiguous in its import, bespeaking reassurance, protectiveness, or punitive satisfaction," as Heung notes.[22] Steve shows that he is more than the insipid Lana-lover who falls head over heals for the imitation of life. It is *his* visual sympathy that conducts desire in this film, *his* glance that collects all the excessive bifurcated plots into one steely trajectory.[23] Meanwhile, the black mother's signifying body is no longer a threat—to Sarah Jane or to the whiteness valued by this film. Annie's particular black female excess is all but erased, noted only in Mahalia Jackson's haunting alto, which swells into a symphonic black chorale, while spectators witness the garish pomp of four white horses, the black hearse and white limousine.

Excessive Mothers and Daughters on
Sally Jessy Raphaël

Excessive femininity and alternating fetishistic terms—closeness and aliena-tion, presence and absence—also dominate mother-daughter relationships portrayed on *Sally,* a syndicated television talkshow that has enjoyed a wide, female-based viewership for well over a decade. Like *Imitation of Life* or countless other maternal-melodrama films, the excessive presence of close but conflicted women on this talkshow caters to female domestic concerns while also objectifying women. The sadistic, fetishistic *Sally* drama is not just isolated to *Sally* alone. On a typical talkshow weekday of channel surfing, we find a *Jenny Jones* show about adolescent girls who physically and emotionally harass schoolmates who win beauty pageants. (The *Jenny Jones* show is in-famous for the murder of one male talkshow guest by another, following a show on which the latter declared romantic homosexual interest in the former.) And we find a *Rikki Lake* show that pits biological moms against stepmoms, while husbands, the biological dads, look on. And we also find a *Jerry Springer* show—reputed to be the most violent TV talkshow to date—on which sisters slug and throw food at one another in a "Holiday Hell Feast" (the show's title), allegedly because one sister abandoned her children for a biker boyfriend. The *Sally* show itself is not overtly violent. But one cannot help but wonder if it did not whet the daytime-television public's appetite for hostile programming. The content of the *Sally* show presumably is geared to help women, in the manner of confessional pop-psychology pa-perbacks and glamour magazines. But its typically macabre mise-en-scène of bizarre female costumery and emotional conflict hooks spectators into their own sadomasochistic dynamic as sadomasochist narratives unfold about female domestic relationships. These narratives are about female sympathy but also about power. Their presentation on the *Sally* show, nevertheless, is reliant upon a male gaze hovering in the wings, bestowing approval through female eyes.

    In the name of female sympathy, women cycle again and again through sadomasochistic conflicts, which, as I have been arguing, have culturally masculine origins. In the style of episodic narratives from the maternal-melodrama film, the *Sally* show revels in a fetishistic "circularity and undecidability . . . characteristic of the talkshow" as a genre, according to Wayne Munson (15). Discussing talkshows in general, Munson suggests that a talkshow's disparate and hyperreal format allows its subjects to "play with contradiction and subversion of sense" (14). I suggest that, in the specific example of the *Sally* show, "contradiction" is used not for the "sub-version of sense," but for the reproduction of a traditional cultural "sense" loaded with masculine connotation. The gaze that controls women might be gendered male. But the gaze is activated by actual females, through a relay point of female spectators on and off the show who encourage all spectators to embrace their own sadistic, fetishistic images.

More female-dominated than a prior generation of male-hosted "feminine" talkshows (Munson's term) like *Donahue* and *Geraldo,* the *Sally* show nevertheless perpetuates the fetish and the gaze as women are asked to control and regulate their own excessive image. This site of control is first located in the image of the talkshow hostess herself, Sally, who functions as a "good-mother" regulator figure toward often wayward female guests. Sally is the sympathetic witness whose judgments about mothers and daughters sustain and proliferate the show's excess, as well as its sympathetic controlling gaze. Through Sally's gaze, the "live" studio audience finds a viewing position, mimicking Sally's moral judgments. And through the studio audience's gaze, the daytime television mass spectator finds a viewing position, as well.

My study of shows aired between 1992 and 1998—*Sally* currently can be seen late afternoons on NBC—indicates that, program after program, a supposedly spontaneous talkshow "script" in fact relies upon the maternal-melodrama icon of excessive mothers and daughters. An overview of these shows suggests that excessive mothers and daughters take curious twists and perverse forms. For example, the *Sally* show will transfer mother-daughter conflict onto sisters' rivalry or fighting "best friends." One such show about two "best friends" suggests that the women stopped speaking to each other because one dislikes the other's husband. Such a show might be read as both a reversal of and slightly displaced version of another type of show about mothers having affairs with daughters' husbands. Sometimes a movie star lends the theme of overt specularity to the repeating theme of spec-ularized female conflict. In a show featuring Ginger Rogers shortly before her death, the actress speaks profusely—a little too profusely—about her great love for and intimacy with her deceased stage mother, a powerful force in Rogers' film career. The star factor can make for strange displace-ments of mother-daughter themes. Estelle Parsons and her daughter are interviewed on a 1992 *Sally* show to discuss that daughter's experience of rape and incest. They appear, however, in the context of discussing the mother's role in supporting her daughter. While this emphasis may offer solace to female victims of sex crimes, it ignores the violence perpetrated by the male predator. The narrative design of almost every *Sally* show, in fact, sublimates social-melodrama themes to the sub-theme of mother-daughter identification and conflict. A 1998 show on mental illness is a more recent case in point. While raising awareness about serious mental diseases like schizophrenia, the show, entitled, "Our Family Secret is Tearing Us Apart," features the mother-daughter (and sister-sister) conflict mental illness creates within families, and features the emotions of the non-ill family member.

A typical *Sally* show consists of three structural elements that seemingly offer different reference points for the spectator. These elements include the staged tableau of program guests, predominantly made up of white women posed as mothers or daughters, and often including a woman therapist, author, or other female "expert" figure; the studio audience, in-house spectators who rise and ask questions of the guests before the camera; and the mediatory presence of Sally herself, whose judgment often dovetails with or sometimes replaces the figure of the expert. Sally's own presence—seemingly calm and detached—subtly instigates the excessive drama, sometimes by a mere opening question but also by control over the daily script. Sally's sympathetic and yet sadistic presence is echoed in the studio audience that offers "common sense" advice to tableau participants. The Sally-female mediator role suggests the sadoerotic potential of Chodorow's "good internal mother" figure, whose role of providing regularity and stability for the child-subject can easily slip into that of moral regulator, as both Nelly from *Wuthering Heights* and Annie from *Imitation of Life* illustrate. Sally makes visible this often invisible, or internal, figure, revealing that the "good mother" is a figure of control as well as nurturing.

Tania Modleski and Linda Williams have discussed the way in which the "good-mother" figure is a function of the differential viewing structure available within television soap operas and film melodrama, respectively. Through the good-mother ideal spectator, they suggest, sympathy can be extended to various—and sometimes unscrupulous—characters; the spectator imitates the disparate viewing positions that are the effects of women's real-life experiences in nurturing families.[24] But I would suggest that, like the episodic structure that "disparate" viewpoints breed, the hermeneutic openness of the good-mother spectator contains elements of voyeuristic sadism and potential violence *through* her disparate manner of extending sympathy. To suggest that the "good mother" is a woman's ideal of spectatorship is to sentimentalize women's experience and to relegate most of women's experience to the domestic. Sally, as a good-mother figure, illustrates the way in which identification and distance is requisite to any form of sympathy. And Sally illustrates that, among other things, the "good mother" is a closet exhibitionist, since this figure is a self-denying masochist supposedly absent from the spectacle scene.

The talkshow hostess replicates this voyeuristic and controlling, masochistically self-denying, figure very well. An unassuming person in professional suits, Sally's business-like attire usually contrasts with the carnivalesque and goofy costumes worn by featured guests. Sally, in fact, reveals only the slightest hint of her own specularity, in the trademark bright red frames of her eyeglasses. The Sally viewpoint, often effaced behind the voice of the guest-expert, is typically understated, articulated by the talkshow hostess's soothing, low voice and unchanging facial features. Sally witnesses, collects, and promises to harmonize the conflictual points of view that become the major source of entertainment on the show. Her presence is a sublimated one within the spectacle arena, where open conflict circulates.

One show aired in December 1992 about daughters who say their mothers are verbally abusive toward them depicts the mother-daughter conflict theme straightforwardly, and it also depicts the subtly regulating presence of Sally. This show stages the emotional problems of daughters whose mothers fail to function in the sentimental good-mother role. It plays upon post-Enlightenment assumptions, recently challenged by feminist social-science research as well as semiotics, that mothers naturally love and care for their offspring.[25] The show exhibits the pop-psychology quick-fix assumption that emerges from *Sally* shows, in general. As daughters confront mothers on the program, the daughters are set up for their own emotional transformation before the spectators. The mothers, perceived as unfit by the audience because of a disinterestedness in nurturing their daughters, are put through a corrective process, confronted by adult but childlike children and audience members alike. The fact that a mother may never have been fit to take care of children to begin with is never debated.

This program features one mother, Bonnie, who is confronted by daughter Skye at the program's start: "I love my mom and I want us to have a great relationship but this is the last straw." Referring both to childhood and adulthood contexts indiscriminately blended, Skye complains that her mother calls her "fat," and that she was left at age eight in the care of a 42-year-old man who her mother should have known was a child molester—in a curious twist on the motherhood theme, because this man still lived with his *own* mother. Skye also complains that her mother called the police, when, as a teenager, she returned home late from a date having "run out of gas." The theme of melodramatic extremes and maternal *lack* of care functions semiotically like the empty gas tank, an old story repeated in various guises. The daughter is interrupted by the contentious protests of the mother, who makes statements like, "Maybe I did say something wrong but I didn't mean it"; and, "Why are we going through this, every little detail?" Indeed, why?

On the same program, another mother, Sandy, is blamed by daughter, Melissa, for not properly loving and emotionally supporting her. In this demonstration of mother-daughter conflict, the excess of emotion is coupled with the excess of a woman's body when the obese daughter cries nonstop during the program. The tears and other physical excesses of the daughter, Melissa, contrast with the cool and collected, physically trim mother, Sandy. Here the mother repeatedly argues that she does not know why the daughter complains about the manner in which she was raised: she gave her daughter a job, a car, and money when her daughter needed it. In this segment of the program, the studio spectators rise up in horrified indignation against the mother. One member of the audience lambasts her confusion of money for love, and other audience members roar with applause. This particular audience member stands up and tells Sandy: "You're the coldest woman I've ever seen." Another audience spectator tries to smooth over the ragged relations between both mother-daughter pairs, and perhaps between these women and audience participants, saying, "Turn to your daughters and give them a kiss if you love them." Sandy, however, in a rare moment of genuine inquiry, replies: "Tell me what that [love] means." Meanwhile, the onstage fix-it therapist is busy trying to harmonize the mother-daughter discord, and to regulate the raucous audience-panel discord as well—chastising the audience member who has accused Sandy of coldness: "That isn't helpful," she says. Sally looks on blankly, her regulatory function displaced onto both audience spectators and psychologist.

A more recent "Sally" show, aired in April 1997, shows the way in which the regulatory function of the usually subdued Sally can take an overtly hostile form. Entitled, "My Mother's in Prison," this show features interviews of daughters whose mothers are incarcerated for felonies. The show tells one story of a mother who says she refused a plea-bargain on a contraband charge, receiving, therefore, a mandatory ten-year federal sentence. The beleaguered grandmother (mother of the incarcerated mother) appears, to tell about the horrors of raising her daughter's children, especially a fifteen-year-old daughter who blames her mother for abandoning the family. The segment presents a videotape, entitled, "Last Day of Freedom," about the mother's final day with her children before entering prison. The video builds sympathy for the mother by emphasizing how much the mother loves her children, playing on the sentimental image of maternal piety and masochism. (The mother says before the presumed camera spectators, her children, "I love you so much. I would die for you.") Following the video tape, Sally chastises the fifteen-year-old, announcing that she "hates her mother, won't babysit" brothers and sisters, "has been violent with babies, won't visit her mother in prison, and refuses to go to school." Sally tells the girl she is "very selfish." Then Sally gives a speech:

> "I come from a world where a sense of family is terribly important. Right or wrong, I'll defend them to the death. The brave person is there to make it all right. The coward, the wrong, selfish one, says 'me first.'"

Appealing to sentimental ideals of the naturalness of close mother-daughter bonds, this speech also appeals to all images of closeness among members of the biological family. Because of nature, Sally suggests that daughters should *identify* with, not be alienated from, their mothers. Applause rings throughout the studio audience, with only one audience member asking why the mother did not accept a one-year sentence through a plea bargain.

This segment makes its theme the unnaturalness of female-familial alienation. It is contrasted with a following segment, featuring the two daughters of another mother-inmate named Theresa Cruz. These daughters cry nonstop on the show, signaling their identification with their mother's plight. They are heralded as the "brave" daughters, because they never think about themselves. The theme of mother-daughter identification through female masochism is perpetuated through a mise-en-scène exploiting excessive affect. The bondage of incarceration is subliminally linked to the various aspects of bondage in traditional mother-daughter relationships.

Competing images of identification and alienation through mother-daughter duos inflect most *Sally* scenarios. These displays of fetishistic affect are matched only by displays of women's bodies, either through excessive obesity or spectacular costumes. On a show aired in February 1993, entitled, "I'm Embarrassed by My Mom," mother-daughter conflict is perversely displayed, under the assumption that it will help to correct and socially regulate "unfit" mothers' excessive behavior. The unfitness of mothers is here projected onto their body functions and appearance. The mothers are supposed to learn from the show how to control their bodies, and to adopt properly feminine, specular roles. The contentious drama unfolds in a particularly carnivalesque way. Four different daughters or pairs of them, from four regionally diverse states, describe their apprehension about their mothers' bodies. The mothers, according to their daughters, wear ludicrous clothing or emit bad odors, or otherwise display antisocial behavior. The pervasiveness of this problem is emphasized by the fact that the families of mothers and daughters come from different regional parts. This geographic excess is the geography of the excessive female body that needs to be "placed" under control by the daughters' indignation. The daughters, after all, are part of the maternal excess, a mimesis they both claim and reject in their corrective stance. The daughter from Louisiana complains that her mother dresses too provocatively, a costume the mother wears on stage and nevertheless defends. The daughter from Massachusetts complains that her mother, dressed on the show as a candy corn, is always taking pictures of her and sings loudly (and poorly) in public. The mother then goes on to demonstrate her lewd behavior in both a powerful spectacle and a drama of social powerlessness: she sings with the suburban housewife's imaginary microphone, a dryer hose. The daughter from Iowa reports she no longer visits her mother because her mother does not bathe properly and fails to wear a brassiere—implied here is that the mother's unregulated odors and free-falling breasts keep the daughter from behaving as a good daughter should, another nurturing woman taking care of her female mimetic counterpart. Finally, the daughters from Pennsylvania (two of them) complain that their mother, whose leg was recently amputated, will not wear a prosthesis when they go out. The mother humiliates her daughters by running down fellow consumers while descending wheelchair ramps in shopping malls. The instructive theme of this show is "how to talk to your mom about embarrassing, but necessary, things."

A social worker, a substitute for the "good-mother" figure of Sally, is on hand to establish a quick sentimental resolution to conflict. The expert sides with the humiliated daughters when preaching to the legless mother, "Tell them [the daughters] that you love them, and you're sorry you ever tried to hurt them." The mother and her two daughters conclude by crying rapturously together, evocative of the group displays of artificial tears Ann Vincent Buffault discusses in reference to eighteenth-century sentimental-novel reading practices.[26] Exhibitionism and emotional sensationalism is especially featured on this show. It demonstrates the extremes of female closeness and alienation encoded by female masquerade in the maternal melodrama, as excessive in its multiplicity of participants as in its symbolic geography of national regions and lacking body parts.

"Lack," of course, is tied to male desires about femininity, through the mother's phallic function. I read the candy-corn mother performing with her dryer hose as holding the dominating mother's imaginary phallus, her shocking void of male body parts excessively replenished by the oedipally fixed, symbolic male spectator. The mother on the *Sally* show, who "has the hose," uses it, singing all the while, enacting a comic if pathetic moment of female power that ruptures the conservative moral narrative of the show, not unlike Sarah Jane in her showgirl routines in *Imitation of Life*. Most of the mothers on this *Sally* show try to defend their bodies and their appearance. But, as usual, the studio audience plays out the regulatory function of Sally herself; they gently instruct the mothers to dress more socially appropriately, to hide their body parts—or lack of parts. While the mothers' defenses go unheeded by the dominant collective voice of the show, we are left with the disruptive image of the legless mother running shoppers down on wheelchair ramps, calling attention, almost gleefully, to the missing leg.

Such moments of disruption, however, are quickly assimilated by the dominant fiction, re-incorporated into the primary text that mothers should regulate their bodies and conceal female-body irregularities. A show aired more recently exemplifies the role Sally plays as sympathetic "expert" and intervention agent in such regulation. In a show that displaces maternal-melodrama conflict onto bullied children at school, Sally plays the counselor-therapist role. Entitled, "Sally, I Hate Being Picked On," aired in July 1996, four children and their mothers—and, in one case, a single-parent father—are presented as dealing with the crisis of children's torments at school. The title itself suggests the role that Sally will play as interlocutor, observer, listener, as well as advisor. She first enacts the listener-advisor role in speaking "alone" (in front of millions of viewers) with the parent of a harassed child; meanwhile, the camera provides a simultaneous half-screen image of the face of the boy or girl backstage alone, fighting tears. Sally then repeats this role when speaking to the child, who emerges from backstage to report stories of being called "fat," "freak," "jerk," or being "slammed into lockers." During her segment with the parent, Sally alternatively consoles and advises with statements like, "Sometimes when you're parenting, you feel so helpless, so absolutely helpless, I know," sympathetically identifying with the parent through Sally's own role as a mother. And she makes statements like, "Let's see what we can do"—implying there is something she *can* do; and other statements like, "I would rush right over to the school [following the beating of the child at the bus stop] . . . find out who did it." (She makes this statement in spite of the fact that the mother reiterates school officials were less than helpful.) At one point, Sally does suggest that the form of therapy she is conducting may not be entirely useful. She advises twelve-year-old Jeff, who is ridiculed for his weight and heart condition, to "turn to the camera" and tell his bullies how he feels. The boy complains of hurt feelings and Sally admits, "I don't know if this is going to help."

While this show may not appear on the surface to reflect the excesses of maternity, or the theme of mother-daughter closeness and alienation that I have suggested is key to the maternal melodrama, I argue that it does do so in a slightly rearranged form. It deals with the topic of being bullied, as in the show featuring Bonnie and Skye, Sandy and Melissa: it presents children as socially feminized victims, whether male of female—like the boy tormented at school because he has a heart condition and is overweight due to medication. This show also emphasizes body specularity, like that of thirteen-year-old Angela's slightly large nose, or other slightly obese children or mothers. From the beginning of the show, the *mother's* experience is emphasized in the child's conflict; Sally, in opening remarks, says: "This has happened to every mother at one time or another in your life . . . at least that's happened to me"—again emphasizing identification as elemental maternal experience. The screen then fills with a series of clips from a show aired the previous May, "My Child Is Being Harassed at School," and next reveals photographs of letters received from mothers praising the show. One letter is read aloud in a female voice-over; the letter—from a woman that identifies herself as a mother—speaks about her own harassment when she was a child, as she began "gaining weight." The letter goes on to praise the singing ability of an adolescent girl from that previous show—we are shown the clip of her tearful singing—harassed by schoolmates.

It is no coincidence that many of the female panelists on *Sally* are often largely built or obese. The purpose of my observation is not to judge women's sizes; it is to suggest that the talkshow plays upon the social dilemma of women through cultural body image. A concern for "proper" female size, as well as a sympathy for those women who have not obtained the culturally accepted ideal, runs through the show's fetishistic narratives. The desire to regulate and control size and weight by the implicit spectator of these shows is revealed in the barrage of diet-plan commercials that punctuate the narrative proper of the *Sally* hour. Targeting daytime female viewers who supposedly feel—or are made to feel—apprehensive about their looks in general, the show substitutes the commodity fetishism of diet programs for female fetishism, promising women they might purchase their way to glossy-magazine looks.

Fetishistic excess in the *Sally* spectacle underlies the pathos of female lack, in general. It momentarily, if illusorily, promises women that they can fulfill their emotional function, like their purchasing function, in celebrated mother-daughter identification and union. Another program aired in November 1992 dramatizes the theme of mother-daughter identification and conflict as part of the issue of female-body image and behavior. This show, which I call "The Madonna Show," plays out the relation of proper female clothing and bourgeois masquerade to female adolescent development.

"The Madonna Show" represents that category of *Sally* shows that pretends to be about something other than mother-daughter melodrama—the latter itself a red herring for what I have been arguing is a sadomasochistic, fetishistic representation of female subjectivity and spectatorship. "The Madonna Show" circuitously advances the theme of mother-daughter bonds and conflict while presenting other issues, presumably the controversy over Madonna's then-recently published book of photographs containing sexually graphic poses and erotic images. The show appears to speculate about the true nature of Madonna's influence upon young teenage girls. In doing so, it presents a host of young Madonna impersonators.

Narratively, this show is quite interesting if unfocused. I read it as a text *about* ruptures, a text that alludes to the potential of the maternal-melodrama text to rupture its own patriarchal images but to also reabsorb the rupturing moment back into the text of female subordination. In this show, Sally first introduces several of the Madonna impersonators, a macabre assembly of teenage girls of various levels of development and assorted sizes. They are all dressed in sexually provocative Madonna-like attire. The show then breaks to the display of conflict by one mother-daughter pair, fighting about the daughter's infatuation with Madonna. The mother criticizes her daughter's clothes. Indeed, the daughter appears a bit absurd, thin and pubescent, a body frame that contradicts the excessive sexual hype the clothing delivers. The daughter in her costume suggests an image of feminine excess as well as paucity.

Most interesting to the theme of rupture as well as physical fetishism and excess is the role of the "expert" figure. This role is played out as a competing dual role, in which two guests present a divided representation of views. One guest happens to be E. Ann Kaplan, the popular-culture critic who has written on the maternal melodrama, the male gaze, as well as a book-length study on cultural representations of maternity. Here she is featured as an expert because she had published a book about Madonna.[27] Appearing on the show, Kaplan argues that Madonna is a positive role model for teenage women. This view is opposed by another expert figure on the show, a male president of Morality in Media, who argues for the regulation of female sexual display and suggests that Madonna's graphic book is simply pornography. Both expert figures are initial displacements of the "good-mother" agency of Sally. But their views are not assimilated equally by the larger narrative strategy of the program. Kaplan is not allowed to present a lucid argument; she is continuously interrupted, if not by the president of Morality in Media then by the mother of a Madonna impersonator with a disabled child. Kaplan's viewpoint is marginalized, presented as that of the permissive mother of the academic left, and taken over by the more dominant viewpoint of the *Sally* program. Indeed, the voice of the president of Morality in Media literally dominates over all of the women's voices on the show, including the voice of Sally herself; all women are silenced for several minutes as this male guest takes over the air time. As a displaced figure for the "good-mother," he reminds us of the conservative cultural masculinity behind her authority. That his call for "morality" is the "Sally" voice, afterall, reveals the hidden agenda in a hidden scriptedness, enhanced by an audience member who gets up and praises Sally as an exemplary "woman" and "mother."

The ruptures and interruptions puncturing the narrative flow of the show emphasize both the drama of excess and its intellectual emptiness. No true debate containing two distinct positions can take place on this show. Furthermore, the show panders to the female fetishism it supposedly condemns in its master narrative. Presumably a show that would illuminate women about the problems of female fetishism, it plays upon the spectacle of scantily clad teenage girls, whose own sexualized images are interpolated by graphic images from Madonna's book, in which black censorship bands only heighten the fetishism and erotic seduction of the program.

One can only speculate why women appear on the *Sally* show to parade their fetishism and sadomasochism before the daytime television camera. The participant women, of course, are paid guests; their "spontaneous" conflicts and specularity produce a ticket into daytime stardom and a paid vacation to New York. But it is the women invisible to the television camera that are the show's more mysterious subjects. Do these women spectators identify with the conflicts of mothers and daughters? Do they displace their mix of identification and alienation about the mother-daughter duo onto the voyeurism and fetishism that marks their day-to-day lives in the spectacle of consumer capitalism?

As Ann Kaplan herself has written, the maternal melodrama re-inscribes "the feminine in its location as defined by patriarchy . . . the narrative may allow brief expressions of female resistance to that positioning, and glimpses of other possibilities for women . . . [but] the 'correct' family order must be re-established by the end of the film" ("Theories of Melodrama" 40). In spite of the excessive emptiness of the maternal melodrama, I would guess that its spectators believe it to be a fulfilling experience. But a narrative designed to build up the female image inevitably becomes the narrative about female lack. And any "lack" that metaphorizes the female spectator's *missing* desire in a text can never be a woman's theme.

SIX

The Spectacular Survival of
Sympathy on *Rescue 911*

In *The Surprising Effects of Sympathy,* David Marshall writes about the theatrical association between sympathy, spectacle, and catastrophic accidents. Marshall borrows his own book title from that of the eighteenth-century French writer Pierre Marivaux, *Les Aventures or Les Effets suprenants de la sympathie,* in which a "strange . . . narrative [is] filled with bloody spectacles, desperate lovers, kidnapped heroines, and Turkish sultans . . . the tableau of someone witnessing an accident becomes Marivaux's figure for the experience of reading a novel." Marshall also cites Rousseau, whose *Confessions* suggest that the philosopher was "the most accident-prone figure of the Enlightenment." In Book 5, Rousseau "tries to make a kind of invisible ink," recounts Marshall, and "accidently corks a bottle and the solution he is concocting explodes in his face, blinding him for several weeks." Marshall says he is "struck by the idea that sympathetic ink—the ink of sympathy— might play a role in the writing or reading of Rousseau's autobiography." I am struck by the idea that the ink, exploding, can become a metaphor for sympathy, requiring one man become blind so that another is more capable of vision.

I have moved in this book from an image of sympathy reproduced by technologies of pen and ink to an image reproduced by technologies literally of vision: the mass media. In this chapter, I consider how the rhetoric and spectacular image of disaster and survival generates sympathetic spectacles on prime-time "reality" television. In pseudodocumentary TV melodramas like *Rescue 911,* the eighteenth- and nineteenth-century legacy of a perverse masculine spectator lives on. Through this program's repeated rendering of disaster and yet survival, sympathy's sadomasochistic contradictions are especially perverse. The "force and vivacity" of the disaster image itself—to invoke Hume's words from the *Treatise*—is only equalled to the lack of "force" of the inert spectator, who, watching his TV monitor, desires more disasters, more sympathy.

Mothers, Cops, and Captain Kirk:
The 911 *Survival Spectacle*

Rescue 911 first aired in 1988 on CBS, a weekly drama that quickly became one of the most highly rated prime-time programs. Produced by documentary television veteran Arnold Shapiro, it features harrowing stories of real-life victims who narrowly but regularly survive traumatic accident injuries by dialing the "911" phone call. Running consecutively for many seasons, *Rescue 911* now can be seen in syndication on cable television's "The Family Channel." Its rescue-reality programming is inventive but not unique, borrowing its hybrid format from Fox Television's *America's Most Wanted (AMW)*.

Rescue 911, like *AMW,* developed during the second Reagan administration and the fight over network monopolization facilitated by then-new Federal Communications Commission (FCC) deregulatory policies. *Rescue 911,* again like *AMW,* presents images of law and order as they affect "the norm of the white nuclear family,"[1] a Reagan-Republican theme. *Rescue 911,* however, displaces the criminal element of *AMW*—one that threatens the family "norm" and yet reveals the violence in domestic life[2]—onto the enemy *within* domestic life: household cleaners that poison infants, or the butane sold in every hardware store that seduces "good" white middle-class teenagers into drug use. Like other reality shows borrowing from the *AMW* format—spin-offs also include *Cops* (Fox), *Unsolved Mysteries* (NBC), and *Top Cops* (CBS)—*Rescue 911* blends narrative-melodrama themes about middle-class domestic life under threat with the authoritarian agencies of law enforcement and medical technology.

It is as an authority figure that William Shatner, whom television viewers will remember as *Star Trek's* Captain Kirk and detective T. J. Hooker, makes his mark as the show's host. Producer Shapiro admits that Shatner was hired precisely because of these previous television roles, "because he's a credible guy . . . an authority figure."[3] Furthermore, an aura of representational authority is enhanced on *Rescue 911* through the use of reproductive technologies. Not only does *Rescue 911* use real victims to restage real accident events; it also uses recorded interviews with victims and their family members, "actual footage" of accident scenes, and original (taped) "911" emergency phone calls. The use of these reality reproductive technologies is accompanied by the use of authoritarian rescue-agency hardware crucial to the program's visual images: speeding paramedic fire trucks and ambulances, whirling panopticonic helicopters, blinking hospital monitors with digitalized screens. Rescue-agency hardware is supplemented by the authority of sentiment's "software": the sights and sounds of sobbing family members, especially the mothers of victims. These mothers, invested with the emotional authority of the show, weep next to hospital beds, their hands—Clarissa-like—folded in prayer.

Each hourlong *Rescue 911* program typically contains four episodes, each telling a rescue-survival tale. These episodes themselves are composed of a series of carefully plotted-out sequences that move from the pre-accident scene to the post-trauma celebration. Sequences follow the rules of continuity editing invented by classic cinema, imposing an imaginary spectator at the 180-degree viewing angle, which lends the program an authentic spatial-temporal veracity. Subjective melodrama camera techniques, like point-of-view shots made from the supposed perspective of the victim or horrified family member, alternate with more static documentary-style film shots: the facade of the domestic house prior to the accident; or post-trauma interviews with mothers, cops, paramedics, and doctors laced throughout the chronology of the story. While melodrama shots build identification and sympathy, the documentary-style shots suggest control of the trauma. The "documentary" shots may build veracity, but they also subliminally reassure the viewer that the victim will survive.

Indeed, *Rescue 911* is more about survival than the disaster itself. In this way, *Rescue 911* imitates Puritan captivity narratives, a uniquely American literary genre and colonial best-seller, which provided autobiographical accounts of whites' capture and eventual release by Native Americans. With titles like *The Redeemed Captive Returning to Zion: A Faithful Narrative of Remarkable Occurrences in the Captivity and the Deliverance of Mr. John Williams* (1707), or the first of the genre, *The Sovereignty and Goodness of God: A True History of the Captivity and Restoration of Mrs. Mary Rowlandson* (1682), captivity narratives postulated a safe haven amidst "savagery." And they gave white American settlers what the television docu-drama gives mass American spectators today: a meaning in disaster through its spiritual redemption or salvation. Like *Rescue 911*, captivity narratives also provided a macabre form of sympathetic entertainment for Puritan audiences, as they vicariously experienced a "faithful" rendering of a life-threatening account. The dual attempts to faithfully record the "reality" of a victim and to mythically grant meaning to someone's tragic plight is Richardson's legacy, as well, in his own Puritan-influenced epistolary "recordings" of maidenly distress—like *Pamela*, in which a young woman faces captivity and harassment, but finally is released from lower-class bondage ("rewarded") through marriage to her aristocratic rake-persecutor; or, like *Clarissa*, whose heroine is released from a house of ill repute to her "Father's House" in a saint's death. On the television program *Rescue 911*, saint-like victims also are captivated by a devastating machinery, but are redeemed through some miracle of grace. What Alden Vaughan and Edward Clark suggest about the conclusion of Puritan captivity narratives, that "Everything had a purpose" (6), is the ideology circumscribing each episode of *Rescue 911*.

Vaughan and Clark suggest that the Puritan captivity narratives reflect stages of the "rite or passage"[4] described by anthropologist Victor Turner:

separation from the natal environment; marginality or "liminality," in which loss is experienced and the world appears to be in physical-psychological disarray; and "reaggregation" back into the culture of origin.[5] Each *Rescue 911* episode, too, unfolds according to similar stages. First, an accident assaults the victim and separates the victim from his or her known world. Second, chaos and liminality sets in, during which the victim faces possible death—but while "911" is dialed and the rescue phase begins. Third, the rescue is performed; and the victim is "reaggregated" or integrated back into the familiarity of family and hegemonic community. The victim, thus, becomes a kind of initiation hero. Like the heroes of popular action films or "thrillers"—for example, the *Die Hard* series, in which actor Bruce Willis plays a New York City cop-as-victim—the "criminal element" is subdued by this figure who endures incredible injuries and sufferings, and survives them all.[6]

By conquering the "criminal element"—the evil German multi-nationals in *Die Hard I*, or the bleach or butane in *Rescue 911*—the victim-hero is reabsorbed back into the pastoral domestic order from whence he comes. (The Bruce Willis cop character reunites with his estranged wife.) Especially on *Rescue 911*, the liminality and uncertainty that the "criminal element" introduces into the narrative is repressed through the fact of the victim's survivability, made possible by equally heroic acts of good mothers and their patriarchal reenforcements. On *Rescue 911*, victims are sym-bolically rescued from the contradictions of their liminal states. So, too, are television viewers rescued from the contradictions, the liminal states, of viewing.

On the surface, stories about saving children from swelling river beds or pulling fathers of three from burning car wrecks would seem positive tales lacking contradictory intent. *Rescue 911*, after all, repeats the historic legacy of melodrama, rooted, as Christine Gledhill has claimed, in the political-economic transformation of the master class of the aristocratic elite and in the maneuvering of "cultural hegemony in the name of 'ordinary citizens'" (14). Gledhill is one of many advocates of melodrama, who distinguishes its populist tradition from that of the "legitimate" schools of theater and literary realism—a distinction I have challenged on structural grounds throughout this book. Gledhill argues that melodrama's exagger-ated gestural and visual-musical excesses "enabled it to apply 'pressure'" to the more "conventional and repressive discourses of the post-Enlight-enment" (30). Therefore, its subjects are peopled by members of oppressed classes and groups, from women to children to the working classes to Afri-can Americans. The freak car accident or suburban-home gas leak that causes "average citizens," housewives and concerned fathers, to be con-fronted by possible tragedy on *Rescue 911* is another instance of melo-

drama's pleading for socially downtrodden victim classes—to assist, recalling Richardson's subtitle to *Pamela*, "virtue in distress."

And *Rescue 911* does save lives, according to a 1994 article in *TV Guide*,
that spokes-vehicle for the prime-time industry. The program has saved "at
least 200 lives" by demonstrating the use of the 911 call and reproducing
life-saving technologies (Weinraub 32). Children, especially, have learned
to dial 911 by watching the show—a fact about which more *911* shows have
been made. Shatner claims, "'I'm as proud of this as anything I've ever
done'"; and we learn about Shatner's alleged encounter with a young boy
and his father, who tearfully told the *Rescue 911* host, "'if it hadn't been for
the show . . . the child would be dead . . . The man was aware of mouth-to-
mouth resuscitation . . . because he had watched the show.'"[7] "More important" than the highly successful ratings for the show, *TV Guide* piously
declares, is the fact that "*Rescue 911* has undoubtedly saved lives" (Weinraub
32). At the time entering its sixth season, *Rescue 911* was praised both for
being an instrument of viewer salvation and for extending beyond its 25-
percent Nielsen ratings.

The show may "save lives," but its success story is based upon the
rationale of scopophilic melodrama entertainment. While studies like
Gledhill's emphasize melodrama's capacity for social activism and virtue
ethics, I have been arguing that its ideology of Puritan salvation, as well as
post-Enlightenment reform, reinforces the authoritarian visual regime that
reigns triumphant on the electronic visual media. It might be more accurate
to see melodrama as embodying the *contradictions* of these ideologies of
salvation and reform. *Rescue 911* illustrates such contradictions aptly. The
sympathy and sentiment that build in each episode are underscored by the
authoritarian, scopophilic agencies that make each rescue—and acts of
television watching—possible. But the more sadistic nature of these agencies, and the commercial motivation behind prime-time television programming, is hidden behind the theme of "saving lives" and helping people.

What *Rescue 911* constructs, with every episode, are millions of TV
rubber-neckers who enjoy the thrill of someone else's disaster from the
safety of their domestic livingrooms, and who identify with the victim's
salvation as a metaphor for their own contradictory viewership. *Rescue 911*
may "save," but it also controls and constructs, "lives." We have seen the way
in which voyeurism is related to sadism; and, certainly, *Rescue 911* plots
about "saving lives" are also plots about sadistically controlling lives through
authority figures—from mothers, to cops, to "Captain Kirk" himself. All of
these figures sublimate and yet help to stimulate aggression released by the
disaster image. Aggression is also sublimated through the surreptitious violence that lurks under the surface of every quotidian suburban landscape
and home, *Rescue 911*'s typical mise-en-scène. The accident just waiting to
happen, lurking in the wings of this mise-en-scène, is also an image of the

puerile-spectator himself, who strangely enjoys the scene of carnage and victimage. The hidden propensity for violence in the spectator is mirrored by the same propensity for violence in the domestic sphere, sublimated by technological wisdom and the inherent passivity of the television and rescue apparatus.

The latent aggression in this passive technology is memorialized in the three primary movements that are evocative of captivity narratives and that generate accident-to-rescue narratives, beginning with the *assault* on an innocent victim. The "natural" innocence of the victim—her spiritually "pure" quality—is emphasized by the fact that she often is an infant or child. The victim's moral innocence is coded into his or her relation to white cultural hegemony—she typically resides in white suburbs or white rural America. As a result of the injury, the victim's innocence is temporarily ravaged; her "purity" is formally penetrated by an outside element. The television viewer temporarily is led to believe that the victim cannot survive the trauma. At the same time, the viewer of *Rescue 911* is informed through various narrative strategies that this is just the preliminary stage of the narrative, and that the victim *will* survive, if the viewer keeps tuned to this station. His act of watching, of voyeuristic sympathy, is symbolically called upon to assist in the survival process.

But, first, a rescue must be performed. This rescue often is initiated by a "local" witness, an innocent bystander or on-site family member, like a mother or sister or a heroic small child who dials "911." But the rescue must be concluded by a patriarchal authority figure, beginning with the "911" dispatch operator, but continuing with firemen, paramedics, doctors—usually all male—and their hardware. The primary attendant to the victim exhibits middle-class resourcefulness reminiscent of Richardson's senti-mental heroine Pamela, who uses broken china cups filled with ink and borrowed quill pens to write letters to her parents about her trials at the hands of the libertine. At this stage of the rescue, sentimental themes about the "good mother" and the amelioration of suffering through maternal "instinct" (as well as the innocence of children and the goodwill of strang-ers), are conflated with sentimental themes about immediacy and access: the notion that everyone has instant access to help and medical assistance simply by dialing "911." The presence of an Everyman-witness, like the "off-duty paramedic" and neighbor who, in one episode, helps to rescue a little girl hit by a car while riding her bicycle, further demonstrates the benev-olence of the Everyman's good nature. The Everyman who just happens be a bystander at the scene illustrates the way in which the law infiltrates the domestic sphere, as well as the gaze that technologically accompanies it.

The "911" distress call signals that an invisible guard is always at hand, whose technological handiwork and sentimental accoutrements—the fully equipped ambulance, the helicopter, and especially the "911" phone lines—are essential to the successful completion of the rescue operation. This part of the *Rescue 911* episode usually features stock-footage of state-of-the-art hospital computers and digitalized screens. The tension between technological veracity and its reproducibility through the multiple images of screens, which repeat the conditions of television viewership, is increased with the replaying of "real footage" or the actual "911" call. The "911" operator herself is often a woman, a transitional figure between the mother-child victim and the Everyman witness who invites the masculine order of law-enforcement, medicine, and technology into the disaster-ridden home. Sympathetically mothering but passively detached, this figure also encodes the symbolic male gaze. "She" is a figure for the dual agency of masochism and sadism that directs the entertainment value of the show—as a mere adjunct to the technological apparatus. The "911" operator is another sort of witness who exhibits a calm passivity only matched by the television rubber-necker him- or herself. Woman or not, the "911" operator offers spectatorial transference for Huyssen's "mass-culture as 'woman,'" the consumer of popular pulp narratives, in this case the *Rescue 911* television spectator.

Every episode of *Rescue 911* concludes with "a miracle," a word repeated over and over at the end of episodes in supposedly spontaneous, taped interviews with family members and authorities. The "miracle" is that the victim has been ravaged and then salvaged—to miraculously survive to help tell the tale. Such survival that supposedly is unexpected is often spectacularly rendered by a shot of cheering friends when the victim is wheeled out of a hospital ward; and then he is seen smiling and playful, in a nature park or a subdivision backyard. The control of nature, replete with spectacular background mountain scenery and trimmed hedges with manicured lawns, signals the end of the rescue phase and the "miracle" closure. The "miracle" is a euphemism for the hegemonic survival of the white middle-class, very much like "salvation" is a euphemism for the hegemonic intactness of "white" captives in Puritan narratives.[8] It is also a euphemism for the closed nuclear family, whose members typically hold hands or wrestle with the victim at the end of every *Rescue 911* episode. It is a miracle on every program that the illusion of a white "mainstream" America survives undivided by race, class, or sexuality. It is through the miracle of sympathy, in its powers of resemblance and identification, that the victim's accident only tightens the hegemonic weave, only brings "the (white) family" closer.

A closer look at a few *Rescue 911* episodes reveals little programmatic variation in this narrative format, a format that enhances the sameness of hegemony as well as the unity of the mass spectator. One episode aired on December 28, 1993, illustrates these three stages or movements in a paradigmatic use of the domestic setting and maternal-melodrama themes. In the episode, two white adult sisters, both mothers, are caring for their children. The episode opens with an external shot of a middle-class suburban house in an undisclosed location; the image of the house is supposed to be so ordinary that it could be any tract home, in any American subdivision. The Shatner voice-over emphasizes that this was just an "average day" for the two sisters, the day before Thanksgiving—the holiday theme reasserting the family tableau *vis-à-vis* the dinner table and American patriotism. An interior shot of the sisters in the kitchen baking cookies with the older children emphasizes this family's patriarchal identity, a family in which mothers stay home as child-feeders. The story itself unfolds in a shot of one sister removing the freshly baked cookies from the oven. That two women are also sisters stresses the idea that maternity is naturally reproducible, a fact in which the sisters, as mothers, share.

However, a danger lurks in this maternal melodrama, as it lurks in the maternal care of mothers whose watchfulness is not watchful enough. A near-fatal domestic tragedy will occur, in which one of two babies sequestered in a bedroom leaves the room and drops her head into a bucket of household bleach. The danger that lurks in the quotidian domestic environment remains yet hidden when the sister in the kitchen announces, "Cookies are done!", and we view a shot of other children shouting joyously. The innocence of both mothers and children is signified in their happy frivolity, a frivolity that nonetheless underscores the fact that it will be one of these children, as well as the subtle neglect of the unwatchful mothers, who will cause the infant's accident. A voice-over of what I will call the sister-mother (the aunt of the infant-victim) invades this cheery domestic scene, recounting a day that began by "catching up" and "just bein' sisters." A shot of two babies in their room suggests both the maternal care given the infants and the potential danger as babies are left alone.

The sister-mother's voice-over continues as she recounts a day of cleaning the house for both babies' birthday parties—the theme of togetherness reasserted when we are told they celebrate baby birthdays together. A shot offered from the perspective of the carpeted floor introduces the subjectivity of the baby as potential victim; an absent spectator watches the sister-mother as she carries a bucket into a laundry room. A shot takes us back to the scene, again, of the babies playing alone in the bedroom. The previous point-of-view shot, from the perspective of the floor, however, has made the spectator identify with the point of view of an infant who might crawl along the floor and leave the room. A new shot then shows the sister-mother pouring bleach into the bucket, then carefully closing the door to the room. An interview segment interrupts this visual narrative as the sister-mother recalls her innocent thought, that "the babies might go through the door and climb on the floor before it is dry." Danger, in her mind, is represented by this benign image, of roving babies who might play on a wet floor.

A new shot introduces both mothers caring for their infants, in a kitchen scene during which they prepare bottles. This shot is interrupted by a shot of one of the older children, a boy, running into the house from the outside, intruding upon the domestic tranquility of the scene, and flinging open the door—behind which the spectator knows stands the bucket of bleach. Meanwhile, a shot of the mothers in the kitchen continues to suggest their maternal continuity of care, as they continue fixing baby bottles. A point-of-view shot from the perspective of what is now supposed to be the crawling infant leaving the bedroom follows the baby's imaginary trajectory as she reaches the open door and spies the bucket of bleach water. A shot again cuts to the mothers in the kitchen, and a follow-up shot shows the child now ominously approaching the bucket. A new shot introduces the baby's unsuspecting mother approaching the bedroom through the hall-way—in an angle from the floor, again, which emphasizes the (now missing) baby's point of view. A shot of the mother as she discovers the baby missing from the bedroom cuts to another shot of the sister-mother in the kitchen lifting cookies off the baking pan. A scream shatters this latter image, signifying the otherwise unrepresentable scene of the horrific accident of a baby in bleach. As the sister-mother recounts in an interview, to which the segment now cuts, the mother was "just screaming as a mother would scream." The scream, indeed, ruptures the happy domestic tranquility signified by the scene of baking cookies.

The assault upon the victim now complete, the episode shifts into the performance of a rescue. This segment begins as a shifting and shaky subjective camera reveals the mother of the infant holding her baby and dropping the baby's head violently over a sink. The trauma recorded by this image is sublimated, however, in the voice-over of the mother, recalling the near tragedy in the voice of calm—a voice that signals to the audience that this is a narrative about survival, not death. She tells the interviewer that "goo came out of her [the baby's] mouth," in a language that recalls the perversity of previous feeding images and maternal metaphors. The calm of the mother in the interview is ruptured, however, as we view shots of the mother ineffectively trying to save the baby, shaking the baby, crying, panicking, and then running for help. The sister-mother intervenes, beginning the initial stage of the rescue by performing CPR. But she indicates her concern that the baby does not "look normal." "911" is called, and we see a paramedic fire truck rolling out of a parking lot, its siren wailing.

Traumatic shots of the baby's wet and blue body are coupled with retrospective interview shots of the baby's mother, who reports that she asked her sister, "'Was there *bleach* in your bucket?'" At this question, the mother reports, her sister "lost it." The twisted visage of the mother at this point in the interview indicates that she "lost it," as well. Disaster still seems impending at this stage of the rescue. Yet a calm prevails in a new cut to the interview with the sister-mother, who reports, philosophically, "I always looked at bleach as a cleaning supply. I never in my wildest imagination thought of someone drinking it or getting it into their system." A shot returns us to the scene of the re-enacted rescue, as a uniform-clad male paramedic carries the infant to an ambulance and confirms the presence of bleach. In a voice-over, the paramedic states that he immediately detected "a strong smell of chlorine in the air"—indicating that his rescue operation is more efficient than that of the two mothers. This is not a rescue that mothers could perform alone. A follow-up shot shows the paramedic in the ambulance and a voice-over that expresses concern about the "added problem of the chemical in the water."

The rescue continues in scenes at the hospital. An emergency-room doctor leans over the baby, while his voice-over repeats the concern of the paramedic, using the more technical terms about "a noxious stimuli," and recalling that the "victim" became "less responsive" at this point. Tension mounts for the viewer of the episode when the doctor implies that the infant could die. A shot of a helicopter suggests that the infant is transported to another hospital. Then a shot of the interior of a hospital room reveals a tableau of the grieving mother, who sits alongside the listless infant's crib in a camera image taken from behind the crib bars—as if the mother herself were "behind bars," suggesting incarceration and implicating the mother in a crime of maternal negligence. Her watchfulness over the bedside of the infant, as hospital monitors blink digitally, suggests that the mother's watchfulness had not been thorough enough. Maternal lack of watchfulness now is punitively substituted by excessively watchful monitors in the hospital mise-en-scène. This image cuts to the mother in interview, recalling her pain when she "couldn't even hold her [the victim-infant]—that was torture!" The mother's eyes roll in recollection. The segment then cuts back to a similar scene in the hospital in which the mother is praying over the baby's crib. This tableau, again, of the grieving and praying mother signifies the transition to the miracle closure of the episode.

The narrative suddenly cuts to an external shot of the hospital facade, and the Shatner voice-over announces that "Sierra" (the infant's name) was "given a clean bill of health" and "released." This shot of the hospital facade cuts, again, to the interview of the mother, who states: "It was truly a miracle." This shot brings the viewer into the closure of the *Rescue 911* episode, in which the victim is miraculously sutured and reintegrated back into middle-class domesticity and the protectiveness of the family. The mother's interview about the "miracle" cuts to a shot of the actual victim-infant—now a young toddler—on roller skates at a skating rink. Harmony and unity in the domestic family appear to be restored, as the little girl is held by the hands of both mother-sisters, dancing together on roller skates. This sequence cuts to an interview with the sister-mother (the aunt), who says, "She's a blessing . . . a miracle," repeating the language of the baby's mother. The interview again cuts back to the scene of the skating rink, where "Sierra," the former victim, performs the "Hokie Pokie," whose lyrics (known to most American school children) emit over a public address system in the background: "You put your head in, you put your head out. . . . " A shot of the doctor, again in interview, discusses the technical problem of infant's head sizes, stressing the ease with which babies lose their balance and fall into objects like buckets. The association of the doctor's lecture on falling heads with the lyrics of the "Hokie Pokie" continues in a shot that shows, again, Sierra on roller skates, putting her head up and down as instructed by the lyrics. This final image is both sentimentally restoring and sadistically macabre, given the accident just survived.

Another episode aired in reruns on July 6, 1993, illustrates the way in which *Rescue 911* displaces images of sympathy, sadistic aggression, and class hegemony onto the implicitly white setting of suburban America. In this particular episode, a small-town Utah teenager inhales Butane and Scotch-guard to "get high," and nearly dies of a toxic overdose. *Rescue 911* does not depict the wide-spread use of drugs among teens in American small towns and cities alike. It certainly does not depict any form of crime stereotypically linked to inner cities. According to the *TV Guide*, "The show's producers have found that rescue authorities in major cities—such as New York and Chicago—are often reluctant to cooperate," citing "bureaucratic complications," or "concern among authorities" that their response to 911 emergencies would be revealed to be less than ideal. However, it is clear that the depiction of inner cities would also not feed the white pastoral rural-suburban ideal of the show—the fantasy of a hegemonic white America living collectively in domestic unity and peace. So, this rare episode about drug abuse focuses on a white teenager in a small Utah town, a person about whom his own father tearfully reports, "We'd never had problems," and about whom the paramedic called to the scene of the teenager's trauma states: "I had known Greg for years. This was a real shock to me. . . . He looked like the all American-type kid." An initial shot provides an external view of the teenager's high school, which, like the suburban home in the episode about the bleach bucket is supposed to be any suburban school.

The assault phase of the program unfolds as a re-enactment by actors, when "Greg" and his teenage companions sniff Butane in the local hardware store, then return "stoned" to school. An interior shot of the school depicts the teen collapsing on the floor, surrounded first by the school athletic director, then the vice-principal, then the paramedic, in a symbolic hierarchy of male authority figures and rescuers. As the rescue operation begins, shots of the teenage victim are cut by shots of a doctor's interview, as well as scenes of a grieving family discussing possible organ donation since it is doubtful Greg will survive. The narrative then cuts to a shot of a CAT-scan in progress, holding out the promise of survival through medical technology. The CAT-scan shot is brief but interesting. The teenage boy's body is seen in double images, in the background as his body is inserted into the scanner machine, and in the foreground as an electronic image on a monitor. The former image of his body in the machine is witnessed through the perspective of the CAT-scan technician's window, and through the monitor, of course, of the TV camera. An external shot of a helicopter and hospital strategically repeats the panopticon metaphor. Then, cutting to a scene with an interview of the father crying, we witness the emotive power of masculine sentiment. A new shot reveals the teenager in bed, now speaking to a family member on the phone. Follow-up shots show the victim in scenes of rehabilitation, surrounded by the mother and female medical technicians. Finally, a shot shows the victim miraculously restored to heath and strolling with family members through a state park, with the majestic Utah mountains in the background and family members playfully rubbing snow in his face.

A voice-over of the teenager's mother emphasizes the way the "crisis" has strengthened family unity: "We're a much stronger family," she declares. A final shot shows the attending doctor in interview, emphasizing the "miracle" aspect of this rescue, suggesting that divine intervention played a role: "I've never seen anybody in as bad a shape as he was and recover . . . that's a miracle." The rescue a success, shots of the family at the park are spliced by shots of the teenage victim and his mother giving lectures to high-school students on drug prevention. The victim's reintegration back into suburban white community and family life now complete, we hear the victim's testimony about the use of Butane and Scotchguard, and the miracle of family sympathy.

Occasionally, nonwhite minority groups are depicted on the *Rescue 911* show. In these rare occurrences, the format of the program changes to suggest racialized difference is at stake. Format variations suggest a *deviance* in social difference outside the white American family "norm." This difference is not just reproduced as difference, but as social marginalization and inferiority. Two such episodes were aired, curiously, on the same show, on December 15, 1993. One tells the story of an out-of-control school bus carrying Native-American Montana firefighters careening down a mountainside. A heroic driver in another bus manages to stop the bus with his own vehicle. While this miraculous rescue avoided the sure loss of many lives, the emotive content of the show is missing or displaced, in the stoic

Native American men's testimonies that reveal little emotion, and in the conspicuous absence of family testimonies, mothers, or reference to technological rescue equipment. A final scene shows tribal members picnicking together in the mountains. This scene suggests the usual *911* reference to pastoral community life and reintegration of the potential victims. But other elements of this episode also emphasize the group's isolation and marginalization from white America, signified by the absence of domestic life, technology, and white law. This episode may not have been aired at all had it not been for the fact that the Native-American men themselves represent some semblance of the "law," as local firefighters.

The other episode combines unusual *911* plot elements to signify African-American racial difference on the show. On this episode, an African-American mother gives birth to a baby in her home on Christmas Day. That black Americans live in domestic homes and celebrate traditional American holidays is emphasized by the holiday framing of this episode. However, the domestic mise-en-scène itself also signifies class-racial difference. The woman is shown giving birth in a darkened room on the floor, a scene that differs significantly from the brightly lit homes depicted in episodes about white suburban life. Furthermore, there is no establishing shot of the suburban facade of the house (or hospital or school) in the beginning of the episode; the occasional shots of the figurally "black" house in the dark suggest the desire to conceal the working-class neighborhood, but also to reveal a different class for blacks.

During this episode, the mother is shown screaming and writhing in pain. This again differs from other *Rescue 911* depictions, in which white women give sudden birth but whose labors themselves are not dramatized. In the birth scene of the African-American mother, the "actual call" containing the sounds of birth is replayed, but partly from the perspective of the "911" dispatch room. There, a middle-aged white woman, the dispatch-operator, calmly contains the image of the writhing woman's agony by giving directives to a panicked father and the woman's own mother assisting the labor—refashioning the tape as a maternal melodrama. As the white dispatcher types "Lady in Labor" on a computer screen, this shot of the monitor sublimates the sounds of crisis that emerge from the tape in the background. The black mother is depicted as lacking control through sexuality, playing into stereotypes about black women as "breeders" about which Patricia Hill Collins has written eloquently.[9] The animal-like screams of this woman are posed against the severe control of the white bureaucracy and its rescue machine. This machine is composed of sedate maternal agents who use computer screens to "title" a birth, and whose maternal usefulness is conscripted to giving telephone instructions and contacting male emergency technicians.

A very curious element included in this episode is a volunteer paramedic dressed in a Santa Claus costume, who attends the birth. The fact that this technician is decked out in St. Nick array is made humorous as neighbors outside the birth scene jeer, or as a fellow paramedic peers out his ambulance window at the Santa Claus apparition in another rescue vehicle and declares he "couldn't believe" his "eyes," that "It was really strange— almost too good to be true [to see Santa Claus] . . . like something out of book or a movie." Indeed, the white Santa Claus apparition in the context of the black woman's birth scene *is* "strange." The attempt at levity, however, reveals that a darker side exists to this juxtaposition of images. Seen through the window of the other vehicle, the Santa Claus paramedic is a carnivalesque reminder of blackface minstrelsy, popular entertainments in which whites have imitated blacks, mimicking and also interrogating American racial difference.[10]

But the final shots of this episode of the Black mother giving birth figurally re-integrate the black family into the white order of law, domesticity, and commerce—still signified by the Santa-Claus metaphor. A shot shows the black family, including the new mother and infant, in a shopping mall. After the family browses through a pet store—the bestial metaphor domesticated and commercialized—the family meets one of the white attending paramedics at a fast-food restaurant, who then proceeds to offer the family a wrapped gift. The concept of the "miracle" in this episode is figurally wrapped in the gift, a token which anthropologist Marcel Mauss has suggested sublimates fear or "poison" (the literal translation of "gift" from the Old German), which the rival group represents. That the "miracle" is offered in the plenitude of a commercial shoppers' paradise is reminiscent of the language of "miracle" from the famous Hollywood classic about Santa Claus, *Miracle on 34th Street*. The importance of Santa Claus as the "real" miracle at the birth scene is recalled in a concluding voice-over of the gift-offering paramedic, who says, "Under the circumstances, it would be hard not to believe in Santa Claus." The Santa Claus myth, and the accompanying suggestion of gift-giving, offers a wholesale absorption of black racial difference into a white-signified realm of commodity fetishism. This episode concludes with an image of sentimental reintegration that suggests the miracle of sympathy can produce this miracle of visual-cultural integration—on behalf of commercial enterprise.

The Catastrophic Witness and the "Miracle" of Sympathy

As these episodes of *911* suggest, the show's stories of rescue, contradiction, aggression and sublimation, are parables about the sympathetic spectator. These shows not only recount the survivability of victims as they are rescued from near-fatal cataclysm. They recount the survivability of the mass spectator, posed as the "individual" who watches *Rescue 911* from inside his own domestic confines during the prime-time "family" hour, the "individual" alone and yet unified, in sympathetic identification with other spectators. The fantasy of oneness and cultural hegemony of the mass spectator can be attributed to the image of an "abundant economy" that Debord suggests drives the "society of the spectacle." Describing the mechanisms of late capitalism, Debord notes that a subtle enslavement to the commodity occurs when "economic necessity" and "the satisfaction of primary human needs . . . [is] replaced by an uninterrupted fabrication of pseudo-needs," in turn "reduced to the single pseudo-need of maintaining the reign of the autonomous economy."[11] To break economic survival away from "primary . . . needs" is to create an economy of abundance and surplus. Debord suggests that a faulty sense of liberation is produced by the "abundant economy":

> the primary question of survival is undoubtedly resolved, but in such a way that it is constantly rediscovered. . . . Economic growth frees societies from the natural pressure which required their direct struggle for survival, but at that point it is from their liberator that they are not liberated. . . . The abundance of commodities, namely, of commodity relations, can be nothing more than *increased survival.*[12]

The differential of class through a master-slave structure is smoothed over by what Debord calls "the shimmering diversions" of the commodified spectacle.[13] Yet the imaginary unity that lies at the "root of the abundant economy" is a false one. It is an image of "unity" built upon "disjunction . . . contradiction," and makes "the entire expanse of society . . . its portrait."[14]

Debord's analysis of the commodity as a megatrope for both spectacle and late-capitalist culture has a provocative application to the spectacle of accident and survival on *Rescue 911*. The spectator's own survival is driven home in each episode as the narrative structure of each episode both contradicts and re-unifies the spectator's sympathetic self-image. The sympathetic spectator experiences identification with these everyday accidents; and yet he is distanced from them by the phenomenon of watching television media. The use of "reality" equipment and reproductive technologies assist the spectator's instant identification with victimage as well as with the sentimental master agents of disaster-control. But, like so many other types of "reality" shows that are disaster-driven—from the nineteenth-century Parisian dioramas of Flaubert's society to today's TV network news programming—*Rescue 911* also represents the division apparent between the spectacular image and the spectator himself, through the spectator's great passivity.

The division is expressed through the "force and vivacity" of the original "impression," recalling Hume's theory, Debord's "shimmering diversions." We remember that Hume describes compassion as a spectator's inertia, when, "safely at land," he contemplates the idea of "those who are at sea in a storm." Sympathy is distinguished from compassion by the greater "nearness" of the spectacle, as the ship actually appears "to be driven . . . near me," and the spectator "can perceive distinctly the horror." Near and direct, but still preserving the spectator's autonomy and intactness, the operation of sympathy requires the very vividness of the "shimmering" horrific image so that its spectator may be assured of his own shimmering luster and representational survival, his own mastering power. The split between the "force" of the sympathetic image and the inertia of the sympathetic spectator addresses deep levels of the subject's hidden fears in a radical-capitalist age. The spectator repeats the psychological paradigm behind filmic suture, in which a problem arises for the spectator seeking monolithic images of his own narcissism and safety, but who is also suspicious of those images because they do not address his reality in being a spectator, which creates distance, a liminal gap. Shimmering disasters and a theater of horrors unfold as a means of expressing the distance the spectator feels. Meanwhile, this distance produces *dis*-ease, a disease of the spectator. He again seeks suture, closure, to survive his own sympathetic viewership.

To survive "reality" in the context of prime-time commercial television is to survive the very reproduction of sentiment through sympathy, and the moral but also epistemological conflicts asserted through master-slave vicissitudes of power. Perhaps more than any other fabrication of masculine sentiment to date, programs like *Rescue 911* hold out the solace, the class transcendence, that the sympathetic spectator has always sought—while ironically demanding the hierarchical conventions that spectatorship inevitably brings. The logic that pervades the spectacle forces the sadistic viewer to watch over the masochistic scene of his own victimage. To save, to rescue, is to submit again and again to the sympathetic halves: to the masculinity of the visual perversion, to the femininity of the victim's scene.

NOTES

Introduction

1. According to *The New York Times,* the stepfather, Beverly Russell, did not testify directly about sexually molesting Smith but read a letter describing his own guilt and suffering, addressed to Smith herself but, of course, intended for an audience of spectators, including the South Carolina judge: "'To see unfolded before my eyes the principle of reaping and sowing, to lose Michael and Alex, to see you and Linda [his wife, Smith's mother] crushed . . . you don't have all the guilt of this tragedy.'" The language reproduces sentimental phrasing when Russell adds: "'My heart breaks for what I have done to you.'"

2. The term "melodrama" is used to refer to theatrical productions of the sentimental tradition, beginning with the eighteenth-century populist theater and peaking during the nineteenth century. As a chiefly theatrical form, melodrama is also a term used by film critics, referring to sentimental forms of American cinema, especially movies targeted at female audiences. The tradition recently has been to separate the terms "melodrama" and "sentiment." Christine Gledhill makes the distinction between the "sentimental"—which she claims is a more rational-based intellectual genre—and "melodrama," which she says arises from out of the sensational aspects of bawdy spectacle. Since I argue that spectacle (and its spectator) is a feature of sentimental genres, I treat the term "sentimental" as a more pervasive and categorical term, and film (and television) melodrama as an important subcategory. Like Gledhill, film critic Thomas Elsaesser distinguishes between the sentimental tradition of literature and film melodrama. This division, I suggest, is based upon an understandable desire by earlier cinema critics to establish their distinct discipline.

3. For other classic works that provide significant discussion upon the topic of sentiment's relation to women and female representation, see Janet Todd's *Sensibility, an Introduction* and *The Sign of Angelica: Women, Writing, and Fiction, 1660–1800;* Shirley Samuels, ed., *The Culture of Sentiment;* Nancy Armstrong, *Desire and Domestic Fiction;* and Suzanne Clark, *Sentimental Modernism.* See also Terry Eagleton's "Introduction" to *The Rape of Clarissa,* which calls Richardsonian sentiment of the eighteenth century a historic "feminization of discourse."

4. My work extends the observations of critics like Nancy Miller, who in *The Heroine's Text* writes about the sentimental heroine as at least partially inspired by masculine cultural determinations about women. What Miller suggests is the "femi-

nocentrism" of sentimental novels is often a "pose," based on an "obsessing," she says, "about an idea called 'woman'" assuaging masculine anxieties. Rachel Brownstein, in *Becoming a Heroine,* also writes ironically at times about several renown sentimental heroines, including those I will study here, Clarissa, as well as Isabel Archer from *The Portrait of a Lady.* Linda Zwinger, in *Fathers, Daughters, and the Novel,* writes about father-daughter sadomasochistic liaisons in both *Clarissa* and Henry James's later novel, *The Golden Bowl;* she suggests that the heterosexual family romance important to novels of sentiment is based upon the sadomasochistic power relations of patriarchy.

5. Shirley Samuels borrows this term from Pierre Bourdieu's *Distinctions* (Paris: Editions de Minuit, 1979). She writes that her volume of essays "traces a genealogy of the culture of sentiment that mobilizes both a rhetorical configuration of emotional excess and a problem of the body and what it embodies: its gendered, racialized, or national affiliation," what Bourdieu might call "the position of disposition of the sentimental subject," its "'habitus'" (6).

6. See Laura Wexler's "Tender Violence: Literary Eavesdropping, Domestic Fiction, and Educational Reform," and Karen Haltunen, "'Domestic Difference': Competing Narratives of Womanhood in the Murder Trial of Lucretia Chapman" (Samuels 9–38, 39–57).

7. See, for example, Kaja Silverman in *Male Subjectivity in the Margins;* and Gaylyn Studlar's work on masochism.

8. In art criticism, however, Jonathan Crary's *Techniques of the Observer: On Vision and Modernity in the Nineteenth Century* does turn to many of these philosophical texts, relating vision to philosophy and medical-technology experiments.

9. See Emile Benveniste's analysis of pronouns in *Problems in General Linguistics.*

10. While Smith's defense built its case upon the allusion to Russell's sexual abuse of his stepdaughter, Smith's husband, David Smith, the father of the murdered boys, constructed a different narrative. In an excerpt of his book in *People Magazine,* David Smith reported his wife writing in a note from the York County Detention Center: "I'm sorry . . . I don't know why I did it" (*People* 81).

11. See Fred Kaplan, who writes that the notion of the existence of *a* "human nature" as "an identifiable entity . . . defined in universally applicable abstract terms" is but a product of Enlightenment reason (12–13). That this concept is more rationalistic than empirical is suggested by R. F. Brissenden.

12. See M. H. Abrams, entry on "Sentimentality," *Glossary of Literary Terms.* As chief editor of *The Norton Anthology of English Literature,* Abrams represents the classic "textbook" point of view on sentiment, prior to feminist revisions of that view.

13. I quote Catherine Gallagher in personal conversation at Stanford University, May 17, 1991, following a lecture on David Hume. Peter Brooks, in *The Melodramatic Imagination,* writes at length about sentimental melodrama as a "mode of excess," in which "excess" becomes a structural feature.

14. Lynn Chancer refers to Jessica Benjamin's *The Bonds of Love: Psychoanalysis, Feminism, and the Problem of Domination*.

15. See Andreas Huyssen's chapter by that title, which discusses the way in which male stereotypes of women as consumers of popular fiction during the nineteenth century attributed "femininity" to all audiences of mass cultural forms.

16. Sigmund Freud titled the first section of his "Three Essays," "The Sexual Aberrations."

17. Freud (68). He includes "inversion" and homosexuality as part of his catalogue of sexual perversions or "aberrations."

18. Silverman cites the polysexuality issue of *Semiotext(e)* 4.1 (1981). More recently published is the example of *Dirty Looks: Women, Pornography, Power*, ed. Pamela Church Gibson and Roma Gibson (London: British Film Institute, 1993), a volume whose essays tend to view a positive relation between pornography and women, suggesting porn is connected to sexual liberation.

19. In *Discipline and Punish*, Michel Foucault famously interprets the implications of Jeremy Bentham's nineteenth-century panopticon figure through its watchtower gaze. The panopticon becomes his model for the reformed prison institution as the exemplary machine of social surveillance.

20. Specific perversions in the Victorian era, for instance, were distinctions *unified* by "a gaze, isolated and animated by the attention they received. Power operated as a mechanism of attraction; it drew out those peculiarities over which it kept watch" (*History of Sexuality* 45).

21. Early sexology presumed sadism and masochism to be "opposite" but interconnected forms of the same sexual perversion, associating "cruelty and violence with lust," according to Richard von Krafft-Ebing. Havelock Ellis's *Studies in the Psychology of Sex* (1903) went further in insisting that "sadism and masochism may be regarded as complementary emotional states" (33). Freud, too, in his earlier writing on the sexual perversions, insisted on a binary complementarity between sadism and masochism, which he gendered as male and female in impulse. Freud, furthermore, linked masochism to the "feminine" instinct. Such assumptions about the natural causes of sadomasochistic sexuality are still widely held today by sociobiologists such as Desmond Morris and C. Owen Lovejoy.

Most sociological accounts of sadomasochism continue to employ the binary term, and convey a double message about the "nature" of S&M. Paul Gebhard, for example, while insisting on the scripted nature of sadomasochistic activities among subcultural groups, does not question the collapse of these categories. The introduction to the volume in which Gebhard's essay is published states the volume's intention to "reach beyond the prevailing narrow and myopic views" that have considered sadomasochism to be a pathology or aberration. However, the editors and writers of the introduction appear to accept sadomasochism as part of "life itself," revealing again the socio-biological fallacy (Weinberg 9, 11).

22. Joseph Boyle (4); he writes in a context of contemporary theories of natural law.

23. See *De Jure Belli ac Pacis* (quoted in Tuck 4–5). Richard Tuck's discussion explains that this passage reveals the fact that "God's will is no longer the unique source of moral qualities: things are good or bad *from their own nature,* and that is logically prior to God commanding or forbidding them (Tuck 68).

24. Norman Kemp Smith, in *The Philosophy of David Hume* (1949), first urged the importance of Frances Hutcheson's work upon Hume's philosophy. More recent accounts of Hutcheson's influence upon Hume include David Fate Norton's *David Hume,* who agrees with Kemp Smith's overarching claim: that Hume should not be read "as providing merely a skeptical extension of empiricism" (Norton, *David Hume* 59), but as influenced by Hutcheson's moral realism. However, Norton calls for a rereading of Hutcheson's moral theory, which refutes the moral skepticism of Thomas Hobbes and Bernard de Mandeville, whose *The Fable of the Bees* (1723) offered a satiric attack upon human nature as hypocritical and wholly egocentric. Like the Earl of Shaftesbury, Hutcheson argued that the "moral sense" makes man "a genuinely moral creature," in Norton's words, through the corrective of reason over sentiment (*David Hume* 61). In Hume, however, the relationship between reason and sentiment appears a much more conflictual one, according to Norton, a point I agree with.

25. *Treatise* (457). All references to Hume henceforth are to the *Treatise,* unless otherwise noted.

26. I quote Norton's more recent account of the Hutcheson-Hume link, in an article entitled, "Hume, Human Nature, and the Foundations of Morality." There Norton suggests that Hume provides such an "unalterable" view of human nature resting "morality on human nature," thereby providing "a stable base for morality." Norton quotes the passage on the passions cited above in my own text. Read straight-forwardly, without irony, this passage might indeed suggest that there is little "variation" in human nature at all.

However, I follow John Valdimer Price in arguing to treat Hume as an ironist. In the above passage, irony becomes Hume's strategy for meeting the objections that his morally skeptic viewpoint would invariably have triggered in his culture. Norton ignores the statement that follow these quotations, which, in the slippery manner of irony, reasserts the important distinction Hume makes between "nature" and "origin."

Another writer on Hume's relationship to natural law, Stephen Buckle, also presumes the close relationship of Hume to Hutcheson, particularly through the notion of the "moral sense." See his discussion of Hutcheson's moral sense "as part of a larger argument about our perceptual capacities" (201–5). Hutcheson argued that "Moral goodness" is related to the impression of "beauty," according to Buckle, and—again, taken straightforwardly—Hume's *Treatise* might be seen as taking this position. However, again, I find Hume much more cynical about that which con-stitutes "beauty" through the eyes of the spectator than Hutcheson, who implies a universal sentiment in this approbation.

See also Gallager's book *Nobody's Story,* which "follows the lead of most writers who have stressed the problematic nature of Hume on sympathy" (168); she argues that sympathy is associated with property, whose effect might "aggrandize the self and its properties, even as it unsettles the concept of a bounded, stable ego" (170).

27. The first edition of the *Enquiry into the Human Understanding* appeared in 1748 and was based largely on Book 1 of the *Treatise;* the *Enquiry concerning the Principles of Morals* appeared in 1751, based partially on Book 3 of the *Treatise*. The *Dissertation of the Passions,* published in 1757, drew much of its material from Book 2 of the *Treatise.*

28. Hutcheson wrote this to Hume in a letter dated September 17, 1739 (Hutcheson quoted in Buckle 273).

29. The emphasis on the sensory is partially attributable to Hutcheson, as Buckle notes. Hume's moral spectator is prefigured in Hutcheson's account of the moral sense, and the concept of the "observer."

30. Price is the one observer of the deeply ironic nature of all of Hume's writing, linking Hume's ironic voice to the age in which he was born, which produced some of the word's greatest irony and satire. Price notes that Hume faced "intellectual and cultural pressure" to conform with the moral values of his day (4). Hume's ironic method of presenting his skeptical ideas was "subtle and effective" (5), serving to protect him from social persecution as well as a brilliant rhetorical strategy. Irony in Hume's writings, in general, conveys symbolic opposition that criticizes his works' more superficial meanings. Price does not remark specifically upon the way in which irony affects Hume's theory of sympathy.

31. See, for example, Diane Waldman's essay, "Film Theory and the Gendered Spectator," which summarizes this position, arguing, in fact, against any gender essentialism toward the viewer at all, and even criticizing those feminist arguments that focus on the *female* spectator. Waldman suggests we remain "wary of any theory that privileges the acquisition of gender identity as the only factor in meaning construction" (90), disregarding, for example, race and class.

32. In "Women and Representation: Can We Enjoy Alternative Pleasure?", Jane Gaines's critique of the Laura Mulvey school makes the suggestive point that women may be "aroused" by this culturally masculine imaginary of pleasure, coupling that point with a subtle side-swipe at a "feminist film criticism, which has reached the point of exasperation with the cataloguing and analyzing of male pleasure" (358). In the "critical vogue to study the cinematic construction of male pleasure," Gaines asserts that only two places remain for women: as fetishized star, or as audience member occupying a point of view reserved for the male gaze.

33. Mary Ann Doane's essay, "Film and the Masquerade," first published in 1982 and then as a chapter in *Femmes Fatales* (1991), argues that the female spectator overidentifies with the image, based in the daughter's overdetermined, pre-oedipal bond with the mother; the distance provided by feminine masquerade becomes a means of creating a necessary distance to the image. Linda Williams's essay, "Something Else Besides a Mother": *Stella Dallas* and the Maternal Melodrama" (1984) argues that the episodic fragmentation for which the maternal melodrama is well

known embodies the multiplicity of the female gaze, as replication women's social experience; Williams applies the model of a shifting and oscillating female gaze to the horror genre in another 1984 essay, "When the Woman Looks" (1984). Mulvey raises these issues of the female spectator—previously unacknowledged in her 1975 essay—in her 1981 "Afterthoughts on 'Visual Pleasure,'" a reading of King Vidor's 1947 film, *Duel in the Sun*. Feminist film criticism has continued to contest Mulvey's focus on the masculine gaze, including Tania Modleski's work on Alfred Hitchcock, *The Women Who Knew Too Much* (1988); and, more recently, Rhona J. Berenstein's *Attack of the Leading Ladies* (1996), which follows Williams's oscillating model of gender in horror-film genres.

34. Mulvey (59). She notes that Freud drew upon "the voyeuristic activities of children, their desire to see and make sure of the private and the forbidden (curiosity about other people's genital and bodily functions, about the presence or absence of the penis, and, retrospectively, about the primal scene)."

35. The Lacanian mirror is a psychical mirror, which both Mulvey and film theorist Christian Metz suggest is (re)duplicated by the cinema screen, one of the most important contributions of the *Screen* school.

36. Mulvey (10—emphasis added). This tension is graphically illustrated by the Lacanian mirror, and it was a tension that was "crucial for Freud," as Mulvey notes, in describing the origin of erotic pleasure.

37. An invaluable critique of Mulvey's focus on sadism as a chief visual pleasure is Gaylyn Studlar's "Masochism and the Perverse Pleasures of the Cinema," which describes masochism as a more pervasive perversion in the viewing experience.

38. See Freud's essay, "Fetishism" (1927).

39. Emily Apter's careful reconsideration of fetishism's Freudian and Marxist legacy links it to the visual-entertainment commodity, as well as to cultural femininity, in *Feminizing the Fetish*. Hal Foster discusses fetishism's relationship to spectatorship of realist painting in "The Art of Fetishism: Notes on Dutch Still Life," published in *Fetishism as Cultural Discourse*, edited by Apter and William Pietz.

40. Immanuel Kant made these comments in his pamphlet, "An Answer to the Question: What Is Enlightenment?", first published in 1784 (90–92). Kant justified his claim on a separation between the public and private use of reason: "By the public use of one's reason I understand the use which a person makes of it as a scholar before the reading public. Private use I call that which one may make of it in a particular civil pose of office which is entrusted to him" (92). Kant perceives that there are many private "affairs which are conducted in the interest of the community," and that they "require a certain mechanism through which some member of the community must passively conduct themselves with an artificial unanimity, so that the government may direct them to public ends." Kant concludes this statement by declaring: "Here argument is certainly not allowed—one must obey" (92). Kant gives examples of those who must "obey," such as the taxpayer who must pay taxes or the military officer who must not question orders.

41. Foucault makes this critique in his own essay, "What Is Enlightenment?", which challenges many of Kant's claims, including the faulty division he makes between public and private. See Waugh volume also (98).

Chapter One

1. Helene Ostovich has written of Clarissa as a positive heroine; Margaret Doody similarly views Clarissa this way, suggesting her dying words are "a manifesto, a declaration of independence from [bourgeois] society" (179). Among not-so-positive portraits of Clarissa is William Warner's. See also Zwinger, who perceives Clarissa as a willing participant in the patriarchal family romance. Brownstein has written ironically about Clarissa's virginal character, suggesting that as "exemplar to her sex," Clarissa's character and actions are always limited to those maintaining the determined image of "heroine."

2. In *Clarissa's Ciphers,* Terry Castle writes of the symbolic fragmentation and disruption in the epistolary document that composes our image of the heroine, exemplified when the amputation and death of the brothel owner, Sinclair, interrupts Clarissa's own extended scene of dying: "In *Clarissa,* the woman's body (prototypically rendered in the dying Sinclair and repeated in the heroine's corpse) is broken, incomplete, motley—disturbingly discontinuous," a fact which "has consequences for a reading of *Clarissa* in its entirety" (35).

3. "Through the keyhole" is Lovelace's phrase, a phrase alluded to by Ian Watt. Watt first quotes a passage from Samuel Coleridge's *Biographia Literaria,* suggesting that Richardson's "'whole *material* and imagery . . . is supplied *ab extra* by a sort of *camera obscura* manufactured at the printing office.'" Watt argues that "much has been said about Samuel Richardson's 'keyhole view of life,' which he undoubtedly used on occasion for unwholesome ends," but for which was "the essential basis of his remarkable opening up of the new domain of private experience for literary exploration." I revisit the keyhole metaphor once again, suggesting that "private experience" is a construct of sentiment.

4. Linda Kauffman (133). This passage also is quoted by John P. Zomchick (59). Fred Kaplan suggests that "Richardson made his appeal to the heart through the heart," alluding to the epistolary convention itself. Kaplan (30) refers not only to the sentimental heroine but to the sentimental conventions of the epistolary itself—in the words of Alexander Pope, "the most impartial Representations of a free heart." (Pope wrote this to correspondent Lady Mary Wortley Montagu several decades before Richardson's publication of *Clarissa,* on August 18, 1716.) See also Tom Keymer for a discussion of this and other passages referring to the epistolary genre of Richardson. Twentieth-century critics have persisted in the myth of the epistolary form as an unmediated and, therefore, truthful expression related to the "heart." The language is echoed by the modern critic Watt, for instance, when he calls the epistolary *Clarissa* "a short-cut . . . to the heart" (195). That the heart's

authentic expression revealed through the epistolary form is connected to *female* interests in the epistolary is suggested in the fine essays by Elizabeth Goldsmith, Katharine Jensen, and Margaret Rosenthal, published in Goldsmith's anthology *Writing the Female Voice.* See also Janet Gurkin Altman, who accounts for the formal properties of "epistolarity" that contribute to the illusion of immediacy and realism.

5. See Warner's controversial deconstruction of the heroine Clarissa in *Reading Clarissa* (17). See also Zomchick, who writes more specifically about natural law and Clarissa and speaks of the heroine's "heart" as a "site . . . driven by the same historical forces that are producing the modern conditions of individualism" (59).

6. *De Officio Hominis . . . (On the Duty of Man . . .* 1.3.12), first published in 1673. Samuel von Pufendorf was known primarily as a theorist of natural law; his masterpiece, *De Jure Naturae* (1672), is condensed by *De Officio Hominis* (1673), and became a standard natural-law text.

7. See *Questions Concerning Natural Law* (131). J. B. Schneewind's essay on John Locke's moral philosophy goes into detail on the subject of Locke's relation to natural law. While his essays on the subject "do not provide a completely coherent ethical theory," in a few places, "Locke speaks of the moral law as innate." At the same time, Locke "devotes much space to arguing that moral knowledge cannot be innate." Schneewind notes that Locke refused to publish his essays on natural law; therefore, "it is not clear how much of what they say we can suppose to represent his own considered opinion" (213).

8. See Sylvia Kasey Marks, who notes that the conduct-book elements of Richardson's epistles were the "forerunners of today's Ann Landers, Miss Manners, and all the other self-improvement books that swell the weekly best-seller list" (3–4). Marks reminds us that the virtuous content of Clarissa's character is related to its conduct-book genre, a popular eighteenth-century manual of moral instruction proposing an idealized representation of human behavior—the genre from which Richardson's epistolary novels first emerged. Richardson's first work, *Familiar Letters* was exemplary of the genre, stating in its forward that the book intends to "inculcate the principles of virtue and benevolence" by which children and parents, apprentices and masters, should conduct themselves by, both as "rules to think and act by, as well as forms to write after" (xxvii–xxix). Richardson's conduct-book interests were retained in his later fiction, as well. The Preface to *Clarissa*, for example, warns its audience that this is no "light novel, or transitory Romance," which some readers may make of its "sole end, rather than as a vehicle to the Instruction" (xxi).

9. *Selected Letters* (151). To illustrate Clarissa's conduct-book virtue, Richardson states also, like a proud father, that "My girl [is] . . . a beacon to warn" (151, 92).

10. *An Inquiry Concerning . . . Virtue or Moral Good* (74). While Hutcheson suggested that the "moral sense" is not innate, he also suggested that it was a "determination of our minds to receive" what he called "Ideas of Actions," whether they be of an "amiable or disagreeable" nature (83).

11. Hutcheson writes that God "has given us a Moral Sense, to direct our Action, and to give us still nobler Pleasures." He adds that "the Author of Nature" is

one who "has determined us to receive, by our external Senses, pleasant or disagreeable Ideas of Objects" (83).

12. Lawrence Klein explains that "land was seen as a form of wealth that insured the reliability of the owner. The permanence of land and its tangible reality were a guarantee of the owner's commitment to the nation since his wealth was physically part of the nation." This kind of wealth was contrasted to "moveable wealth," which "seemed to make its owner's relation to the polity contingent: the commercial human was too plastic a being" (223).

13. *Clarissa* (486). Clarissa's faith in natural-law's universal morality is reiterated when she tells Anna, "Surely he had not the insolence to *intend* to tease me" (490).

14. *De Jure Belli ac Pacis,* first published in Paris in 1625 and translated as *The Rights of War and Peace,* ed. J. Barbeyrae, trans. anon (London 1738—*De Jure* quoted in Richard Tuck 78). In analyzing these statements by Grotius, Tuck suggests this "Janus-faced" book contains "two mouths" through arguments for "absolutism," whereby "men no longer have a right to defend themselves against the person of the sovereign," and in its "libertarian arguments" (Tuck 79). Stephen Buckle argues differently, suggesting that in Grotian theory, "absolutism was seen as a key to liberty" (3).

15. See Zomchick's discussion of the entail (62). He cites Lawrence Stone's discussion from *The Family, Sex and Marriage in England, from 1500–1800* (New York: Harper & Row, 1977), to suggest the increasing effectiveness of legal entails in binding the estate to the masculine line after 1660, thereby precluding female inheritance as "preserving estate integrity" (Zomchick 62). In *Clarissa,* suggests Zomchick, the "grandfather's devise . . . appears to go against the actual trends of the time" (62). Nevertheless, "the will is in accord with William Blackstone's belief that the freedom to alienate one's lands at will was conducive to economic growth," and to the value of "possessive individualism" (62), in which the grandfather's bequest serves as a reward to Clarissa both for her affection and her labor in caring for the grandfather and the estate.

16. Clarissa's property inheritance is essential to the plot, as suggested in Richardson's first novel title, *The Lady's Legacy.* The favoritism shown Clarissa by the family patriarch instigates the rivalry of her siblings and the determination of them against her.

17. See Christina Marsden Gillis, who points out that writing represents Clarissa's spatial privacy, a privacy, in turn, that informs her notion of "self."

18. Brownstein intuits these connections between the novel's plot, the plot of property, and the plot of the grave, writing that "Clarissa is the ideal of a materialistic society based on the preservation of private property through monogamy, a relationship sanctified by its religion" (43–44). Doody plays upon the links between the themes of "will," "death," and "property" that echo throughout the novel. Perceiving this link to be based in "the spirit of Locke and of post-Revolutionary England . . . reflected in the interest in property . . . a symbol of power," the association of all

these terms in the novel exemplify "a legal and social contract, easily definable in Locke's language about the nature of property, but absurdly frail in the world of active wills engaged in the struggle for power" (Doody 123).

19. Kant's famous invective (90) was borrowed from Horace's *Epistles*, I.2.40. While I quote from the essay anthologized by Patricia Waugh, I borrow from the translation used, instead, by Flax, in "Postmodernism and Gender Relations" (43). The line from Horace, however, is more literally translated from the Latin "dare to be wise," according to Waugh, although the notion of "reason" or "understanding" is Kant's use of the German.

20. Flax also suggests that this illusion "still predominates in contemporary Western thought" and involves gender "self-deception," adding "all such transcendent claims reflect and reify the experience of a few persons—mostly white, Western males" (43).

21. I quote Benjamin's condensed version of her argument on sadomasochism, "The Bonds of Love: Rational Violence and Erotic Domination" (62).

22. Chancer writes: "one has had to guarantee by fiat that the other upon whom one depends will not disappear. Clearly, the dominating or the dominated fear abandonment if they are not manipulating or consenting to be controlled" (73).

23. See Louise J. Kaplan for a discussion of masochism as a primarily *male* practice, from a clinical point of view.

24. Eagleton suggests that the bourgeois sentimental novel, in general—as exemplified by *Clarissa*—may have repudiated aristocratic ideals, but it sought to incorporate many of those ideals, as well. In this scene, I suggest that Clarissa illustrates the desires of the bourgeoisie to authorize its recent economic ascendancy by imitating upper-class attitudes as well as artistic traditions.

25. *Clarissa*, quoted in the edition edited by George Sherburn (Boston: Houghton Mifflin, 1962: 202). This passage is not included in the Penguin edition, otherwise cited here; the Penguin is based upon Richardson's original manuscript, and therefore does not reproduce letters superadded to later editions by Richardson.

26. *Clarissa*, both quotes in Sherburn edition (169—Richardson's emphasis).

27. Studlar's essay counters the claim of Mulvey's classic account of filmic sadism in "Visual Pleasure and Narrative Cinema," arguing that masochism also informs visual desire—but as an "alternative" pleasure, a giving up rather than a holding onto "self."

28. *Clarissa*, Sherburn edition (171). If this seems but posturing for Clarissa's sake only, Lovelace also reportedly plays the masochist for Lord M, writing Belford, after being ordered to marry the maiden, "All obedience, all resignation—no will but hers, I withdrew, and wrote directly to my lord" (249).

29. *Clarissa*, Sherburn edition (172, 184—Richardson's emphasis).

30. *Clarissa*, Sherburn edition (202).

31. *Clarissa*, Sherburn edition (263).

32. Freud writes that debasement of the feminine ideal is necessary for "men" experiencing "romantic love." These subjects preserve the object's ideal status by creating an obstacle "to keep their sensuality away from the object they love." Romantic debasement is the result, derived from what Freud calls "an ascetic current in Christianity" that could be argued is historically fundamental to the development of masochism (*Three Essays* 251).

33. William Wehrs (761) makes this claim, arguing that all poststructural readings of *Clarissa* tend to place "letters in a narrative vacuum," failing to regard the fact that "each letter stands in a collection, created by an author, that shapes the way individual letters are read."

34. Eagleton (71—emphasis added). He takes up the "unfashionable" sword in the war against deconstruction by dueling the critic (Eagleton's own metaphor) who would make of Clarissa a "mere" representation.

35. Foster (261) writes that, while the fetish is always the object of luster that attempts to restore, or reinvent, the imagined object lost—the castrated penis, in the reductive Freudian sense—the fetish also enacts a perpetual tension that the woman's body encodes.

36. See Rosenthal's account of Franco, who comments on the importance of Veronica Franco to the female letter tradition through the way in which Franco redefines "the courtesan's profession as contrary to mercenary and duplicitous love" (4).

37. See Jensen, who writes that the *Lettres portugaises*, in meeting with "enormous enthusiasm" in their female display "of torment and desire," served as "a litmus test for the public's reading of female identity in love" (26).

38. See Madame de Sévigné's *Letters of Madame de Robertin Chantal, Marchioness de Sévigné, To the Comtess de Grignan, Her Daughter* (1727).

39. Madame de Sévigné's granddaughter is quoted in Goldsmith's essay (16). Artifice, associated in the Salon school with the evils of dissimulation that only "bad" or sexually licentious women would approbate, was unbecoming and unfeminine. Therefore, these women adopted what Goldsmith calls "a charming carelessness, a facility of expression."

40. Jean de La Bruyère, *Les caractères ou les moeures de ce siècle* (*The Characters, or Manners of the Age*—79–80), first published in 1688. I borrow the English translation of this passage from Goldsmith's essay on women and the epistolary tradition (46). See also Jensen, who writes that male "admirers" viewed "women's nature" as "characterized by emotion." This allowed women "to express 'naturally' what men must work to convey" (29).

41. See Jacques Lacan's "The Signification of the Phallus" in *Ecrits,* in which he writes: "the phallus is a signifier, a signifier whose function, in the intrasubjective economy of the analysis, lifts the veil perhaps from the function it performed in the mysteries" (285).

42. See Keymer, who agrees with the concept of "competing epistolary voices," but uses this approach as a call to "active participation of his [Richardson's] readers"

(xviii). The emphasis on *Clarissa's* hermeneutic openness, focusing "on the subjectivity of meaning and interpretation," as April London suggests, Richardson himself would have found "highly suspect." She notes that Clarissa's recovery of a "spiritual intactness may seem an argument for the final victory of . . . subjectivism"; yet the novel's conclusion "does little to alleviate the overwhelming sense of Clarissa's victimization by the anarchic individualism of Lovelace and the collective authority of the Harlowes" (279). Wehrs concurs with this position in his reading of narrative "irony" in *Clarissa*.

43. Montagu says this in a letter to Sir James Steuart; Pope says this when writing to John Caryll. See Keymer, who comments upon the use of "undress" in these letters and associates them with the letter's seeming immediacy of presentation.

44. See Scott Cutler Shershow, who has written about the use of the puppet as symbol of power, a power imbued in the puppeteer but also the spectator who watches (138–39). Puppet theaters, which were popular in England during the eighteenth century, are one of the many entertainment precursors to cinema.

45. See Walter Benjamin, "The Work of Art in the Age of Mechanical Reproduction," where he employs this term to refer to the image of "aura" granted the object perceived as original, unreproduceable.

46. Richardson quoted in James Carson (98—emphasis added), who also comments upon Richardson's interest in absorption.

47. See Janet Bergstrom's discussion of this use of segmentation in *The Birds* (168).

48. Stephen Heath, "Film and System" (10).

Chapter Two

1. From letter written by Flaubert on March 8, 1857, to Mademoiselle LeRoyer de Chantepie (164—my translation). "It" refers to Gustave Flaubert's novel *Madame Bovary*.

2. For one classic account of Flaubert's "free indirect style," see Roy Pascal.

3. The usual definition of the "free, indirect" style is that method by which speech is quoted indirectly. However, Victor Brombert notes its more structural effects in his concept of "disappearance."

4. D. A. Williams notes that Flaubert perfected the technique of narrative "impersonality" in *L'Education sentimentale*, which he describes as "the virtual elimination of opinions, value judgments and commentary of a generalized nature which would have helped to endow the narrator with a recognizable personality" (3).

5. "Economic" (276). Freud emphasizes that his clinical experience with this type of fantasy is featured in male patients.

6. Kaplan (12). Such "strivings" serve to conceal the masculine fear of "a terrifying primitive violence," which sexual activity invokes for some.

7. Kaplan adds that perversions permit men to identify with the degrading position assigned to women in the social order, "but without losing face" (25).

8. In this sense, my argument reconsiders the concept of masochism detailed by Studlar, who identifies it with female pleasure. While I agree with Studlar's important distinction between a post-oedipal "genitally organized sadism, for which women, the object of sadistic voyeurism, represent the threat of castration," and a pre-oedipal masochism that is the "pregenital sexuality" suggestive of a "symbiotic bond with the mother, who represents the promise of plenitude and unity" (603), I disagree with the suggestion that masochism is differently gendered than sadism. "The mother," as Studlar describes her, is a fantasy not only of male masochism but of male fetishism. In this sense, masochism returns us to the theme of castration, which underlies the perversion of voyeuristic sadism.

9. *Venus in Furs* (*Venus im Petz*) was the first volume of *The Heritage of Cain,* a study in sexuality. According to Gilles Deleuze's study of Leopold von Sacher-Masoch's work, it was not translated into English or French until 1902; the latter was an "inaccurate" translation by economist R. Ledos de Beaufort. My own quotations of *Venus in Furs* come from Deleuze's volume, originally derived from a subsequent translation of the French by Aude Willm.

10. *L'Education sentimental* (63). All page numbers refer to the French edition of the novel and are my own translation.

11. "*Une lorette*" is a type of high-class female prostitute, a term for which there is no equivalent in English.

12. This passage (57) is colloquial and difficult to translate. In demanding that his companions "be Gauls," Hussonnet recalls cultural stereotypes about the churlishness of their French male ancestors; he wants his friends to behave as happy rogues, "Gauls," uncivilized.

13. Roland Barthes (140). Jonathan Culler refers to this statement by Barthes in making his own argument for Flaubert's postmodernity and deconstructive quality. Brooks sums up the postmodern view of Flaubert, calling Flaubert a "radical ironist," establishing a modern deconstructive style in which the "self" is "all stripped of significant status, shown to be unauthentic or illusory." For Brooks, Flaubert is not a melodrama writer like Honoré de Balzac or James, citing a distinction between the "melodramatic imagination" of these authors and a "counter-tradition" represented by Flaubert. I will argue against this distinction in chapter 3.

14. Robert Scholes and Robert E. Kellog (268) quote Flaubert's March 1857 letter to Mademoiselle de Chantepie.

15. Frank Gees Black suggests that *Evelina* provides "a rich and realistic picture of London society of the 1770s, with a foreground occupied by a heroine so human that one could believe in her." This novel, he suggests, was the last attempt to use the epistolary for the purpose of serious fiction, after which the epistolary became "the provender of 'light readers'" (1–2).

16. In *Pride and Prejudice,* for example, the letter serves as an important narrative device in the form of Darcy's letter to Elizabeth, which helps her to dispel her illusions about Wickham, as well as other minor familial letters that assist plot. In *Wuthering Heights,* Isabella's letter to Nelly recounts her own disillusion with Heathcliff and the Wuthering Heights household.

17. Black gives examples of the latter, including Oliver Goldsmith, *An History of England, in a Series of Letters from a Nobleman to his Son* (1764); and William Richardson, *Anecdotes of the Russian Empire, in a Series of Letters, Written a Few Years Ago, from St. Petersburgh* (1784).

18. Not only did Richardson declare the importance of verisimilitude in his epistles in the Preface to *Clarissa,* but so did Denis Diderot in his 1761 eulogy to Richardson, which emphasized the quality of veracity and exactitude to be found in Richardson's novels.

19. The Praxinoscope is of particular interest to film historians because it was a projecting Praxinoscope model that Reynaud employed in his Théâtre Optique, a popular spectacle that ran continuously at the Paris wax museum, the Musée Grévin, and whose projective apparatus is considered to be one of two main precursors to the first cinematic projection machine, the cinematograph, from which the first film was shown in 1895.

20. Charles Wheatstone's inquiry into the problem of binocular parallax resulted in stereoscope technology.

21. One in a series of early French aeronautical experiments, the dirigible (built by Henry Giffard) landed 30 kilometers outside of Paris.

22. The guide was a two-volume series of essays about the city of Paris, including contributions by Georges Sand, Charles Augustin Sainte-Beuve, and an introduction by Victor Hugo. The drawing of the Hippodrome is at the end of volume 1 of the guide.

23. See Lisa Lowe's discussion of orientalism in *L'Education sentimentale* and *Salammbô,* which links the forbidden other that non-European societies represented in nineteenth-century literature and art to the "hetero-erotic" other of "woman," or "gendered relationship" (215). The reference to Bou-Maza in tandem with the female spectators at the Hippodrome is another illustration of these "oriental" gendered references in *L'Education.*

24. See Denis Bordat and Francis Boucrot for a history of the importance of the *théâtres d'ombres* in Paris beginning with the eighteenth century.

25. Lotte Reiniger (31) also notes that "the European puppeteers took great care that the sources of their puppets' movements should be hidden," thereby inventing elaborate "systems of strings and wires" attached to the puppet-figure's back to move "them vertically from below with more or less ingenuity."

26. See Stathis Damianchos (251) on the history of the *Chat Noir* club, organized by the entrepreneur Rodolphe de Salis, and for other information on shadow theaters.

27. Shershow quotes Plato (14), and also notes that "the puppet or perform-

ing object is figurally implicated in Western discourse about theatre," about "theatrical and literary authorship, about representation itself" (14–15).

28. This is the language of David Bordwell and Kristen Thompson (6) in describing film emulsion processes.

29. For a history of the universal expositions held during the Paris nineteenth century, see Ory Pascal. See also Philippe Bouin and Christian-Philippe Chanut.

30. From a pamphlet by G. Lenotre, *Voyages merveilleux à l'exposition universelle de 1889,* a copy of which is part of world-fair archives at the Bibliothèque de la Ville de Paris.

Chapter Three

1. Sandra Winner (60).

2. The Art of Fiction" (609—emphasis added).

3. "Gustave Flaubert," in *Minor French Novelists* (82). James asks rhetorically: "Why did Flaubert choose, as special conduits of the life he proposed to depict, such inferior and in the case of Frédéric such abject human specimens?" (*Minor French Novelists* 81–82).

4. "Charles de Bernard and Gustave Flaubert," published in a volume entitled *French Poets and Novelists.*

5. R.P. Blackmur's 1950 introduction to *The Art of the Novel,* his collection of James's critical prefaces, focuses on what the prefaces seem to say overtly about James's views on the novel as art; it does not focus upon how the prefaces might suggest an artistic practice of their own—a reading of the prefaces sustained by Donna Przybylowicz, who suggests that James's prefaces are "a justification of his novelistic techniques and innovations" (201). Carol Schloss takes up the issue of James's "poignantly informed debate" (59) about aesthetic visuality and power in his novels, as does Mark Seltzer's Foucauldian analysis of James's fascination with surveillance in *The Princess Casamassima* and *The Golden Bowl.* Susan Griffin discusses Jamesian "vision" as it affects both psychological perception and the "eye" of realism in *The Golden Bowl* and *The American Scene.* Edgar Dryden reads the Preface to *The Portrait of a Lady,* specifically, as a statement on James's relationship to romance.

6. We recall that Benveniste distinguishes two kinds of subjects involved in language acts in "The Nature of Pronouns," in *Problems in General Linguistics:* the "I" as speaker or "referent" and the "referee," which, according to Silverman, is "the discursive element with which that discoursing individual identifies, and in doing so finds his or her subjectivity" (*The Subject of Semiotics* 45–46). The third subjectivity distinction, the "spoken" subject of the audience, arises from but never is articulated directly by Benveniste's theory; this subject is "constituted through identification" with the other narrative subjects (*The Subject of Semiotics* 47), and arises from a cinematic elaboration of Benveniste's theory—based upon the image of an audience spectator in a darkened theater.

7. Eagleton suggests that the rise of the sentimental novel in the eighteenth century represented a "feminization of discourse," emphasizing female subjectivity (13). Others also align sentimental novels with women and their interests, most notably Janet Todd (on the eighteenth-century British tradition), Jane Tompkins (on the American nineteenth-century tradition), and Suzanne Clark (on the relationship of modernism to sentimentality and women). Criticism on *The Portrait of a Lady* tends to assume that Isabel's subjectivity directs the course of the novel, like Brownstein, who views Isabel somewhat ironically. Miller wisely has suggested that novels of what she calls "feminocentrism" are often a "pose," based upon an "obsessing," she says, "about an idea called 'woman'"; and Zwinger has called attention to the more sadistic aspects of James's sentimental portrayal of women in her reading of *The Golden Bowl*.

8. Huyssen writes that the "great male artists" of the nineteenth century stereotyped "woman" as the consumer-driven popular reader, in a chapter provocatively titled, "Mass Culture as Woman: Modernism's Other."

9. Jean-Jacques Rousseau's "natural man" is part of his pastoral view of nature. He argues in *Emile* for a "natural man" (the ideal citizen) raised in the nature of rural provinces, remaining free of urban corruption, and breastfed by a "natural" mother.

10. The Emersonian resonances in Isabel's character in *The Portrait of a Lady* have been noted by many James critics, including Richard Poirier, who writes that Isabel's "action is absolutely within the logic of her Emersonian idealism" (35); and Elizabeth Sabiston, who argues that Isabel is an Emersonian heroine because she plays the role of "the Transcendental innocent" (117).

11. Although James provocatively complicates his notion of experience, questioning "what kind of experience is intended" and suggesting that "experience," like "the sense of reality," is difficult to classify, he also asserts that "experience" is "never limited," suspended in the "chamber of consciousness" ("The Art of Fiction" 609).

12. Preface (4–5). James's friend Ivan Turgenieff was a writer for whom James expressed considerable admiration. About Turgenieff's work, James said: "His vision is of the world of character and feeling; the world of the relations throws up at every hour and on every spot. . . . his work was all delicate and fancy, penetration and compression" (120–21).

13. *The Portrait of a Lady* (360). For a discussion of Isabel's character and the various houses she inhabits, see R.W. Stallman and Sabiston.

14. See John Bender for a discussion of the relationship between prison design—particularly important is his discussion of the panopticon—and the development of the modern novel form.

15. Schloss (68) adds that Coburn carried the author's "elaborate notes" on assignment, and James himself accompanied Coburn when in London.

16. In Lacanian theory, the subject leaves the Imaginary phase, associated with narcissistic attachment to the mother's body, to enter the Symbolic phase, associated with separation and the Father's Law of castration. From the viewpoint of

the Symbolic, the subject experiences what Jacques Lacan, in *Ecrits,* calls "anatomical incompleteness" (9); the "subject" sees himself only as image.

17. In "Three Essays on Sexuality," Freud remarks that "Every active perversion is . . . accompanied by its passive counterpart: anyone who is an exhibitionist in his unconscious is at the same time a voyeur" (81).

18. Adele Tinter, *The Cosmopolitan World of Henry James* (3).

19. James quoted in John Auchard (xx), who suggests that James was very affected by the deaths in Venice of musicians and poets like Richard Wagner and Robert Browning, and that this colored his appreciation for the city.

20. This dual image of Venice is echoed in another passage Tinter quotes, written by James following a visit to Venice in 1887. Alluding to his international party at the Palazzo Barbaro, where James himself was a guest, he wrote that Venice represented "all Europe as having at one time and another revelled or rested, asked for pleasure or for patience there; which gives you the place supremely on the refuge of endless strange streets, broken futures, and wounded hearts." Like Auchard, Tinter uses such a quote to support the idea of James's admiration of Venice, ignoring his ironic images of its alienation and darkness.

21. Huyssen (46) ironically makes this association between women and entertainment fiction when reporting on nineteenth-century claims about "high" versus "low" art. See also Silverman, who suggests that the Jamesian approach to "vision" often bends the rigid cultural divisions marking gender. The supposed Jamesian "Master" figure "is never unequivocally male," she writes, because James's "recourse to vision" is more generative of "trauma than of power" (*Male Subjectivity* 180).

22. Jacques Derrida's comment is made in the context of an analysis of the problematic of philosophical language, in its tendency to lose metaphorical capacity. This observation seems echoed by James, in the "overspent" metaphoricity of the Preface's final paragraphs.

Chapter Four

1. Pufendorf, "On the Natural State of Men" (114).

2. Editor's Preface to *Wuthering Heights* (second edition). Sister Charlotte Brontë wrote this famous editor's Preface under the pseudonym Currer Bell for the second edition of the novel, which appeared in 1850, three years after its original publication.

3. Reviews included those in the popular *Douglas Jerrold's Weekly Magazine* that acknowledged the "'power'" in *Wuthering Heights* but suggested it is a "'purposeless power which we feel a great desire to see turned to a better account . . . the reader is shocked, disgusted, almost sickened by details of cruelty, inhumanity and the most diabolical hate and vengeance'" (quoted in Katherine Frank 236). Similarly harsh in their assessment, the critic at *Britannia* wrote of "'so much rude ability

displayed yet in which there is so much to blame' "; and at *Graham's Magazine's*, another contemplated " 'how a human being could have attempted such a book . . . without committing suicide' " (quoted in Frank 237). As Maggie Berg points out, a novel full of what reviewers called " 'misshapen' characters" and structurally crude and " 'disjointed' " was "assumed to proceed from the 'rough shaggy uncouth power' of the artist herself (or rather himself)," in an attack upon the author personally (Berg 12). (*Wuthering Heights* was originally published under the sexually ambiguous pseudonym Ellis Bell, who most critics assumed to be male.) Charlotte's Brontë's Preface, written soon after Emily's death, however well intended, did little to dispel this image of her sister.

4. Audrey Jaffe (260) bases her argument about the sympathetic image-making process upon a Marxist discussion of "modern capitalism's construction of a temporarily diffuse, or narrativized, subject." For this subject, "only the moment of consumption offers an illusion of presence, giving the self that consumes the opportunity to coincide, phantasmatically, with the idealized and temporally detached self projected onto the object consumed" (260).

5. Beth Newman, in her article on vision and visuality in the novel *Wuthering Heights,* remarks that "the relation between Nelly's story and Lockwood's enframing diary . . . can be articulated in visual terms." Newman believes that it is "Lockwood's scopic drive" that "links the frame of *Wuthering Heights* to the narrative it introduces," as he "hears a story about the object of his desire," Catherine Heathcliff (1033). Newman suggests a correlation between metaphors about vision and the storytelling process, but does not discuss sympathy.

6. The '90s has seen many new, lavish movie productions of nineteenth-century novels, including many films adapted from Jane Austen novels, and director Jane Campion's 1996 production of *The Portrait of a Lady.*

7. Dudley Andrew describes this process in making films based upon novels, which requires both a conceptual, global view of a novel's meaning, but also a textual reinvention of the textual process.

8. I quote the *OED* entry on "whether."

9. In but one classic example of the Romantic use of nature, William Wordsworth's *Lyrical Ballads* uses the image of the "sylvan Wye" river valley in the poem about Tintern Abbey, to suggest a relatively stable referent point—as visual icon—for the poet-speaker who has himself experienced change.

10. J. Hillis Miller makes this point in his reading of *Wuthering Heights;* Hillis Miller perceives the novel to be a detective story, a mystery, enshrouded in the hermeneutic problems endemic to language and its deconstructive qualities.

11. "The pleasure of inflicting cruelty and torture" is the libertine's "Nature," he who believes it is his nature to torment others—akin to Richardson's Lovelace. The libertine's "pleasure" is one law of nature that counters natural-law's philosophical optimism. But this "pleasure," as I noted in my analysis of Lovelace, relies upon an image of nature as biological determinant. *Wuthering Heights* implicitly counters

this kind of reading of nature in natural-law theory. It neither sides with the Hobbesian view—that human nature is essentially self-preservationist or selfish—or the proto-sentimental view of Shaftesbury and Hutcheson—that nature provides an inner moral sense as rational guide. Instead, *Wuthering Heights* reveals the actual mechanisms by which human nature, *in social bondage,* finds "pleasure" in "cruelty and torture"—by the very bonds of resemblance that create social liaisons, harmonious, protectionist, or otherwise.

12. This is Chancer's description of Margaret Mahler's work.

13. See "The Absent Mother in *Wuthering Heights,*" in Emily Brontë, *Wuthering Heights,* edited by Linda H. Peterson (318); an earlier and different version of this essay was published under the same title in *American Imago* 42.2 (Summer 1985): 143–64.

14. Brontë quoted in Wion (323). The writings of both D.W. Winnicott and Lacan emphasize the child's relationship to the "mother," or primary caretaker, is one of a mirror, which helps to constitute the child's sense of identity.

15. Chancer summarizes Nancy Chodorow (78). See also Chodorow's article, "Psychoanalytic Perspectives on Gender Difference."

16. Charlotte Brontë's Preface to *Wuthering Heights* (xxvii).

17. John K. Mathison (143) and David Cecil (43), respectively; Cecil includes in his remark both "spectators" of the novel, a term he applies to Lockwood as well as Nelly.

18. Melvin R. Watson (91).

19. See James Hafley, "The Villain in *Wuthering Heights.*"

20. See Frank's biography of Emily Brontë, which describes the adult Charlotte as a Tory sympathizer and royalist, while the adult Emily expressed more revolutionary (and Romantic) views. The sisters' political views were often expressed by the fantasy worlds they created, Angria and Gondal, respectively, in adolescence and early adulthood.

21. George J. Worth (175, 171) sums up these views of Lockwood, arguing that while his ordinariness makes him a "representative of the great body of ordinary readers," he is also a comic character, "an often unconscious commentator" steering us toward recognizing Brontë's thematic concerns (175).

22. *De Jure Naturae et Gentium Libri Octo* (1.1.3).

23. Buckle (88) makes these observations about Pufendorf's state of nature in his contemporary study of natural law.

24. Newman has provided an excellent analysis of this scene, suggesting that the young woman's "look" is a female reversal of the male gaze, invoking "the terror of castration in the male spectator, a terror that turns him to stone," like Medusa. To have the woman "look" invokes a particular terror for the male protagonist, Newman writes (1031).

25. See Newman for her comments on this "looker-on," as well as Hillis Miller and Terence McCarthy. What Hillis Miller calls narrational "unreliability" and Mc-

Carthy calls "incompetence" is a strange form of reliability and competence through the compensatory, the supplementary, drama of visual sympathy.

26. *Wuthering Heights* was voted by New York film critics best picture of the year, over competitors *Gone with the Wind* and *Mr. Smith Goes to Washington.*

27. Gregg Toland won an Academy Award for his cinematography in *Wuthering Heights.*

28. See Willliam Wyler's biographer Jan Herman for more details about the *Wuthering Heights* production (195).

29. André Bazin (107) also offers his well-known analogy of theatrical adaptations, a process of refraction like that of "'a crystal chandelier' "—he quotes Charles Baudelaire. Bazin writes:

> If one were called upon to offer in comparison a symbol other than this artificial crystal-like object, brilliant, intricate, and circular, which refracts the light which plays around its center and holds us prisoners of its aureole, we might say of the cinema that it is the little flashlight of the usher, moving like an uncertain comet across the night of our waking dream. (106)

Bazin also wrote that "A good translation" is the work of a "genius. . . . In short, to adapt is no longer to betray but to respect" (69). Commenting specifically on Wyler's films, Bazin argued for the artistry of film adaptation: "The effective fidelity of a Cocteau or Wyler is not evidence of a backward step, on the contrary, it is evidence of a development of cinematographic intelligence," which in Wyler results from "the asceticism of his editing, the refining down of the photography, the use of the fixed camera and of deep focus" (69).

30. I quote the unpublished screenplay from an original hand-edited script used during the production of *Wuthering Heights,* available in the Wyler Collection of the Special Collections of the Arts Library, UCLA. Although written by Charles MacArthur and Ben Hecht, the screenplay was revised by Wyler, friend John Huston, and *Wuthering Heights* producer Sam Goldwyn.

31. Krafft-Ebing quoted in Thomas S. Weinberg's sociological study of sadomasochism (25), which the latter ultimately describes as a socially scripted phenomenon. See also Margaret Jackson's discussion of twentieth-century sexology and its marriage manuals, which have inculcated domination and submission into the ideal of heterosexual love.

32. Freud quoted in Weinberg, in the latter's study of sadomasochism (30—Freud's emphasis).

33. This includes Juliet Mitchell, who argues, in the words of Chancer, "that feminists ought not overlook the theoretical significance of basic Freudian insights into the workings of the unconscious and the centrality of sexuality." Mitchell believes that Freud "diagnosed (rather than approved of) the results of cultural inculcation" (Chancer 127).

34. Chancer (140). Paula J. Caplan is one of several psychologists who has criticized the image of female masochism that dominates even serious psychological

literature and clinical practice alike. She calls it a "myth" that women act upon these masochistic impulses. But this "myth," she argues, nevertheless "contributes to a difference in attitude toward suffering women and men . . . the focus of many therapists tends to be on discovering how women supposedly bring suffering on themselves" (9). Michele Massé writes about the way the gothic novel genre portrays the female stereotype of masochism. Summing up the cultural rationale for female masochism, Massé notes, "Masochism is the end result of a long and varying successful cultural training. This training leaves its traces upon individual characters and upon the Gothic itself" (3).

35. She plays the classic moral masochist in her orientation away from herself and her strict devotion to another. But that there is a touch of sadism underlying the surface of this masochism is suggested when Dr. Kenneth visits Wuthering Heights in an earlier episode, telling Isabella that she should go to Edgar, because Cathy is dying. Isabella glances toward the distance, her eyes seemingly on fire, and says, "If she died, I might begin to live." In an aesthetically parallel episode that comes a bit later, it is Ellen who arrives at Wuthering Heights, again, to tell Isabella she is wanted at the Grange, that Cathy is dying. As Heathcliff starts for the door, Isabella flings herself at him and begs him to stay, reasoning that if Cathy is dying, "she belongs in Edgar's arms." Her reasoning is sympathetically disarming but duplistic. It suggests concern for her brother, Edgar, as well as a desire to keep Heathcliff away from Cathy for herself.

36. Wyler opposed this "happy ending" scene. According to Herman, Goldwyn demanded that Wyler add a shot of the resurrected couple to the final film frame, marking the film's sentimental conclusion. Wyler refused to shoot the scene. So Goldwyn hired another filmmaker, H.C. Potter, to add a pair of Laurence Oliver-Merle Oberon doubles, seen from the back, climbing up the hill together—resulting in the film's final sequence (199).

Chapter Five

1. According to Brooks, the melodrama "mode of excess" developed out of the rise of the bourgeoisie, when it became the dominant economic class during the seventeenth and eighteenth centuries, displacing romance fictions about aristocratic heroes and heroines into quotidian tales of middle-class domesticity.

2. Elsaesser opposes melodrama "categories" of startling visual and sound effects to "categories" he calls "intellectual or literary ones," a distinction Gledhill also makes.

3. See "Film and the Masquerade" (23). Doane invokes the Metz concept that "voyeuristic desire" of the gaze "symbolically and spatially evokes this fundamental rent" between nearness and closeness, subject and object. But she challenges Mulvey's contention that the oppositional structure of the voyeur in mainstream cinema is passive versus active only, suggesting that proximity and distance provide a more important and pervasive oppositional structure.

4. Judith Butler names this figure of white Hollywood femininity "Lana/ Lora." Sirk, referring to other characters by their fictive name when interviewed about the film, steadfastly refers to the Lora Meredith character as "Lana Turner."

5. John Halliday interview, "Sirk on Sirk" (228).

6. Sandy Flitterman-Lewis made these comments in a talk entitled, "Discourses of Desire and Difference: Configurations of Sexuality and Race in the Classical Hollywood Cinema," for the Columbia Film Seminar, New York City, January 1993. See also her comments on *Imitation of Life* in the article "*Imitation(s) of Life:* The Black Woman's Double Determination as Troubling Other."

7. Thomas Schatz notes that "The initial success of romantic tearjerkers reflects the collective capacity to stroke the emotional sensibilities of suburban housewives, but recent analysts suggest that the '50s melodramas are actually among the most socially self-conscious and covertly 'anti-American' films ever produced by the Hollywood studios" (151).

8. In Fannie Hurst's novel, only Jessie, Bea's daughter, is described as blonde, at seven years old "a rather lanky, knob-kneed little girl, whose first blondness had dimmed into a freckled sort of eclipse from which it was to emerge again" (164). In John Stahl's close adaptation of the Hurst novel, neither the Bea character (played by Claudette Colbert) nor the Jessie character are blondes.

9. Halliday interview (228).

10. Michael Selig takes a different approach to this film than many feminist critics, arguing that Douglas Sirk's *Imitation*, like so many other domestic melodramas, circumscribes the power of social commentary to the domestic realm populated by women alone.

11. Sirk's visual system is renown for establishing as much distance as it does proximity or identification. Through actual visual images, like those of mirrors and other hyper-references to "spectacle," Sirk creates irony, as Paul Willemen notes. Butler's analysis of how Sirk achieves this irony with the representation of gender, representing itself through the figure of Lana/Lora in *Imitation of Life*, begins with a reading of the credits scene, in which diamonds are dropped into a glass of water— suggesting the connections between illusion, commodity wealth, visuality, and "life" that will mark both themes and image-making in this film.

12. Michael Stern comments on this use of "mannered" color in the Sirkian visual scheme in the film. He suggests that the "baroque patterns of intense, enameled color" that typified another Sirk film, *Written on the Wind,* "are formalized in this film [*Imitation*] into a procession of specific tonal emblems" (286). By "tonal emblems," he refers to the blue used to depict the cold-water flat or the "dominant black of the funeral"—here Stern points out that "blackness" signifies mourning, but it also signifies "the racial issue as well" associated with Annie.

13. Butler reads Steve as a stupid "Lana lover," who does not understand that she is an "imitation of life," an image. I read Steve as more sadistic in his "stupidity," a sentimental voyeur with whom the melodrama audience identifies.

14. These accoutrements are well relayed in the film by Lana Turner's

sweater-girl shoulders plumping out of glittering, low-cut frocks, and Sarah Jane's imitation of those frocks in her scanty vaudeville costumes.

15. I quote Rhona Berenstein from a 1993 conference talk, entitled, "White Skin, White Masks: The Monstrosity of Race in 1930s Jungle Films." Berenstein further develops these ideas in *Attack of the Leading Ladies: Gender, Sexuality, and Spectatorship in Classic Horror Cinema.*

16. Tania Modleski's commentary on this scene from *Blonde Venus* is evocative of Berenstein's on the blonde's role in jungle films; Modleski writes: "the sexual charge of the spectacle derives from the disavowal, the doubleness . . . structure whereby she [the Marlene Dietrich character] is posited as *simultaneously* animal and human, as well as simultaneously white and not white" (*Feminism without Women* 128).

17. The image of Turner in *The Postman Always Rings Twice* informed the development of the Marilyn Monroe image, which came much later and I would argue is a Turner imitation. By the late '50s and early '60s, blonde female figures like Kim Novak, Tippy Hedrin and Marilyn Monroe would continue to eroticize "blonde-ness" as both sadistic and masochistic, "helpless" constructs in which women are evil, frightening and wayward—but also easily masterable and punishable for their sadistic qualities.

18. In Flitterman-Lewis's article *"Imitation(s) of Life,"* she writes that Sarah Jane's show in the nightclub is "a manipulation . . . doomed to failure." Moreover, Sarah Jane conceives of assimilation as "acting a part," and thereby asserting self-identity as a "parody of a highly conventional notion of female sexuality" (334). Such criticism of Sarah Jane's performance again follows one level of the Sirkian ideology in the film: that a falsity masks a truth, that there is a true female and/or black female "self-identity" in the film.

19. Mulvey (12). She further notes, "A woman performs within the narrative, the gaze of the spectator and that of the male characters in the film are neatly combined without breaking narrative verisimilitude."

20. See Bergstrom's "Rereading the work of Claire Johnston." Claire Johnston first speculates about a type of "rupture" endemic to Hollywood cinema, especially in the representation of women, in her article "Women's Cinema as Counter-Cinema," published in pamphlet form in 1973. She teams up with Pam Cook to elaborate upon this theory in the classic essay on director Raoul Walsh's films, "Woman in the Cinema of Raoul Walsh."

21. Attributed to Louis Comolli and Jean Narboni, this editorial was published in *Cahiers due Cinéma,* October 1969. See Cook and Johnston's use of this quote in "Woman in the Cinema of Raoul Walsh" (35), where they identify this moment as a "de-naturalization." These critics perceive in some classic cinema the capacity to show that the fetishized "woman" has been constructed as a patriarchal sign ("Woman in the Cinema of Raoul Walsh" 34).

22. Although Marina Heung sees Sarah Jane as "a catalytic force" in the film," who "dismantles the film's basic strategy of displacement and obfuscation" (318), she nevertheless perceives the ending of the film, in which Sarah Jane is ushered into

a limousine, as a conservative gesture, as well, making the three women reconstitute the nuclear family.

23. Heung's reading of this scene is similar, suggesting that *Imitation of Life* can be interpreted as an attempt to offer an image of positive black-white relations. The film was released five years after the Supreme Court ruled in *Brown v. Board of Education of Topeka* (1954), a landmark decision that sought to end public school segregation. Flitterman-Lewis interprets the scene differently, writing: "Sarah Jane no longer resists her determined social position; rather, she assumes her black identity by fitting into the 'family' in her designated place" (334). I agree that Sarah Jane fits into "her designated place," but it is the place she has fantasized about— that of the undifferentiated white daughter, not as black servant.

24. See Williams, "'Something Else Besides a Mother': *Stella Dallas* and the Maternal Melodrama"; and Modleski, "In Search for Tomorrow in Today's 'Soap Operas'" in *Loving with a Vengeance*.

25. See, for example, E. Ann Kaplan's *Maternity and Representation,* which attempts to historicize our view of motherhood, beginning with a discussion of Rousseau's "natural mother" in *Emile.* See also the essays in Donna Bassin's volume, *Representations of Motherhood;* they promote multiple images of maternity as cultural constructions, images circulating and yet transformed by culture. Also see anthropological accounts of mother "love" in studies such as that of Nancy Scheper-Hughes, *Death without Weeping: The Violence of Everyday Life in Brazil.* This study of child-rearing practices among impoverished mothers in Brazil suggests that mothers often withhold affection and emotional commitment to children who face the probability of infant mortality during their first year; it again suggests that notions of "mother love" are social, not biological.

26. See *The History of Tears: Sensibility and Sentimentality in France.*

27. See Kaplan, *Motherhood and Representation: The Mother in Popular Culture and Melodrama* (New York: Routledge, 1992); and *Rocking around the Clock: Music, Television, Postmodernism, and Consumer Culture* (New York: Methuen, 1987).

Chapter Six

1. Anna Williams uses this phrase in her discussion of *America's Most Wanted* (99).

2. See Williams's discussion of *AMW* (99–105).

3. Arnold Shapiro quoted in *TV Guide* (32).

4. Summarizing Victor Turner, Alden Vaughan and Edward Clark define the rite of passage as "an initiation process by which a person moves from one set of perceptions to another" (11).

5. Turner defines these stages for "rites of passage" in *Dramas, Fields, and Metaphors: Symbolic Action in Human Society* (Ithaca, NY: Cornell UP, 1974), 231–32. See Vaughan and Clark's discussion (11).

6. In classic "thrillers," like those of the *Die Hard* trilogy, a character who represents the marginal fringes of law and order undergoes a series of assaults and injuries always to survive them intact, and to become reintegrated back into the domestic order of wife and family. These films almost inevitably cast a male-hero as protagonist. However, a recent thriller, *The Long Kiss Goodnight* (1996), made by director Renny Harlin of the second and third *Die Hard* films, casts a female "hero" figure played by Geena Davis, who, as a hard-core CIA detective-assassin, suffers amnesia and discovers her identity while living out the conventions of a suburban mother's domestic role. (She "kills" the assassin role and lives out the housewife conventions in the end.) The commercial success of these "thrillers" of the 1990s, I would argue, is related to the rise of the "reality" show on commercial television, with its survival themes.

7. William Shatner quoted in Bernard Weinraub's article in *TV Guide* (34).

8. June Namias writes about the ethnocentric mythologies embodied in texts of white North Americans' captivity by Indians in *White Captives*. She points out that these narratives describe "a forced, prolonged imprisonment with the enemy," suggesting "a fearful contamination" with a brutal, savage culture—an unspeakable deed "against an innocent, civilized, and superior foe" (that of the European settlers), which was forced into "communion with or at least relentless exposure to representatives of the devil" (2–3).

9. See Patricia Hill Collins, *Black Feminist Thought: Knowledge, Consciousness, and the Politics of Empowerment* (New York: Routledge, 1990).

10. See Eric Lott, *Love and Theft: Blackface Minstrelsies and the Working Class* (New York: Oxford UP, 1993) for an analysis of white imitation of blackness in the nineteenth as well as twentieth centuries.

11. Guy Debord (Paragraph no. 51).

12. Debord (Paragraph no. 40—Debord's emphasis).

13. Debord (Paragraph no. 59).

14. Debord (Paragraph nos. 54, 50).

WORKS CITED

Abrams, M. H. *A Glossary of Literary Terms.* New York: Holt, Rinehart, 1957.

Adorno, Theodor W., and Max Horkheimer. "The Culture Industry: Enlightenment and Mass Deception." *Dialectic of Enlightenment.* Trans. John Cumming. New York: Continuum, 1991: 120–67.

Altman, Janet Gurkin. *Epistolarity: Approaches to a Form.* Columbus: Ohio State UP, 1982.

Andrew, Dudley. "Adaptation." In *Film Theory and Criticism.* 4th ed. Ed. Gerald Mast et al. Oxford UP: New York, 1992: 420–28.

Apter, Emily. *Feminizing the Fetish: Psychoanalysis and Narrative Obsession in Turn-of-the-Century France.* Ithaca, NY: Cornell UP, 1991.

Aquinas, Saint Thomas. *On Law, Morality, and Politics.* Ed. William P. Baumgarth and Richard J. Regan. Indianapolis: Hackett, 1988.

Armstrong, Nancy. *Desire and Domestic Fiction: A Political History of the Novel.* New York: Oxford UP, 1987.

Auchard, John. "Introduction." *Italian Hours.* By Henry James. Ed. John Auchard. University Park: Pennsylvania State UP, 1992: ix–xxx.

Augustine, *Concerning the City of God against the Pagans.* (412–27). Trans. Henry Bettenson. London: Penguin, 1984.

Barthes, Roland. *S/Z.* Trans. Richard Miller. New York: Hill and Wang, 1974.

Bassin, Donna, et al. eds. *Representations of Motherhood.* New Haven, CT: Yale UP, 1994.

Baudelaire, Charles. "*Exposition universelle 1855—Beaux-Arts.*" (1855.) In *Critique d'art.* Vol. I. Ed. Claude Pichois. Paris: Armand Colin, 1965: 185–210.

Baumeister, Roy F. *Masochism and the Self.* Hillsdale, NJ: Lawrence Erlbaum, 1989.

Bazin, André. *What Is Cinema?* Trans. Hugh Gray. Berkeley: U of California P, 1967.

Bender, John. *Imagining the Penitentiary: Fiction and the Architecture of Mind in Eighteenth-Century England.* Chicago: U of Chicago P, 1987.

Benjamin, Jessica. *The Bonds of Love: Psychoanalysis, Feminism, and the Problem of Domination.* New York: Pantheon, 1988.

———. "The Bonds of Love: Rational Violence and Erotic Domination." In *The Future of Difference.* Ed. Hester Eisenstein and Alice Jardin. New Brunswick, NJ: Rutgers UP, 1985: 41–79.

Benjamin, Walter. "The Work of Art in the Age of Mechanical Reproduction." *Illuminations.* Ed. Hannah Arendt. Trans. Harry Zohn. New York: Schocken, 1969: 217–51.

Benveniste, Emile. *Problems in General Linguistics.* Trans. Mary Elizabeth Meek. Coral Gables, FL: U of Miami P, 1971.

Berenstein, Rhona. *Attack of the Leading Ladies: Gender, Sexuality, and Spectatorship in Classic Horror Cinema.* New York: Columbia UP, 1996.

———. "White Skin, White Masks: The Monstrosity of Race in 1930s' Jungle Films." Conference talk delivered at the Society for Cinema Studies, February 1993 (New Orleans).

Berg, Maggie. *Wuthering Heights: The Writing in the Margin.* New York: Twayne, 1996.

Bergstrom, Janet. "Enunciation and Sexual Difference." Rpt. in *Feminism and Film Theory.* Ed. Constance Penley. New York: Routledge, 1988: 159–85.

———. "Rereading the Work of Claire Johnston." *Camera Obscura* 3–4 (1979). Rpt. in *Feminism and Film Theory.* Ed. Constance Penley: 80–88.

Berlant, Lauren. "National Brands/National Body: *Imitation of Life.*" In *Comparative American Identities: Race, Sex, and Nationality in the Modern Text.* Ed. Hortense J. Spillers. London: Routledge, 1991: 110–40.

Bersani, Leo, and Ulysse Dutoit. *The Forms of Violence: Narrative in Assyrian Art and Modern Culture.* New York: Schocken, 1985.

Black, Frank Gees. *The Epistolary Novel in the Late Eighteenth Century.* Eugene: U of Oregon P, 1940.

Blackmur, Richard P. "Introduction." In *The Art of the Novel: Critical Prefaces by Henry James.* New York: Scribners, 1950: vii–xxxix.

Blair, Sara. "Henry James and the Paradox of Literary Mastery." *Philosophy and Literature* 15. 1 (1991): 89–102.

Bordat, Denis, and Francis Boucrot. *Les théâtres d'ombres: histoire et techniques.* Paris: L'Arche, 1956.

Bordwell, David, and Kristin Thompson. *Film Art: An Introduction.* 4th ed. New York: McGraw-Hill, 1993.

Bouin, Philippe, and Christian-Philippe Chanut. *Histoire française des foires et des expositions universelles.* Paris: Baudouin, 1980.

Boyle, Joseph. "Natural Law and the Ethics of Traditions." In *Natural Law Theory.* Ed. Robert P. George. Oxford: Clarendon P, 1992: 3–30.

Brissenden, R. F. *Virtue in Distress: Studies in the Novel of Sentiment from Richardson to Sade.* New York, 1974.

Brombert, Victor, "Flaubert and the Status of the Subject." In *Flaubert and Postmodernism.* Ed. Naomi Schor and Henry F. Majewski. Lincoln: U of Nebraska P, 1984: 100–15.

Brontë, Charlotte. "Editor's Preface." (1850.) *Wuthering Heights.* By Emily Brontë. Boston: Houghton Mifflin, 1956: xvii–xxiii.

Brontë, Emily. *Wuthering Heights.* (1847.) Boston: Houghton Mifflin, 1956.

Brooks, Peter. *The Melodramatic Imagination: Balzac, Henry James, and the Mode of Excess.* New York: Columbia UP, 1985.

Brophy, Elizabeth Bergen. *Samuel Richardson: The Triumph of Craft.* Knoxville: U of Tennessee P, 1974.

Brownstein, Rachel M. *Becoming a Heroine: Reading about Women in Novels.* New York: Viking, 1982.

Buckle, Stephen. *Natural Law and the Theory of Property: Grotius to Hume.* Oxford: Clarendon P, 1991.

Butler, Judith. "Lana's 'Imitation': Melodramatic Repetition and the Gender Performative." *Genders* 9 (Fall 1990): 1–17.

Caplan, Paula J. *The Myth of Women's Masochism.* New York: Dutton, 1985.

Carson, James. "Narrative Cross-Dressing and the Critique of Authorship in the Novels of Richardson. In *Writing the Female Voice: Essays on Epistolary Literature.* Ed. Elizabeth C. Goldsmith. Boston: Northeastern UP, 1989.

Castle, Terry. *Clarissa's Ciphers: Meaning and Disruption in Richardson's Clarissa.* Ithaca, NY: Cornell UP, 1982.

Cecil, David. "Emily Brontë and *Wuthering Heights.*" In *Early Victorian Novelists.* Indianapolis, IN: Bobbs-Merrill, 1935. Rpt. in *A Wuthering Heights Handbook.* Ed. Richard Lettis and William E. Morris. New York: Odyssey: 20–49.

Chancer, Lynn S. *Sadomasochism in Everyday Life: The Dynamics of Power and Powerlessness.* New Brunswick, NJ: Rutgers UP, 1992.

Chodorow, Nancy. "Gender, Relation, and Difference in Psychoanalystic Perspective." In *The Future of Difference.* New Brunswick, NJ: Rutgers UP, 1980.

Clark, Suzanne. *Sentimental Modernism: Women Writers and the Revolution of the Word.* Bloomington: Indiana UP, 1991.

Comolli, Louis, and Jean Narboni. "Cinema/Ideology/Criticism." *Cahiers du Cinéma* (October 1969). Rpt. in *Film Theory and Criticism.* Ed. Gerald Mast et al. New York: Oxford UP, 1992: 682–89.

Cook, Pam, and Claire Johnston. "Woman in the Cinema of Raoul Walsh." Rpt. in *Feminism and Film Theory.* Ed. Constancy Penley: 25–35.

Crary, Jonathan. *Techniques of the Observer: On Vision and Modernity in the Nineteenth Century.* Cambridge, MA: MIT P, 1991.

Culler, Jonathan. "The Uses of Madame Bovary." In *Flaubert and Postmodernism.* Ed. Naomi Schor and Henry F. Mejewski: 2–12.

Damianakos, Stathis, and Christine Hemmet, collaborator. *Théâtre d'ombres: Tradition et modernité.* Paris: Editions L'Harmattan, 1986.

Dayan, Daniel. "The Tudor Code of Classical Cinema." *Film Quarterly* 28.1 (Fall 1974): 22–31.

Debord, Guy. *Society of the Spectacle.* Detroit: Black and Red, 1983.

DeCordova, Richard. "From Lumière to Pathé: The Break-Up of Perspectival Space." In *Early Cinema: Space, Frame, Narrative.* Ed. Thomas Elaesser with Adam Barker. London: British Film Institute, 1990: 76–85.

Deleuze, Gilles. *Coldness and Cruelty.* New York: Zone Books, 1989.

DeRougemont, Denis. *Love in the Western World.* Trans. Montgomery Belgion. Princeton: Princeton UP, 1940.

Derrida, Jacques. "White Mythology: Metaphors in the Text of Philosophy." In *The Margins of Philosophy.* Trans. Alan Bass. Chicago: U of Chicago P, 1982: 207–71.

Doane, Mary Ann. *The Desire to Desire: The Woman's Film of the 1940s*. Bloomington, IN: Indiana UP, 1987.

———. "Film and the Masquerade: Theorizing the Female Spectator." In *Femmes Fatales: Feminism, Film Theory, Psychoanalysis*. London: Routledge, 1991: 17–32.

Doody, Margaret Anne. *A Natural Passion: A Study of the Novels of Samuel Richardson*. London, Oxford UP, 1974.

Douglas, Ann. *The Feminization of American Culture*. New York: Avon, 1977.

Dryden, Edgar. *The Form of American Romance*. Baltimore: Johns Hopkins UP, 1988.

Eagleton, Terry. *The Rape of Clarissa: Writing, Sexuality, and Class Struggle in Samuel Richardson*. Minneapolis: U of Minnesota P, 1982.

Ellis, Havelock. *Studies in the Psychology of Sex*. (1903).

Elsaesser, Thomas. "Tales of Sound and Fury: Observations on the Family Melodrama." *Movies and Methods, Vol. II*. Ed. Bill Nichols. Berkeley: U of California P, 1985: 165–89.

Emerson, Ralph Waldo. *Nature*. (1836.) In *Selections from Ralph Waldo Emerson*. Ed. Stephen E. Whicher. Boston: Houghton Mifflin, 1957: 21–56.

Evenson, Norma. *Paris: A Century of Change, 1878–1978*. New Haven: Yale UP, 1979.

Flaubert, Gustave. *Correspondence*. 4ème série (1854–1861). Paris: Louis Conard, 1927.

———. *L'Education sentimentale*. (1869.) Paris: Editions Garnier, 1961.

Flax, Jane. "Postmodernism and Gender Relations." In *Feminism/Postmodernism*. Ed. Linda J. Nicholson. New York: Routledge, 1990: 39–62.

Flitterman-Lewis, Sandy. "The Black Woman's Double Determination as Troubling 'Other.'" In *Imitation of Life*. Ed. Lucy Fischer. New Brunswick, NJ: Rutgers UP, 1991: 325–38.

———. "Discourses of Desire and Difference: Configurations of Sexuality and Race in the Classical Hollywood Cinema." Talk delivered at the Columbia Film Seminar (Museum of Modern Art), New York City, January 28, 1993.

Foster, Hal. "The Art of Fetishism: Notes on Dutch Still Life." In *Fetishism as Cultural Discourse*. Eds. Emily Apter and William Pietz. Ithaca, NY: Cornell UP, 1993: 251–65.

Foucault, Michel. *Discipline and Punish: The Birth of the Prison*. Trans. Alan Sheridan. New York: Vintage, 1979.

———. *The History of Sexuality, Vol. I: An Introduction*. Trans. Robert Hurley. New York: Vintage, 1980.

———. "What Is Enlightenment?" Rpt. in *Postmodernism: A Reader*. Ed. Patricia Waugh. London: Edward Arnold, 1992: 96–108.

Frank, Katherine. *A Chainless Soul: A Life of Emily Brontë*. Boston: Houghton Mifflin, 1990.

Freud, Sigmund. *Beyond the Pleasure Principle*. (1920.) In *The Standard Edition of the Complete Psychological Works of Sigmund Freud*. Vol. 18. Ed. James Strachey. London: Hogarth P, 1953–74.

———. "The Economic Problem of Masochism." (1924.) In *Essential Papers on Masochism.* Ed. Margaret Ann Fitzpatrick Hanly. New York: New York University P, 1995: 274–85.

———. "Fetishism." (1927.) In *On Sexuality: "Three Essays on the Theory of Sexuality" and Other Works.* Ed. Angela Richards. Trans. James Strachey. London: Penguin, 1953: 345–57.

———. "Instincts and Their Vicissitudes." (1915.) *The Standard Edition of the Complete Psychological Works of Sigmund Freud.* Vol. 14: 111–40.

———. "Three Essays on the Theory of Sexuality." (1905.) In *On Sexuality:* 45–170.

Gaines, Jane. "Women and Representation: Can We Enjoy Alternative Pleasure?" In *American Media and Mass Culture: Left Perspectives.* Ed. Donald Lazere. Berkeley: U of California P, 1987.

Gallagher, Catherine. *Nobody's Story: The Vanishing Acts of Women Writers in the Marketplace, 1670–1820.* Berkeley: U of California P, 1994.

Gaudreault, André. "Film, Narrative, Narration: The Cinema of the Lumière Brothers." In *Early Cinema: Space, Frame, Narrative.* Ed. Thomas Elaesser with Adam Barker: 68–75.

Gebhard, Paul H. "Sadomasochism." In *S & M: Studies in Sadomasochism.* Ed. Thomas Weinberg and G. W. Levi Kamel. Buffalo, NY: Prometheus, 1983: 36–39.

Gillis, Christina Marsden. *The Paradox of Privacy: Epistolary Form in* Clarissa. Gainesville: U of Florida P, 1984.

Gledhill, Christine. "The Melodramatic Field: An Investigation." In *Home Is Where the Heart Is: Studies in Melodrama and the Woman's Film.* London: British Film Institute, 1987: 5–39.

Golden, Morris. *Richardson's Characters.* Ann Arbor: U of Michigan P, 1963.

Goldsmith, Elizabeth C. "Authority, Authenticity, and the Publication of Letters by Women." In *Writing the Female Voice.* Ed. Elizabeth C. Goldsmith: 46–59.

Gordon, Scott Paul. "Voyeuristic Dreams: Mr. Spectator and the Power of Spectacle." *The Eighteenth Century* 36.1 (1995): 3–23.

Griffin, Susan M. *The Historical Eye: The Texture of the Visual in the Late James.* Boston: Northeastern UP, 1991.

Grotius, Hugo. *De Jure Belli ac Pacis (1625—On the Law of War and Peace.)* Ed. J. Barbeyrae. Trans. anon. London: 1738.

Hafley, James. "The Villain in *Wuthering Heights.*" *Nineteenth-Century Fiction* 13.3 (1958): 199–215.

Halliday, Jon. "Sirk on Sirk." In *Imitation of Life.* Ed. Lucy Fischer: 226–36.

Haltunen, Karen. "'Domestic Difference': Competing Narratives of Womanhood in the Murder Trial of Lucretia Chapman." In *The Culture of Sentiment: Race, Gender, and Sentimentality in Nineteenth-Century America.* Ed. Shirley Samuels. New York: Oxford UP, 1992: 39–57.

Heath, Stephen. "Difference." *Screen* 19.3 (1978): 51–112.

———. "Film and System: Terms of Analysis." *Screen* 16.1 (1975): 7–77.

————. "On Suture." From *Questions of Cinema*. Bloomington: Indiana UP, 1981.

Hegel, Georg Wilhelm Friedrich. *The Phenomenology of the Spirit*. In *The Philosophy of Hegel*. Ed. Carl J. Friedrick. New York: Random House, 1953.

Herman, Jan. *A Talent for Trouble: The Life of Hollywood's Most Acclaimed Director, William Wyler*. New York: Putnam, 1995.

Heung, Marina. "'What's the Matter with Sarah Jane?': Daughters and Mothers in Douglas Sirk's *Imitation of Life*." In *Imitation of Life*. Ed. Lucy Fischer: 302–24.

Hobbes, Thomas. *Leviathan*. (1651.) Ed. C. B. Macpherson. London: Penguin, 1968.

Hugo, Victor. "Introduction." *Paris par les principaux écrivains des artistes de la France*. (1867.) Rpt. in *Paris Guide*. Ed. Victor Hugo. Paris: Calmon Lévy, 1879.

Hume, David. *An Enquiry Concerning the Principles of Morals*. (1751.) In *Enquiries Concerning Human Understanding and Concerning the Principles of Morals*. 3rd ed. L.A. Selby-Bigge. Oxford: Clarendon P, 1975.

————. "My Own Life." *Dialogues Concerning Natural Religion*. Ed. Norman Kemp Smith. New York: Macmillan, 1947: 233–40.

————. *A Treatise of Human Nature*. (1739–40.) 2nd ed. Ed. L. A. Selby-Bigge and P. H. Nidditch. Oxford: Oxford UP, 1978.

Hurst, Fannie. Excerpts from *Imitation of Life*. In *Imitation of Life*. Ed. Lucy Fischer: 161–72.

Hutcheson, Frances. *An Inquiry concerning Moral Good and Evil*. (1725.) In *British Moralists: Being Selections from Writers Principally of the Eighteenth Century*. Vol. I. Ed. L. A. Selby-Bigge. New York: Dover, 1965: 68–187.

Huyssen, Andreas. *After the Great Divide: Modernism, Mass Culture, Postmodernism*. Bloomington: Indiana UP, 1986.

Irigary, Luce. *Speculum of the Other Woman*. Trans. Gillian C. Gill. Ithaca, NY: Cornell UP, 1985.

Jackson, Margaret. "'Facts of Life' or the Eroticization of Women's Oppression?" In *The Cultural Construction of Sexuality*. Ed. Pat Caplan. London: Tavistock, 1987: 52–81.

Jaffe, Audrey. "Specular Sympathy: Visuality and Ideology in Dickens's *A Christmas Carol*. *PMLA* 109.2 (1994): 254–65.

James, Henry. "The Art of Fiction." (1884.) In *Anthology of American Literature*. Vol. 2. Ed. George McMichael et al. New York: Macmillan, 1989: 604–18.

————. "Charles de Bernard and Gustave Flaubert." (1878.) In *French Poets and Novelists*. Intro. Leon Edel. New York: Grosset and Dunlap, 1964: 186–210.

————. "Gustave Flaubert." In *Minor French Novelists*. (1876.) Rpt. in *Notes on Novelists*. New York: Scribners, 1914: 65–108.

————. *Italian Hours*. Ed. John Auchard. University Park: Pennsylvania State UP, 1992.

————. "Ivan Turgenieff (1818–1883)." In *The Art of Fiction and Other Essays*. New York: Oxford UP, 1948: 117–23.

————. *The Portrait of a Lady* and Preface. (1880–81; 1908.) Ed. Robert D. Bamberg. New York: Norton: 1975.

Jensen, Katharine. "Male Models of Feminine Epistolarity; or, How to Write Like a Woman in Seventeenth-Century France." In *Writing the Female Voice*. Ed. Elizabeth C. Goldsmith: 25–45.

Johnston, Claire. "Women's Cinema as Counter-Cinema." In *Notes on Women's Cinema*. Ed. Clarie Johnston. London: Society for Education in Film and Television, 1973: 24–31.

Kant, Immanuel. "An Answer to the Question: What Is Enlightenment?" Rpt. in *Postmodernism: A Reader*. Ed. Patricia Waugh: 89–95.

Kaplan, E. Ann. "Is the Gaze Male?" In *Women and Film: Both Sides of the Camera*. Ed. E. Ann Kaplan. New York: Methuen, 1983: 23–35.

————. "Theories of Melodrama: A Feminist Perspective." *Women and Performance: A Journal of Feminist Theory* 1 (Spring/Summer 1983): 40–48.

Kaplan, Fred. *Sacred Tears: Sentimentality in Victorian Literature*. Princeton: Princeton UP, 1987.

Kaplan, Louise J. *Female Perversions: The Temptations of Emma Bovary*. New York: Doubleday, 1991.

Kauffman, Linda. *Discourses of Desire: Gender, Genre, and Epistolary Fictions*. Ithaca, NY: Cornell UP, 1986.

Keymer, Tom. *Richardson's* Clarissa *and the Eighteenth-Century Reader*. New York: Cambridge UP, 1992.

Klein, Lawrence E. "Property and Politeness in the Early Eighteenth-Century Whig Moralists: The Case of the Spectator." In *Early Modern Conceptions of Property*. Ed. John Brewer and Susan Staves. New York: Routledge, 1995.

Kraft-Ebing, Richard von. *Psychopathia Sexualis, with especial reference to the antipathic sexual instinct; a medico-forensic study*. Trans. Franklin S. Klaf. New York: Bell, 1965.

La Bruyère, Jean de. *Les caractères ou les moeurs de ce siècle*. Paris: Garnier, 1962.

Lacan, Jacques. *Ecrits: A Selection*. Trans. Alan Sheridan. New York: Norton, 1977.

LaPlanche, Jacques. "Aggressiveness and Sadomasochism." *Essential Papers on Masochism*. Ed. Margaret Ann Fitzpatrick Hanly: 104–24.

Lenotre, G. *Voyages merveilleux a l'exposition universelle de 1889*. Paris: Librairie Universelle d'Alfred Duquesne et Fils, 1889.

Locke, John. *An Essay Concerning Human Understanding*. (1700.) Ed. Peter H. Nidditch. Oxford: Clarendon P, 1975.

————. *Questions Concerning the Law of Nature*. Intro. and Trans. Robert Horwitz et al. Ithaca, NY: Cornell UP, 1990.

London, April. "Enclosing Clarissa." *English Studies in Canada* 13 (1987): 271–80.

Lowe, Lisa. "Nationalism and Exoticism" Nineteenth-Century Others in Flaubert's *Salammbô* and *L'Education sentimentale*. In *Macropolitics of Nineteenth Century Literature: Naturalism, Exoticism, Imperialism*. Ed. Jonathan Arac and Harriet Ritva. Philadelphia: U of Pennsylvania P, 1991.

Lyotard, Jean-François. *The Postmodern Condition: A Report on Knowledge*. Trans. Geoff Bennington and Brian Massumi. Minneapolis: U of Minnesota P, 1984.

MacArthur, Charles, and Ben Hecht. "*Wuthering Heights* Screenplay." Samuel Goldwyn, Inc., 1938.

McCarthy, Terence. "The Incompetent Narrator of *Wuthering Heights*. *Modern Language Quarterly* 42 (1981): 48–64.

Marks, Sylvia Kasey. "*Clarissa* as Conduct Book." *South Atlantic Review* 51.4 (1986): 3–16.

Marshall, David. *The Surprising Effects of Sympathy: Marivaux, Diderot, Rousseau and Mary Shelley*. Chicago: U of Chicago P, 1988.

Massé, Michele A. *In the Name of Love: Women, Masochism, and the Gothic*. Ithaca, NY: Cornell UP, 1992.

Mathison, John K., "Nelly Dean and the Power of *Wuthering Heights*." *Nineteenth-Century Fiction* 11.2 (1956): 106–29. Rpt. in *A Wuthering Heights Handbook*. Ed. Richard Lettis and William E. Morris: 143–63.

Metz, Christian. *The Imaginary Signifier: Psychoanalysis and the Cinema*. Trans. Celia Britton et al. Bloomington: Indiana UP, 1982.

———. "Story/Discourse: Notes on Two Kinds of Voyeurism." In *Movies and Methods, Vol. II*. Ed. Bill Nichols. Berkeley: U of California P, 1985: 543–48.

Miller, J. Hillis. "*Wuthering Heights*: Repetition and the 'Uncanny.'" In *Fiction and Repetition: Seven English Novels*. Cambridge, MA: Harvard UP, 1982: 42–72.

Miller, Nancy K. *The Heroine's Text: Readings in the English and French Novel*. New York: Columbia UP, 1980.

Modleski, Tania. *Feminism without Women: Culture and Criticism in a "Postfeminist" Age*. New York: Routledge, 1991.

———. *Loving with a Vengeance: Mass-Produced Fantasies for Women*. New York: Methuen, 1984.

———. *The Women Who Knew Too Much: Hitchcock and Feminist Theory*. New York: Methuen, 1988.

Montagu, Lady Mary Wortley. *The Complete Letters of Lady Mary Wortley Montagu*. Ed. Robert Halsband. Oxford, 1967.

Mulvey, Laura. "Afterthoughts on 'Visual Pleasure and Narrative Cinema' Inspired by *Duel in the Sun*." *Framework* 15–17 (1981). Rpt. in *Feminism and Film Theory*. Ed. Constance Penley. 69–79.

———. "Visual Pleasure and Narrative Cinema." *Screen* 16.3 (1975): 6–18.

Munson, Wayne. *All Talk: The Talkshow in Media Culture*. Philadelphia: Temple UP, 1993.

Musser, Charles. *The Emergence of Cinema: The American Screen to 1907*. Berkeley: U of California P, 1990.

Namias, June. *White Captives: Gender and Ethnicity on the American Frontier*. Chapel Hill: U of North Carolina P, 1993.

Newman, Beth. "The Situation of the Looker-On: Gender, Narration, and Gaze in *Wuthering Heights*. *PMLA* 105.5 (1990): 1029–41.

The New York Times, "Defending Smith, Stepfather Says He Also Bears Blame; Reads a Letter Saying, 'My Heart Breaks.'" July 28, 1995: 1.

Norton, David Fate. *David Hume: Common-Sense Moralist, Sceptical Metaphysician.* Princeton, NJ: Princeton UP, 1982.

———. "Hume, Human Nature, and the Foundations of Morality." In *The Cambridge Companion to Hume*. Ed. David Fate Norton. New York: Cambridge UP, 1993: 148–81.

Ostovich, Helene. M. "'Our Views Must Now Be Different': Imprisonment and Friendship in *Clarissa*." *Modern Language Quarterly* 52.2 (1991): 153–69.

Pascal, Ory. *Les expositions universelles de Paris: Panorama raisonné, avec des aperçus nouveaux et des illustrations par les meilleurs auteurs.* Paris: Ramsay, 1982.

Pascal, Roy. *The Dual Voice: Free Indirect Speech and Its Functioning in the Nineteenth-Century European Novel.* Manchester, England: Manchester UP, 1977.

Poirier, Richard. *The Comic Sense of Henry James.* London: Oxford UP, 1960.

Price, John Valdimir. *The Ironic Hume.* Austin, TX: U of Texas P, 1965.

Pritchett, V.S. "Introduction." *Wuthering Heights*. By Emily Brontë. Boston: Houghton Mifflin, 1847, 1956: v–xiii.

Przybylowicz, Donna. *Desire and Repression: The Dialectic of Self and Other in the Late Works of Henry James.* University: U of Alabama P, 1986.

Pufendorf, Samuel. *De Jure Naturae et Gentium Libri Octo.* (1672.) Trans. C. A. and W. A. Oldfatum. New York: Oceana, 1964.

———. *De Officio Hominis et Civis, Juxta Legem Naturalem Libri Duo.* (1673.) Trans. F. G. Moore. New York: Oxford UP, 1927.

———. "On the Natural State of Men." In *On the Natural State of Men: The 1678 Latin Edition and English Translation.* Trans. and Intro. Michael Seidler. Lewiston, NY: Edwin Mellen P, 1990.

Reiniger, Lotte. *Shadow Puppets, Shadow Theatres, and Shadow Films.* Boston: Plays, Inc., 1970.

Rendell, Jane. "Virtue and Commerce: Women in the Making of Adam Smith's Political Economy." In *Women in Western Political Philosophy: Kant to Nietzsche.* Ed. Ellen Kennedy and Susan Mendus. New York: St. Martin's, 1987: 44–77.

Richardson, Samuel. *Clarissa, or The History of a Young Lady.* (1747–48.) Ed. Angus Ross. London: Penguin, 1985.

———. *Familiar Letters on Important Occasions.* (1741.) Ed. Brian W. Downs. Philadelphia: R. West, 1928.

———. *Selected Letters.* Ed. John Carroll. Oxford: Clarendon P, 1964.

Rosenthal, Margaret F. "A Courtesan's Voice: Epistolary Self-Portraiture in Veronica Franco's *Terze Rime*." In *Writing the Female Voice*. Ed. Elizabeth C. Goldsmith: 3–24.

Rousseau, Jean-Jacques. *Emile.* (1762.) Trans. Barbara Foxley. London: J. M. Dent and Sons, 1992.

Sabiston, Elizabeth. "Isabel Archer: The Architect of Consciousness." In *The Prison of Womanhood: Four Provincial Heroines in Nineteenth-Century Fiction*. New York: St. Martin's P, 1987: 43–54.

Sacher-Masoch, Leopold von. *Venus in Furs*. New York: Zone Books, 1989.

Samuels, Shirley. "Introduction." *The Culture of Sentiment*. Ed. Shirley Samules: 3–8.

Schatz, Thomas. "The Family Melodrama." In *Imitations of Life: A Reader on Film and Television Melodrama*. Ed. Marcia Landy. Detroit, MI: Wayne State UP, 1991: 148–67.

Scheper-Hughes, Nancy. *Death without Weeping: The Violence of Everyday Life in Brazil*. Berkeley: U of California P, 1992.

Schneewind, J. B. "Locke's Moral Philosophy." In *The Cambridge Companion to Locke*. Ed. Vere Chappell. New York: Cambridge UP, 1994: 199–225.

Scholes, Robert E., and Robert Kellogg. *The Nature of Narrative*. New York: Oxford UP, 1966.

Schor, Naomi. "Fetishism and Its Ironies." In *Fetishism as Cultural Discourse*. Ed. Emily Apter and William Pietz: 92–100.

Schwartz, Vanessa R. "Cinematic Spectatorship before the Apparatus: The Public Taste for Reality in *Fin-de-Siècle* Paris." In *Viewing Positions: Ways of Seeing Film*. Ed. Linda Williams. New Brunswick, NJ: Rutgers UP, 1995: 87–113.

Seidler, Michael. "Introduction to 'On the Natural State of Men.'" In *Of the Natural State of Men*. Trans. and Intro. Michael Seidler: 13–57.

Selig, Michael E. "Contradictions and Reading: Social Class and Sex Class in *Imitation of Life*." *Wide Angle* 10.4 (1988): 14–23.

Seltzer, Mark. *Henry James and the Art of Power*. Ithaca, NY: Cornell UP, 1984.

Shaftesbury, Third Earl of. *An Inquiry Concerning Virtue*. (1699.) In *British Moralists*. Vol. 1. Ed. L. A. Selby-Bigge: 1–67.

Shershow, Scott Cutler. *Puppets and "Popular" Culture*. Ithaca, NY: Cornell UP, 1995.

Shloss, Carol. *In Visible Light: Photography and the American Writer: 1840–1940*. New York: Oxford UP, 1987.

Silverman, Kaja. *Male Subjectivity at the Margins*. New York: Routledge, 1992.

———. *The Subject of Semiotics*. New York: Oxford UP, 1983.

Smith, Adam. *The Theory of Moral Sentiments*. (1759.) New York: Augustus M. Kelley, 1966.

Smith, David. "The Reckoning." *People Magazine*. August 7, 1995: 73–82.

Smith, Norman Kemp. *The Philosophy of David Hume: A Critical Study of Its Origins and Central Doctrines*. London and New York: Macmillan, 1941.

Spiegel, Alan. *Fiction and the Camera Eye: Visual Consciousness in Film and the Modern Novel*. Charlottesville: UP of Virginia, 1976.

Stallman, R. W. "The Houses that James Built—*The Portrait of a Lady*." *Texas Quarterly* 1 (Winter 1958): 176–96.

Staves, Susan. *Married Women's Separate Property in England, 1660–1833*. Cambridge, MA: Harvard UP, 1990.

Stern, Michael. "*Imitation of Life.*" In *Imitation of Life.* Ed. Lucy Fischer: 279–88.

Stone, Lawrence. *The Family, Sex, and Marriage in England, 1500–1800.* New York: Harper & Row, 1977.

Studlar, Gaylyn. "Masochism and the Perverse Pleasures of the Cinema." Rpt. in *Movies and Methods, Vol. II.* Ed. Bill Nichols. Berkeley: U of California P, 1985: 602–21.

Tinter, Adeline R. *The Cosmopolitan World of Henry James: An Intertextual Study.* Baton Rouge: Louisiana UP, 1991.

———. *The Museum World of Henry James.* Ann Arbor: U of Michigan P, 1986.

Todd, Janet. *Sensibility, an Introduction.* London: Methuen, 1986.

———. *The Sign of Angelica: Women, Writing, and Fiction, 1660–1800.* New York: Columbia UP, 1986.

Tompkins, Jane. *Sensational Designs: The Cultural World of American Fiction, 1790–1860.* New York: Oxford UP, 1987.

Tuck, Richard. *Natural Rights Theories: Their Origin and Development.* Cambridge: Cambridge UP, 1979.

Van Ghent, Dorothy. *The English Novel: Form and Function.* New York: Rinehart, 1961.

Vaughan, Alden T. and Edward W. Clark. "Cups of Common Calamity: Puritan Captivity Narratives as Literature and History." In *Puritans among the Indians: Accounts of Captivity and Redemption 1676–1724.* Ed. Vaughan and Clark. Cambridge, MA: Harvard UP, 1981: 1–28.

Vincent-Buffault, Anne. *The History of Tears: Sensibility and Sentimentality in France.* London: Macmillan, 1991.

Waldman, Diane. "Film Theory and the Gendered Spectator: The Female or the Feminist Reader?" *Camera Obscura* 8 (1988): 80–94.

Warner, William Beatty. *Reading* Clarissa: *The Struggles of Interpretation.* New Haven, CT: Yale UP, 1979.

Watson, Melvin R. "Tempest in the Soul: The Theme and Structure of *Wuthering Heights.*" *Nineteenth-Century Fiction* 4.4 (1949). Rpt. in *The Wuthering Heights Handbook:* 83–95.

Watt, Ian. *The Rise of the Novel: Studies in Defoe, Richardson, and Fielding.* Berkeley: U of California P, 1957.

Wehrs, Donald R. "Irony, Storytelling, and the Conflict of Interpretations in *Clarissa.*" *EHL* 53.4 (1986): 759–77.

Weinberg, Thomas S., and G. W. Levi Kamel. "S&M: An Introduction to the Study of Sadomasochism." In *S & M: Studies in Sadomasochism.* Ed. Thomas Weinberg and G. W. Levi Kamel: 17–24.

Weinraub, Bernard. "Getting Ratings from *Rescue 911.*" *TV Guide.* April 9, 1994: 32–35.

Wexler, Laura. "Tender Violence: Literary Eavesdropping, Domestic Fiction, and Educational Reform." In *The Culture of Sentiment.* Ed. Shirley Samuels: 9–38.

Willemen, Paul. "Towards an Analysis of the Sirkian System." In *Imitation of Life*. Ed. Lucy Fischer: 273–79.

Williams, Alan. *Republic of Images: A History of French Filmmaking*. Cambridge, MA: Harvard UP, 1992.

Williams, Anna. "Domestic Violence and the Aetiology of Crime in *America's Most Wanted*." *Camera Obsura* 31 (1993): 97–117.

Williams, D. A. *"The Hidden Life at Its Source": A Study of Flaubert's* L'Education sentimentale. Pickering, North Yorkshire: U of Hull P, 1987.

Williams, Linda. "'Something Else Besides a Mother': *Stella Dallas* and the Maternal Melodrama." *Cinema Journal* 24.1 (Fall 1984): 2–27.

———. "When the Woman Looks." In *Re-Vision: Essays in Feminist Film Criticism*. Ed. Mary Ann Doane, Patricia Mellencamp, and Linda Williams. Frederick, MD: AFI Monograph Series, University Publications of America, 1984: 83–99.

Winn, James Anderson. *A Window in the Bosom: The Letters of Alexander Pope*. Hamden, CT: Archon Books, 1977.

Winner, Viola Hopkins. *Henry James and the Visual Arts*. Charlottesville: UP of Virginia, 1970.

Winnicott, D. W. "The Use of an Object and Relation through Identification." In *Playing and Reality*. Middlesex, NY: Penguin, 1974: 101–11.

Wion, Philip K. "The Absent Mother in *Wuthering Heights*." In *Wuthering Heights*. By Emily Brontë. Ed. Linda H. Peterson. New York: Bedford/St. Martin's P, 1992: 315–29.

Worth, George J. "Emily Brontë's Mr. Lockwood." *Nineteenth-Century Fiction* 12.4 (1958). Rpt. in *The Wuthering Heights Handbook*. Ed. Richard Lettis and William E. Morris: 171–75.

Wyatt, Thomas. "Sonnet XVII." ("I Find No Peace and All My War Is Done.") *Sir Thomas Wyatt: The Complete Poems*. Ed. R. A. Rebholz. New Haven: Yale UP, 1978: 80.

Zomchick, John P. *Family and the Law in Eighteenth-Century Fiction: The Public Conscience in the Private Sphere*. New York: Cambridge UP, 1993.

Zwinger, Linda. *Fathers, Daughters, and the Novel: The Sentimental Romance of Heterosexuality*. Madison: U Wisconsin P, 1991.

INDEX